Legal Skills

Legal Skills

Lisa Cherkassky
Lecturer in Law, Bradford University Law School

Julia Cressey
Lecturer in Law, Bradford University Law School

Christopher Gale
Director of Legal Studies and Head of Department, Bradford University Law School

Jessica Guth
Lecturer in Law, Bradford University Law School

Ilias Kapsis
Lecturer in Law, Bradford University Law School

Robin Lister
Senior Lecturer in Law, Bradford University Law School

William Onzivu
Lecturer in Law, Bradford University Law School

Steve Rook
Formerly Career Development Adviser at Bradford University; now Postgraduate Careers Adviser at Nottingham University Business School

palgrave
macmillan

First published 2011 by PALGRAVE MACMILLAN

Palgrave Macmillan in the UK is an imprint of Macmillan Publishers Limited, registered in England, company number 785998, of Houndmills, Basingstoke, Hampshire RG21 6XS.

Palgrave Macmillan in the US is a division of St Martin's Press LLC, 175 Fifth Avenue, New York, NY 10010.

Palgrave Macmillan is the global academic imprint of the above companies and has companies and representatives throughout the world.

Palgrave® and Macmillan® are registered trademarks in the United States, the United Kingdom, Europe and other countries.

ISBN 978-0-230-23008-8 paperback

This book is printed on paper suitable for recycling and made from fully managed and sustained forest sources. Logging, pulping and manufacturing processes are expected to conform to the environmental regulations of the country of origin.

A catalogue record for this book is available from the British Library.

10   9   8   7   6   5   4   3   2   1
19   18   17   16   15   14   13   12   11   10

Printed in China.

If you would like to comment on this title, or on any other law textbook published by Palgrave Macmillan, please write to lawfeedback@palgrave.com.

Preface

'Legal Skills' is an area of law that many students are unsure about. It is taught in many different ways, making it difficult to identify as an independent unit of study. Sometimes legal skills is integrated into other modules and sometimes it is offered as a standalone unit, but no matter where it is placed, 'Legal Skills' always seems to stick out as the module that doesn't fit into the same 'academic' mould of other law modules. The subject can't decide what it wants to be and is often interpreted differently by students and teachers alike. Is it concerned with 'professional' skills, 'academic' skills or 'career' skills? Does it cover 'personal' skills or could it be a combination of all four?

In truth, 'Legal Skills' cannot be shoehorned into a short module description or even into a whole module, for it covers all of the professional, academic, career and personal skills needed to progress on a law course and to succeed in a future legal career.

It is with that in mind that this book has come to be written. The authors are, with one exception, members of the teaching team at Bradford University Law School. As members of a new school, we felt we were in a unique position to consider carefully how to teach legal skills to our students and this book is an attempt to share our practice with others. Drawing on our extensive experience as lecturers of law, this fresh and innovative textbook showcases a unique approach to the teaching and learning of legal skills in all their diverse forms. Using a form of activity-based learning, this comprehensive legal skills guide aims to build the confidence of law students and help them to achieve their academic and professional goals in a structured and friendly way. Our new textbook explains in simple yet practical detail just what legal skills are, how they can be utilised successfully on a law course and how they apply in their many different guises to legal practice. Each chapter is packed with stimulating activities to allow readers to identify and build upon their transferrable legal skills, and the text is written in a fun and approachable way.

The content of this book falls into four distinct areas. Chapter 1 considers the question 'What is law?' and provides a valuable introduction to the English Legal System and its sources. Chapters 2, 3 and 4 cover the essential academic skills of using a law library, reading and researching the law and critical thinking. Chapter 5 covers all aspects of written and oral communication, while Chapter 6 contains much useful material on study skills, including revision and time management. Chapters 7 and 8 turn to the more practice-orientated skills that students need to develop, such as professional communication, advocacy (including mooting) and people skills such as networking and negotiation. Lastly, and very importantly, Chapter 9 focuses on the vital subject of career development and planning and contains invaluable information and advice that should be of help to students both during their degree and beyond.

Throughout, we have adopted an imaginative approach to legal skills that is both creative and practical. Within each chapter there are a wide range of activities and tasks which will enable the reader to self-assess, to develop his or her personal and academic legal skills, and to harness the vital tools necessary for the successful study and practice of law.

The book can be read in the order presented and the skills discussed are specifically placed to follow on logically from each other. Primarily, however, the book is intended for 'dipping into' and for readers to choose those sections they wish to spend more time on than others.

This book is intended to be of help to all students studying law either as part of an undergraduate law degree, postgraduate diploma or similar course, or as part of other subjects and degree paths. The book is designed to accompany readers throughout their studies and aid them in the development of their academic and professional skills. While it can certainly be used as a course textbook to accompany a specific module in legal skills, it should also add value to the study of law more generally and remain a useful source of information well beyond the first year of study.

Whilst the majority of this material is best presented in book form, useful supporting material is available online. We have created extra resources for the Companion Website. These include self-assessment activities, case studies and, for some chapters, comprehensive skills guides. The address of this site is www.palgrave.com/law/legalskills. Readers will also find much of interest on the site that accompanies Palgrave Macmillan's general study skills list at www.palgrave.com/skills4study.

This book could not have been written without the support of a number of people. The authors would like to thank Colin Neville and Martin Sedgley for allowing us to adapt material from the Bradford University School of Management Effective Learning Service Guides, all written by Colin Neville, thereby saving us from having to reinvent the wheel.

We would also like to thank Neil Carter for writing the chapter on using a law library, and for his input more generally. Further thanks for their contributions and comments must go to Jackie Ford and Lorraine Lucas, and to all of the reviewers who commented on the manuscript during its development. Thank you also to Jasmin Naim, Rob Gibson and the team at Palgrave Macmillan for their patient support and invaluable advice throughout the construction of this project. We would also like to thank our families.

Any errors or omissions are, of course, our own.

Lisa Cherkassky	Jessica Guth	William Onzivu
Julia Cressey	Ilias Kapsis	Steve Rook
Christopher Gale	Robin Lister	

Bradford University Law School
November 2010

Contents

3 Legal research

5 Written and oral communication

6 Study skills

1

An introduction to the English Legal System and its sources

Learning outcomes

> To understand the legal system of England and Wales in its European and international context

> To appreciate our legal system as a common law system

> To understand the term 'common law' and its various different meanings

> To understand how our law is made, applied and developed

> To be able to explain and apply the skills of statutory interpretation

> To be able to explain and apply the doctrine of precedent

Introduction

'What is law?' is a question that has exercised philosophers, legal theorists, social scientists and poets down the ages and across continents and cultures. It remains a central question in legal theory, as you will discover if and when you study legal theory during your degree. The answer you give will depend on who you are and why you are asking the question.

A short answer is that law means *the body of rules and procedures established by a state to regulate the conduct of its citizens.* This law decides whether we have legally enforceable rights and duties in all areas of our lives. This law determines whether a particular act or omission is criminal, whether an agreement is enforceable, a tax payable, a harm remediable, a property owned, a copyright breached. Individuals and corporate entities, like companies, charities, schools, hospitals and universities, need to know the law in order to guide their conduct. Governments, national and local, need to know the law that regulates their conduct and controls their powers. Because law's rules and procedures are so many and diverse, individuals and corporations rely on lawyers to advise and represent them in all kinds of private and commercial transactions, arrangements and in courts and tribunals.

Activity What is law? In the space below, explain what law means to you by identifying the areas of your life which are influenced by it. Can you identify any benefits from the intervention of the law in these areas? If not, why not?

Areas of life   Benefits of law

....

....

....

....

....

....

....

Knowing what the law is and how to apply it is obviously fundamental for law students and practising lawyers. Researching the law and legal reasoning are core legal skills, and two chapters of this book are devoted to these subjects respectively (see **Chapters 3** and **4**). However, our initial, very narrow, definition of law comes with a warning about its limitations. Apart from the important omission of European Union and international law from this definition (see **1.3** and **1.4** below) you should recognise from the start that there is much more to law than its formal, technical, institutional aspect.

In learning and practising the law we can easily forget its human dimension. Law affects people's lives, by no means always for the better. Legal services are expensive and many people cannot afford them. Litigation can drag on for years and outcomes are unpredictable. Sometimes the law can seem unsatisfactory, inadequate and unfair.

Developing our legal skills should be about more than becoming expert legal technicians, but this may be easier said than done.

1.1 THE COMMON LAW AND OTHER CATEGORIES

Why start a book about legal skills with a chapter about the English Legal System and its sources? The aim is to put your learning of legal skills in the context of the law that you are studying. We want you to start by thinking about the kind of system the English Legal System is and the main sources of the law of England and Wales. How is our law made, applied and developed? How does our common law system work, and how does it sit in the context of European Union and international law and in terms of different legal theories?

The law of England and Wales is the product of gradual, pragmatic development over the last millennium. That is to say the development of both our law and legal system has been largely unplanned. The process has been one of evolutionary adaptation rather than a planned design, despite the periodic interventions of central government to reform and modernise the law in a more systematic way (for example with the Supreme Court of Judicature Acts 1873–1875 and the Constitutional Reform Act 2005).

What do we mean by 'common law'?

The English Legal System is a 'common law' system, and we need to consider what we mean by common law and the common law tradition before we go on to consider the main sources of our law. You are, after all, engaged in the academic study of our common law, and many readers will go on to become common lawyers.

The expression 'common law' was first used in the late-thirteenth century to denote the law that applied throughout the kingdom as opposed to local laws that applied in different parts of the country. Common law was the law developed by the royal common law courts that was common to all the king's subjects. Sir William Blackstone (*Commentaries on the Laws of England,* 1765–1769) describes 'the common law properly so called' as 'unwritten law' contained in ancient customs and maxims (broad statements of general principle) 'common to all the realm'. According to Blackstone and his predecessors, successive generations of judges gradually revealed this unwritten law as they drew on it to decide the cases before them. A combination of long-standing customs and maxims thus developed through legal argument and judgments into principles and rules of law.

Today, our common law is made up of a distinctive combination of statutes, judge-made law, and adversarial trial procedure, that is different to other European civil law traditions.

Definitions and categories: common law and other terms

The term 'common law' can be initially confusing because it means a number of different things. You will avoid confusion if you take the time to familiarise yourself with the various meanings of 'common law' in their different contexts, as well as with some other distinctions in legal terminology.

(a) 'Common law' system versus 'civil law' system

(i) Civil law system

In civil law systems the law is largely codified, meaning that it is laid down as legislation in the form of codes and constitutions which set out a comprehensive body of abstract legal principles and rules to regulate conduct and for the courts to apply. Courts within civil law systems have to apply the codified legal rules and principles to the legal disputes which come before them with a much more limited reliance on precedent (following previous decisions) than in common law systems.

(ii) Common law system

In its broad meaning 'common law' refers to a system of law in which legal principles and rules have been developed by judges in the process of determining specific legal disputes. In modern common law systems, legal rules and principles are a combination of judge-made law, developed through the doctrine of precedent, legislation (law enacted by the state) and, in many jurisdictions, constitutions. Although the bulk of English law is now statutory (legislated by Parliament), a substantial part remains common law in the sense that it is judge-made law based on precedent. As a good example, our law of civil obligations – contract and tort – is essentially judge-made, as are the rules of equity and the core principles of criminal law. Furthermore, in relation to legislation, the judges have a significant role to play in the application of the law because of their responsibility for statutory interpretation.

(b) Common law and equity

Equity developed in response to the excessive formalism and unfairness that could result from the early common law courts' refusal to deal with cases which did not fit within their own strict procedures. Equity, as the court of conscience under the direction of the Chancellor (leading to the court of Chancery), developed doctrines and principles to provide justice in cases where the common law produced unfair outcomes. Until the Judicature Acts of 1873–1875, which brought the common law courts and the court of Chancery together into the High Court, equitable remedies were only available in the court of Chancery. Although common law and equitable remedies are still distinct, they now operate as complementary systems of law applicable within all our courts.

(c) Common law and statute law

'Common law' here refers to the legal rules and principles which emerge from judgments in cases decided by the courts according to the doctrine of judicial precedent (meaning that the judges make the law through their decisions). Common law (or case law as it is sometimes known) is distinguished from Acts of Parliament (statutes) and delegated legislation (statutory instruments). In the sense that 'common law' means case law, common law also includes equity:

> 'The common law, which in a constitutional context includes judicially developed equity, covers everything which is not covered by statute.' (Lord Scarman, *McLoughlin v O'Brian* [1983] 1 AC 410 at 429–30)

(d) Private law and public law

These terms are used to distinguish legal relationships. Cases between legal individuals (including both individual citizens and corporate legal bodies) are known as private law, and cases between individuals and the state are known as public law. The distinction between private and public law is common to both civil law and common law traditions. Public law is often described as constitutional and administrative law.

(e) Civil law and criminal law

These categories, like private law and public law, are distinguished within the legal systems of most countries. Criminal law refers to conduct which the state disapproves of and which it formally prohibits (for example, murder). Civil law concerns legal relations between legal individuals, for example disputes over the terms of a contract or ownership of property.

The distinction between civil and criminal law is important. Civil cases involve disputes between the claimant (this is the person making the claim, formerly called the plaintiff) and the defendant (the person receiving the claim) over legal rights and remedies. In criminal cases, a prosecutor representing the Crown (ie the Queen) from the Crown Prosecution Service seeks to prove that a defendant – the accused – is guilty of a criminal offence. Standards of proof and rules of evidence differ for civil and criminal actions. The same set of facts, acts and omissions can give rise to both criminal and civil law consequences; a standard example is a road traffic accident involving negligent or dangerous driving.

Activity In the space below, list the main differences between statute law and common law

Statute law	Common law

(f) UK law and European law

Both these terms can be misleading. 'UK law' might apply to England and Wales and Northern Ireland but not Scotland, or might apply throughout the United Kingdom. Scotland and Wales now have their own political institutions, meaning that UK law might only apply to England. Scotland has retained its own legal system, based on a combination of Roman law and common law traditions, which distinguishes it from the common law systems of the rest of the United Kingdom. We are primarily concerned with English law.

'European law' was once used as a term to describe the law of continental European countries such as France and Germany. Now it generally refers to European Union law, although it is sometimes loosely used to refer to European human rights law as well. Both European Union law and human rights law (based on the European Convention on Human Rights and Fundamental Freedoms) are now significant sources of English law in particular and UK law.

(g) Domestic law and international law

There are many different types of international law, as distinct from domestic (also known as municipal) law. Domestic law (meaning 'inside the country') refers to the law of a particular state, applicable within its jurisdiction (ie UK law). There is international trade law, shipping law, intellectual property law, aviation law and so on, as well as international public law, including human rights law, criminal law and environmental law. We have provided an introductory account of international law at **1.4** below.

Activity Take some time to reflect on the previous section by considering the following questions:

1 What do we mean by describing a legal system as a common law system?

....

....

2 What is the difference between common law and statute law?

....

....

3 What is the difference between common law and equity?

....

....

4 How could Lord Scarman state that common law includes equity when equity was invented to provide an alternative to common law?

....

....

5 How many different meanings can you find for the term 'common law'? Are any of these meanings contradictory?

....

....

6 What was the original meaning of common law and why is that not relevant today?

....

....

The administration of justice and the courts

Courts have an integral role in any legal system. Legal proceedings must be started in the court or tribunal which has the authority to hear or try the particular legal issues involved. Various courts of first instance (also referred to as trial courts, meaning the courts in which legal disputes are first heard and decided) have different avenues of appeal. The different courts stand in a hierarchical relationship to each other, meaning that the decisions of higher courts are binding on the lower courts.

It is a good idea to become familiar with the structure of the courts and their jurisdiction when you study the English Legal System.

Of course, a court can only develop the law by setting a new precedent if its judgment is published for later courts to consider. It is the cases heard in the High Court, Court of Appeal and Supreme Court (formally known as the House of Lords), along with those heard in specialist tribunals like the Employment Appeal Tribunal and the Upper Tribunal (Immigration and Asylum Chamber) that dominate law reports. The magistrates' and county courts deal with the bulk of criminal and civil cases, yet cases heard in these courts are rarely reported.

In the context of European Union law, decisions of the European Court of Justice in Luxembourg are binding on the courts of England and Wales and all other Member States. By the same token, the European Court of Human Rights in Strasbourg stands as the final court of appeal for the determination of human rights violations. Decisions of the European Court of Human Rights on the application of the European Convention on Human Rights must be followed by our national courts. A common error of students studying the European dimension of English law for the first time is to muddle up the jurisdiction of these two European courts. Make sure that the function and jurisdiction of each court is clear in your mind from the start: the European Court of Justice is concerned with European Union law which applies to the 27 Member States of the European Union. The European Court of Human Rights is concerned with the human rights of the people of the 47 Member States of the Council of Europe who are signatories to the European Convention on Human Rights.

Activity Tick the following boxes once you have read and understood the listed points. You can carry out further research at your law library to help you understand:

- ☐ I know what 'common law' is and can describe it myself
- ☐ I know where the UK common law comes from
- ☐ I know how the common law is a primary source of law
- ☐ I know what 'civil law' is and can describe it myself
- ☐ I know what 'equity' is and can describe it myself
- ☐ I can explain how equity is different from other UK law systems
- ☐ I know what 'statute law' is and can describe it myself
- ☐ I understand how statute law is different to common law

- ☐ I know what 'private law' is and can describe it myself
- ☐ I know what the 'criminal law' is and how it is different to civil law
- ☐ I can list the differences between criminal law and civil law
- ☐ I know what 'domestic law' is and can describe it myself
- ☐ I understand how international law is different from domestic law
- ☐ I understand the basic UK court structure

1.2 THE MAIN SOURCES OF ENGLISH LAW

The main sources of English law in the twenty-first century are UK legislation, judicial precedent (case law), European Union law and human rights law.

1.2.1 Legislation

This is the major source of our law today since Parliament, as the legislature, is the supreme law-making body in the United Kingdom. Parliamentary sovereignty is a fundamental principle of the United Kingdom's unwritten constitution. Parliament, as a general constitutional principle, has an unlimited power to make or unmake any law it chooses (subject to any overriding European Union law as a result of the European Communities Act 1972).

Activity 'Legislation' is a daunting word for those of you who have never studied law before. Can you describe 'legislation' in your own words and write down what you think it means?

....

....

....

....

....

Since the Human Rights Act 1998 came into force on 2 October 2000, our courts can declare legislation to be incompatible with the European Convention on Human Rights (Human Rights Act 1998, s 4), but this does not invalidate the legislation nor require Parliament to take corrective action.

A number of senior judges have indicated that the courts should be prepared to intervene if Parliament were to abuse its constitutional supremacy, for example by passing laws allowing arbitrary arrest and imprisonment, preventing judicial review of administrative action, or enacting other forms of 'oppressive and wholly undemocratic legislation':

- Lords Steyn, Hope and Hale in *R (Jackson and others) v Attorney-General* [2005] 1 AC 262;
- Extra-judicial commentary by Lords Woolf and Steyn in 'Judicial Review – The Tensions between the Executive and the Judiciary' (1998) 114 LQR 579;
- Lord Steyn, 'Democracy, the Rule of Law and the Role of Judges' (2006) EHRLR 243 at 253;
- 'Civil Liberties in Modern Britain' (2009) PL 228 at 231–2.

Primary and secondary legislation

Legislation consists of primary legislation, namely Acts of Parliament (statutes), and secondary legislation, which is usually termed 'delegated legislation'. Acts of Parliament have to be passed by both Houses of Parliament, following full scrutiny and debate, before they become law. Because of the limits on parliamentary time and the sheer volume of modern law making, many statutes contain provisions which authorise an individual or body to make further rules and regulations. Typically, a statute will delegate (or 'shift') law-making power to the Secretary of State whose government department is responsible for initiating the legislation. This is delegated legislation.

Activity In the space below, list the main sources of UK law as you believe them to be:

Primary sources of UK law	Secondary sources of UK law
....	....
....	....
....	....
....	....
....	....
....	....

Acts of Parliament

These take the form of Public General Acts and Private Acts. Public Acts are the principal form of primary legislation, usually starting life as draft Public Bills and presented to Parliament by the government minister whose department is responsible for the relevant area of regulation. A smaller proportion of Acts are introduced to Parliament by individual Members in the form of Private Members' Bills. A frequently-cited example of an important Act which was introduced as a Private Members' Bill is the Abortion Act 1967, presented by David Steel.

Private Acts of Parliament are proposed by corporate bodies such as local authorities and public companies and are designed to give such bodies the right to do things not permitted under the general law, for example to construct a road or railway or a power or water network.

 Activity Go to www.parliament.uk/factsheets. Under Legislation Series L3, 'The Success of Private Members' Bills', you will find a full list of all Private Members' Bills to have been enacted since 1945. Find the titles of the three Acts, referred to above, which started life as Private Members' Bills in the current century.

1 ....

2 ....

3 ....

Delegated legislation

When a statute – the parent Act – authorises a Secretary of State or Minister to make further legal rules and regulations, this is known as delegated legislation. It may have a purely technical function, for example setting the dates on which the various provisions of the parent Act come into force as law, or play a significant part in the making of detailed law.

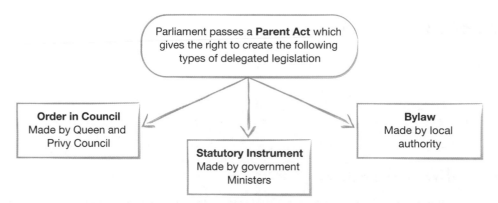

Technical statutory instruments (SIs) are not subject to any parliamentary scrutiny and become law on the date they are signed by the responsible Minister. Substantive SIs (those which actually make law under the delegated authority of the parent Act) are generally subject to some form of scrutiny by both Houses of Parliament (although the sheer mass of such legislation means that there is little time to do this in any detail).

Activity Your local council is able to pass many of its own laws (bylaws) because of the 'parent Act' that is passed by Parliament. Can you list in the space below the regulations and laws in your local area that are passed by your council?

....
....
....
....

See our **Companion Website** at www.palgrave.com/law/legalskills for further details about how to access Acts of Parliament and delegated legislation.

Self-assessment

Tick the statement that applies to you...

	I can do this with confidence	I am learning at a steady pace to do this
I can find the House of Commons Information Office Factsheet, Legislative Series L7, 'Statutory Instruments' at www.parliament.uk/factsheets	☐	☐
I can find Acts of Parliament and statutory instruments online at the Statute Law Database run by the Ministry of Justice at www.statutelaw.gov.uk	☐	☐
I can also find Acts of Parliament and statutory instruments on the Office of Public Sector Information website at www.opsi.gov.uk/acts.htm	☐	☐
I can find statutes on *LexisLibrary* at my institution	☐	☐
I can find statutes on *Westlaw* at my institution	☐	☐
In order to find prospective legislation, I can find Bills currently before Parliament (and Bills from recent sessions) when I visit http://services.parliament.uk/bills	☐	☐

Are you happy with your current research skills?

....
....
....
....

Legislative procedure

The great bulk of legislation is introduced by the government to implement its policies, now set out in a draft legislative programme at the beginning of each parliamentary session. The aim of the legislation may be to give effect to policies declared in an election manifesto or generated by the work of a government department. Alternatively, it may be a reaction to current events and issues or an attempt to improve and modernise the law, for example as a result of a recommendation by the Law Commission after a process of review and consultation.

The following summary and examples of the background to major legislation in two areas of legal regulation are intended to give you a flavour of the forces behind and the process of making statutory law.

The UK legislative process

Stage 1 – Green Paper

↓

Stage 2 – White Paper

↓

Stage 3a – First Reading (of three)

Stage 3b – Second Reading (of three)

Stage 3c – Committee Stage

Stage 3d – Report Stage

Stage 3e – Third Reading (of three)

↓

Stage 4 – House of Lords

↓

Stage 5 – Queen gives Assent

Example in practice

The Regulation of Assisted Reproduction and Embryological Research: the Human Fertilisation and Embryology Acts of 1990 and 2008

The birth of the first so-called 'test-tube baby', Louise Brown, in Oldham on 14 July 1978 was a landmark for medical science. At the same time, the possibility of in-vitro fertilisation and other developments in embryology raised significant medical and ethical issues. As Lord Bingham put it:

> 'There is no doubting the sensitivity of the issues. There were those who considered the creation of embryos, and thus of life, in vitro to be either sacrilegious or ethically repugnant and wished to ban such activities altogether. There were others who considered that these new techniques, by offering means of enabling the infertile to have children and increasing knowledge of congenital disease, had the potential to improve the human condition, and this view also did not lack religious and moral arguments to support it. Nor can one doubt the difficulty of legislating against a background of fast-moving medical and scientific development. It is not often that Parliament has to frame legislation apt to apply to developments at the advanced cutting edge of science.' (*R (Quintavalle) v Secretary of State for Health* [2003] 2 AC 687 at para 12)

Following extensive consultation, the Warnock Committee published its report as a command paper presented to Parliament in July 1984: Report of the Committee of Inquiry into Human Fertilisation and Embryology (Cmnd 9314). Following debate and further review, a White Paper, based on the Warnock Report was presented to Parliament in 1987: Human Fertilisation and Embryology: A Framework for Legislation (Cm 259). The White Paper provided the basis for the Human Fertilisation and Embryology Bill passed as the Human Fertilisation and Embryology Act on 1 November 1990.

Since the 1990 Act came into force there have been further dramatic advances which have raised new medical and ethical issues. These developments, combined with changing attitudes to same-sex parenthood, led to a comprehensive review of the 1990 Act and major amendments in a new statute, the Human Fertilisation and Embryology Act 2008, passed on 13 November 2008. The extended process of review and consultation leading to the new legislation is summarised below:

- HC Science and Technology Committee Fifth Report of Session 2004–05, Human Reproductive Technologies and the Law
- Government Response; Cm 6641, August 2005
- Review of the HFEA – A Public Consultation – August 2005
- Report on the Consultation, March 2006
- White Paper: Review of the HFEA December 2006; Cm 6989
- Human Tissue and Embryos (Draft) Bill; Cm 7087, 17 May 2007
- Joint Scrutiny Committee Report, 1 August 2007; HL Paper 169–1; HC Paper 630–1
- Government Response to Joint Committee Report; Cm 7209, October 2007
- Human Fertilisation and Embryology Act 2008 (passed 13 November 2008)

Legislation and the Human Rights Act 1998

According to s 19 of the Human Rights Act 1998, before the Second Reading of a Bill in either House of Parliament the Minister responsible for the legislation must make a statement that in his or her view its provisions are compatible with Convention rights under the European Convention on Human Rights 1950 (ECHR); or that the legislation is not compatible but the government wishes to proceed. Under Article 15 of the ECHR, a Member State (of the European Council):

'In time of war or other public emergency threatening the life of the nation ... may take measures derogating from its obligations under this Convention to the extent strictly required by the exigencies of the situation, provided that such measures are not inconsistent with its other obligations under international law'.

Section 14 of the Human Rights Act 1998 delegates this power to derogate (ie 'walk away') from ECHR obligations to the Home Secretary. The Belmarsh case (*A v Secretary of State for the Home Department* [2005] 2 AC 68) provides an excellent example – for a detailed explanation of this case, see our **Companion Website**.

 It's research time! The following exercise will significantly deepen your knowledge of human rights, which underpin the whole of English law:

1 Find the text of the European Convention on Human Rights on the European Court of Human Rights website at www.echr.coe.int/echr. Read Articles 3, 5, 14 and 15.

2 Then locate the House of Lords judgment in *A v Secretary of State for the Home Department* [2004] UKHL 56. Go to the UK Parliament website at www.parliament.uk and follow the link to 'Judicial Work', then 'Judgments' to access the judgments archive.

3 For a summary of the reasons of the majority, read the opinion of Baroness Hale at paras 232–9.

4 Look out for the following passages, and write your own short essay about what you think:

– A number of the judges went to some length to explain that the protection of individual liberty is a central common law tradition (going back to Magna Carta) and not simply a result of the Human Rights Act 1998. Indeed, much of the ECHR, including Article 5, enshrines long-established common law principles.

– However well intentioned (in terms of protecting the security of the nation and population), it is not for the executive to decide who should be detained and certainly not who should be detained indefinitely. See, for example, Lord Bingham at para 36, Lord Hoffmann at paras 86–91 and Baroness Hale at para 222.

5 What is your understanding of the impact of this case on English law?

1.2.2 Statutory interpretation

Although legislation is the supreme source of law, it is the courts that have to interpret statutes when they come to be applied. As with any text, the precise meaning of a statutory provision can be uncertain. The courts therefore have an important role in determining what the law is, even when that law is made by Parliament (including, in the case of European Union law, the European Court of Justice).

The courts spend a large proportion of their time interpreting legal texts. These range from different kinds of contracts and deeds (such as leases, mortgages, transfers, employment contracts, wills, partnership agreements, company articles and so on), Acts (statutes enacted by Parliament) and delegated legislation (where an Act authorises a government Minister or other appropriate person or body to make law on matters specified by the Act). A high proportion of Supreme Court and Court of Appeal cases are about disputed interpretation of statutes and delegated legislation.

The courts' approach to the interpretation of any legal text is essentially the same. They wish to find the true meaning. But is that meaning what the words plainly say or what the drafter intended to say? And is there such a thing as a plain meaning?

The courts' function is to apply the law as laid down by Parliament, paying attention to the principle of parliamentary sovereignty. But this inevitably involves interpretation, ie deciding what the law is. To say that judges merely apply the law made by Parliament and have no active role in making that law is an oversimplification. How creatively do the courts interpret statutes and how creative should they be?

The purposive approach to interpretation

Today's judges recognise that they have a limited creative role to play in applying legislation. They will stick to a literal approach when the words of a statute or statutory instrument are unambiguous. But, however carefully legislation is drafted, its 'meaning' is rarely plain and draftsmen cannot anticipate all outcomes in a courtroom.

(a) The 'purposive' approach

> 'Take the broader approach!'
>
> '[The purposive approach is] filling in gaps and making sense of the enactment.' (*Magor and St Mellons v Newport Corporation* [1952] AC 189, per Lord Denning)

There are other methods that judges can use under the purposive approach when reading legislation. Look at these traditional legal Latin phrases:

- the *ejusdem generis* rule. Where a specific list of words is followed by general words, the general words will follow the same meaning.
- *expressio unius est exclusio alterius* (English translation: 'the mention of one thing excludes all others'). Where there is a list of words, the Act applies to these words only.
- *noscitur a sociis* (English translation: 'a word is known by the company it keeps'). Words are looked at in the context of the words surrounding them.

Lord Bingham in *R (Quintavalle) v Secretary of State for Health* [2003] 2 AC 687

'7 Such is the skill of parliamentary draftsmen that most statutory enactments are expressed in language which is clear and unambiguous and gives rise to no serious controversy.

8 The basic task of the court is to ascertain and give effect to the true meaning of what Parliament has said in the enactment to be construed. But that is not to say that attention should be confined and a literal interpretation given to the particular provisions which give rise to difficulty. The court's task, within the permissible bounds of interpretation, is to give effect to Parliament's purpose. So the controversial provisions should be read in the context of the statute as a whole, and the statute as a whole should be read in the historical context of the situation which led to its enactment.'

The job of the courts, according to Lord Bingham, is to interpret and apply legislation in line with that its purpose. Traditionally, courts restricted themselves to the words of the legislation in order to determine what the purpose of the legislation was. They would not allow themselves, for example, to go behind the legislation to examine what may have been said about it in parliamentary debate. This self-imposed restriction was eventually removed, as we will see, by *Pepper v Hart* [1993] AC 593.

Today's senior judges remain highly sensitive to the judiciary's subordinate role in relation to legislation. It is for our elected Parliament to make the law and for the courts to apply it. At the same time, however, modern courts recognise that the traditional distinction between making law and applying law is sometimes unsound. The courts must identify the real purpose behind the legislation and seek an interpretation which is clearly consistent with that purpose.

(b) The traditional rules of statutory interpretation

All students of English law are taught the traditional rules of statutory interpretation: the literal rule, the golden rule and the mischief rule. In addition, there is an extensive range of accessories – other rules, principles, presumptions and aids – that the courts have developed to help them fulfil their task of deciding what legislation means.

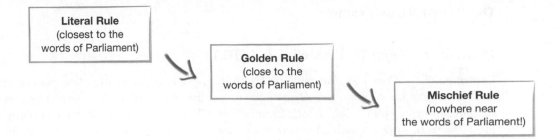

Literal Rule
(closest to the
words of Parliament)

Golden Rule
(close to the
words of Parliament)

Mischief Rule
(nowhere near
the words of Parliament!)

You should have a good grasp of these rules. They will help you understand how the judiciary has developed its role historically, highlight the problems which face judges as interpreters, and they may even help you when you have to interpret a statute yourself.

Bear in mind, however, that these rules and principles of statutory interpretation are not legally binding. They are simply interpretative guidelines and principles which the courts have developed over time. The principles of statutory interpretation are not clearly set out in any judgment, and judges frequently use them without stating that that is what they are doing. The approach favoured by an individual judge will not necessarily be fixed.

Donaldson J in *Corocraft Ltd v Pan American Airways Inc* [1969] 1 QB 622 at 638

'The duty of the courts is to ascertain and give effect to the will of Parliament as expressed in its enactments. In the performance of this duty the judges do not act as computers into which are fed the statutes and the rules for the construction of statutes and from whom issue forth the mathematically correct answer. The interpretation of statutes is a craft as much as a science and the judges, as craftsmen, select and apply the appropriate rules as the tools of their trade. They are not legislators, but finishers, refiners and polishers of legislation which comes to them in a state requiring varying degrees of further polishing.'

(i) The literal rule

The first rule requires that the words used in a statute must be given their 'plain and obvious meaning' in the context of the Act, whether an everyday meaning or a technical meaning. In a number of notorious cases, this approach has led to outcomes that were probably not intended by Parliament when it passed the legislation in question (because the judgment made no logical sense!).

The case discussed below resulted in the defendant's acquittal, despite the fact that he had clearly committed what the legislation intended to criminalise, namely electoral fraud.

The literal rule: an example

Whiteley v Chappell (1868–69) LR 4 QB 147

Under s 3 of the Poor Law Amendment Act 1851 a person impersonating 'any person entitled to vote at an election' of guardians of the poor was guilty of an offence punishable by a maximum sentence of three months in prison. The appellant, Chappell, had been charged with impersonating J Marston, a person entitled to vote at an election for guardians of the poor for Bradford. As a ratepayer Marston had indeed been entitled to vote but he had died before the election was held. Chappell, who had used Marston's ballot paper to vote, was convicted of the offence under s 3 at Manchester magistrates' court. On appeal to the Queen's Bench Division the judges held that Chappell could not have been guilty. Since a dead man cannot vote Chappell had not impersonated 'a person entitled to vote' and therefore his conviction should be quashed. As Lush J put it at 148–9:

> 'I do not think we can, without straining them, bring the case within the words of the enactment. The legislature has not used words wide enough to make the personation of a dead person an offence. The words "a person entitled to vote" can only mean, without a forced construction, a person who is entitled to vote at the time at which the personation takes place.'

See our Companion Website for another famous example, *Fisher v Bell* [1961] 1 QB 394.

Activity Look closely at the extract from *Quintavalle* above. Do you think that the decision is morally right? Have the Lords, in your opinion, used the law correctly, or incorrectly? Why do you think they have interpreted the law in the way that they have?

....
....
....
....
....

(ii) The golden rule

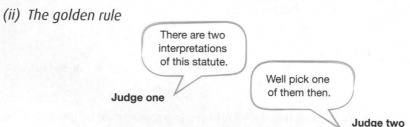

This rule has traditionally been said to apply where the application of the literal rule proves impossible. The golden rule is sometimes described as an accessory to the literal rule, in that it is used where the literal rule fails. With the narrow application of the golden rule, the court will find a meaning from a limited selection of alternatives. With the wider application, the court will find a meaning that fits with the purpose of the statute.

The golden rule: an example

Adler v George [1964] 2 QB 7

Section 3 of the Official Secrets Act 1920 provides that 'No person in the vicinity of any pro-hibited place shall obstruct, knowingly mislead or otherwise interfere with or impede, the chief officer or a superintendent or other officer of police, or any member of His Majesty's forces engaged on guard, sentry, patrol, or other similar duty in relation to the prohibited place, and, if any person acts in contravention of, or fails to comply with, this provision, he shall be guilty of a misdemeanour.' The defendant, George, had entered a Royal Airforce Station and obstructed a member of the Airforce. George was convicted in the magistrates' court under s 3 and appealed on the basis that he was 'in' a prohibited place, not 'in the vicinity' of one, and therefore could not be guilty of the offence. Although literally correct as to the meaning of 'in the vicinity', George's argument was unsuccessful. The court held unanimously that Parliament cannot have intended to create the s 3 offence to apply outside but not within prohibited places. In the words of Lord Parker CJ (at 9–10):

> 'I am quite satisfied that this is a case where no violence is done to the language by reading the words "in the vicinity of" as meaning "in or in the vicinity of". Here is a section in an Act of Parliament designed to prevent interference with members of Her Majesty's forces, among others, who are engaged on guard, sentry, patrol or other simi-lar duty in relation to a prohibited place such as this station. It would be extraordinary, I venture to think it would be absurd, if an indictable offence was thereby created when the obstruction took place outside the precincts of the station, albeit in the vicinity, and no offence at all was created if the obstruction occurred on the station itself.'

See our **Companion Website** for another famous example of the golden rule: *R v Allen* (1872) LR1 CCR 367.

Activity Jot down your thoughts on the following:

In what way is the golden rule case different from the example given for the literal rule above? Could the same reasoning as that applied in *Adler v George* have been deployed in *Whiteley v Chappell* to convict Chappell? Why was George convicted where Chappell had been acquitted? Are the different interpretative approaches justified?

(iii) The mischief rule

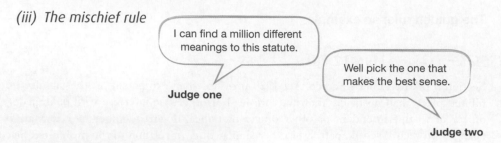

Under the third rule of statutory interpretation, the court looks at *why* an Act was passed in order to enable it to interpret that Act. In the classic statement of this rule, by the Barons of the Court of Exchequer in *Heydon's Case* (1584) 3 Co Rep 7a, judges must identify and consider four things in order to interpret a statute: the common law before the Act came into force, the mischief or defect the common law did not cover, the remedy the Act provided and the reason for that remedy.

When the mischief rule was first developed, the courts did not have to look further than the Act itself to discover the mischief that it was intended to 'cure'. That is not the case with modern statutes, and judges need to be cautious about looking outside an Act for guidance as to its intended meaning:

Lord Diplock in *Black-Clawson International Ltd v Papierwerke Waldhof-Aschaffenburg Aktiengesellschaft* [1975] AC 591 at 639

'The rule was propounded by the judges in an age when statutes were drafted in a form very different from that which they assume today. Those who composed the Parliaments of those days thought it necessary to incorporate in the statute the reasons which justified the changes in the common law that the statute made. Statutes in the sixteenth century and for long thereafter in addition to the enacting words contained lengthy preambles reciting the particular mischief or defect in the common law that the enacting words were designed to remedy. In construing modern statutes which contain no preambles to serve as aids to the construction of enacting words, the "mischief" rule must be used with caution to justify any reference to extraneous documents for this purpose.'

Since modern Acts no longer contain lengthy preambles which describe the purpose of the legislation, the judiciary has to look elsewhere to find out what, precisely, Parliament intended. The general purpose of an Act may well be clear from the Act itself, but the purpose of a particular word in a particular section may be uncertain without going behind the Act to examine the background to it and the reasons why it was drafted as it was. Since 1999, Explanatory Notes have been published to explain the purposes and key provisions of Bills and subsequently passed Acts of Parliament. Although Explanatory Notes are not part of the Act itself and not endorsed by Parliament, they can provide a useful guide to statutory interpretation.

For Lord Steyn's opinion on Explanatory Notes, see *R (Westminster City Council) v National Asylum Support Services* [2002] 1 WLR 2956 on our **Companion Website**.

An example of the mischief rule

Smith v Hughes [1960] 1 WLR 830

Under s 1(1) of the Street Offences Act 1959 'It shall be an offence for a common prostitute to loiter or solicit in a street or public place for the purpose of prostitution.' The defendants in the case had been advertising their services by standing on the balcony or at the windows of their premises and attracting the attention of men passing along the street outside. Although the defendants were not themselves physically present in the street they were nevertheless convicted of the s 1(1) offence at Bow Street magistrates' court. The defendants appealed and the Queen's Bench Division upheld their convictions. Explicitly applying the mischief rule Lord Parker CJ was happy to hold that the words 'solicit in a street' covered the situation where the prostitutes were soliciting from premises on a street to men passing by in the street:

> 'The sole question here is whether in those circumstances each defendant was soliciting in a street or public place. The words of s 1(1) of the Act of 1959 are in this form: "It shall be an offence for a common prostitute to loiter or solicit in a street or public place for the purpose of prostitution." Observe that it does not say specifically that the person who is doing the soliciting must be in the street. Equally, it does not say that it is enough if the person who receives the solicitation or to whom it is addressed is in the street. For my part, I approach the matter by considering what is the mischief aimed at by this Act. Everybody knows that this was an Act intended to clean up the streets, to enable people to walk along the streets without being molested or solicited by common prostitutes. Viewed in that way, it can matter little whether the prostitute is soliciting while in the street or is standing in a doorway or on a balcony, or at a window, or whether the window is shut or open or half open; in each case her solicitation is projected to and addressed to somebody walking in the street.' (at 832)

See our Companion Website for another famous example of the mischief rule: *Royal College of Nursing v Department of Health and Social Security* [1981] AC 800.

 Now it is your turn to be a judge! In the space below, make a comment about how you believe all the cases above would have ended depending on the rule of interpretation the judges might have applied:

	The literal rule	The golden rule	The mischief rule
Whiteley v Chappell (1868–69) LR 4 QB 147			
Fisher v Bell [1961] 1 QB 394			

	The literal rule	The golden rule	The mischief rule
R v Allen (1872) LR1 CCR 367			
Adler v George [1964] 2 QB 7			
Smith v Hughes [1960] 1 WLR 830			
Royal College of Nursing v Department of Health and Social Security [1981] AC 800			

(c) *Hansard*, the exclusionary rule and *Pepper v Hart*

In cases where the meaning of a statute is unclear, courts have long accepted that they can look at preparatory materials, such as official reports and command papers, to clarify what mischief the legislation was intended to remedy.

Hansard is the official daily report of proceedings in both Houses of Parliament, but it can only be used according to the strict criteria established in *Pepper v Hart* [1993] AC 59: (a) legislation is ambiguous or obscure, or leads to an absurdity; (b) the material relied upon consists of one or more statements by a Minister or other promoter of the Bill together if necessary with such other parliamentary material as is necessary to understand such statements and their effect; (c) the statements relied upon are clear. Otherwise, it must be excluded from consideration by judges when interpreting Acts of Parliament.

For further information about *Hansard* and how *Pepper v Hart* changed the legal landscape, see our Companion Website for further cases and judgments.

Activity Statutory interpretation is a large area of the English Legal System to take in. So, it's time to consolidate your knowledge.

Find the following case in your law library:

R (Jackson and others) v Attorney-General [2005] UKHL 56.

This case – about the validity of the Hunting Act 2004 which bans hunting wild animals with dogs – was of major constitutional importance. An appellate committee of nine judges was convened to decide it instead of the usual five judges. The case turned on the interpretation of s 2(1) of the Parliament Act 1911 as amended by s 1 of the Parliament Act 1949. This allows legislation to be enacted without the consent of the House of Lords, preventing the Upper House from blocking legislation approved by the House of Commons. The appellants argued that the 1949 Act was itself invalid, making the Hunting Act, passed under the amended procedure, invalid. The House of Lords unanimously held that the 1949 amendment and the 2004 Act were valid.

Locate the report of the case on the parliamentary website at www.parliament.uk. Follow the link to 'Judicial Work' then 'Judgments' to access the judgments archive.

The majority of judges who considered the issue felt that this was not a case in which reference to *Hansard* was required. Lord Nicholls, on the other hand, argued that ministerial statements during the passage of the 1911 Act through Parliament provided useful confirmation of its intended meaning.

Read paras 65–6 and 97–8 and compare them. Answer the following essay questions:
- What is the difference between the views expressed by Lord Nicholls and Lord Steyn?
- Why did the former approve the use of *Hansard* in the case while the latter judged it unnecessary?

See, for example, Lord Nicholls at 65–6 and Lord Steyn at 97–8 and Lord Phillips in *R v JTB* [2009] UKHL 20 at 35.

(d) Statutory interpretation and the effect of the Human Rights Act 1998

Section 3(1) of the Human Rights Act 1998 provides that: 'So far as it is possible to do so, primary legislation and subordinate legislation must be read and given effect in a way which is compatible with the Convention rights.'

The European Convention on Human Rights and Fundamental Freedoms is partly incorporated into English law by the 1998 Act. If a UK court cannot find an interpretation of a statutory provision that is compatible with the Convention, it may make a declaration of incompatibility under s 4 to bring the incompatibility to the attention of Parliament, but it must still apply the legislation. Our courts do not have the power to strike down incompatible legislation.

Statute

Declaration of incompatibility!!!

In *Ghaidan v Godin-Mendoza* [2004] 2 AC 557 a majority of four judges in the House of Lords construed the words 'a person who was living with the original tenant as his or her wife or husband' in para 2(2) of Sch 1 to the Rent Act 1977 as meaning 'as if they were his or her wife or husband'. This was in order to ensure that the Rent Act was compatible with Article 8 (right to respect for a person's ... home) in conjunction with Article 14 (right not to be discriminated against in respect of substantive Convention rights). Otherwise, the Rent Act would have provided security of tenure for the surviving partner of a deceased heterosexual co-habitant tenant where it would not for the surviving partner of a deceased homosexual cohabitant tenant.

- Your first task is to locate the report of the case on the parliamentary website at www.parliament.uk. Follow the link to 'Judicial Work' then 'Judgments' to access the judgments archive. The full text of the case is cited as *Ghaidan v Godin-Mendoza* [2004] UKHL 30.

Lord Millett, dissenting, considered it impossible to interpret the words 'a person who was living with the original tenant as his or her wife or husband' in a way that covered homosexual relationships. He nevertheless agreed with the majority that discrimination between straight and gay couples, in the context of statutory rights to succeed to a tenancy, would be a clear violation of the respondent's Convention rights under Article 8 in conjunction with Article 14.

- Read para 82 of Lord Millett's opinion and para 144 of Baroness Hale's opinion. Who do you think is right? Is the answer a matter of language or of your own attitude to issues of sexual orientation?

Now go to www.opsi.gov.uk/acts.htm and find the Civil Partnership Act 2004. Read para 13(3) of Sch 8.

- How has this amended para 2 of Sch 1 to the Rent Act 1977?
- Is this consistent with the decision of the House of Lords in *Ghaidan v Godin-Mendoza*?

Note that in the same case the Court of Appeal had already chosen not to follow the previous decision of the House of Lords in *Fitzpatrick v Sterling Housing Association* [2001] 1 AC 27.

- Why do you think that the Court of Appeal did not follow the House of Lords?

1.2.3   Case law and precedent

So far we have considered statute law, made up of Acts of Parliament and delegated legislation, and the essential role of the judiciary in deciding what statute law actually means. The other main source of English law, and the one that is fundamental to our common law system, is case law, or 'judge-made' law.

The scope of judicial law making: setting and following precedents

You may be familiar with the notion of 'setting a precedent'. Precedents are rules that others must follow when in a similar situation.

My precedents! Make a note in this space of previous decisions you have made and then followed ever since when the same problem or situation has arisen:

....

....

....

....

....

....

....

A great deal of what we do is regulated by precedent. Think about how in the family, school, university, workplace and sporting context, precedent operates to regulate our relationships and behaviour. Parents, teachers, employers, sports authorities and referees are quickly made aware of inconsistent decisions by those subjected to them. Fairness demands equal treatment which requires consistency. Treating like cases alike is central to the rule of law.

When, in the famous trial scene in Shakespeare's *The Merchant of Venice*, Bassanio begs Portia to bend the law to prevent Antonio's death by denying Shylock's strict legal rights, Portia, disguised as the legal expert Balthazar, points out that this would undermine the entire legal edifice of Venice and the state itself:

> Bassanio: *And I beseech you*
> *Wrest once the law to your authority, –*
> *To do a great right, do a little wrong, –*
> *And curb this cruel devil of his will.*

> Portia: *It must not be, there is no power in Venice*
> *Can alter a decree established:*
> *'Twill be recorded for a precedent,*
> *And many an error by the same example*
> *Will rush into the state, – it cannot be.*

> *The Merchant of Venice* (ll.210–218)

The rule of law, therefore, must be respected. It would be unconstitutional for the court to override legislation or depart from established precedent. Law must be transparent, predictable and consistently applied.

It has not always been accepted that judges make law at all:

> 'There is in fact no such thing as judge made law, for the judges do not make the law though they frequently have to apply existing law to circumstances as to which it has not previously been authoritatively laid down that such law is applicable.' (Lord Esher, *Willis v Baddeley* [1892] 2 QB 324 at 236)

The obvious flaw in that argument is that it begs the question of where our common law rules came from in the first place. Many principles have in fact been formulated and developed by the courts:

'The whole of the rules of equity and nine tenths of the common law have in fact been made by judges.' (Mellish LJ, *Allen v Jackson* (1875) 1 ChD 399 at 405)

This idea was captured by Lord Goff in a passage headed 'The declaratory theory of judicial decisions' in his opinion in *Kleinwort Benson v Lincoln City Council* [1999] 2 AC 349:

Lord Goff in *Kleinwort Benson Ltd v Lincoln City Council* [1999] 2 AC 349 at 377–8

'When a judge decides a case which comes before him, he does so on the basis of what he understands the law to be. This he discovers from the applicable statutes, if any, and from precedents drawn from reports of previous judicial decisions. Nowadays, he derives much assistance from academic writings in interpreting statutes and, more especially, the effect of reported cases; and he has regard, where appropriate, to decisions of judges in other jurisdictions. In the course of deciding the case before him he may, on occasion, develop the common law in the perceived interests of justice, though as a general rule he does this "only interstitially," to use the expression of O. W. Holmes J. in Southern Pacific Co. v. Jensen (1917) 244 U.S. 205, 221. ... he must act within the confines of the doctrine of precedent, and the change so made must be seen as a development, usually a very modest development, of existing principle and so can take its place as a congruent part of the common law as a whole.

Occasionally, a judicial development of the law will be of a more radical nature, constituting a departure, even a major departure, from what has previously been considered to be established principle, and leading to a realignment of subsidiary principles within that branch of the law.'

 Activity In your own words, interpret (translate into a more simple form) Lord Goff's idea:

....

....

....

....

....

The real issue for our courts has always been how far judges should go in developing the common law. Sometimes, judges find themselves compelled to go further and they make a decision which represents an evolutionary leap in law rather than another small step.

In 1932, there came a very big common law leap. Prior to the majority decision of the House of Lords in *Donoghue v Stevenson* [1932] AC 562, the circumstances in which the courts had held a defendant liable for causing damage to a claimant when not in a contract with the defendant were limited to specific, established categories of relationship and circumstance.

In *Donoghue v Stevenson*, the House of Lords held that a manufacturer is liable for personal injury or property damage to any person who uses his good if his good is negligently produced. The Law Lords were divided three to two. Tellingly, the leading majority and minority opinions of Lord Atkin and Lord Buckmaster respectively used the same previously decided cases on negligence as legal authorities to support their opposite conclusions!

On occasions, the courts will state that it is not their function to alter the law in response to changes in society and morality. That is the job of Parliament. As a good example, the House of Lords decided that it was legitimate to withdraw life support from a patient in a persistent vegetative state in Airedale *NHS Trust v Bland* [1993] 1 All ER 821. Lord Browne-Wilkinson and his fellow Law Lords were clear that it would be more appropriate for the legislature to make the law on this issue:

> '... the moral, social and legal issues raised by this case should be considered by Parliament. The judges' function in this area of the law should be to apply the principles which society, through the democratic process, adopts, not to impose their standards on society. If Parliament fails to act, then judge-made law will of necessity through a gradual and uncertain process provide a legal answer to each new question as it arises. But in my judgment that is not the best way to proceed.' (Lord Browne-Wilkinson, *Airedale NHS Trust v Bland* [1993] 1 All ER 821 at 879)

Activity The decision in *Bland* is just as controversial today as it was in the 1990s. Why do you think judges avoid making controversial laws? Does it frustrate you – as a potential lawyer – that sometimes judges simply walk away from a difficult case and leave difficult decisions to Parliament?

What is judicial precedent?

You will sometimes find the doctrine of precedent referred to as the doctrine of *stare decisis*. *Stare decisis et non quieta movere* means 'stand by decided cases and do not disturb established practices'. The rule has been self-imposed by the courts in the interests of certainty, predictability and maintaining their own authority.

The essential ingredients of precedent for a court are:

- *The hierarchy of the courts.* If a precedent comes from a decision of a higher court then the lower courts must follow it in the present case (it is a binding precedent). If a precedent is a previous decision of a lower court, it will have persuasive force only and the present court is not bound to follow it.

- *Ratio decidendi.* For a precedent to be binding, the principle of law that it establishes must form part of the *ratio decidendi* (the essential reason for the decision) of the judgment and not be *obiter dictum* (something said 'by the way' that is incidental to the actual decision).

- *Applicable.* For a precedent to be binding, the principle of law it establishes must be relevant to the facts of the present case (distinguishing the facts of the present case from the previous one – the precedent case – is the standard way of avoiding being bound by a precedent).

- *Valid.* For a precedent to be binding, it must not have been repealed or altered by statute or a later court (ie a higher court which has power to overrule the decision).

(a) Finding the *ratio* in a judgment

Under the doctrine of precedent, courts use previous decisions to provide the legal answers to new cases before them. The precedent is not the previous decision itself (in the sense that Mr X won the case); the precedent is the element which determined *why* the case reached the outcome it did, also known as the *ratio decidendi* of the case.

Activity Can you pick out the *ratio* – or the 'deciding sentence' – out of the whole paragraph below?

'Tilly plagiarised her entire assignment – everything was copied from the parliamentary website. I called her and she wasn't home. Her mother hung up on me! Therefore, as a result of the plagiarism combined with the poor study skills, Tilly will have to re-take her assignment. She has no one to blame but herself. Next year, her study skills should be much better.'

Hint: The *ratio* is usually the 'final decision' of the speaker or the writer.

....

....

....

....

....

It is widely agreed that finding the *ratio* is often far from easy. Recently, in cases of particular constitutional importance, the Law Lords (now Justices of the Supreme Court) have sat as a committee of nine (following the model of the US Supreme Court) in order to give their decisions the greatest possible authority: for example in *A v Secretary of State for the Home Department* [2005] 2 AC 68 and *R (Jackson and others) v Attorney-General* [2006] 1 AC 262.

Activity Let's get practical. Do you think you could recognise a *ratio* in a case judgment? Pick out the *ratio decidendi* from the following collection of quotes:

'The defendant stabbed the victim. He fled the scene. He showed no remorse – in fact, there is evidence that he planned the attack. It is held that the defendant is guilty of this assault.'

....

'The plaintiff cannot possibly expect to win this case – she provided no consideration for the item and her acceptance was delayed by an unreasonable time. Action for the appellant.'

....

'The previous case law seems to assert that as long as the defendant is intoxicated, he is still in possession of a reckless state of mind. I cannot argue with this notion. The defendant drank 10 units of alcohol in two minutes. He harmed himself and others. He was reckless in his alcohol consumption. The defendant is guilty of this offence.'

....

'The appellant admitted he hated the victim. This alone constitutes a blameworthy state of mind.'

....

The *ratio decidendi* has to be picked out from the judgment or judgments given by the court and, in truth, will only fully emerge in time as it is considered, applied and developed by later courts in later cases.

Let us take *Donoghue v Stevenson* as an example, which may be the most famous case in the development of our common law. The facts are set out in the headnote to the judgment:

Donoghue v Stevenson [1932] AC 562 at 562–3

'The appellant, who was a shop assistant, sought to recover damages from the respondent, who was a manufacturer of aerated waters, for injuries she suffered as a result of consuming part of the contents of a bottle of ginger-beer which had been manufactured by the respondent, and which contained the decomposed remains of a snail. The appellant by her condescendence averred that the bottle of ginger-beer was purchased for the appellant by a friend in a café at Paisley, which was occupied by one Minchella; that the bottle was made of dark opaque glass and that the appellant had no reason to suspect that it contained anything but pure ginger-beer; that the said Minchella poured some of the ginger-beer out into a tumbler, and that the appellant drank some of the contents of the tumbler; that her friend was then proceeding to pour the remainder of the contents of the bottle into the tumbler when a snail, which was in a state of decomposition, floated out of the bottle; that as a result of the nauseating sight of the snail in such circumstances, and in consequence of the impurities in the ginger-beer which she had already consumed, the appellant suffered from shock and severe gastro-enteritis. The appellant averred that it was the duty of the respondent to provide a system of working his business which would not allow snails to get into his ginger-beer bottles, and that it was also his duty to provide an efficient system of inspection of the bottles before the ginger-beer was filled into them, and that he had failed in both these duties and had so caused the accident.'

Because the appellant (Donoghue) had no contractual relationship with the café owner (Minchella), her only possible legal claim was against the respondent manufacturer (Stevenson) in negligence. Despite the lack of clear precedents, the House of Lords held that Stevenson would be liable if the alleged facts were proved at trial. The case therefore decided that a manufacturer of certain products owed a duty to the end consumer (ie no contract was needed) to take reasonable care in their preparation.

So what does the *ratio* of *Donoghue* look like? The legal principle on which liability in negligence is based is very widely stated by Lord Atkin (at 580) in the so-called 'neighbour test':

'The liability for negligence, whether you style it such or treat it as in other systems as a species of "culpa," is no doubt based upon a general public sentiment of moral wrongdoing for which the offender must pay. The rule that you are to love your neighbour becomes in law, you must not injure your neighbour; and the lawyer's question, Who is my neighbour? receives a restricted reply. You must take reasonable care to avoid acts or omissions which you can reasonably foresee would be likely to injure your neighbour. Who, then, in law is my neighbour? The answer seems to be – persons who are so closely and directly affected by my act that I ought reasonably to have them in contemplation as being so affected when I am directing my mind to the acts or omissions which are called in question.'

Activity *Donoghue v Stevenson*: **now that you have read all about this special case that changed the law so dramatically, write in the space below, in Lord Atkin's exact words, what his** *ratio* **of the case is. Remember, a** *ratio* **is the 'final decision', and it is usually very short.**

....

....

....

....

....

....

....

For further activities on distinguishing precedents, see our Companion Website.

(b) Precedent and the hierarchy of the courts

In England, we have a special 'pyramid' of courts, which consists of smaller courts at the bottom and really important, powerful courts at the top. Cases start at the bottom, and they travel up through the court system if the parties keep appealing against the decisions. The Supreme Court, at the very top, then decides on important points of law.

(i) The Supreme Court

In the Supreme Court, formerly known as the House of Lords, decisions are binding on all courts except the Supreme Court itself. The House of Lords historically regarded itself as bound by its own previous decisions. If the law needed changing it was for Parliament to change it. This practice was affirmed in *London Tramways v London County Council* [1898] AC 375.

In reality, when it chose to, the House of Lords could and did get around inconvenient binding precedents by distinguishing them creatively from the case before it. In 1966 the House of Lords decided that its previously rigid public position failed to strike the right balance between certainty and the need for change in the common law. The Law Lords therefore declared that they had the power to overrule their own previous decisions:

Practice Statement [1966] 3 All ER 77, 1 WLR 1234

'Their Lordships regard the use of precedent as an indispensable foundation upon which to decide what is the law and its application to individual cases. It provides at least some degree of certainty upon which individuals can rely in the conduct of their affairs, as well as a basis for orderly development of legal rules.

Their lordships nevertheless recognise that too rigid an adherence to precedent may lead to injustice in a particular case and also unduly restrict the proper development of the law. They propose, therefore, to modify their present practice and, while treating former decisions of this House as normally binding, to depart from a previous decision when it appears right to do so.'

(ii) The Court of Appeal

The Court of Appeal is bound to follow Supreme Court/House of Lords decisions, even where it disagrees with them. The current position is that the Court of Appeal must follow the highest court's authority unless it can distinguish the case before it from the precedent case, or the House of Lords decision has been overruled by statute or by a decision of the European Court of Justice or because of the requirements of the Human Rights Act 1998.

The Court of Appeal is bound to follow its own decisions subject to strictly limited exceptions. The classic statement of this rule was set out by Lord Greene MR, giving judgment for a full court of six judges in *Young v Bristol Aeroplane Co Ltd* [1944] KB 718 at 723–5.

The long-established exceptions are:

1   Where previous Court of Appeal decisions conflict, the present Court must decide which to follow and which to reject.

2   The Court of Appeal must refuse to follow a decision of its own which cannot stand with a House of Lords decision, ie where it has been impliedly overruled.

3   The Court of Appeal is not bound to follow a decision of its own if it is satisfied that the previous decision was given *per incuriam* (in ignorance of the relevant law: where some relevant authority – a statutory provision or precedent – which would have led to a different decision has not been taken into account by the court).

A well-known example of a Privy Council decision effectively overruling a Court of Appeal precedent, on the test for foreseeability of damage in negligence, is *Overseas Tankship (UK) Ltd v Morts Dock Engineering Co Ltd (The Wagon Mound No 1)* [1961] AC 388, overruling *Re Polemis & Furness, Withy & Co Ltd* [1921] 3 KB 560. Privy Council judgments are said to be of persuasive precedent force only, as the Privy Council sits as the final appeal court for (a decreasing number of) Commonwealth jurisdictions. However, as the Justices of the Supreme Court are the judges for the Judicial Committee of the Privy Council, its decisions are highly persuasive.

Activity As you can see, the Court of Appeal is a very busy court, with its own divisions and some authoritative powers. Jot down in this space your own definition of the role of the Court of Appeal in the UK English Legal System:

....

....

....

....

....

....

....

....

....

....

(iii) Other courts

Below the Court of Appeal, there are criminal and civil courts which follow their own pathway.

Murder!		Breach of contract!

Criminal courts   **Civil courts**

Self-assessment

Me and the law! Tick the statement that applies to you...	Very confident	Would like to be more confident
I know how the English Legal System works	☐	☐
I know where to find research on the English Legal System	☐	☐
I know how to express my views about the law in my country	☐	☐
I understand what my lecturer means when he or she talks about 'other jurisdictions'	☐	☐
I understand what my lecturer means when he or she talks about 'common law'	☐	☐
I understand how the common law is developed	☐	☐
I understand how the common law constitutes a primary source of English law	☐	☐

My biggest concern at the start of my course:

....

....

....

....

....

....

....

....

....

1.3   THE IMPORTANCE OF EUROPEAN UNION LAW

Law students need to understand the English Legal System in the context of the UK's membership of the European Union.

What is the European Union?

The European Union as we know it today has 27 Member States and encompasses a number of policy areas and areas of cooperation. However, it started life much smaller and with a much narrower focus. In 1951 six countries (Germany, France, Italy, Belgium, Luxembourg and The Netherlands) signed up to the European Coal and Steel Community (ECSC) which had as its core the shared control of coal and steel production in the territory. The original Treaty set up a number of institutions to oversee the ECSC and laid the foundation for what was to come.

The institutional structure

The four most important EU institutions – the Commission, the Council, the Parliament and the Court of Justice – are institutions with which you need to be familiar because they are involved in the making, as well as enforcement, of EU law.

The Commission proposes new laws and has a fundamental role to play in the enforcement of EU law and has been called 'The Guardian of the Treaties'. The term 'Commission' is used in two distinct ways. First, it refers to the 27 Commissioners, one from each Member State, who each take responsibility for a policy area such as trade or the environment. Secondly, the term refers to all the staff who work in the Commission and do the bulk of the day-to-day work.

The Council and the Parliament share the main legislative power within the institutional structure. The Parliament is directly elected by nationals of the Member States and represents their interests. The Council represents the interests of the individual Member States. Up to four times a year, the heads of the national governments meet. These summits do not provide a forum for law making but are important in terms of policy making and outlining the general direction the Member States wish the EU to take.

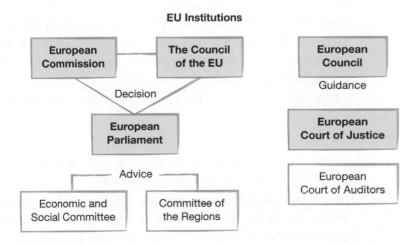

The fourth institution is the European Court of Justice (ECJ), which also encompasses the General Court (formerly the Court of First Instance) to help cope with an ever-increasing caseload. Its job is to make sure that EU legislation is interpreted and applied in the same way in all EU countries, and to make sure that EU Member States and institutions do what the law requires. The Court has the power to settle legal disputes between EU Member States, EU institutions, businesses and individuals.

Self-assessment

How confident am I on the European Union? Tick the statement that applies to you...	Very confident	Would like to be more confident
I know what the European Union is	☐	☐
I understand why the UK's membership of the EU affects our UK law	☐	☐
I know how the EU influences UK law	☐	☐
I am aware of the basic structure of EU law	☐	☐
I know of the main bodies within EU law	☐	☐
I know what jobs each of the institutions have within the EU law-making process	☐	☐
I know how to research EU law	☐	☐

My action plan for the understanding of EU law:

....

....

....

....

....

Law making in the EU

Law making is increasingly exercised on multiple levels: local, regional, national, European and international. The European Union is a body of limited powers. It enjoys powers *only* in those areas where the Member States have agreed to pool their national sovereignty. The European Union therefore does not have a completely free hand to decide how, and what, it will legislate on; it can only act where it has the *competence* to do so. Where it does have competence, the EU can make law which is then supreme over national law. In situations where national law and EU law conflict, the EU provision should prevail.

Enforcing EU law

Individuals do not go before the European Court of Justice to enforce their EU law rights. Instead, they do this before their national courts.

National courts can make references for preliminary rulings to the ECJ on questions of EU law. The ECJ then answers the questions put by the national court, and the national court continues to hear the case in accordance with the ECJ's ruling.

The principle of Union loyalty or fidelity (Treaty on European Union, Article 4(3)) means there is an obligation on Member States to enforce EU law, and Member States cannot introduce or maintain national laws which conflict with commitments contained within EU law. If a Member State breaches EU law obligations, the institutions or another Member State can take legal action against that State.

Francovich and Bonifaci v Italy (Cases 6 & 9/90) [1990] ECR I-5357 at 5415

'It must be held that the full effectiveness of Community rules would be impaired and the protection of the rights which they grant would be weakened if individuals were unable to obtain compensation when their rights are infringed by a breach of Community law for which a Member State can be held responsible.'

Different types of law: sources of EU law

EU law comes in a variety of formats and this section will discuss them in turn:

- The Treaties
- Secondary legislation
- Decisions of the Court of Justice
- General principles of EU law

(a) The Treaties

The Treaties provide the framework of EU law. They are considered to be the primary legislation and the primary source of EU law. What are now referred to as 'the Treaties' actually began life as two treaties which were signed in Rome in 1957. The primary treaty is therefore often referred to as the 'Treaty of Rome'. This Treaty has been updated and amended many times over the years by a succession of treaties and other important legal acts:

- Merger Treaty 1965
- Acts of Accession
  - 1972 (UK, Ireland and Denmark)
  - 1979 (Greece)
  - 1985 (Spain and Portugal)
  - 1995 (Austria, Finland and Sweden)
  - 2003 (Eight Eastern European States, Malta and Cyprus)
  - 2005 (Bulgaria and Romania)
- Single European Act 1986
- Treaty of Maastricht (Treaty on European Union (TEU)) 1992
- Treaty of Amsterdam 1997
- Treaty of Nice 2000
- Treaty of Accession 2003
- Constitutional Treaty 2004 (failed)
- Lisbon Treaty 2009

(b) Secondary legislation

The Treaties are supported, clarified and expanded upon through various forms of secondary legislation. The process of adoption and impact of the secondary legislation varies according to its type, so it is important to know what sort of secondary legislation you are dealing with.

(i) Regulations

Regulations are the most all-encompassing form of EU secondary legislation, and they leave Member States with little power in terms of implementation and application. Regulations apply in their entirety to all Member States. They are 'directly applicable', which means that there is no need for implementing legislation. Instead Regulations become law in all the Member States automatically. Member States have to make provisions in their own legal systems to accommodate this principle of direct applicability. In the UK the relevant legal instrument is the European Communities Act 1972 (as amended).

(ii) Directives

Directives are widely used in EU law making. They are only binding on those Member States to which they are addressed, although this often includes all 27 Member States. Directives differ in one important respect from Regulations. They are binding only as to the result to be achieved. This requires the Member States to implement the Directive through their national legal systems. This allows Member States to choose their own form and methods of achieving the objectives set out in the Directive taking account of national traditions, customs and contexts.

(iii) Decisions

The third type of secondary legislation is Decisions. Decisions are binding in their entirety on those to whom they are addressed. They may be addressed to Member States, companies or individuals. There is no need for any implementing legislation but the Decision must be notified to those addressed in it.

(iv) Recommendations and Opinions

Recommendations and Opinions are non-binding secondary legislation, but they can be persuasive and can also often act as a forerunner to binding secondary legislation. Recommendations and Opinions are a form of 'soft law'.

(c) Jurisprudence of the European Court of Justice

The ECJ and General Court together produce quite an impressive number of judgments each year. It is important to remember that while these decisions form binding law in the Member State, the doctrine of precedent does not operate in EU law and the ECJ is thus not technically bound by its own decisions in the same way that courts in England and Wales are bound by previous decisions. Conflicting decisions in EU law or similar cases being argued along different lines are not uncommon, and the judges do not often explain fully why they are departing from previous decisions. Because there is no doctrine of precedent, there is no need for the ECJ to explicitly overrule, confirm or distinguish earlier decisions, and while this allows for a flexible and purposive approach to deciding cases and interpreting legislation it can also be a little confusing at times.

Issue

I understand what Treaties are and how much power they have ☐

I understand how Regulations are made and what they do ☐

I know how Directives are made and how much power they have ☐

I am aware of the various Decisions that can possess an authority in EU law ☐

I know that Recommendations and Opinions can have an influence in EU law ☐

I understand that the ECJ has significant power in EU law ☐

I know what the general principles of EU law are and why they are important ☐

Interpretation of European Union legislation in the UK

Section 2(1) of the European Communities Act 1972 provides that directly applicable European Union law is immediately part of UK law without any further legislation to incorporate it, even where it conflicts with national law. This means that all Treaty articles, Regulations and Decisions are directly applicable, while under the doctrine of direct effect Directives may be directly applicable in English law. In order to have direct effect in national law, Treaty provisions and other forms of legislation must be clear, precise, unconditional and require no further action by the State for implementation: *Van Gend en Loos* 26/62 [1963] ECR 1.

Under s 2(2) of the European Communities Act 1972, any European Union obligation can be implemented by an Order in Council or statutory instrument. Thus the executive uses delegated legislation to implement relevant EU Directives, frequently amending UK law, without the need for primary legislation.

Since all directly applicable EU law is immediately part of national law under s 2(1) of the European Communities Act 1972, all parliamentary legislation, whenever passed, must be interpreted and applied consistently with EU law. Any provisions of national law that conflict with EU law are inapplicable (s 2(4)).

R v Secretary of State for Transport ex parte Factortame (No 2) [1991] 1 AC 603 demonstrated the supremacy of Community (now EU) law in those areas to which it applies:

> 'Under the terms of the 1972 Act it has always been clear that the duty of a United Kingdom court, when delivering final judgment [is] to override any rule of national law found to be in conflict with any directly enforceable rule of Community law. ...' (Lord Bridge at 659)

What does this mean for legal skills?

We hope that this section has given you a little bit of background to help you better understand where EU law comes from and how it finds its way into our domestic law. This understanding should help you identify and locate sources more easily when you are conducting legal research, and it should also help you think more critically about the sources once you have found them.

Activity Work in small groups of 3–4 students. Identify and discuss the main legal consequences of the UK's membership of the EU. Consider issues such as the impact of the membership on the English doctrines of parliamentary sovereignty and precedent. Do you agree that UK institutions should comply with the decisions of EU bodies?

....

....

....

....

....

1.4   THE IMPORTANCE OF INTERNATIONAL LAW

Private international law

Private international law, sometimes referred to as conflict of laws, refers to a body of rules of domestic law (such as UK statutes and other laws) which applies when a legal problem contains a foreign element and it needs to be decided whether a UK court should apply foreign law or the case should be left to be decided by a foreign court. Private international law also seeks to harmonise domestic rules on conflict of laws, and this has led to the adoption of up to 36 treaties in this area.

Public international law

International law is sometimes referred to as public international law to differentiate it from private international law. It is clearly distinguished by the fact that it is not the product of any national legal system but of the over 192 states that make up our world. It used to be referred to as the Law of Nations that has been developing over many centuries. Public international law is manifested in a variety of ways. For example, international treaties establishing and regulating the operation of international organisations such as the United Nations, the EU and NATO are elements of public international law.

Is international law actually law?

Because there is no international police force or army or an effective sanctions mechanism to enforce international law on disobedient states, some people view it as not real law. The term 'soft law' may be more appropriate in some circumstances.

The basis of international law is that relations between states should be governed by common rules and principles. Early examples of the use of international law include the freedom to use the high seas and protection of foreign diplomats. Therefore, the binding nature of international law does not derive from the police, courts or prisons as in domestic legal systems. Rather, it is based on the consent/agreement of states and the protection of each state's interest. States do not wish to ignore international law because they do not wish other states to ignore it.

Sources of international law

Unlike domestic law, which is easily located in legislation and court decisions, international law is not so coherent and certain. There is no single global legislature, no formal hierarchy of courts comparable to domestic courts. International law is derived from various sources, which are authoritatively listed in Article 38(1) of the Statute of the International Court of Justice (which is an Annex to the Charter of the United Nations). These sources include the following:

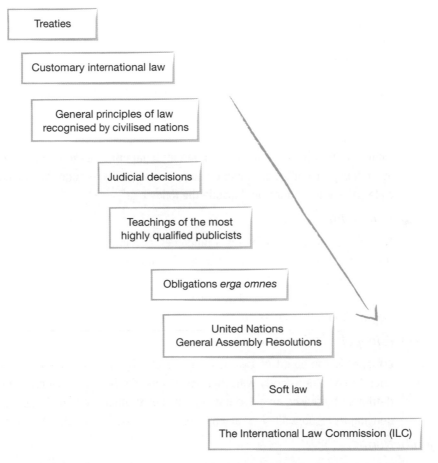

Treaties

Customary international law

General principles of law recognised by civilised nations

Judicial decisions

Teachings of the most highly qualified publicists

Obligations *erga omnes*

United Nations General Assembly Resolutions

Soft law

The International Law Commission (ILC)

(a) Treaties

Treaties constitute the most popular way for creating binding legal obligations between states in international law. Article 38(1) of the Statute of the International Court of Justice refers to international 'conventions' instead of treaties, whereas other terms such as 'protocol' or 'pact' have also been used in international agreements. There are bilateral and multilateral treaties. In a bilateral treaty, there are only two parties involved, whereas in multilateral treaties several states are involved. Treaties involve states and/or international organisations but not individuals or non-state actors (companies, NGOs etc). The treaty is one of the most important sources of international law because it also codifies (consolidates) custom and other sources of international law.

(b) Customary international law

Customary international law, or simply custom, must be distinguished from the domestic customary law of some countries. Custom in international law evolves from state practices over a long or short period of time. In fact, there must be evidence of substantial and consistent uniform practice by a substantial number of states. Evidence of state practice includes: governmental actions in relation to other states, legislation, diplomatic notes, ministerial and other official statements, government documents and resolutions of governments, such as in the United Nations General Assembly.

For a new rule to be established, besides practice, there must also exist a general recognition by states that the practice is settled enough to amount to an obligation on states in international law. This is known as *opinio juris*.

(c) General principles of law recognised by civilised nations

The term 'civilised nations' above is not a term to demean other nations. It simply refers to states that have reached an advanced state of legal development. International courts and tribunals often borrow and apply important legal principles to relations between states, and in so doing have filled gaps and enhanced weaknesses through the application of legal principles. These legal principles include the following:

(i) Good faith

The duty to act in good faith is a fundamental principle of international law. The Charter of the United Nations (Article 2(2)) as well as the Vienna Convention on the Law of Treaties, 1969 (Articles 26, 31(1)) require member parties to perform their treaty obligations in good faith. The principle also applies to all other legal obligations of states in international law derived from other sources of law other than treaties.

(ii) Estoppel

Estoppel is composed of two aspects. A state that has taken a particular position is duty bound to act consistently with that position in all other cases. When a state has acted to its detriment by relying on a declaration/action of another state, the latter may be stopped from denying its responsibility for any adverse consequences from its declaration or actions.

(iii) Norms

This refers to standards and is used loosely to include principles and rules. Sir Robert Jennings, sometime President of the International Court of Justice, once said that he would not recognise a norm if he met one in the street.

(d) Judicial decisions

Judgments of courts and tribunals, both international and domestic, while formally a subsidiary source of international law, exercise substantial influence in practice as a source of international law. Judgments of these courts and tribunals, especially appellate or highest courts, often provide a persuasive legal authority on matters of international law. Their role is significant because the international community lacks law-making bodies and procedures similar to domestic legal systems. The courts through their decisions help to clarify legal issues and to create international customary rules, which are then accepted by all states.

(e) Teachings of the most highly qualified publicists

Writers on international law provide a subsidiary source of international law and were influential in shaping the early development of international law. Writers analyse facts and opinions and help to draw conclusions on binding customary rules and on trends of their evolution.

(f) Obligations *erga omnes*

These are certain obligations of states that are owed to all other states (the whole world). These include obligations often referred to as *jus cogens*, which include important human rights and certain treaties. *Jus cogens* are absolute rules of general international law defined in the Vienna Convention on the Law Treaties, 1969. This Treaty defines *jus cogens* as 'a norm accepted and recognised by the international community of States as a whole as a norm from which no derogation is permitted and which can be modified only by subsequent norm of general international law having the same character' (Article 53). For example, international law rules that prohibit torture or slavery have attained the legal status of *jus cogens*.

(g) United Nations General Assembly Resolutions

While not initially envisaged under Article 39(1) of the Statute of the International Court of Justice, some writers consider General Assembly Resolutions as informal treaties, or as indicating general principles of law or contributing to the formation of custom.

(h) Soft law

Soft law refers to international instruments that the makers recognise are not treaties but use treaty language to pass norms of general or universal application. These instruments are referred to in various forms, such as guidelines, principles, declarations, recommendations, codes of practice, etc. They are common in environmental, social and economic aspects of international relations between states. The Rio Declaration on Environment and Development, 1992 and the Universal Declaration of Human Rights, 1948 are good examples of soft law.

(i) Recommendations of international bodies that progressively codify international law: the International Law Commission

In 1946, the General Assembly acting under the Charter of the United Nations created the International Law Commission (ILC). The ILC is tasked with promoting the progressive development and codification of international law. The ILC has prepared several draft conventions (treaties) which have formed the basis of adopted treaties. For example, the several treaties on the Law of the Sea, the Vienna Convention on the Law of Treaties and the Statute of the International Criminal Court have incorporated drafts and recommendations prepared by the International Law Commission. In this regard, the codification efforts of the ILC have contributed to other sources of the law such as treaties.

 **How well do you understand international law? Plot your present position on the line with an X:**

I still need to research this		I know this off-by-heart
I am not sure what private law is	– – – – –	I know all about private law
I am not sure what public law is and how it is different to private law	– – – – –	I know all about public law and I can distinguish it from private law
I am struggling to remember all the sources of international law	– – – – –	I can name all the sources of international law
I am not sure what treaties are and what they do	– – – – –	I can list important international treaties and what they do
I am not aware of what customary international laws are	– – – – –	I understand the principles of customary international law
I still need to research the general principles of law recognised by civilised nations	– – – – –	I know that the general principles of law recognised by civilised nations play a big role in international law
I am not sure how the principle of good faith affects international law	– – – – –	I know how important the principle of good faith is in international law
I an not sure what estoppel is in the context of international law	– – – – –	I know how estoppel is used in international law
I am still unsure about the norms in international law	– – – – –	I know all about the norms in international law
I am not yet fully aware of the influence of judicial decisions	– – – – –	I am aware of the influence that judicial decisions have in international law
I am not sure how teachings of the most highly qualified publicists have an authority in international law	– – – – –	I understand how teachings of the most highly qualified publicists have an authority in international law
I do not know what obligations *erga omnes* are	– – – – –	I understand what obligations *erga omnes* are
I am not sure what United Nations General Assembly Resolutions do	– – – – –	I know what United Nations General Assembly Resolutions do
I am struggling to understand the concept of soft law	– – – – –	I know what soft law is in the context of international law
I do not know what the International Law Commission (ILC) is	– – – – –	I know what the International Law Commission (ILC) is and what it does

Group activity Identify and discuss the main bodies and sources of international law and compare them to the bodies and sources of English law. What are the main differences and how can they be explained?

....

....

....

....

....

2

Using a law library

Learning outcomes

> To locate different types of materials in your law library

> To differentiate between primary and secondary legal sources

> To decode case citations and locate cases in your library and online

> To find statutory materials in your library and online

> To find journal articles and other secondary materials in your library and online

> To use different types of database searchers

You may think that the library in the institution in which you are studying is 'no big deal', or 'just a library', but your law library will help you to pass your course. In fact, you will not pass your course without it! You have to be able to navigate your way around a law library, and they are complex, because of the strange and varied documents that they stock. However, once you have located the particular resources that you need, you will use that resource for the rest of your course.

A common criticism from lecturers when they mark assignments is 'not enough research'. When was the last time you went to your law library? All the answers are there!

2.1 USING THE LIBRARY

I hate libraries!!

As a law student, it is vital that you are able to use your law library effectively. Not only must you be able to locate primary and secondary sources of law, but you must learn how to read case citations and locate other important legal resources online.

Why do you need to use your law library?

Using a law library for the first time can be a daunting experience. You will be faced with such a mass of printed materials that, initially, you will find it difficult to locate specific items. But don't despair – library staff will be there to give you assistance, and once you find your resource for the first time you'll know exactly where to look throughout the rest of your course.

You must therefore familiarise yourself with the layout of your law library. It is in your own interests to know exactly how the material is organised and where items are shelved. This will save you time and effort in the future.

- Do attend training sessions that the library organises.
- Don't be afraid to ask library staff for help – the law librarian will know where everything is!

In the table below, make a note of key information relating to the law library:

What I need to know	Information
Library location on campus	
Library home page	
Library opening times	
Available training sessions	
Where the law textbooks are	
Where the law journals are	
How to take books out of the library	
Where the silent reading room is	

As a student studying law, it is essential that you know how to find both the primary sources and the secondary sources of law that are held by your library.

Primary and secondary sources of law

In your law assessments, you will need to show that you have researched the law. 'Primary' sources of law are the laws themselves – cases and statutes. 'Secondary' sources of law are not the law; they are simply documents describing or criticising the law (ie textbooks and journals). Students are often criticised for stating that 'secondary' sources of law are authoritative sources of law, but only 'primary' sources of law are authoritative sources of law.

Primary sources of law	*Written by*	Secondary sources of law	*Written by*
Statutes	Parliament	Textbooks	Academics
Cases	Judges	Journals	Academics

The organisation of your law library

In the table below, tick the different sources of law once you are happy that you know where they are located in your institution's library:

Sources of law	Written by	Located in your law library
Statutes	Parliament	☐
Cases	Judges	☐
Textbooks	Academics	☐
Journals	Academics	☐

2.2 FINDING CASES

Why is case law so important?

Because the English legal system is heavily dependent upon the *doctrine of precedent*, case law is a major source of law in English and Wales. We have considered precedent at some length in **Chapter 1** so you might want to return to our discussion there once you have worked through this section. The doctrine of precedent determines that: 'The courts, within certain limits, must follow earlier decisions made by the higher courts.'

To understand the doctrine of precedent, it is necessary for you to understand the structure of the court system in England and Wales. The following gives a very simplified diagram and basic account of the hierarchy of the courts. For a more detailed diagram of the hierarchy of the courts, see the HMCS website at www.hmcourts-service.gov.uk/aboutus/structure/index.htm. For detailed analysis of the work of each of the courts, see Ministry of Justice (2008), *Judicial and Court Statistics, 2007*, Cm 7467 at www.justice.gov.uk/publications/docs/judicial-court-stats-2007-full.pdf.

The court hierarchy enables the doctrine of precedent to take effect and allows cases decided at a lower level to be taken on appeal to a higher level court.

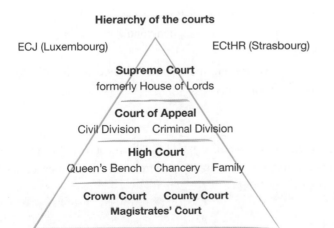

Hierarchy of the courts

ECJ (Luxembourg)   ECtHR (Strasbourg)

Supreme Court
formerly House of Lords

Court of Appeal
Civil Division   Criminal Division

High Court
Queen's Bench   Chancery   Family

Crown Court   County Court
Magistrates' Court

(a) The Supreme Court (House of Lords)

The Supreme Court is the ultimate court for England and Wales. It opened in October 2009 in the Middlesex Guildhall, London, opposite the Houses of Parliament and is presided over by the 12 most senior judges in the land who, each year, will deal with around 60 cases of the utmost importance. Decisions made here are binding on all the other courts in the hierarchy (the exception being the Supreme Court itself – it is not necessarily bound by its own previous decisions). You should be aware of the following issues:

- The Supreme Court has assumed the jurisdiction of the former Appellate Committee of the House of Lords (which was located within the upper House of Parliament), with the intention of further separating the judiciary from the legislature.
- The Supreme Court has only recently replaced the House of Lords as the most senior court in England and Wales, and decisions from the House of Lords will continue to be binding. This is because the House of Lords was formerly the final court of appeal on points of law in civil and criminal cases for England and Wales.

(b) The Court of Appeal

The Court of Appeal sits in the Royal Courts of Justice, The Strand, London, and comprises two divisional courts: the Civil Division and the Criminal Division. The Civil Division hears appeals from the High Court and the county courts, whilst the Criminal Division handles appeals from the Crown Court. The Court of Appeal thus deals only with appeals from courts lower in the hierarchy, but it is bound to follow decisions made by the Supreme Court and its predecessor, the House of Lords.

(c) The High Court

The High Court also sits in the Royal Courts of Justice, London, and in addition has eight provincial centres, for example in Manchester and Birmingham. The High Court presides over the most serious cases and is separated into three divisions:

- *Queen's Bench Division*: deals with cases concerning matters such as tort (eg negligence, nuisance, defamation) and breach of contract.
- *Chancery Division*: deals with cases concerning matters such as equity and trusts, contentious probate (wills), tax, bankruptcy, patents, and land registration.
- *Family Division*: deals with trials concerning matrimonial proceedings (eg divorce), plus matters such as child custody and adoption.

(d) The Crown Court

Around 90 cities and major towns have been designated as Crown Court centres to deal with the more serious criminal cases that are committed to trial from the magistrates' courts, plus criminal appeals from the magistrates' courts.

(e) The county courts

Two hundred and thirty cities and major towns have county courts to deal with civil matters such as land disputes, will disputes, civil debts, bankruptcy and claims for personal injury that do not exceed £50,000.

(f) The magistrates' courts

In England and Wales there are around 600 magistrates' courts wherein 28,000 voluntary magistrates (who are not qualified lawyers) deal with around 96% of all criminal cases – an astonishing statistic. These are cases deemed to be *'not so serious'*, ie if a single offence merits more than six months' imprisonment, or more than a £5,000 fine, then it is sent to a higher court.

What is meant by the 'higher courts' and the 'lower courts'?

The Supreme Court, the House of Lords, the Court of Appeal and the High Court are sometimes referred to as the higher courts because of their position in the hierarchy. Decisions made in these courts are reported in various series of law reports (but only where they are of *'significant legal interest'*, see below).

The courts further down the hierarchy – the Crown Court, the county courts and the magistrates' courts – are sometimes referred to as the lower courts. These courts do not make precedents. Instead, they must follow judgments made in the higher courts. Consequently, their cases are rarely recorded in any series of law reports.

The European courts

In our diagram of the courts' hierarchy you will notice, outside the triangle showing the courts of England and Wales, both the European Court of Justice (ECJ) and the European Court of Human Rights (ECtHR).

(a) European Court of Justice (ECJ)

In January 1973 the UK became a member of the European Community (EC), and hence of the European Union (EU). Consequently, the courts of England and Wales are bound by the ECJ (which sits in Luxembourg) on matters relating to EU law. Much of our national law remains unaffected by membership of the EC and the EU, except in significant areas such as environmental law, consumer law and employment law. In such areas, if our national law conflicts with EU law then our courts are required to apply EU law in preference to national law. Due to their importance, all cases from the ECJ are recorded in official law reports.

(b) European Court of Human Rights (ECtHR)

Because the UK is a signatory to the European Convention of Human Rights, the courts of England and Wales are bound by decisions of the ECtHR (which sits in Strasbourg) to observe certain standards concerning human rights. Thus an individual claiming a violation of the Convention may take his or her case to the ECtHR. Decisions made here are binding over judgments made in our national courts. All cases from the ECtHR are recorded in official law reports.

Law reporting

We have spoken at length about the hierarchy of the courts, noting in particular those courts whose cases are recorded in law reports. Law reports are absolutely crucial to the doctrine of precedent because they allow judicial decisions to be accessed by future courts. The doctrine of precedent can only operate effectively if there is an accurate and well established system of law reporting. Law reports are our access to case law, and you should familiarise yourself with the main law reports held in your library. As part of your studies, you will be asked to read cases, and if you learn how to locate them now you will save yourself a lot of time and effort later on.

Activity In the table below, put a number next to each court, placing it in the correct order. Number them from 1 to 7, with the highest court numbered '1'. Some entries will have the same number.

High Court ☐   Supreme Court (House of Lords) ☐
Queen's Bench Division ☐   European Court of Human Rights ☐
Crown Court ☐   Court of Appeal ☐
Chancery Division ☐   European Court of Justice ☐
county court ☐   Family Division ☐
magistrates' court ☐

Activity Suppose that you have had your bike stolen and a criminal law case is being brought in the courts. The law surrounding stolen bikes has a provision in it that may breach your human rights. Which trail of courts will you fight through in order to get to the very top?

....

....

....

....

....

Law reports and case transcripts

Law reports are narratives of the facts, legal discussions and judgments of individual cases. It might surprise you to learn that only a small number of cases from the higher courts of England and Wales are actually published as law reports. The cases published as law reports are those deemed to be of 'significant legal interest', ie they are cases which create a new precedent, or which modify, or which clarify, an existing principle of law.

Law reports are quite user-friendly, adding features such as:

- *Catchwords*: a list of key legal issues addressed by the case.
- *Headnotes*: a summary of the main themes of the case.
- *Tables of cases*: cases cited by the present case.
- *Tables of legislation*: statutes and other legislation cited by the present case.

Be aware of the difference between a 'law report' and a 'case transcript':

(a) Law reports

As mentioned above, a law report is a narrative of the facts and judgment of a case of significant legal interest; law reports are edited to give additional value in the form of catchwords, headnotes, and tables of relevant cases and legislation.

(b) Case transcripts

A case transcript is the 'raw' court version of a case. Although transcripts may appear on various websites, case transcripts ostensibly remain 'unreported' unless they are published within a recognised law report series. Since 2001, transcripts of cases heard before the higher courts have each been given a *neutral case citation* to make them easier to find.

Many law reports and case transcripts can now be found online. Your own institution will be able to give you details at the library help desk. You will have to log in with your own password to use its services. You can also visit www.bailii.org, the website of the British and Irish Legal Information Institute, which provides free access to case transcripts.

Law reports: major series and specialist series

Your law library will provide access to various series of law reports, both in paper format and online. Each law report series has its own abbreviated citation. You need to know the meanings of these abbreviations before you can find the actual law report. Here are a few examples:

- Appeal Cases (Supreme Court/House of Lords and Court of Appeal) [AC] (1865 onwards)
- Chancery Division [Ch]
- Queen's Bench Division [QBD] (1865 onwards)
- Family Division [Fam]
- Weekly Law Reports [WLR] (1953 onwards)
- All England Law Reports [All ER] (1936 onwards)
- The English Reports [ER] (1220–1873)
- Family Law Reports [FLR] (1980 onwards)
- Butterworths Human Rights Cases [BHRC] (1996 onwards)
- Housing Law Reports [HLR] (1976 onwards)

Self-assessment

Are you feeling confident now that you could identify the following abbreviations in a textbook or an article?

Abbreviation	Volume
AC	Appeal Cases (House of Lords/Supreme Court and Court of Appeal)
Ch	Chancery Division (of the High Court)
QBD	Queen's Bench Division (of the High Court)
Fam	Family Division (of the High Court)
WLR	Weekly Law Reports
ER	The English Reports (really old cases)
All ER	All England Law Reports
FLR	Family Law Reports
BHRC	Butterworth's Human Rights Cases
HLR	Housing Law Reports

Case citations and finding law reports

As we said earlier, selected cases from the higher courts are recorded in various series of law reports, and each series has its own abbreviation. Each reported case has its own unique case citation. At first sight, a case citation might appear confusing. Don't worry – you will soon learn to 'decode' the various elements. Consider the examples below:

Case citation example 1

> • *Farley v Skinner* [2001] 4 All ER 801

The above citation is decoded as follows:

Elements of a case citation

> • *Farley v Skinner*[1] [2001][2] 4[3] All ER[4] 801[5]
>   1   Names of parties; the party initiating proceedings is placed first
>   2   Year the case was reported
>   3   Number of volume in which it was reported
>   4   Abbreviation of the law report in which it was reported, ie the *All England Law Reports*
>   5   Page number
> You will find the full report of this case in the appropriate volume of the *All England Law Reports* in your law library.

Cases are cited as briefly as possible:

Case citation example 2

> • [2001] 1 AC 27
> • [2002] 3 All ER 209
> • (1987) 84 LSG 2530

These citations refer to the following cases:
> • *Fitzpatrick v Sterling Housing Association Ltd*, reported in *The Law Reports, Appeal Cases,* 2001, vol 1, starting at p 27.
> • *Kuwait Airways Corp v Iraqi Airways Co*, reported in the *All England Law Reports*, 2002, vol 3, starting at p 209.
> • *Balgobin and Francis v Tower Hamlets LBC*, reported in the *Law Society Gazette,* 1987, vol 84, starting at p 2530.

Some case citations can appear quite daunting. This is because the same case has been reported in a number of different series of law reports. When you see a citation such as the example below, don't panic! All the abbreviations are very easy to decode.

Case citation example 3

> • *OBG Ltd v Allan* [2005] EWCA Civ 106; [2005] QB 762; [2005] 2 WLR 1174; [2005] 2 All ER 602; [2005] 1 BCLC 711; [2005] BLR 245; [2005] BPIR 928; [2005] PNLR 27; (2005) 102 (14) LSG 27; *The Times*, 24 February 2005; *The Independent*, 18 February 2005.

In case citation example 3, the abbreviations show where the case was reported, which appear in the activity table below:

Activity Find the following reports in your law library, or locate them elsewhere, and tick the box when done.

Abbreviation	Report	Found it!
EWCA Civ	Court of Appeal (Civil Division)	☐
QB	Law Reports, Queen's Bench	☐
WLR	Weekly Law Reports	☐
All ER	All England Law Reports	☐
BCLC	Butterworths Company Law Cases	☐
BLR	Business Law Reports	☐
BPIR	Bankruptcy and Personal Insolvency Reports	☐
PNLR	Professional Negligence and Liability Reports	☐
LSG	*Law Society's Gazette*	☐
Times	*The Times* newspaper	☐
Independent	*The Independent* newspaper	☐

All law libraries provide access to various series of law reports, both online and in paper format, so you should be able to track down all, or most, of the reports cited above. But to do this, you do need to know what the abbreviations mean.

(a) Neutral case citations

In case citation example 3, the first citation, [2005] EWCA Civ 106, is called a *neutral case citation*. Neutral case citations were introduced in 2001 to make it easier to identify judgments published on the Internet. They look very similar to law report citations, but a neutral case citation is not a reference to a commercial law report. Instead, it is a unique identifier assigned to the transcript of a case heard before one of the higher courts, ie the Supreme Court, the House of Lords, the Court of Appeal (Civil and Criminal Divisions), and all divisions of the High Court (Queen's Bench; Chancery; Family).

As an example:

- [2005] EWCA Civ 106 shows the case was heard in 2005 in the *England and Wales Court of Appeal, Civil Division,* and that it is case number 106.

Examples of neutral case citations

- [2008] UKHL 10 means the case was heard in 2008 in the *United Kingdom House of Lords,* case number 10.
- [2003] EWHC 1274 (Ch) means the case was heard in 2005 in the *England and Wales High Court, Chancery Division,* case number 1274.
- [2008] EWHC 1532 (Fam) means the case was heard in 2008 in the *England and Wales High Court, Family Division,* case number 1532.

Neutral case citations do not have page numbers. Instead, the text of each case has numbered paragraphs. You must include the paragraph reference (para) in your essay if you are referring to a specific place in the record of the case.

Example

In the case of *Grobbelaar v News Group Newspapers* [2002] UKHL 40, at para 28, Lord Steyn stated 'that the jury verdict of £85,000 in favour of Mr Bruce Grobbelaar was an affront to justice and had to be quashed'.

Activity Write the full reference for the following neutral case citations:

Neutral citation	Where to find it
[2006] EWHC 453 (QB)	
[2003] UKHL 556	
[2008] EWCA Civ 879	
[2007] EWCA Crim 334	
[2004] EWHC 365 (Fam)	

(b) Square or round brackets?

Note how in case citation example 3, the *OBG Ltd v Allan* case, most of the citations have square brackets [ ], but one citation has round brackets ( ). Square brackets are used when the date is absolutely essential to finding the report. Round brackets are used when the date is merely of assistance in giving an idea of when the case was reported in a law report series (or in a legal journal) that has cumulative volume numbers.

Example

- [1998] 2 WLR 225
- (1998) 30 HLR 576

The *WLR* date is crucial to finding the *Weekly Law Report* case report which hence has square brackets, but because the *Housing Law Reports* are published in an ongoing sequence of volumes, the date (given in round brackets) is not essential to finding the report.

(c) Law reports in legal journals and newspapers

Note how, in case citation example 3, there are case citations to a legal journal (LSG) and to two newspapers. Brief law reports and case notes appear in various practitioner journals, notably in the *Law Society's Gazette* (LSG) and in the *New Law Journal* (NLJ). Many law libraries will keep these journals in paper format. These reports can be useful because they appear within days of a judgment being made.

Cases are also reported in the 'quality' newspapers. These reports can also be useful because they appear a day or so after a judgment is heard. *The Times* newspaper is of particular note and contains short case reports (look for the heading 'Law Report') which are collated and issued in annual volumes and cited as the *Times Law Reports* (TLR).

Exercise 1: Finding old cases (pre-1873)

Find the following cases in the *English Reports.* Write the case names in the space below.

- (1784) 168 ER 279
- (1865) 55 ER 860
- (1840) 49 ER 132

Answers

....

....

....

Exercise 2: *The Law Reports*

Find the following cases in *The Law Reports.* Write the case names below.

- [1972] 1 QB 198
- [1993] AC 789
- [1964] 1 Ch 413
- [2001] Fam 473

Answers

....

....

....

....

Exercise 3: *Weekly Law Reports*

Find the following cases in the *WLR.* Write the case names below.

- [1960] 1 WLR 733
- [1978] 1 WLR 215

Answers

....

....

....

Exercise 4: *All England Law Reports*

Find the following cases in the *All ER.* Write the case names below.

- [2004] 3 All ER 411
- [2001] 4 All ER 801

Answers

....

....

....

(d) European courts that affect the law of England and Wales

You noted above how our diagram of the courts' hierarchy shows, outside the triangle, both the European Court of Justice (ECJ) and the European Court of Human Rights (ECtHR). As part of your course you will study cases from both of these courts. Why?

● Because the UK is a member of the European Union (EU), the courts of England and Wales are bound by the ECJ on matters relating to EU law. If there is a conflict between national law and EU law then our courts are required to follow decisions made by the ECJ.

● Because the UK is a signatory to the European Convention of Human Rights, the courts of England and Wales are bound by the ECtHR to observe certain standards concerning human rights. Thus, in principle, individuals claiming a violation of the Convention may take their case to the ECtHR. Decisions made there are binding over judgments made in our national courts.

It is absolutely essential for you to know that the ECJ (based in Luxembourg) is an EU institution and it has *no* connection whatsoever with the ECtHR based in Strasbourg. Do not confuse the two!

(i) *Finding and citing European Court of Justice law reports*

The European Court of Justice (ECJ) quickly built up a heavy caseload. To ease its workload, the Court of First Instance (CFI) (now the General Court) was established in 1989 to hear cases brought by private parties only. Consequently, European cases are split into two parts:

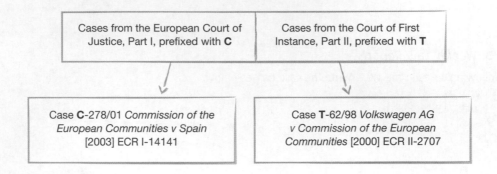

European cases can be decoded as follows:

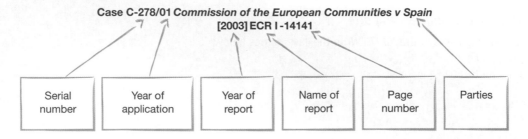

Notice in the example above that the serial number, C-278, indicates that the case is from the European Court of Justice. ECR means *European Case Reports*.

(ii) European human rights cases

Cases from the European Court of Human Rights (ECtHR) are recorded in several series of law reports:

- European Court of Human Rights law reports (ECHR)
- European Human Rights Reports (EHRR)

The ECHR cases can be decoded as follows:

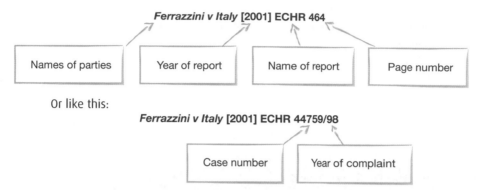

Ferrazzini v Italy [2001] ECHR 464

Names of parties	Year of report	Name of report	Page number

Or like this:

Ferrazzini v Italy [2001] ECHR 44759/98

Case number	Year of complaint

The European Human Rights Reports are edited by publishers, and you will find them much easier to comprehend than the official reports. Citation is straightforward.

The EHRR cases can be decoded as follows:

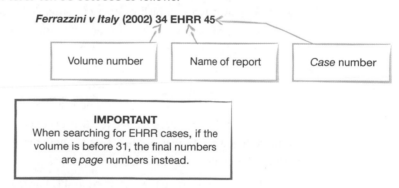

Ferrazzini v Italy (2002) 34 EHRR 45

Volume number	Name of report	Case number

IMPORTANT

When searching for EHRR cases, if the volume is before 31, the final numbers are *page* numbers instead.

Activity Write out in full the following abbreviations:

Abbreviation: Case C-278/01 *EC v Italy* [2005] ECR I-15782

Meaning: ....

Abbreviation: *Melenga v Spain* [2002] ECHR 489

Meaning: ....

Abbreviation: *Smith v United Kingdom* [2000] ECHR 46234/99

Meaning: ....

....

Abbreviation: *Kapatia v Ireland* (2004) 52 ECRR 29

Meaning: ....

2.3 FINDING STATUTORY MATERIALS

What is primary legislation?

Statutes (Acts of Parliament) are primary legislation. They are the most important source of law for England and Wales. Statutes are published individually in paper format and also on the free Internet by the Office of Public Sector Information (OPSI) and by the UK Statute Law Database (SLD). They are also available online via various subscription databases (see below at **2.5**). See **Chapter 1** for further information about how Acts of Parliament are made and what they do.

Primary legislation constantly changes. Legislation is certainly not static – entire Acts can be repealed and individual sections can be amended or revoked. In most cases you will need to quote current law, so it is vital that you use statutes *currently in force*. However, at times you may need to consult the original wording of a statute, so you also need to know how to find the original text of statutes as enacted.

Finding statutes in force

In most cases you will be required to use statutes currently in force. If you are relying on paper format, then you might consult *Halsbury's Statutes*.

- *Halsbury's Statutes* are published by LexisNexis Butterworths and made up of 50 grey-coloured Main Volumes which contain the amended text of all current statutes arranged alphabetically by major subject area, eg Vol 1 Admiralty, Agency, Agriculture; Vol 50 Value Added Tax, War & Emergency, Weights & Measures, Wills.
- *Halsbury's Statutes* are updated monthly by the Noter-up Service and then updated each year by the Annual Cumulative Supplement. The Main Volumes are reissued periodically when the number or importance of changes affecting them warrants this.
- Note also the Current Statutes Service: six loose-leaf binders labelled A to F that correspond to the subject areas of the Main Volumes. These provide the text of recent Acts not yet included in the Main Volumes.

To use *Halsbury's Statutes,* follow the steps in this flowchart:

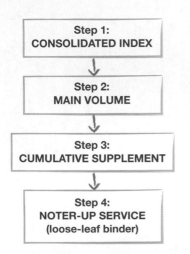

- **Step 1:** Look up the Act you require in the Consolidated Index (a softback volume) which lists all statutes alphabetically and chronologically. This will give you a reference in bold to the Main Volume, followed by a page number in lighter type.
- **Step 2:** Follow this reference to the relevant Main Volume. There are 50 Main Volumes, arranged in an alphabetical scheme of over 160 subjects. The entry in the Main Volume gives the text of the statute as it stands on the date that the individual Main Volume was published.
- **Step 3:** Check the annual Cumulative Supplement for any revisions which post-date the Main Volume. The Cumulative Supplement is arranged in the same volume, title and page order of the Main Volumes.
- **Step 4:** Check the Noter-up Service (a loose-leaf binder) for any recent developments.

Finding secondary legislation (statutory instruments)

In **Chapter 1** we mentioned that secondary legislation is important for implementing legislative details which are not feasible to incorporate into the main Act of Parliament. Remember the following points:

- If you are referred to a regulation, an order or a rule, this usually means a statutory instrument.
- Statutory instruments (SIs) are sometimes called 'subordinate legislation' or 'delegated legislation' because the original statute has delegated power to some other authority (usually a Minister of the Crown) to make detailed rules and regulations on a general principle determined by the statute, for example the various Road Traffic Acts allow the Secretary of State for Transport to impose speed limits on certain stretches of road, and to vary those limits if appropriate.

You can find SIs on the free Internet, or you can use the online subscription databases (see below). Because so many SIs are produced each year (around 3,000–3,500), only the largest law libraries will maintain a complete collection in paper format. Smaller libraries will not stock individual SIs. Instead, they will keep *Halsbury's Statutory Instruments,* a series which reproduces the most important SIs.

- *Halsbury's Statutory Instruments* are made up of 22 grey-coloured Main Volumes, which contain the full text of all major general SIs, plus summaries of others.
- They are arranged by subject to match *Halsbury's Statutes* (and also to match the authoritative legal encyclopaedia, *Halsbury's Laws of England*).
- They can be searched either by subject, or by SI number.

To use *Halsbury's Statutory Instruments,* follow the steps in this flowchart:

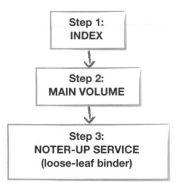

- **Step 1:** Look up the SI you require in the Consolidated Index (a softback volume) which lists all SIs alphabetically and by subject area. This will give you a reference in bold to the Main Volume, followed by a page number in lighter type.
- **Step 2:** Follow this reference to the relevant Main Volume. There are 22 Main Volumes, arranged in an alphabetical subject scheme. The entry in the Main Volume gives the text of the statute as it stands on the date that the individual Main Volume was published.
- **Step 3:** Check the Noter-up Service (a loose-leaf binder) for any recent revisions.

Activity Next time you go to your law library, take this book with you. Tick the following boxes if you are able to:

- ☐ Find items using the Library catalogue
- ☐ Understand the meaning of case citations
- ☐ Find the meanings of legal abbreviations
- ☐ Find cases in the various series of printed law reports

- ☐ Find statutes (Acts of Parliament)
- ☐ Understand how to use *Halsbury's Statutes*
- ☐ Understand how to use *Halsbury's Laws of England*

You should also have acquired knowledge and understanding of the following online legal databases:

☐ *Lawtel*   ☐ *Westlaw UK*   ☐ *LexisLibrary*

You should be able to use these online databases to find:

☐ Statutes   ☐ Legal journal articles   ☐ Newspaper articles
☐ Cases   (abstracts and full text)

Finding European Union legislation

In 1973 the UK became a member of the European Community, which itself is now part of the wider European Union. Consequently, EU legislation is an integral part of UK law. We discussed the different types of sources of EU law in **Chapter 1**. Here we are concerned with locating the Treaties as well as the secondary sources (Regulations, Directives and Decisions).

Because most EU legislation is available on the free Internet, and also due to the vast amount of printed material involved, many law libraries will not hold all EU legislation in paper format. However, a number of university libraries have been designated as European Documentation Centres. This means they receive the official publications and working documents of the European Union, including legislative and judicial material. There are more that 40 European Documentation Centres in the UK, and more than 500 worldwide, so it might be worthwhile for you to check if you have an EDC nearby. You can locate EDCs by checking on the following website: http://ec.europa.eu/europedirect/visit_us/interactive_map/index_en.htm.

For most law students, a compilation of the main EU Treaties and legislation will suffice, and two such titles are:

- Foster, N (ed) (2009) *Blackstone's: EU Treaties and Legislation 2010–11,* 21st edn (Oxford: Oxford University Press); and

- Busby, N and Smith, R (eds) (2010) *Core EU Legislation 2010–11* (Basingstoke: Palgrave Macmillan).

For free online access to the EU Treaties and to most secondary sources of EU legislation, you can use the *EUR-Lex* website.

- *EUR-Lex:* part of the *Europa* website, the freely available official database of the EU. It provides access to *CELEX,* the official legal database of the EU. Go to http://eur-lex.europa.eu/en/index.htm. When you have entered the database, click on the type of record you want to search.

- *Eurolaw:* a commercial database containing the full text of all EU Treaties, Regulations, Directives, Decisions and proposed legislation (COM docs).

- *Westlaw UK:* to find EU legislation, you must first click on the EU tab which is displayed on *Westlaw's* homepage.

- *LexisLibrary:* to find EU legislation, you must first click on the Legislation tab which is displayed on *LexisLibrary's* homepage, and then choose International Legislation.

- *Lawtel EU:* provides direct access to EU legislation.

Finding and citing Committee Reports and Royal Commission Reports

Committee Reports and *Royal Commission Reports* are papers that various interested parties and committees may submit to Parliament. Such reports outline the current state of affairs about a particular area of concern and then discuss details to improve or to amend legislation.

- *Committee Reports:* Parliament often commissions Committee Reports to elucidate or to influence the drafting of Green Papers, White Papers and Bills. Such papers are sometimes published as Command Papers because they are formally presented to Parliament *'By Her Majesty's Command',* whilst other Committee Reports may be called *'Session Papers'* after the particular House of Commons or House of Lords sessions from which they originate.

- *Royal Commission Reports:* these are published much less frequently than Commission Reports. Royal Commissions are created by the Monarch on the advice of Parliament to look into prescribed areas of profound concern. Royal Commissions, which can last for several years, have considerable power and their reports are taken very seriously when Parliament considers new legislation.

Example of a Royal Commission Report

Royal Commission on Criminal Justice (1993) *The Royal Commission on Criminal Justice: report* (London: HMSO).

Finding Law Commission papers

The Law Commission is the statutory independent body created by the Law Commissions Act 1965. Its purpose is to keep the law under review and to recommend reform where needed. The Law Commission regularly issues:

- Law Commission Consultation Papers (originally called 'Working Papers')
- Law Commission Reports

Law Commission Consultation Papers are, of course, precursors of the actual Law Commission Reports which are then put before Parliament to recommend reforms to legislation.

In your Bibliography, you must cite Law Commission Consultation Papers using the following formula as a template:

- Corporate author (ie Law Commission); Date of publication (in brackets); Title; Law Commission number (LC No); Command Paper or House of Commons Session number.

Examples of Law Commission Consultation Paper

Law Commission (2003) *Partial defences to murder: summary paper.* Consultation Paper No 173 (London: TSO).

Example of Law Commission Reports

Law Commission (2006) *Murder, manslaughter and infanticide, Project 6 of the Ninth Programme of Law Reform: Homicide.* Law Com No 304/HC 30 (London: TSO).
Law Commission (2008) *Housing: proportionate dispute resolution* (LC 309, Cm 7377) (London: Stationery Office).

To see a full list online of all Law Commission Reports, go to www.lawcom.gov.uk/lc_reports. htm. This list gives the Law Commission number for each report, plus the full title, plus the Command Paper number (Cmnd/Cm) or the House of Commons Sessions Paper number (HC).

All Law Commission Reports from 1996 onwards are published online. Go to www.law-com.gov.uk/publications.htm. Click on the link to 'Law Commission Reports'.

Self-assessment Tick the boxes when you have tried and succeeded in finding one of each of the below:

Source	Found!
Command Paper Department of Trade and Industry (1985) *Financial Services in the United Kingdom: a New Framework for Investor Protection* (Cmnd 9432) (London: HMSO)	☐
Command Paper Department of Health (2006) *Review of the Human Fertilisation and Embryology Act* (Cm 6989) (London: TSO)	☐
Committee Report Department of Health & Social Security (1984) *Report of the Committee of Inquiry into Human Fertilisation and Embryology* (Cmnd 9314) (London: HMSO)	☐
Committee Report Joint Committee on Human Rights (2008) *Counter-Terrorism Policy and Human Rights (Tenth Report): Counter-Terrorism Bill. Twentieth Report of Session 2007–08.* HL 108/HC 554 (London: TSO)	☐
Royal Commission Report Royal Commission on Criminal Justice (1993) *The Royal Commission on Criminal Justice: report* (London: HMSO)	☐
Law Commission Consultation Paper Law Commission (2003) *Partial defences to murder: summary paper*. Consultation Paper No 173 (London: TSO)	☐
Law Commission Report Law Commission (2008) *Housing: proportionate dispute resolution* (LC 309, Cm 7377) (London: Stationery Office)	☐

Notes for future reference:

....

....

....

....

....

Finding *Hansard*: the official reports of parliamentary debates

Parliamentary debates allow MPs to discuss, deliberate and then make decisions upon questions of national interest. Parliamentary debates are intended to allow each MP the right to voice opinions. Decisions are then arrived at by the process of voting. *Hansard* is considered in further detail in **Chapter 1**.

If you are required to follow debates in Parliament, then you must consult *Hansard*, which is is divided into two parts:

- *Commons Hansard:* covers proceedings in the Commons Chamber, Westminster Hall and Standing Committees.
- *Lords Hansard:* covers proceedings in the Lords Chamber and its Grand Committees.

The debates of both Houses are available online at www.publications.parliament.uk/pa/pahansard.htm. *Hansard* online is divided into three main parts:

- *Daily Debates:* the daily debates of Parliament are published on this website the next working day at 8.00am.
- *Commons Hansard:* allows you to browse House of Commons debates, including Parliamentary questions, going back to November 1988.
- *Lords Hansard:* allows you to browse House of Lords debates going back to December 2000.

Self-assessment Tick the boxes when you have tried and succeeded in finding one of each of the below:

Source	Found!
Find a Public Bill introduced by a Government Minister	☐
Find a Private Members' Bill put forward by a member of the House of Commons, or by a member of the House of Lords	☐
Find a Private Bill promoted by an organisation such as a local authority or a private company	☐
Find *Hansard's* 'Daily Debates' online	☐
Find 'Commons *Hansard*' online	☐
Find 'Lords *Hansard*' online	☐

Notes for future reference:

....

....

....

....

2.4 FINDING JOURNALS AND OTHER PUBLICATIONS

What are secondary sources of law?

Publications such as textbooks, journals, encyclopaedias and yearbooks which describe, comment upon and interpret the law are called secondary sources of law. Secondary sources of law can also include newspaper articles.

Textbooks

To find textbooks appropriate to your studies, look at the reading lists given to you by your tutors. Your law library should have all (or most) of the books listed. In addition to copies available for you to borrow, your library may keep some copies of core items in a special short loan collection. Other core titles may be kept as reference only items to help ensure they are available for consultation in the library at all times.

Purchasing law books

If your tutor recommends that a textbook is an essential title then you should consider buying a copy. Currency of information is of utmost importance in law, and new editions of major legal textbooks are issued every one to three years. Consequently, you are recommended *not* to purchase second-hand texts unless they are current editions.

Legal journals

To support you in your studies, your library will subscribe to various legal journals in paper format. Many of these titles, and hundreds of others, are also available online.

Why are legal journals important?

In addition to publishing articles on various branches of the law, many journals also contain sections devoted to recent and proposed legislation, to case analysis, and to reviews of recently published law textbooks.

Also, journals are published much more quickly than textbooks. Consequently, the information they contain is usually more up-to-date than that found in academic textbooks. So, for example, if you want current opinion on a piece of legislation, or on a recent case, then you are more likely to find this in a recent journal than in a textbook. Law journals are also more likely to contain detailed analysis or theoretical examination of the law and will often consider a topic in much more detail than a textbook could. You should therefore get into a habit of consulting the key journals relating to the subjects you are studying and reading as widely as possible. Not only will this deepen your understanding of the topic, but the more academic work you read, the more you will develop your own reading, reasoning and writing skills.

Legal journals can be divided into two categories:

- *Professional titles:* intended primarily for practising lawyers.
- *Academic titles:* intended more for scholars studying and researching the law.

Thus the *Law Society's Gazette* (published weekly) and the *New Law Journal* (weekly) are professional titles, whilst journals such as the *Cambridge Law Journal* (published three times a year) and *Modern Law Review* (six times a year) are academic titles. However, articles in each type of journal will be of interest to both law students and practising lawyers.

How to find articles from legal journals

To find journal articles on specific topics, you can use various *Indexes*, available in paper format and online via the subscription databases. The quickest and most efficient way to find journal articles on a specific legal topic is to use the online indexes.

Journal indexes: online

The following are the most popular online indexes:

'Legal Journals Index' on *Westlaw UK.*
'Journals Search' on *LexisLibrary.*
'Articles Index' on *Lawtel.*
'Search Index' on *HeinOnline Law Journal Library*

For further information about different types of indexes for paper journals which may be in your law library, visit our **Companion Website** at www.palgrave.com/law/legalskills.

Activity Decode these references to journal articles:

- Walker (2002) MLR 65 (3) 317
- James (2005) J Crim L 69 (3) 264
- Cowan (2003) J Law & Soc 30 (2) 283

Find each journal on the library shelves. Look inside each journal to locate the actual articles and, below, write a full reference for each article

....

....

....

....

2.5 USING ONLINE LEGAL DATABASES

A modern law library will subscribe to various legal databases which are usually available to students 24 hours each day, both on and off campus. Because the subscription legal databases are expensive to provide, access will be password controlled. At the time of writing, most academic libraries in the UK Higher Education sector control access to subscription databases by means of the 'Athens' authentication scheme:

- *Athens* is the name given to the electronic service which authenticates a user as a bona fide student of a particular university or college, and then authorises that user to have individual access to online services paid for by the university or college.
- All new students in the scheme receive a personal *Athens* username and password upon registration, usually sent to each individual student email address.
- You can only use your own *Athens* username and password to access the online subscription services that your library pays for.
- For further information about which legal databases you are entitled to access, contact your own law library.

What do the online legal databases contain?

The subscription legal databases provide professional, up-to-date, and quality-assured legal information. They provide online access to a tremendous array of:

- primary sources of law: legislation and law reports
- secondary sources of law: notably the full text of articles from major (and lesser-known) legal journals, and also (if extra subscriptions are paid) to other services such as:
  - the legal encyclopaedia *Halsbury's Laws of England*
  - practitioner texts such as *Chitty on Contracts*
  - international law materials
  - newspaper articles from the national and provincial press

From the very start of your course you should learn how to use the legal databases that your library subscribes to. Your law librarian will offer instruction on how to use the databases, so do ensure you attend any training sessions that are provided. It is very much in your own interests to do so. Once you know how to use the legal databases, you should find the legal research necessary for lecture, tutorial and assessment preparation much easier!

The online legal databases in more detail

Different law libraries will subscribe to different databases and, indeed, to different services within each database. What follows is a very brief summary of the major online databases that your library may subscribe to.

For the UK legal market, the major databases are:

Lawtel

Lawtel is owned by Sweet & Maxwell. A good starting point for legal research which includes:

- UK cases: over 56,000 full text law reports in an archive that dates back to 1980, including the ICLR *Law Reports* (from 2003 onwards), *Weekly Law Reports* (from 1980 onwards), *All England Law Reports* (from 1980 onwards), and *Times Law Reports* (from 1980 onwards), plus the full text of many UK cases not reported elsewhere.
- UK legislation: includes all Acts (1987 onwards); Statutory Instruments (1984 onwards); Public Bills (1993 onwards); Command Papers (1997 onwards), plus the Statutory Status Table which allows you to track changes in legislation.

- Articles index: provides summaries (abstracts) of articles from over 60 specialist legal journals.
- *Lawtel Human Rights*: claims to be the most comprehensive information service on the Human Rights Act 1998.
- *Lawtel EU*: a useful gateway to European legal material.

Westlaw UK

Westlaw UK is also owned by Sweet & Maxwell. A powerful database which includes:

- UK and EU cases, including ICLR *Law Reports* (1865 onwards), *Weekly Law Reports* (1953 onwards), *Criminal Appeal Reports* (1995 onwards) and *Common Market Law Reports* (1962 onwards).
- UK and EU legislation.
- Legal journals index: provides summaries (abstracts) of many thousands of legal journal articles.
- The full text of articles from over 80 legal journals, including *Criminal Law Review*, *Law Quarterly Review* and *Public Law*.
- UK newspapers.
- Links to international law, including US law and Asiatic law.
- Allows users to create email alerts about specific legal topics.

 Complete the *Westlaw* exercise below.

Exercise
- To find cases, click on the 'Cases' tab at the top of the screen.
- Search for the case *Mullin v Richards*, Court of Appeal (Civil Division), 1998.
- In the 'Party Names' search box, type the keywords: **mullin v richards**. Click on 'Search'.

Screen display (1)
- Click on 'Case Analysis' to get a summary of the case.
- Below, write down the case citations (where the case has been reported). Also write down the names of the three judges who heard the case.

....

....

....

Screen display (2)
- In the left-hand frame titled 'Documents on Westlaw', click on the hyperlink to see the full text of the case as reported in the *Personal Injuries and Quantum Reports*.
- Below, write down the four catchphrases (the list of legal issues the case addresses).

....

....

....

....

LexisLibrary

LexisLibrary is owned by LexisNexis Butterworths. A powerful database which includes:

- UK and EU cases, including ICLR *Law Reports* (1865 onwards), *All England Law Reports* (1936 onwards) and *Times Law Reports* (1988 onwards).
- UK and EU legislation.
- The full text of articles from over 85 legal journals, including the *Journal of Criminal Law, Law Society Gazette* and *New Law Journal*.
- UK newspapers.
- *Halsbury's Laws of England* (online version of the legal encyclopaedia).
- Links to international law, including US law and Asiatic law.
- Allows users to create email alerts about specific legal topics.

The above databases are tailor-made for the UK market. Whilst there is some overlap in their content, if you have access to each database then you are advised to familiarise yourself with all three services.

The journal content on *Westlaw* and *LexisLibrary* is particularly significant. *Westlaw* is licensed to hold legal journals titles that are published by Sweet & Maxwell (around 30 titles, including major titles such as *Law Quarterly Review* and *Public Law*), which you won't find on *LexisLibrary*. On the other hand, *LexisLibrary* holds major journals published by Jordans (eg *Family Law, Child and Family Law Quarterly*) and Vathek (eg *Environmental Law Review*) which you won't find on *Westlaw*. Consequently, you should use both *Westlaw* and *LexisLibrary* if you are running a search for the full text of journal articles on a specific topic.

 Complete the *LexisLibrary* **exercise below:**

Exercise

- On the red 'Search' tab (top left-hand side of screen), click on 'Cases'.
- Search for the case *Carlill v Carbolic Smoke Ball Co*.
- In the 'Enter Search Terms' box, type **carlill and carbolic smoke ball co**.
- Click on 'Search'. Below, write down the number of results you get.

....

To return to previous screen

- **DON'T** use the Back button on your PC (if you do, you will soon be 'timed out' from *LexisLibrary*).
- **DO** click on the so-called 'bread-crumb trail' – the blue hypertext links that appear under the *LexisLibrary* logo in the top left-hand of the screen.
- Now go to the 'Case name' box, and type **carlill and carbolic smoke ball co**.
- Click on 'Search'. How many results do you get this time?

....

- Click on the hypertext link to find the **1893** report of the case. This brings you to a page showing various case citations.
- Click on hypertext link **[1893] 1 QB 256** to see the full case report.

Answer the following questions:

- In which court and on what dates was the case heard?

....

- What are the first three **catchwords** for the case (ie the phrases indicating the key legal issues raised by the case)?

....

....

To support other aspects of legal research, your law library may subscribe to the following:

HeinOnline

HeinOnline is owned by the American legal publisher, William Hein & Co. A large, image-based legal research database, which includes:

- Access to the back-files of over 800 legal journals; although the emphasis is on US titles, many UK titles are included, eg *Cambridge Law Journal* and *Modern Law Review*.
- The full text of *The English Reports* (1220 –1873): these early cases played an important role in formulating the basis of our common law as we know it today.
- The full text of Statutes of the Realm: English statutes from 1235 to 1713; this is the authoritative source for older UK statutes. Access via 'Subscribed Libraries' list; click on 'English Reports, Full Reprint'; then click on 'Statutes of the Realm'.
- Access to the *Legal Classics Library*: contains law-related items from the late 19th and early 20th centuries.

Justis

Justis is owned by Justis Publishing. A powerful full text online legal library which includes:

- The full text of UK, Irish and EU case law dating back to 1163, including ICLR *Law Reports* (1865 onwards), *Weekly Law Reports* (1953 onwards) and *The English Reports* (1220–1873).
- The full text of all UK legislation from 1235, including all repealed Acts.
- State Trials: coverage of over seven centuries of higher criminal jurisprudence covering English trials between 1163 and 1858. A wide variety of cases are covered, including high treason, sedition, riot, piracy and witchcraft!
- A noted advantage of *Justis* is that the database allows you to download and print the exact replica of documents in Portable Document Format (PDF) (essential for presentation in court, and useful for mooting).

JustCite

JustCite, a powerful legal research tool, is owned by Justis Publishing.

- Essentially, *JustCite* is a search engine and an electronic citator which quickly allows users to identify legal information from other online legal databases.
- It links to case law, legislation and legal journal articles from numerous publishers, providing citations and a drop-down list showing the various electronic sources that hold the full text.
- If your own law library subscribes to the relevant databases, then *JustCite* will provide you with deep links straight into the full texts you require (thus reducing the need for you to do separate searches of individual legal databases).

Eurolaw

Eurolaw is owned by SAI Global – ILI Publishing. A powerful tool for tracing European Union law which provides the full text of primary sources of EU law, including the official CELEX database with substantial additions made by the International Law Institute (ILI). The databases includes:

- Primary legislation (Treaties); secondary legislation (Directives, Regulations and Decisions); national implementation details.
- The full text of case law from the European Court of Justice (Luxembourg) and the European Court of Human Rights (Strasbourg).
- The full text of the Official Journal, 1998 onwards.

Useful tips for online searching

Searching online databases can be extremely time-consuming and frustrating. Many students lack confidence when it comes to searching, and it can be difficult to know what terms to use to get the best results. If you can refine your search techniques and reduce the time spent searching, you should be able to reduce the time you waste and increase the time you have available to actually engage with the material you find. To make your online search techniques more efficient, you should learn to use the following:

> (a) Synonyms and related terms
> (b) Case name and case citation searches
> (c) Author and Title searches
> (d) Exact phrase searching using double quotation marks
> (e) Truncation
> (f) Wild card characters

(a) Synonyms and related terms

In common with most databases, the legal databases allow you to do a general keyword search, sometimes called a free text search. A free text search will look for the terms that you type, wherever they occur in the documents you have selected to search (eg law reports, legislation, journal articles).

When doing a free text search, think of *synonyms* (different words that have the same, or similar, meaning) and other related terms.

Example

- If you type the keyword **damages** you will miss other important documents that discuss the same topic. Try using the synonym **compensation**, plus related phrases such as **exemplary damages** and **compensation awards**.
- If you cannot think of any synonyms or related terms, consult a (law) dictionary or thesaurus.

(b) Case name and case citation searches

If you are looking for a specific law report, and you have the party names, then use the appropriate search boxes to find the case. On *Westlaw* use the 'Party Names' search box. On *LexisLibrary* use the 'Case Names' search box. On *Lawtel* use the 'Case Law' search box. If you have the case citation, then use the 'Citation' search box.

Example

To find this case, *Bradford City Council v Arora* [1991] 2 QB 507, do the following (note it is not essential to include capital letters):
- In the 'Party Names' search box type: **bradford city council and arora**
Alternatively, you can search by case citation:
- In the 'Citation' search box type: **1991 2 QB 507**
Note. Do not include the square brackets as included in the actual citation as this will confuse the search engine and yield no results.

(c) Author and Title searches

If you are required to find specific journal articles, and you have the appropriate details, then use 'Author' and 'Title' searches to look for known items.

Example

If you are using *LexisLibrary* to search for the journal article 'Disciplinary uniformity in uniform: a success of the Human Rights At 1998?' by Chris Gale, published in the *Journal of Criminal Law* in April 2008, then do the following:
- In the 'Author' search box type: **gale**
- In the 'Title' search box type: **disciplinary uniformity**
Typing the author surname, plus just two or three leading words of the title, should retrieve the article you require.

(d) Exact phrase searching using double quotation marks

If you type a phrase, ie a small group of words, the database may pick up the string of words as a complete phrase. More likely, however, the database will search for each individual word and you will retrieve a large number of results, many of which will be irrelevant to your topic. So, if you are searching for a particular phrase, enclose the string of words between double quotation marks:

" "

This will enable an exact phrase search, ie the database will find only those words that you have typed in the exact order within the double quotation marks.

Examples

- If you are searching for cases concerning unfair dismissal then enclose the phrase in double quotation marks, ie type **"unfair dismissal"**
- If you are searching for documents concerning the Judicial Committee of the Privy Council then enclose the phrase in double quotation marks, ie type **"judicial committee of the privy council"**

(e) Truncation

Truncation means running a search with a shortened (ie truncated) keyword followed by either of the following characters:

*

!

Using these symbols will widen your search because the truncation symbol will find all derivatives of the word stem, including the infinitive, the plural, and the past tense of the word. The symbol to use, whether an asterisk (*) or an exclamation mark (!), differs between databases. *Westlaw* and *LexisLibrary*, for example, use the exclamation mark (!) as the truncation symbol, whilst *Lawtel* uses the asterisk (*).

Example

- On *Westlaw* and *LexisLibrary*, typing **legislat!** will pick up: legislate, legislates, legislated, legislating, legislation, legislator, legislature, legislative.
- On *Lawtel* typing **prosecut*** will pick up: prosecute, prosecutes, prosecuted, prosecuting, prosecutor, prosecution.

(f) Wild card characters

To find words with variable characters, use the wild card character, symbolised by an asterisk:

*

The asterisk can be used as substitute for any letter (just as a blank tile is used in the Scrabble board game).

Example

- Typing **withdr*w** will pick up: withdraw and withdrew
- Typing **wom*n** will pick up: woman and women

If you are looking for a case name with variable spelling, the wild card character can help:
- Typing **sm*th** will pick up: Smith and Smyth
- Typing **don*ghue** will pick up: Donoghue and Donaghue

Self-assessment **Tick the following boxes when you have completed the task:**

- ☐ I am able to use online legal resources in my studies
- ☐ I have done a *Lawtel* search
- ☐ I have done a *Westlaw* search
- ☐ I have done a *LexisLibrary* search
- ☐ I have done a *HeinOnline* search
- ☐ I have used *Justis*
- ☐ I have used *JustCite* (if my library has access to it)
- ☐ I have used *Eurolaw*

- ☐ I can use synonyms and related terms in a search
- ☐ I can carry out case name and case citation searches
- ☐ I can do author and title searches
- ☐ I can do exact phrase searching using double quotation marks
- ☐ I can use truncation in a search
- ☐ I can use wild card characters in a search

3

Legal research

Learning outcomes

> To be able to read material effectively
> To be able to use different legal sources in your research and writing
> To decide whether alternative approaches to research might be helpful in your own legal research

> To begin to evaluate the validity and reliability of other research studies you might come across

This chapter aims to equip you with the expertise to carry out independent legal research into any area of law. Developing these skills from the start will underpin your academic study of law and prepare you for practical legal research in the future. When you have read this chapter and worked through the exercises included, you should feel confident that you have met the learning outcomes listed above.

The development of the legal regulation of many areas of our lives involves a combination of public policy decisions, legislation and adjudication, may well involve significant political, moral and ethical as well as legal aspects, and may require an international as well as a municipal (national) legal perspective. Legal research can therefore involve the exploration of all these different aspects of a particular issue and of the interrelationship of the different aspects.

Self-assessment How good am I at reading?

Tick the statement that applies to you...	This is me!	This is not me
I love books!	☐	☐
I read often for leisure	☐	☐
I own a lot of books	☐	☐
I have a favourite subject and own many books on it	☐	☐
I buy items on my law reading lists	☐	☐
I find it easy to read law books	☐	☐

I do my weekly reading for my course	☐	☐
I can remember facts and figures when I am reading	☐	☐
I learn a lot by reading	☐	☐

My thoughts on my results:

....

....

....

3.1 EFFECTIVE READING

In order for you to make the most of your research and library skills, you need to learn how to read effectively. As a law student you will be required to work through a lot of material, and this section provides you with some tips and tricks to do so in the most effective and efficient way.

Students often struggle with the volume of reading required, and there are two main reasons for this. Some students struggle to make time for reading or to work out how much time you should spend reading in preparation for lectures and tutorials, as general background or for assignments. Consider having a look at the time management section in **Chapter 6** to improve your skills in this area.

Other students struggle with the reading itself. You might spend a lot of time trying to work out unfamiliar words or jargon, you may keep going back over what you've just read to make sure you understand the point being made, or you may feel like you are going very slowly, especially if you are reading aloud under your breath. Some of these issues will be even more prominent if your first language is not English. To help you improve your reading skills, this section presents you with six steps to becoming a more effective reader:

1 Feeling right about reading

2 Develop the 3 Rs of reading

3 Become a more selective reader

4 Become a smarter reader

5 Become a more focused (and faster) reader

6 Become a more active reader

Step 1: Feeling right about reading

First things first: how do you feel about reading? Tick the most accurate statement below to describe how you feel about reading. Be honest!

Self-assessment

I enjoy reading all types of things and read often for pleasure as well as for work or study purposes	☐
I quite like reading, depending on the subject etc, and will get on with doing it, particularly for work/study purposes – but I would not say it was my first priority for pleasure	☐
I am not very keen on reading, but will do it because I have to for work or study purposes. I might, occasionally, do it for pleasure!	☐

If you don't feel that any of these statements connects with the way you feel about reading, write your own feelings in the space below:

....

....

....

....

....

Your feelings about reading

Your feelings about reading can affect the way you approach and manage it. People who generally enjoy the experience of reading and read for pleasure have often learned instinctively to manage the process. They know that maintaining and enhancing their enjoyment of reading is often about:

- finding the right time and place to read;
- getting into the right mood;
- getting involved actively with what they read;
- picking the right text to read.

However, many students either have mixed feelings about reading, or dislike the experience, and only do it because they have to! If you are in this latter category, you could begin to address the issue by trying to increase your enjoyment of reading. If you begin to enjoy reading more, this will help you to develop more effective reading and reading management techniques. If you actively dislike the experience of reading, you will not respond as well as you might to the techniques, as your aversion to reading can act as a barrier to change.

Three ways of making the experience of reading more enjoyable

- Try going once a week to buy something to read that really interests you. The brighter, the lighter, the more frivolous, rude, controversial or humorous the better. Try and look forward to this moment in the week. Read it and enjoy it. Stop when you get bored.
- Try to encourage a friend or partner to read the same thing you have selected and then have a discussion about what you have read.
- Set yourself strict limits for reading things you have to read. Set yourself a limit of no more than 40–50 minutes reading at any one stretch. And as you read, try to engage more actively with the text.

Step 2: Develop the 3 Rs of reading

It is important to have a purpose for reading before you start. This advice may seem self-evident, but when time is limited, it is important to consider beforehand why you intend to read a particular text and what you hope to gain from it. Different reading purposes require different levels of engagement with texts: the 3 Rs of reading.

- Reading to reveal
- Reading to review
- Reading to remind

To reveal ...

Reading (a) to prepare for lectures and tutorials to reveal main points, and (b) to reveal new sources and data to add to knowledge gained from lectures and tutorials, in preparation for writing assignments or taking examinations.

Reading approach

Reading in preparation for a lecture or tutorial will help you to anticipate and understand some of the ideas and practices that the tutor will present and discuss. At this stage, you do not need a great depth of knowledge. A fairly quick scan and review of the main ideas and practices associated with a particular topic will give you the basic understanding of the key ideas that you need to know to follow the lecture.

To review ...

Reading to review what was learned and to reinforce understanding after a lecture or tutorial.

Reading approach

It requires an active and more rigorous approach to reading to ensure you have grasped the main points presented by the lecturer and to follow up other sources suggested. This reading purpose is often neglected. However, arguably it is the most important purpose of all, as it can save you much time and effort later in the course, particularly when you have to write assignments.

To remind ...

Reading to remind yourself what you read previously, eg for examination revision purposes.

Reading approach

If you have engaged well with reading at the review stage, the revision reading task should be much less formidable, as you will have gained a good grasp of the assignment topic from earlier reading.

A reading plan

Why do you need a reading plan? Look at the table below. Do you fall into the left column?

Non-readers!	Readers!
✘ Reading is boring	✓ I love reading
✘ I get distracted	✓ I can concentrate when I read
✘ Law books are too heavy	✓ I don't mind carrying law books
✘ Law books are too complex	✓ I don't mind the complexity
✘ I don't understand the content	✓ I re-read until I understand
✘ There are words I don't know	✓ I have a dictionary at hand
✘ I don't learn through reading	✓ I learn more through reading
✘ I'm too impatient	✓ I can find the time to read

It is wise to plan ahead each week, as the study of law requires a lot of reading. This is particularly relevant for review reading, which will save you time later when you have to write assignments and revise for exams. A reading plan will encourage you to schedule blocks of time, eg 40–50 minutes per topic, on selected days throughout the week.

Fill in the table below to start creating your own reading plan.

Module/ topic	Background/general reading	Directed reading
Contract law	Mondays 3.15pm–4pm	Wednesdays 9am–11.30am with 2 breaks of 15 minutes Saturdays 11am–11.50am

Step 3: Become a more selective reader

Jenny: Which book are you reading tonight? I'm reading Contract Law.

Katherine: I'm reading Legal Skills – the assignment's coming up.

You are *not* expected to read recommended books from cover to cover. You are meant to read with a particular learning purpose in mind and refer to them selectively in your assignments. Don't be afraid to deviate from recommended texts. Some books are easier to read than others (and it is worth asking yourself why that is). If you find it hard to grasp ideas presented in one textbook, try looking at another to compare how ideas are presented. You may, for example, prefer books that illustrate ideas with pictures or graphics to those that are more text based. The important thing is to develop your understanding of theories, ideas and practices in a way that is best for you.

If you are clear about your purpose for reading and what it is you want from a text before you start reading, you can then select the most appropriate source and concentrate on the part of this that will give you the information you seek. Refer back to the **Chapter 2** for some guidance on where to search for legal information on the Internet.

Step 4: Become a smarter reader

You can become a smarter reader in the following way:

- Read the summaries or conclusions of chapters or articles first to gain an overview of a chapter – or even the book itself. For 'reveal' reading purposes, this may be enough to give you the key point(s) that you need.
- For other reading purposes, this initial look at summaries or conclusions will help you to gain an overall sense of the main points made by the author. This will help prepare you for the more thorough reading you will need to give to the text, as you will be mentally primed and prepared for the key point(s) that emerge.

   'What are key points? Where do I find them?'

Most books, articles and other well written sources are broken up into paragraphs or sections. Within each paragraph or section you can try to identify the key point, which is the sentence or sentences upon which the others are built.

Other ways to become a smarter reader

1 Smart reading is also about discovering the right time to connect with your energy levels. Some people find they read better early in the day; others prefer to read late at night.

2 Smart reading is also about knowing when to stop. It is often better to schedule short bursts of reading (40–50 minutes), rather than go on for long periods without a break. If you set yourself a relatively short time for any one period of reading, you then have to get on with it and really concentrate on the topic selected. If you don't set yourself a time limit, you may be inclined to be less focused, lose your concentration and be open to distractions.

3 Distraction problems can also occur when the subject being studied appears totally removed from the 'real world'. To overcome this, one approach is to keep asking yourself, *'how does this relate to real life?'* Try to connect the subject to the world about you and your previous work experience. If you are reading primary sources of law, think about how they might affect you or people you know.

4 Listening to music while you read may help some students but can be an irritant to others. You need to work out what works best for you.

5 If you are reading in preparation for a written assignment, it is sensible not to surround yourself with too many books that cover the same topic. It is more effective to find one or two books and use these as your main sources for other relevant reading on the assignment topic.

Step 5: Become a more focused (and faster) reader

Do you ever do one or more of the following as you read:

- mouth words or read under your breath;
- keep going back over words just read to reassure yourself you understood their meaning; or
- frequently stop reading to check unfamiliar words?

If you answer 'Yes' to any of these, you may find the following ideas helpful to speed up the reading process.

Do you mouth words or read under your breath?

If you mouth words, you can only read as fast as you speak. If you try to stop doing this, you may then find that your reading speed increases. Try the technique below to help train your eyes to follow more quickly a line of reading.

Do you keep going back over words you have just read?

Anxiety can cause students to re-read sentences to reassure themselves that they have understood. This can slow the reading process down and lead to frustration at the slow progress made. One way out of this problem is to cover the text with an A3 or A4 card or sheet of paper with a rectangle, approx 3" in depth, cut out about a third of the way down. The card or sheet is then placed across the item to be read and moved downwards over the text.

After a while, when your confidence and reading speed has increased, you can stop using this aid. This technique, combined with active reading techniques, can really help you increase both reading speed and understanding. This may seem a very 'low-tech' idea in a high-tech age, but it does work!

Do you frequently stop reading to check unfamiliar words?

Many students who encounter unfamiliar or difficult words stop reading at that point and check the meaning of the word in a dictionary. However, it is often better to keep reading, as you can often gain more information later from the text, which can then clarify the points you did not initially understand. You should make a note of words you do not immediately understand, and if their meaning does not become clear from continued reading you should look them up later.

Self-assessment Tick the boxes below when you have finished the task:

☐ I now know how I really feel about reading
☐ I now know what I have to do to improve my reading on my course
☐ I can now read to reveal, review and remind myself
☐ I have developed a reading plan for my studies

☐ I can now be a selective reader
☐ I have trained myself to become a smarter reader
☐ I am a focused reader now
☐ I am a faster reader – I can speed-read

Reminder!

You will remember that it is a better strategy to look quickly for a key point or idea in each paragraph, rather than reading texts word by word. The main ideas are usually supported by primary words in a text. These are words that play an important role in developing the key points or ideas in a text.

Focusing on primary words

As emphasised earlier, an important skill in reading is to be able to identify key points or ideas and primary words in reading. If you can try and isolate first the main point or points in any section of text, you can then try and pick out the words that support the main point(s) and try and give less attention to the rest. This can speed your reading and help you gain a sense of the subject matter more quickly.

Speed-reading

Speed-reading is the purported ability to read as many as 10,000 to 25,000 words a minute.

It is one thing to recognise the meanings of words, but another to really understand (and even enjoy or appreciate) the context in which those words are presented. The basic idea of speed-reading, however, is that you rapidly scan each line, focusing on the centre of the page, moving your eyes as quickly as possible down the page, never regressing, and picking out verbs and nouns.

But success in speed-reading is mainly determined by how fast a reader can recognise the meanings of the words on the page. These tend to be those who have a very good command of the language in which they are studying, and have developed the ability to differentiate between the meanings of same or similar words.

Speed-reading techniques have their role though, if:

- you want or need to skim quickly through a text to isolate something very specific from it; and
- you have already developed a good vocabulary and can differentiate between words spelt the same or in a similar way (for example between 'their' and 'there', or 'effect' and 'affect', 'practise' and 'practice').

But, as stressed earlier, slower, more analytical and critical reading is often required. The speed at which you read for all purposes can certainly be increased, but for success in the academic world, the real trick is to know when to skim and when to read every word.

Adjusting the pace of reading to suit the purpose

You would not drive a car at one speed; you would adjust to the road conditions. It is the same with reading. There are times when you can and should speed up, and other times when you need to slow down.

Speed up: when you scan text or notes to identify main ideas, for example in preparation for a lecture or tutorial, or to pick out key ideas in texts in preparation for a more detailed reading.

Steady on: a slower, more detailed reading is often necessary, for example to ensure you have understood lectures and tutorials, and to add to the knowledge presented by the tutor. This is a key phase of reading, as it will save you time later when you have to prepare for assignments and revise for examinations.

Step 6: Become a more active reader

Active reading is about becoming more involved with what you read. One important way of getting involved is by making notes. Note making means summarising or highlighting what you feel is important or relevant to note.

Students who make notes will often ask themselves:

'Do I really need this information? If so, which bit?'
'Will I ever use the notes? If so, when and for what purpose?'

Whether you make written notes yourself, or highlight what is printed, the principle of effective note making is the same: look for the main points in the text. Students who make notes often add their own thoughts to the notes made. They may experiment with different note-making formats, including voice notes or visual forms of note making. You might want to have a look at our section on note making in **Chapter 5** to develop your skills in this area.

Becoming a better reader: my action plan

In the space below write down what you are going to do to improve your reading skills. Try to break down your action plan into small steps and tick them off when you have achieved them.

My step to better reading

Achieved!

.... ☐

.... ☐

.... ☐

.... ☐

.... ☐

.... ☐

.... ☐

.... ☐

.... ☐

Effective reading: key points

Step 1: Feel right about reading

- Find the right time and place to read
- Get into the right mood
- Get involved actively with what you read
- Pick the right text to read

Step 2: Develop the 3 Rs of reading

- Read to reveal
  - o main points
  - o new sources and data
- Read to review what was learned
- Read to remind yourself what you learned previously

Step 3: Become a more selective reader

- Read selectively with a particular learning purpose in mind

Step 4: Become a smarter reader

- Read summaries and conclusions first
- Try to identify the key points of the text by searching for sentences upon which the others are built
- Find the right time to read and know where to stop
- Focus your reading on the most relevant books
- Seek a connection between the studied topic and the 'real world'

Step 5: Become a more focused (and faster) reader

- Use speed-reading
- Adjust the pace of reading to suit the purpose

Step 6: Become a more active reader

- Make notes
- Draw a reading plan

3.2 USING CASES

In order for you to become an efficient legal researcher, it is important that you find your way around legal sources quickly and easily. You should be able to evaluate quickly whether the source will help you further in your investigation or whether it is irrelevant. This section and the following sections at **3.3** and **3.4** therefore focus on the anatomy of cases, statutes and journals. Once you understand these, you will find that other sources such as statutory instruments, case transcripts and reports also follow similar patterns allowing you to decode the information in front of you. This chapter does not deal with the analysis, interpretation or evaluation of sources in detail; this is covered in **Chapter** 4, 'Critical Thinking'.

 **You might already know quite a lot about legal sources, and the table below will help you work out where your strengths and weaknesses lie in this area. Fill in the table once now (Mark 1), and then come back to it after you have read this chapter (Mark 2). See how much you have improved. For each skill give yourself a mark out of 10 depending on your level of confidence (where 1 is not at all confident and 10 is very confident)**

	Mark 1	Mark 2
I know where to find the parties' names in a case report	☐	☐
I know where to find the name of the person reporting the case	☐	☐
I know what the headnote is	☐	☐
I know where to find the judges' names	☐	☐
I know where to find the neutral case citation	☐	☐
I know where to find the long title of a statute	☐	☐
I know where to find the date of Royal Assent	☐	☐
I know how to find out when a statute came into force	☐	☐
I know how a statute is organised	☐	☐
I know how EU legislation is organised	☐	☐
I know where to find the authors' names in journal articles	☐	☐
I know what an abstract is for	☐	☐
I know where to find the publication details of a journal article	☐	☐
Total	....	....

Reading cases takes practice and it takes some time to get used to the language used. It may therefore seem cumbersome when you first start. However, you will get better with practice and should soon begin to enjoy reading cases. They are after all real-life stories which give you an insight into legal disputes, their resolution and legal reasoning.

It is often useful to scan the headnote first to get an idea of what the case is about, but you must bear in mind that this is the editor's interpretation of the judgments and you must read the full report yourself to come to your own conclusions.

Cases can be used in a variety of ways in your studies. Reading cases will help you develop your legal reasoning skills and will make you more familiar with legal language. Reading cases, analysing them and evaluating the arguments put forward by judges will allow you to build effective legal arguments based on primary sources. In order to read a case effectively, you have to know what you are looking at and what each bit of a law report means.

The anatomy of a law report

As you will have seen in **Chapter 2**, there are a number of different law reports. However, the reports follow a similar structure, so once you have understood clearly what each part of the report presented is you will not have to relearn this for each different series of reports. The example given on the following pages highlights the most important parts of a law report. The extracts are taken from the case of *R (on the application of Quintavalle) v Human Fertilisation and Embryology Authority* [2005] 2 All ER 555.

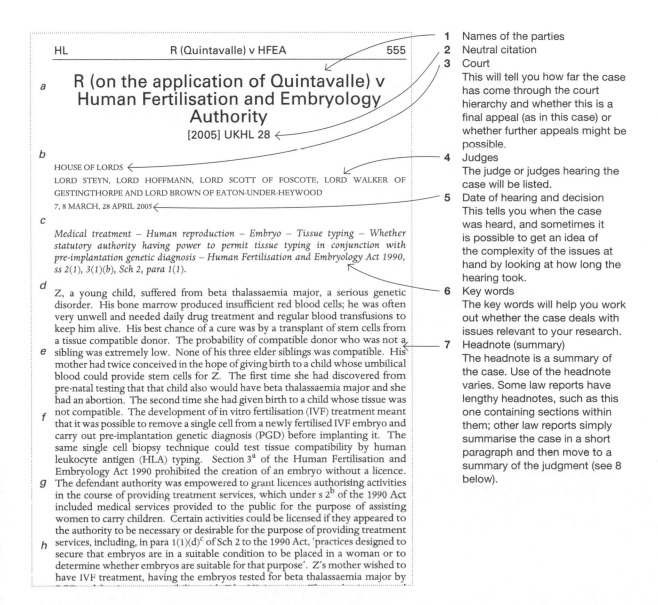

HL   R (Quintavalle) v HFEA   555

a

R (on the application of Quintavalle) v Human Fertilisation and Embryology Authority
[2005] UKHL 28

b

HOUSE OF LORDS

LORD STEYN, LORD HOFFMANN, LORD SCOTT OF FOSCOTE, LORD WALKER OF GESTINGTHORPE AND LORD BROWN OF EATON-UNDER-HEYWOOD

7, 8 MARCH, 28 APRIL 2005

c

Medical treatment – Human reproduction – Embryo – Tissue typing – Whether statutory authority having power to permit tissue typing in conjunction with pre-implantation genetic diagnosis – Human Fertilisation and Embryology Act 1990, ss 2(1), 3(1)(b), Sch 2, para 1(1).

d

Z, a young child, suffered from beta thalassaemia major, a serious genetic disorder. His bone marrow produced insufficient red blood cells; he was often very unwell and needed daily drug treatment and regular blood transfusions to keep him alive. His best chance of a cure was by a transplant of stem cells from a tissue compatible donor. The probability of compatible donor who was not a

e

sibling was extremely low. None of his three elder siblings was compatible. His mother had twice conceived in the hope of giving birth to a child whose umbilical blood could provide stem cells for Z. The first time she had discovered from pre-natal testing that that child also would have beta thalassaemia major and she had an abortion. The second time she had given birth to a child whose tissue was not compatible. The development of in vitro fertilisation (IVF) treatment meant

f

that it was possible to remove a single cell from a newly fertilised IVF embryo and carry out pre-implantation genetic diagnosis (PGD) before implanting it. The same single cell biopsy technique could test tissue compatibility by human leukocyte antigen (HLA) typing. Section 3[a] of the Human Fertilisation and Embryology Act 1990 prohibited the creation of an embryo without a licence.

g

The defendant authority was empowered to grant licences authorising activities in the course of providing treatment services, which under s 2[b] of the 1990 Act included medical services provided to the public for the purpose of assisting women to carry children. Certain activities could be licensed if they appeared to the authority to be necessary or desirable for the purpose of providing treatment

h

services, including, in para 1(1)(d)[c] of Sch 2 to the 1990 Act, 'practices designed to secure that embryos are in a suitable condition to be placed in a woman or to determine whether embryos are suitable for that purpose'. Z's mother wished to have IVF treatment, having the embryos tested for beta thalassaemia major by

---

1 Names of the parties

2 Neutral citation

3 Court
This will tell you how far the case has come through the court hierarchy and whether this is a final appeal (as in this case) or whether further appeals might be possible.

4 Judges
The judge or judges hearing the case will be listed.

5 Date of hearing and decision
This tells you when the case was heard, and sometimes it is possible to get an idea of the complexity of the issues at hand by looking at how long the hearing took.

6 Key words
The key words will help you work out whether the case deals with issues relevant to your research.

7 Headnote (summary)
The headnote is a summary of the case. Use of the headnote varies. Some law reports have lengthy headnotes, such as this one containing sections within them; other law reports simply summarise the case in a short paragraph and then move to a summary of the judgment (see 8 below).

Held – Both PGD and HLA typing could lawfully be authorised by the authority   *d*
as activities to determine the suitability of the embryo for implantation within the
meaning of para 1(1)(d) of Sch 2 to the 1990 Act. The concept of suitability was
broad enough to include suitability for the purposes of the particular mother.
Parliament had not intended to confine the authority's powers to unsuitability on
grounds of genetic defect; the limits of permissible embryo selection were for the
authority to decide. The fact that decisions left by the 1990 Act to the authority   *e*
might raise difficult ethical questions was no objection; it had been specifically
created to make ethical distinctions and, if Parliament should consider it to be
failing in that task, it had regulatory powers in reserve. The appeal would,
accordingly, be dismissed (see [1], [14], [24], [26], [28], [29], [35], [39]–[41], [52],
[56], [61]–[63], below).
  Decision of the Court of Appeal [2003] 3 All ER 257 affirmed.   *f*

Notes
For prohibitions on the use of embryos and for licences for treatment, see
30 *Halsbury's Laws* (4th edn reissue) paras 59, 62.
  For the Human Fertilisation and Embryology Act 1990, ss 2, 3, Sch 2, para 1,   *g*
see 28 *Halsbury's Statutes* (4th edn) (2001 reissue) 291, 332.

Cases referred to in opinions
Leeds Teaching Hospital NHS Trust v A [2003] EWHC 259 (QB), [2003] 1 FCR 599.
Pepper (Inspector of Taxes) v Hart [1993] 1 All ER 42, [1993] AC 593, [1992] 3 WLR   *h*
  1032, HL.
R (on the application of Quintavalle) v Secretary of State for Health [2003] UKHL 13,
  [2003] 2 All ER 113, [2003] 2 AC 687, [2003] 2 WLR 692.
Royal College of Nursing of the UK v Dept of Health and Social Security [1981] 1 All ER
  545, [1981] AC 800, [1981] 2 WLR 279, HL.   *j*

Cases referred to in list of authorities
Black-Clawson International Ltd v Papierwerke Waldhof-Aschaffenburg AG [1975] 1 All
  ER 810, [1975] AC 591, [1975] 2 WLR 513, HL.
R (on the application of Westminster City Council) v National Asylum Support Service
  [2002] UKHL 38, [2002] 4 All ER 654, [2002] 1 WLR 2956.

Appeal
The claimant, Josephine Quintavalle acting on behalf of Comment on Reproductive
Ethics, appealed with permission of the House of Lords Appeal Committee given on   *c*
21 January 2004 from the decision of the Court of Appeal (Lord Phillips of Worth
Matravers MR, Schiemann and Mance LJJ) on 16 May 2003 ([2003] EWCA Civ 667,
[2003] 3 All ER 257 allowing the appeal of the Human Fertilisation and Embryology
Authority from the decision of Maurice Kay J on 20 December 2002 ([2002] EWHC
2785 (Admin), [2003] 2 All ER 105) giving judgment in favour of the claimant in
d judicial review proceedings concerning the power of the authority to grant licences
for human leukocyte antigen tissue typing under para 1 of Sch 2 to the Human
Fertilisation and Embryology Act 1990. The Secretary of State for Health appeared
as an interested party. The facts are set out in the opinion of Lord Hoffmann.

e *Lord Brennan QC* and *Clive Lewis* (instructed by *Ormerods*, Croydon) for the
    claimant.
  David Pannick QC and *Dinah Rose* (instructed by *Morgan Cole*, Cardiff) for the
    authority.
  James Eadie (instructed by the *Solicitor to the Departments of Health and Work and*
    Pensions) for the Secretary of State.
f
  Their Lordships took time for consideration.

  28 April 2005. The following opinions were delivered.

8 Summary of judgment
(technically part of the
headnote)
This will give you a summary
of what the judges held.
Remember it is a summary
only and the editor's
interpretation only.

9 Notes
The notes provide clarification
or references and often refer
to additional information which
you may want to follow up.

10 Cases referred to
A list of cases referred to. This
list is sometimes split into
cases cited in the judgments
and those cited in argument.

11 Prodedural history
This section describes the
stages in the claim prior to the
current hearing.

12 Legal representatives
It is usual for the legal
representatives for both sides
to be listed.

13 Date of judgment
The date of the judgment is not
necessarily the same as the
date of the hearing as judges
will often want to take their
time to consider the case in
detail.

g **LORD STEYN.**

[1] My Lords, I have had the advantage of reading the opinions of my noble and learned friends Lord Hoffmann and Lord Brown of Eaton-under-Heywood. For the reasons they have given I would dismiss the appeal.

h **LORD HOFFMANN.**

[2] My Lords, Zain Hashmi is a little boy, now aged six, who suffers from a serious genetic disorder called beta thalassaemia major. His bone marrow does not produce enough red blood cells and in consequence he is often very poorly and needs daily drugs and regular blood transfusions to keep him alive. But he
j could be restored to normal life by a transplant of stem cells from a tissue compatible donor.

[3] The problem is to find compatible tissue which Zain's immune system will not reject. The chances of finding a compatible donor who is not a sibling are extremely low. Even in the case of siblings, the chances are only one in four. None of Zain's three elder siblings is compatible. In addition, the donor must be free of the same disorder. That lengthens the odds even more. Zain's mother,

14 Judgments
The bulk of most reports is made up of the judgments. Sometimes all judges will write their own judgments; sometimes one judge will write the judgment and the others will simply agree, and occasionally you will see joint judgments. If a judge does not agree with the majority, he or she will write his or her own dissenting judgment.

jurisdiction could be invoked.
[63] For these reasons, most of which are more fully explained in Lord Hoffmann's speech with which I entirely agree, I too would dismiss this g appeal.

Appeal dismissed

Kate O'Hanlon   Barrister.

15 Outcome
This is usually a one-line statement confirming the legal outcome of the case.

16 Author of report

EU cases

As well as the law reports reporting cases heard in the English courts, you are likely also to have to consider EU law cases. European law reports look slightly different to English law reports. Consider the example below.

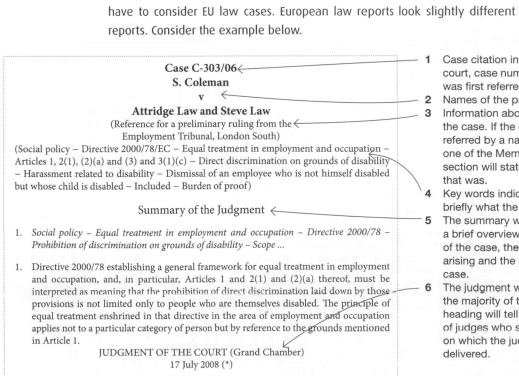

Case C-303/06

S. Coleman

v

Attridge Law and Steve Law

(Reference for a preliminary ruling from the Employment Tribunal, London South)

(Social policy – Directive 2000/78/EC – Equal treatment in employment and occupation – Articles 1, 2(1), (2)(a) and (3) and 3(1)(c) – Direct discrimination on grounds of disability – Harassment related to disability – Dismissal of an employee who is not himself disabled but whose child is disabled – Included – Burden of proof)

Summary of the Judgment

1. *Social policy – Equal treatment in employment and occupation – Directive 2000/78 – Prohibition of discrimination on grounds of disability – Scope ...*

1. Directive 2000/78 establishing a general framework for equal treatment in employment and occupation, and, in particular, Articles 1 and 2(1) and (2)(a) thereof, must be interpreted as meaning that the prohibition of direct discrimination laid down by those provisions is not limited only to people who are themselves disabled. The principle of equal treatment enshrined in that directive in the area of employment and occupation applies not to a particular category of person but by reference to the grounds mentioned in Article 1.

JUDGMENT OF THE COURT (Grand Chamber)
17 July 2008 (*)

1 Case citation indicating the court, case number and year it was first referred to the court.

2 Names of the parties.

3 Information about the origins of the case. If the case has been referred by a national court of one of the Member States, this section will state which court that was.

4 Key words indicating very briefly what the case is about.

5 The summary will usually give a brief overview of the facts of the case, the legal issues arising and the outcome of the case.

6 The judgment will then take up the majority of the report. The heading will tell you the number of judges who sat and the date on which the judgment was delivered.

...

THE COURT (Grand Chamber),

composed of V. Skouris, President, P. Jann, C.W.A. Timmermans, A. Rosas, K. Lenaerts and A. Tizzano, Presidents of Chambers, M. Ilešič, J. Klučka, A. Ó Caoimh (Rapporteur), T. von Danwitz and A. Arabadjiev, Judges,

Advocate General: M. Poiares Maduro,

Registrar: L. Hewlett, Principal Administrator,

having regard to the written procedure and further to the hearing on 9 October 2007,

after considering the observations submitted on behalf of:

– Ms Coleman, by R. Allen QC and P. Michell, Barrister,

7 The next section deals with the personnel involved in the case, listing the judges first as well as the Advocate General and the parties' representatives.

8 It is usual in cases heard before the ECJ to have an Advocate General give an opinion on the case prior to the hearing. The Advocate General is impartial and considers the legal issues arising and then delivers an opinion to the ECJ. The ECJ does not have to follow the opinion given but Advocate Generals are often very persuasive. This part of the judgment tells you that an opinion was received and considered by the court before making its judgment.

Judgment

This reference for a preliminary ruling concerns the interpretation of Council Directive 2000/78/EC of 27 November 2000 establishing a general framework for equal treatment in employment and occupation (OJ 2000 L 303, p. 16).

Legal context

Community legislation

...

National legislation

The dispute in the main proceedings and the questions referred for a preliminary ruling

19 Ms Coleman worked for her former employer as a legal secretary from January 2001.

27 Since the Employment Tribunal, London South, considered that the case before it raised questions of interpretation of Community law, it decided to stay the proceedings and refer the following questions to the Court of Justice for a preliminary ruling:

'(1) In the context of the prohibition of discrimination on grounds of disability, does [Directive 2000/78] only protect from direct discrimination and harassment persons who are themselves disabled?

The questions referred for a preliminary ruling

The first part of Question 1, and Questions 2 and 3

33 By these questions, which should be examined together, the referring tribunal asks, in essence, whether Directive 2000/78, and, in particular, Articles 1 and 2(1) and (2)(a), must be interpreted as prohibiting direct discrimination on grounds of disability only in respect of an employee who is himself disabled, or whether the principle of equal treatment and the prohibition of direct discrimination apply equally to an employee who is not himself disabled but who, as in the present case, is treated less favourably by reason of the disability of his child, for whom he is the primary provider of the care required by virtue of the child's condition.

9 You now finally get to the judgment itself.

10 You will often find that much of the information given above is repeated in the first sections of the judgment.

11 Although the order of sections may vary from judgment to judgment, you will always find a summary of the legal issues arising towards the beginning of the text. These summaries are split into the national legal issues arising and the Community (now EU) law issues raised as a result. These sections provide useful explanations of the contentious legal questions that the court is being asked to resolve.

12 The judgments then usually move on to a consideration of the facts of the case before them. This section will end with a list of the specific questions the national court requires answers to from the ECJ.

13 The ECJ will consider each of the questions referred in turn, and this will usually form the bulk of the judgment.

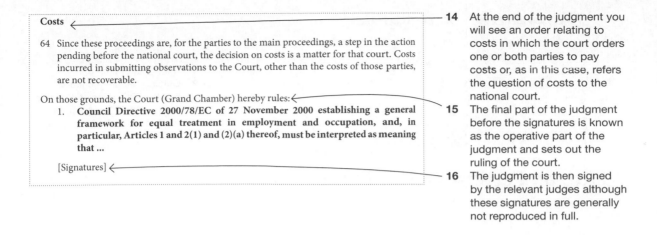

Costs

64 Since these proceedings are, for the parties to the main proceedings, a step in the action pending before the national court, the decision on costs is a matter for that court. Costs incurred in submitting observations to the Court, other than the costs of those parties, are not recoverable.

On those grounds, the Court (Grand Chamber) hereby rules:

1. **Council Directive 2000/78/EC of 27 November 2000 establishing a general framework for equal treatment in employment and occupation, and, in particular, Articles 1 and 2(1) and (2)(a) thereof, must be interpreted as meaning that ...**

[Signatures]

14 At the end of the judgment you will see an order relating to costs in which the court orders one or both parties to pay costs or, as in this case, refers the question of costs to the national court.

15 The final part of the judgment before the signatures is known as the operative part of the judgment and sets out the ruling of the court.

16 The judgment is then signed by the relevant judges although these signatures are generally not reproduced in full.

 Go to your law library and find the most important case in one of your modules so far. Find the law report on the shelf, not an online version. Photocopy the opening pages of the case and annotate the copy as in the examples above.

3.3   USING STATUTORY MATERIAL

Reading a statute is very different from the kind of reading you might be used to. It is not the kind of document you want to read from start to finish! The long title of the Act can assist you in working out whether you have found the relevant Act, and many statutes now have a contents page at the beginning which will help you find the sections relevant to your research more quickly. Do not automatically assume that, simply because it is in print, the Act remains in force and unaltered.

As with cases, it is important to understand what you are looking at and what sections of text mean. Once you have learned to do this, you should be able to find the information you are looking for efficiently.

All Acts of Parliament share the same structure. The main provisions of the Act are contained in numbered sections which may be subdivided into subsections and paragraphs. Acts may be divided into Parts which deal with distinct subject-matter, although the sections are still numbered continuously throughout the main body of the Act. Acts will often end with Schedules, which provide a level of detail which may be too bulky to fit into the main body of the Act. Schedules often give details of the effect of the Act on existing legislation in terms of amendments and repeals.

The following extracts from the Human Fertilisation and Embryology Act 2008 cover the standard format for the opening and closing parts of the main body of an Act.

Human Fertilisation and Embryology Act 2008

2008 CHAPTER 22

An Act to amend the Human Fertilisation and Embryology Act 1990 and the Surrogacy Arrangements Act 1985; to make provision about the persons who in certain circumstances are to be treated in law as the parents of a child; and for connected purposes.   [13th November 2008]

B E IT ENACTED by the Queen's most Excellent Majesty, by and with the advice and consent of the Lords Spiritual and Temporal, and Commons, in this present Parliament assembled, and by the authority of the same, as follows:—

PART 1

AMENDMENTS OF THE HUMAN FERTILISATION AND EMBRYOLOGY ACT 1990

Principal terms used in the 1990 Act

1   Meaning of "embryo" and "gamete"

(1)   Section 1 of the 1990 Act (meaning of "embryo", "gamete" and associated expressions) is amended as follows.

(2)   For subsection (1) substitute—

"(1)   In this Act (except in section 4A or in the term "human admixed embryo")—

(a)   embryo means a live human embryo and does not include a human admixed embryo (as defined by section 4A(6)), and

(b)   references to an embryo include an egg that is in the process of fertilisation or is undergoing any other process capable of resulting in an embryo."

1   Short title of the Act

2   Official citation or chapter number. This denotes that this Act was the 22nd Act to be passed in 2008. This form of citation occurs only in Acts passed after 1963.

3   This is the long title of the Act and will give some indication as to its purpose.

4   This indicates the date on which Royal Assent was given and the Act was passed. A statute will become law on this date unless the Act says otherwise.

5   This is known as the enacting formula. It is the standard wording used to indicate that an Act has successfully passed through all necessary legislative stages.

6   Each section of an Act will contain a specific legal provision. When referring to a particular provision, you should state the section or Schedule in which it is contained, as well as the subsection (s 1(1)) or paragraph applicable.

While the beginning of an Act of Parliament is important, there are also usually provisions towards the end of the Act which are important. The extract below is taken from the end of the Human Fertilisation and Embryology Act 2008.

67 Extent

(1) Subject to the following provisions, this Act extends to England and Wales, Scotland and Northern Ireland.

(2) Any amendment or repeal made by this Act has the same extent as the enactment to which it relates (ignoring extent by virtue of an Order in Council).

(3) Subsection (2) is subject to paragraph 1(2) of Schedule 6.

(4) Her Majesty may by Order in Council provide for any of the provisions of this Act to extend, with or without modifications, to the Bailiwick of Guernsey.

(5) Subsection (4) does not authorise the extension to the Bailiwick of Guernsey of a provision of this Act so far as the provision amends an enactment that does not itself extend there and is not itself capable of being extended there in exercise of a power conferred on Her Majesty in Council.

(6) Subsection (4) does not apply in relation to the extension to the Bailiwick of Guernsey of a provision which extends there by virtue of subsection (2).

(7) Subsection (3) of section 61 applies to the power to make an Order in Council under this section as it applies to any power of the Secretary of State to make an order under this Act, but as if the references in that subsection to the Secretary of State were references to Her Majesty in Council.

68 Commencement

(1) The following provisions of this Act come into force on the day on which this Act is passed—
    sections 61 to 64;
    section 67, this section and section 69.

(2) The remaining provisions of this Act come into force in accordance with provision made by the Secretary of State by order.

7 All Acts have an Extent section indicating whether the Act applies to all or part of the UK.

8 All Acts have a Commencement section indicating when the Act, or parts of the Act, come into force as law.

Schedules

Some Acts of Parliament have one or more Schedules at the end. These may contain provisions not found in the main body of the Act, or merely summarise legal rules or changes to rules found elsewhere in the Act. Eight Schedules follow the main body of the Human Fertilisation and Embryology Act 2008.

EU legislation

You may have to use European Union material too, and statutory material from the EU looks a little different. Consider the example below. This should help you to decode the information you see and work out what type of material you are looking at and where you will find the bits relevant to your research.

30.4.2004   EN   Official Journal of the European Union   L 158/ 77

DIRECTIVE 2004/38/EC OF THE EUROPEAN PARLIAMENT
AND OF THE COUNCIL
of 29 April 2004

on the right of citizens of the Union and their family members

to move and reside freely within the territory of the Member States

amending Regulation (EEC) No 1612/68 and repealing Directives 64/221/EEC,

68/360/EEC, 72/194/EEC, 73/148/EEC, 75/34/EEC, 75/35/EEC,

90/364/EEC, 90/365/EEC and 93/96/EEC

(Text with EEA relevance)

THE EUROPEAN PARLIAMENT AND THE COUNCIL OF THE EUROPEAN UNION,

Having regard to the Treaty establishing the European Community, and in particular Articles 12, 18, 40, 44 and 52 thereof,

Having regard to the proposal from the Commission [1],

Having regard to the Opinion of the European Economic and Social Committee [2],

Having regard to the Opinion of the Committee of the Regions [3],

---

1   The Official Journal citation details appear at the top of each page. You can use this to help you cite the materials you use correctly and to locate items if you are given a citation. See **Chapter 2**, 'Using a Law Library' and the referencing guide on the Companion Website for more detail.

2   The title of the legislation tells you the type of legislation that it is. This example is a Directive, but a Regulation, for example, would look much the same. This bold title also gives you the citation, made up of the year and number of the piece of legislation, and tells you which European institutions have adopted the law. This depends on the procedure that was used to make the law and need not concern us any further here.

3   This bit of the legislation is its full title and the section labelled [2] in this example is technically part of that title. As you can see, the title is fairly cumbersome, and it is customary simply to refer to the Directive by its citation – in this case Directive 2004/38. However, this does not help you know what the piece of law is about, so it is important to know how to find secondary legislation to check the details when you come across it in your reading.

4   The next part of EU secondary legislation relates to the law-making procedures and consultation requirements that are required in order to pass the relevant law. The section sets out that the institutions have due regard to those procedures and have consulted with the required bodies.

Whereas:

(1) Citizenship of the Union confers on every citizen of the Union a primary and individual right
     to move and reside freely within the territory of the Member States, subject to the limitations
     and conditions laid down in the Treaty and to the measures adopted to give it effect.

(2) The free movement of persons constitutes one of the fundamental freedoms of the
     internal market, which comprises an area without internal frontiers, in which freedom is
     ensured in accordance with the provisions of the Treaty.

(3) Union citizenship should be the fundamental status of nationals of the Member States when
     they exercise their right of free movement and residence. It is therefore necessary to codify
     and review the existing Community instruments dealing separately with workers,
     self-employed persons, as well as students and other inactive persons in order to simplify and
     strengthen the right of free movement and residence of all Union citizens.

HAVE ADOPTED THIS DIRECTIVE:

5 The section beginning 'whereas' and consisting of numbered paragraphs is known as the recitals (or sometimes the preamble). These recitals list background information and considerations which provide the context for the piece of secondary legislation which follows. The recitals do not form part of the binding law, but they do give an indication of the purpose and spirit of it and this may aid interpretation.

6 When you see these words, you know the text which follows is the legally binding part of the piece of legislation you are considering.

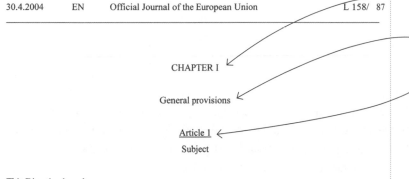

CHAPTER I

General provisions

Article 1

Subject

This Directive lays down:

(a) the conditions governing the exercise of the right of free movement and residence within the
     territory of the Member States by Union citizens and their family members;

7 EU secondary legislation is organised into numbered Chapters.

8 These Chapters have a heading which will give you a general idea of the topic dealt with in them.

9 The provisions within Chapters are split into Articles. Note that EU legislation does not use 'sections' as statutes do in England and Wales and that you should always refer to Articles when writing about EU material.

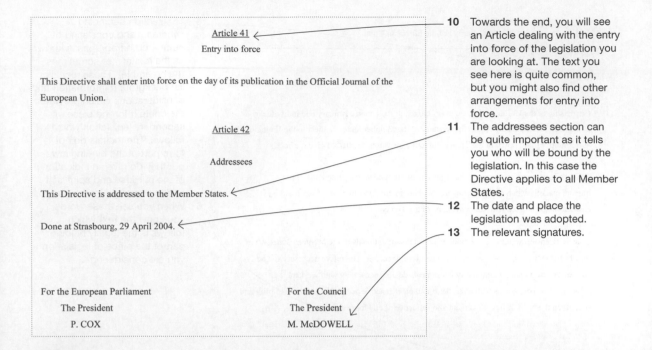

10 Towards the end, you will see an Article dealing with the entry into force of the legislation you are looking at. The text you see here is quite common, but you might also find other arrangements for entry into force.

11 The addressees section can be quite important as it tells you who will be bound by the legislation. In this case the Directive applies to all Member States.

12 The date and place the legislation was adopted.

13 The relevant signatures.

Activity Go to your law library and find the most important piece of legislation in one of your modules so far. Find the printed copy on the shelf, not an online version. Photocopy the front pages of the source and annotate the copy as in the examples above.

3.4 USING JOURNAL ARTICLES AND OTHER PUBLICATIONS

Journal articles are intended for you to read from the beginning, but if you read every article that you think might be relevant from the beginning you will spend a lot of time reading material which does not add anything to your research. You should therefore get into the habit of reading the abstract (where available) or the introduction and then scan the conclusion and decide whether the article is relevant to your research. Once you have found articles that are relevant, you should read them actively. In order to further your research, it is worth paying close attention to the references as they will help you locate material referred to in the articles, including cases, statutes and other journal articles.

The anatomy of a journal article

Journal articles are less alien to us as they are similar to the newspaper articles, magazines or books that we might be more used to reading. However, it is still useful to have a good understanding of where to find relevant information in a journal article. The example below highlights the most important aspects you should be familiar with.

MY 'CONVERSATIONS, CHOICES AND CHANCES'[1]: BECOMING A LAW LECTURER IN THE 21ST CENTURY

JESSICA GUTH*

This paper reflects on my first year as a law lecturer. It considers the conversations, chances and choices that have shaped my growing into the role of legal academic. Based on my personal reflections, the paper examines what it is that I think I am trying to do in carrying out the business of the university and how that fits within the institutional framework in which I operate. Mirroring the realities of my time as a lecturer so far, the paper focuses on my development as a teacher.

Key words: academic identity; legal academics; legal education; reflective practice; autobiography

INTRODUCTION

… what really matters is what we think we are trying to do when we conduct the business of the university. Until and unless we satisfactorily identify what that business is, and thus identify what the business of the law school is, discussion of other matters is entirely redundant. (Bradney 2003: 63)

In August 2007 I took up my first lecturing post after having worked as a researcher for three years previously. This paper reflects on my first year as a law lecturer. It considers the conversations, chances and choices that have shaped my growing into the role of legal academic.

Although my research and PhD focused on other issues, I have been interested in aspects of legal education for some time. Having to attend the Postgraduate Certificate in Higher Education Practice course gave me a forum as well as a starting point to begin exploring some of my interests. In doing so I became increasingly aware of how my background, my experiences and my knowledge of educational theories and best practices influenced not only the way I taught but also how I thought about teaching. It was then the first sentence of the quotation given above that formed the starting point for in-depth reflection.

AUTOBIOGRAPHY AS REFLECTIVE PRACTICE

Schön (1983) defined the concept of reflective practice as a critical process in refining one's skill in a specific discipline. The concept of reflective practice is familiar in educational practice in particular in America (see for example Leitch and Day 2000;

---

*Lecturer in Law, Bradford University Law School, School of Management, Emm Lane, Bradford BD9 4JL, UK. Email: J.Guth@bradford.ac.uk.
1   Bradney (2003).

Volume 6, Number 1, April 2008, pp 41–54
ISSN 1476-0401 print/ISSN 1750-662X online © 2008 Taylor & Francis
DOI: 10.1080/14760400802335763

1 The title of the article will give you an indication of its relevance to your research, but be careful: not all titles accurately reflect the content, or you may be interpreting the title in a different way to that which was intended.

2 The author is usually listed following the title, and it is fairly common to find a footnote providing details of the author's affiliation. You might also find acknowledgements here.

3 The abstract provides you with a brief summary of the article. Not all articles have them, but when they do, this should give you a clear idea whether it is worth reading on.

4 Key words should also help you work out whether the article is relevant to your work.

5 Introductions are useful, especially if no abstract or key words are available. The introduction should set the scene, and you should get a good idea of what the article is about and its main argument.

6 References take many different forms in journal articles, and journals all have their individual house styles. In this case, references are given author/date style in the text and are later fully set out in a Bibliography. Many law journals will, however, contain all reference material in the footnote and will therefore not have a references or bibliography section at the end. It is important that you find out how your tutors want you to reference your work and that you follow a style guide provided by your institution (see the referencing guide on the Companion Website.

7 This section gives the publication details, including the name of the copyright holder and the citation details of the article, which will help you reference it accurately and/or find it again in the future.

As with many sources of information relevant to legal research, you can find additional important information at the end of a journal article. The example below is taken from the same article as the extract above.

8 Journal name
This often appears on every other page at the top.

how they can mean different things to different people. However, the studies have been chosen only in part because I was interested in them. Availability of funding and responding to tenders played a major part in choosing research topics and research questions. My research has been shaped by a policy agenda that determines which questions are put to tender and which projects are funded. I have not yet been able to do a research project simply to follow an interest. While I am hugely proud of the research I have carried out so far, I am conscious that I would like to do myself exactly what I am trying to get my students to do and that is follow an interest, pursue knowledge for knowledge's sake whether or not that interest has any point in policy terms or not.

CONCLUSIONS

9 Conclusions
Conclusions will help you quickly evaluate what the author's main arguments are and can often help you determine if you should read the article in full or whether it is taking you to an area on which you do not wish to focus.

My first two semesters as a law lecturer have been about working out who I am as a teacher. Yes I have struggled with how much time everything takes. Teaching has for periods taken over my life; finishing my PhD, research, private life have all taken a back seat at times during the last year. I am beginning to realise that 'becoming a law lecturer in the 21st century' means many different things not only to different people but also to me. The key to my academic identity lies in what I understand a liberal legal education to be. As I learn more about educational theories, teaching techniques and life as an academic, I grow in confidence and feel better able to defend my ideals. By continuing to attend to the conversations within the university and elsewhere I am becoming aware of ever more chances and choices open to me (Bradney 2003: x) and at the same time I am crystallising what it is I am trying to do; what it is to provide a liberal legal education in the 21st century.

References

Bailey, PD (2008) 'Should "teacher centred teaching" replace "student centred learning"?', *Chem. Educ. Res. Pract.* 9, 70–74.

Biggs, J (1999) *Teaching for Quality Learning at University*, Buckingham: SHRE/Open University Press.

Boud, D and Walker, D (1998) 'Promoting reflection in professional courses: The challenge of context', *Studies in Higher Education* 23 (2), 191–206.

Bradney, A (2003) *Conversations Choices and Chances: The Liberal Law School in the Twenty-First Century*, Oxford: Hart.

Burridge, R, Hinett, K, Paliwala, A and Varnava, T (2002) *Effective Learning and Teaching in Law*, London: Kogan Page.

Campbell, A and Norton, L (2007) (eds) *Learning, Teaching and Assessing in Higher Education: Developing Reflective Practice*, Exeter: Learning Matters Ltd.

Cownie, F (1999a) 'Searching for theory in legal education' in Cownie, F (ed), *The Law School: Global Issues, Local Questions*, Aldershot: Ashgate.

10 Page number

52

Activity Go to your law library and find the most important article in one of your modules so far. Find the printed copy on the shelf, not an online version. Photocopy the front page of the article and annotate the copy as in the example above. Even better – find an article that one of your lecturers has published!

To complete a self-assessment activity on your ability to use legal materials to build legal arguments, see our **Companion Website** at www.palgrave.com/law/legalskills.

3.5 OTHER APPROACHES TO RESEARCH: SOCIO-LEGAL AND EMPIRICAL RESEARCH

As mentioned earlier in this chapter, legal research can also be given a much broader meaning to incorporate research related to legal issues more generally. This section of the chapter deals with this broader approach. Research on legal issues which goes beyond purely legal sources is sometimes referred to socio-legal research, and if it involves the collection of first hand data it can also be empirical. There is no agreed definition of what exactly socio-legal means, but it is generally accepted that this sort of approach goes beyond an analysis of legal texts and considers the application of legal provisions from a multi- or interdisciplinary perspective (see, for example, the Socio-Legal Studies Association website at www.slsa.ac.uk). While this can be purely theoretical and 'desk-based', it often involves the collection of data from people or other sources depending on the topic of research. What follows is an introduction to a number of key issues and debates in social research which should help you to:

- better understand the context in which many of the journal articles you read have been researched and written;
- consider whether you want to carry out this type of research for a dissertation or legal project;
- consider the approach you might take to a socio-legal empirical research project;
- evaluate existing studies and recognise their strengths and weaknesses.

Different types of research

There are various types of research, and which type is appropriate will depend on the topic of study and the amount of work already carried out in that area, as well as on the timescale in which your study has to be completed. Generally, research can be categorised as exploratory, descriptive, analytical or predictive. One research project may involve one, more than one or even all types of research. For example, you may want to study the impact of new legislation. You might start with an exploratory study which will help you define questions and issues to take further; you may then follow that with a descriptive study considering, for example, the number and type of cases brought in relation to the legislation. Following on from that, you could consider why the cases are being brought and/or why others are not, and finally you might consider what this means for the future. In a student project, however, it is unlikely that you will have time to cover all types, so you should be clear in your mind about what type of research you are trying to carry out and therefore what you hope to achieve.

Exploratory	Descriptive	Analytical	Predictive
Exploratory research is undertaken when few or no previous studies exist. The aim is to look for patterns, hypotheses or ideas that can be tested and will form the basis for further research. Typical research techniques would include case studies, observation and reviews of previous related studies and data.	Descriptive research can be used to identify and classify the elements or characteristics of the subject, eg number of days lost because of industrial action. Quantitative techniques are most often used to collect, analyse and summarise data.	Analytical research often extends the descriptive approach to suggest or explain *why* or *how* something is happening, eg underlying causes of industrial action. An important feature of this type of research is in locating and identifying the different factors (or variables) involved.	The aim of predictive research is to speculate intelligently on future possibilities, based on close analysis of available evidence of cause and effect, eg predicting when and where future industrial action might take place.

Research approaches

Research can be approached in many different ways, and although in reality the lines between these approaches are often blurred, it is still important to understand the following distinctions:

- Quantitative/Qualitative
- Applied/Basic
- Deductive/Inductive

> Many research projects combine a number of approaches, eg they may use both quantitative and qualitative approaches.

(a) Quantitative/qualitative research

Quantitative	Qualitative
The emphasis of **quantitative** research is on collecting and analysing numerical data; it concentrates on *measuring* the scale, range, frequency etc of phenomena.	**Qualitative** research is more subjective in nature than quantitative research and involves examining and reflecting on the less tangible aspects of a research subject, eg values, attitudes, perceptions.
This type of research, although not easy to design initially, is usually highly detailed and structured, and results can be easily collated and presented statistically. This type of research may be criticised for being too 'clinical' and not really providing a contextual understanding of the issues investigated.	This type of research also has to be set up carefully and takes a lot of preparation, although some consider it to be easier to design than quantitative research. This type of research can be difficult to interpret, and you will have to consider carefully what your findings show and how to present them.

(b) Basic/applied research

The primary aim of basic research is to improve knowledge generally, without any particular purpose in mind at the outset. Applied research is designed from the start to apply its findings to a particular situation, such as legal or policy development.

(c) Deductive/inductive research

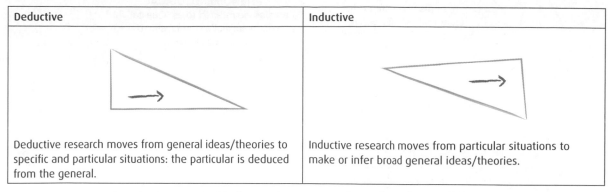

Deductive	Inductive
Deductive research moves from general ideas/theories to specific and particular situations: the particular is deduced from the general.	Inductive research moves from particular situations to make or infer broad general ideas/theories.

Imagine you wanted to learn what a range of people understood the term 'law' to mean.

Deductive approach

You have a clear theoretical position prior to collection of data. You might therefore research the subject and discover a number of definitions of 'law' from, for example, writers on jurisprudence, sociology or even professional associations. You could then test this definition on a range of people, using a questionnaire, structured interviews or group discussion. You could carefully select a sample of people on the basis of age, gender, occupation, etc. The data gathered could then be collated and the results analysed and presented. This approach offers researchers a relatively easy and systematic way of testing established ideas on a range of people.

Inductive approach

If you adopted this approach, you might start by talking to a range of people asking for their ideas and definitions of 'law'. From these discussions you could start to assemble the common elements and then start to compare these with definitions gained from desk-based research. The data gathered could then be collated and the results analysed and presented. This approach might lead you to arrive at a new definition of the word – or it might not! This approach can be very time-consuming, but the reward might be arriving at a fresh way of looking at the subject.

Research philosophies

Research is not 'neutral', but reflects a range of the researcher's personal interests, values, abilities, assumptions, aims and ambitions. In the case of your own research, your own mixtures of these elements will not only determine the subject of the research, but will influence your approach to it. It is important to consider in advance what approach you take with your research – and why.

There are essentially two main research philosophies (or positions), although there can be variations of the two and overlap between the two – and both positions may be identifiable in any research project. Traditionally, certain methods for carrying out research have been associated with one or other research philosophy, and these relationships are detailed below.

PHENOMENOLOGICAL
(can also be referred to as 'Qualitative',
'Subjectivist', 'Humanistic' or
'Interpretative')

The research philosophy can impact on the *methodology* adopted for the research project.

The term *methodology* refers to the *overall approaches and perspectives* to the research process as a whole and is concerned with the following main issues:

- **Why** you collected certain data
- **What** data you collected
- **Where** you collected it
- **How** you collected it
- **How** you analysed it

(A research **method** refers only to the various specific tools or ways data can be collected and analysed, eg a questionnaire; an interview checklist; data analysis software etc.)

Research methodologies

The main research methodologies are summarised below and take the form of two different approaches. However, as mentioned earlier, research often contains both approaches, eg a survey that also contains qualitative work from participant observation.

Positivistic	Phenomenological
<ul><li>Surveys</li><li>Experimental studies</li><li>Longitudinal studies</li><li>Cross-sectional studies</li></ul>	<ul><li>Case studies</li><li>Action research</li><li>Ethnography (participant observation)</li><li>Participative enquiry</li><li>Feminist perspectives</li><li>Grounded theory</li></ul>

(a) Surveys

Surveys involve selecting a representative and unbiased sample of subjects drawn from the group you wish to study. The main methods of asking questions are by face-to-face or telephone interviews, by using questionnaires, or a mixture of the two.

There are two main types of survey: a descriptive survey, concerned with identifying and counting the frequency of a particular response among the survey group, or an analytical survey, to analyse the relationship between different elements (variables) in a sample group. You may, for example, want to study how many different types of family law cases taken on by solicitors are resolved without the involvement of the courts; or you may want to go further and try to identify factors which influence whether court involvement is the chosen course of action.

(b) Experimental studies

Experimental studies are carried out in carefully controlled and structured environments and enable the causal relationships of phenomena to be identified and analysed. The variables can be manipulated or controlled to observe the effects on the subjects studied. Studies done in laboratories tend to offer the best opportunities for controlling the variables in a rigorous way, although field studies can be done in a more 'real world' environment.

(c) Longitudinal studies

These are studies over an extended period to observe the effect that time has on the situation under observation and to collect primary data (data collected at first hand) of these changes. Longitudinal studies are often conducted over several years, which make them unsuitable for students. However, it is possible to base short timescale research on primary data collected in longitudinal studies by, for example, government agencies, and focusing research on a close analysis of one or more aspect or elements of this data. You might want to study how specified legal cases progress over time, or you might be interested in how law students progress in their careers over 10 years, for example.

(d) Cross-sectional studies

This is a study involving different organisations or groups of people to look at similarities or differences between them at any one particular time. For example, you might want to compare the caseload of county courts in different areas or the implementation of EU equality law across a number of countries. Cross-sectional studies are done when time or resources for more extended research, eg longitudinal studies, are limited. It involves a close analysis of a situation at one particular point in time to give a 'snapshot' result.

(e) Case studies

A case study offers an opportunity to study a particular subject, eg a solicitors' office, a court or divorce cases in a particular county court, and usually involves gathering and analysing information that may be both qualitative and quantitative. Case studies can be used to formulate theories, or be:

- **Descriptive** (where current practice is described in detail)
- **Illustrative** (where the case study illustrates practices adopted)
- **Experimental** (where difficulties in adopting new practices or procedures are examined)
- **Explanatory** (where theories are used as a basis for understanding and explaining practices or procedures)

Researchers are increasingly using autobiography as a means of collecting information from small groups of respondents to seek patterns, underlying issues and life concerns. This method could be used, for example, to trace the influences of variables, such as social class, gender and educational experiences on legal decision-making. It can, however, be a time-consuming process as it requires access to respondents and trust to be built between researcher and the people concerned.

At the bullet points below, list the fields of law you are studying that you think would benefit from the research methodologies explained so far:

- ....
- ....
- ....

(f) Action research

Action research involves an intervention by a researcher to influence change in any given situation and to monitor and evaluate the results. The researcher, working with a client, identifies a particular objective (for example, ways of improving telephone responses to 'difficult' clients), and explores ways this might be done. The researcher enters into the situation by introducing new techniques, and monitors the results. This research requires active cooperation between researcher and client and a continual process of adjustment to the intervention in the light of new information and responses to it from respondents.

(g) Ethnography (participant observation)

This form of research evolved from anthropology and the close study of societies. Ethnography is more usually described as participant observation, and this is where the researcher becomes a working member of the group or situation to be observed. The aim is to understand the situation from the inside: from the viewpoints of the people in the situation. The researcher shares the same experiences as the subjects, and this form of research can be particularly effective in the study of small groups. Participant observation can be overt (everyone knows it is happening) or covert (when the subjects being observed for research purposes are unaware it is happening).

(h) Participative enquiry

This is about research within one's own group or organisation and involves the active involvement and cooperation of people who you would normally work and associate with on a daily basis. The whole group may be involved in the research, and the emphasis is on sharing, agreeing, cooperating and making the research process as open and equal as possible. Clearly, this type of research can work when the student is already an active and known member of any group. For example, you might want to study the benefits of being a member of a student law society when you are a member yourself and can involve your fellow members in the research process.

(i) Feminist perspectives

Research, from a feminist perspective, focuses on knowledge grounded in female experiences and is of benefit to everyone, but particularly women. Feminist research perspectives have a number of common starting points. First, women and their contributions to social and cultural life have been marginalised and this is reflected in past research practice. Secondly, men and male perspectives or norms have dominated previous research. And thirdly, gender, as a significant factor in understanding the world, has been absent from understandings and interpretations of social phenomena in favour of other categories, eg social class.

Examples of research projects

Have a look at the examples below and see if you can add two or three of your own.

Project	Approach	Method
Personal injury compensation in settled cases and court judgment	Positivistic approach	Survey
Sentencing in the magistrates' court	Positivistic and phenomenological approaches	Survey, cross-sectional study and participant observation
Disability awareness training within leisure organisations	Phenomenological approach	Participant observation
Age discrimination in the workplace	Positivistic and phenomenological approaches/feminist perspectives	Survey and case study
Child contact and domestic violence from the lawyer's perspective	Phenomenological approach	Interviews
1		
2		
3		

Methods

We now need to consider research methods. Methodology relates to the overall approach taken to the research project. Methods, on the other hand, are the concrete tools used to put the methodology into practice. In this section we briefly introduce the most commonly used methods.

(a) Interviews

Interviews can be grouped into three main types:

- Structured
- Semi-structured
- Unstructured

(i) Structured interviews

Structured interviews involve the use of questionnaires based on a predetermined and identical set of questions. The questions are usually read out by a researcher in a neutral tone of voice to avoid influencing or prompting a particular response from a participant (see also the section on questionnaires below).

(ii) Semi-structured interviews

The interviewer will have a list of themes and areas to be covered, and there may be some standardised questions, but the interviewer may omit or add to some of these questions or areas, depending on the situation and the flow of the conversation.

(iii) Unstructured interviews

These are informal discussions where the interviewer wants to explore in depth a particular topic with another person in a spontaneous way. However, even in unstructured interviews, it is likely that the researcher will have a pre-decided range of topics to cover in the discussion.

Activity What types of research project might favour a structured interview approach? Write in the space below.

....

....

....

....

Activity What types of research project might favour a semi-structured or unstructured interview approach? Write in the space below.

....

....

....

Activity Interviews, whether they are structured or semi-structured/unstructured, can sometimes be problematic. What factors might affect the outcome of any particular interview? Write in the space below.

....

....

....

(b) Focus groups

Focus groups are used to gather data, usually in the forms of opinions, from a selected group of people on a particular and pre-determined topic. The researcher facilitates discussion and records in some way what is being said (eg by use of a tape-recorder, video, note-taker, etc). The purpose of the discussion is introduced and discussion ground rules are agreed. The researcher encourages free discussion, but is ready to intervene if necessary to resolve group problems.

Focus groups can be a useful way of finding out what the main issues and concerns of any group are. This can help in questionnaire design or to develop a future interview strategy. They can be a useful way, too, of bringing to the surface issues that might not otherwise have been discovered: the dynamics of a group can often make people bolder in advancing their opinions. They are also useful in situations where research participants might feel intimidated or awkward being interviewed individually and can be of great help to researchers wanting to work with children. For example, focus groups have been used successfully to help understand children's perception of their rights and to research people's perceptions of 'consent' in medical treatment.

Activity What might happen in a focus group to cause the researcher to intervene? Write in the space below.

....

....

....

....

(c) Participant observation

As discussed earlier, participant observation is when a researcher attempts to *observe* in some way the group being researched and to share in the experiences being recorded and analysed. It can be used in association with other research approaches or as the primary way of gathering data. It can be a good way of getting below the surface of any situation and to help reveal or unravel complex causal social processes.

The researcher can play an *overt* or *covert* role, and the role the researcher can adopt in this situation has been summarised by Gill & Johnson (2010) *Research Methods for Managers*, 4th edn, Sage Publications Ltd:

- Complete participant
- Complete observer
- Observer as participant
- Participant as observer

(i) Complete participant

- The identity and purpose of researcher is not revealed to other group members
- The researcher attempts to become a full covert member of the group

Example: Client in a personal injury class action researching the process of bringing class actions

(ii) Complete observer

- The purpose of the research activity is not revealed to those being observed
- The researcher does not take part in the activities being observed

Example: Observing rape trials

(iii) Observer as participant

- The researcher's role is known to others in the group
- Researchers participate in activities, but their engagement with group activities may be fairly superficial or spasmodic, as their role is to observe the 'real' participants

Example: Student on work experience researching how a family law practice operates

(iv) Participant as observer

- The researcher's role is known to all others in the group

- The researcher engages fully in all the activities, and observes and talks to other participants about their experiences

Example: Client in a personal injury class action researching the process of bringing class actions

 At the bullet points below, list the kinds of participant and observer roles you have played in the past:

- ....
- ....
- ....

Data collection as a participant observer can be in the form of:

- **Primary observations**: where the researcher notes what actually happened or what was actually said at the time
- **Secondary observations**: interpretative statements by observers of what happened
- **Experiential data**: a record of the researcher's feelings/values and how these changed, if applicable, over time

All three forms of data collection might be included in a research project report.

 Participant observation can present a researcher with a range of advantages and disadvantages to consider in advance or afterwards. What might these be? Write your comments in the space provided below:

Advantages/Positives	Disadvantages/Negatives
•	• ....
•	• ....
•	• ....
•	• ....
•	• ....
•	• ....
•	• ....
•	• ....
•	• ....
•	• ....

(d) Questionnaires

Main points to remember when designing and using questionnaires

- Questionnaires facilitate the collection of data by asking all, or a sample of people, to respond to the same questions.
- There are five types of questionnaire methods:
  - online (electronic)

- postal (printed)
- delivery and collection (printed)
- telephone (electronic/printed)
- interview face to face/group (electronic/printed)

- You need to absolutely clear before you design a questionnaire what it is you want to learn and what data you need to obtain to enlighten you in your search.

- The validity (the extent to which the data accurately measures what they were intended to measure) and reliability (the extent to which the data collection method will yield consistent findings if replicated by others) of the data you collect depends on the design of the questionnaire and the words you use.

- Questions can be open or closed:
  - *Open questions:* a question is posed, but space is left for the respondent's own answer.
  - *Closed:* a limited number of alternative responses to the set question are provided. These can be in list, category, ranking, scale/rating, grid or other quantitative form.

- The order and flow of questions should be logical to the respondent.

- There can be a low rate of return with questionnaires, so they need to be introduced carefully and courteously to potential respondents. Offering a prize or other inducement can also improve the rate of return of questionnaires.

- All questionnaires should be piloted, if possible, with a small group before the main research to assess their value, validity and reliability.

(Adapted from Saunders, Lewis and Thornhill (2009) *Research Methods for Business Students*, 5th edn, Prentice Hall)

 What do you think are the respective research advantages and disadvantages of asking open questions and closed questions?

Open questions	Closed questions
Advantages:	Advantages:
Disadvantages:	Disadvantages:

Some general rules for designing questionnaires

1 Explain the purpose of the questionnaire to all participants
2 Keep your questions as simple as possible
3 Do not use jargon or specialist language (unless the recipients really prefer and understand it)
4 Phrase each question so that only one meaning is possible
5 Avoid vague, descriptive words, such as 'large' and 'small'
6 Avoid asking negative questions as these are easy to misinterpret
7 Only ask one question at a time
8 Include relevant questions only
9 Include, if possible, questions which serve as cross-checks on the answers to other questions
10 Avoid questions which require participants to perform calculations
11 Avoid leading or value-laden questions which imply what the required answer might be
12 Avoid offensive questions or insensitive questions which could cause embarrassment
13 Avoid asking 'difficult' questions, eg where the respondent may struggle to answer (people hate to look stupid by not knowing the 'answer')
14 Keep your questionnaire as short as possible, but include all the questions you need to cover your purposes

(Collis & Hussey (2009) *Business Research: A Practical Guide For Undergraduate & Postgraduate Students*, Palgrave)

Asking the right questions in the right way

When carrying out empirical research and collecting data from research participants, it is really important that you express yourself clearly and say what you mean. Sometimes this is easier said than done. To illustrate the point, please comment on the wording of the following open questions taken from a range of questionnaires.

1 *How satisfied were you with the service you received from your solicitor today?*	
2 *What is your place of residence?*	
3 *Some people say legal aid is a waste of money. Do you agree or disagree?*	
4 *How much time did you spend reading the newspaper yesterday?*	
5 *What is your religion?*	
6 *How old are you?*	
7 *Does your employer make adequate provision for maternity/paternity leave?*	

Size and sampling

To elicit the views of groups of more than 50, some form of sampling is usually necessary to attempt to gather opinions that are likely to be representative of the whole group. Sampling strategies are divided into two main groups: *probability* and *non-probability* sampling.

Probability sampling

Where the researcher has a significant measure of control over who is selected and on the selection methods for choosing them.

Sampling methods allow for representative cross-sections or particular groups to be identified or targeted.

Main methods

Simple random sampling

(selection at random by the researchers from a choice of subjects)

Systematic sampling

(selection by the researchers at numbered intervals, eg every one person in five in the target group)

Stratified sampling

(sampling within particular sections of the target groups, eg you target a specific number of people based on the percentage of the total group that share the same characteristics)

Non-probability sampling:

Where the researcher has little initial control over the choice of who is presented for selection, or where controlled selection of participants is not a critical factor.

Main methods

Convenience sampling

(sampling those most convenient; those immediately available)

Voluntary sampling

(the sample is self-selecting; they come forward voluntarily in response to an appeal)

Purposive sampling

(enables you to use your judgement to choose people that are presented or are available that best meet your objectives or your target groups)

'Snowball' sampling

(building up a sample through informants. You start with one person – who then suggests another and so on)

Event sampling

(using the opportunity presented by a particular event, eg a conference, to make contacts)

Time sampling

(recognising that different times or days of the week or year may be significant, and sampling at these times or days)

Response rates

As a general rule, a response rate of 30 per cent or greater for a postal/externally sent questionnaire is generally regarded as reasonable. However, a goal of 50 per cent or more responses should be attempted in any questionnaire that involves face-to-face interviews.

There are techniques that can help improve response rates to postal or electronic questionnaires:

- *Follow-up calls* (especially telephone reminders and special delivery letters)
- *Pre-contact with respondents* (telling them about the questionnaire)

- *Type of postage* (special delivery is superior to ordinary mail; there is also some evidence that hand-written white envelopes are more likely to be opened than brown/typed)
- *Rewards:* prizes or, better still, cash incentives
- *Personalising the questionnaire:* writing to the person by name, eg 'Dear John', etc
- *Emphasising confidentiality:* ensuring that all views to be published remain anonymous, if appropriate
- *Appeals to the respondent:* based on the social, personal or other benefits that might flow from the participation of a respondent

Postal questionnaires should *always* include a stamped return envelope and have a covering letter explaining the purpose of the questionnaire and the use intended for the findings in the future.

The researcher should include full contact details and an offer to discuss the questionnaire with any respondent who has doubts or queries about it.

The researcher should always offer to share the research findings with any participant, if requested, and this offer is best made in the covering letter.

Ethical considerations in research

Ethical concerns may emerge at all stages of research, from the planning to the writing up and publication of the research. Saunders, Lewis and Thornhill ((2009) *Research Methods for Business Students*, 5th edn, Prentice Hall) summarise the main issues to consider, although the ethical issues surrounding these issues are not always clear-cut:

- rights of privacy
- the voluntary nature of participation – and the rights of individuals to withdraw partially or completely from the process
- consent and the possible deception of participants
- maintenance of the confidentiality of data provided by individuals or identifiable participants and their anonymity
- reactions of participants to the ways in which researchers seek to collect data
- effects on participants of the way in which data is analysed and reported
- the behaviour and objectivity of the researcher

However, your obligations towards your research participants is not the only area where ethics need to be considered. The Socio-Legal Studies Association (SLSA) has published a 'Statement on Ethical Research Practice' on its website. This statement stresses the need for integrity and ethical behaviour throughout the research process, and although it is aimed at academic research more than at student projects, many issues raised will apply to you too.

(a) Appropriateness of methods and competence

Part of ethical research practice is, put simply, knowing what you are doing and recognising the complexities and sometimes difficult issues involved in carrying out research. You should make sure that the methods you use are appropriate for your project and that you are confident that you have the skills to carry out the research. There is no point in saying you will carry out a telephone survey if you have a telephone phobia!

If you intend to ask sensitive or difficult questions in an interview, you need to be sure that you can communicate in such a way as to make your participants feel secure rather than intimidated or threatened. You also need to think about how what you hear or observe will impact on you and whether you can deal with your findings on an emotional level. You need to be competent in the method of analysis you intend to use. If you cannot analyse statistics, you may not be in a position to carry out complex quantitative research. If you are not confident in handling large amounts of quite unstructured data, qualitative research may not be for you

(b) Consent

Consent is one of the most important considerations in ethical research practice. Negotiating consent if not a one-off task to be ticked off a list, but an ongoing process which may need to be revisited throughout the research process. Consent should be fully informed consent, and it is your responsibility to ensure that your research participants understand fully what they are consenting to. You therefore need to think carefully about how you will use the material you collect and make clear whether your participants are consenting simply to you collecting and analysing the data for your own project and the writing of the dissertation, whether the data might be used by others such as your supervisor/tutor, or whether it will be published in any other format, for example as a journal article in a student journal, on a website or other medium.

When you are seeking consent, you should make it clear that there is no expectation that people will participate and that they have a right not to do so, and if they decide they want to participate and later change their minds that they can withdraw at any time. If possible, you should try to get written consent, and it is often useful to prepare a consent form which clarifies what exactly the participant is consenting to.

(c) Confidentiality

Confidentiality is the second big issue in social research. It is at the heart of ethical practice but can be more difficult an issue than you might first think. The SLSA statement stresses the importance of confidentiality: 'Socio-legal researchers have obligations regarding respect for anonymity, privacy, confidentiality and data protection' (Principle 8). Generally speaking, you should not disclose the identity of your research participants either during the research process or afterwards. You should also make sure that you present your research in such a way that preserves the anonymity of your participants, and if you are using quotations from interviews, for example, you should ensure that they cannot be traced back to a respondent or that the respondent cannot be identified from the quote or a series of quotes.

However, you also need to be careful not to make unrealistic claims about confidentiality. For example, you should not say that the data is confidential between you and the research participant if your supervisor might see some of the data collected before it has been analysed and anonymised. You also need to be aware of your legal obligation to break confidentiality and report, for example, information relating to a serious criminal offence. If you think this may be an issue in your research, you need to speak to your tutor immediately and consider whether your project is really suitable as a student project.

(d) Integrity

In your studies generally, but particularly when carrying out research, you should always maintain integrity. This means that you should act ethically and maintain high academic, professional and personal standards. In particular, you should respect the research of others and adhere to academic conventions for referencing and citing previous research and other sources. You should obviously not pass off others' work as your own; this is plagiarism and is discussed further in **Chapter 5**.

Another issue concerning integrity concerns researchers exaggerating or even falsifying research findings, and there have been a few past cases of researchers willing to falsify their findings to gain publicity. This is, of course, unethical and absolutely unacceptable at whatever level you are at. You should therefore make sure that your research design meets academic standards and is rigorous as well as suitable for the study you wish to carry out. You should take your research task seriously and try to gain as much of an understanding of the impact you and your role will have on the research and the participant.

You need to consider carefully how the research is going to be viewed by the people participating in it and whether there is any risk of harm, physically or emotionally, to the participants or to you. If there is, you need to be very clear about those risks and how you are going to minimise and manage them. We are not suggesting you should abandon your research ideas in those circumstances, but you should think about whether what you are proposing is realistic in the time you have and where you are going to get the training and/or support you might need to carry out a rigorous and ethical piece of research.

(e) Ethics scenarios

 Below are four scenarios. For each, make a list of the ethical issues raised and how you might resolve them.

1 Kate is writing a dissertation about the general public's awareness of the Consumer Protection Act. She has designed a short questionnaire which she goes through face to face with people stopped in the street. She has a target of 200 responses and has so far collected 80. She was due to go out to collect more today, but it has been raining all day so she has stayed at home and phoned friends and family members and now has 140 responses. She is spending her evening with her sister, and they are filling in the remaining questionnaires at random.

2 Asif is doing a legal project in Semester 2, his report is to be no more than 4,000 words and he has four months to do the project. He is planning to do a survey to get some initial ideas about his topic and then he wants to interview 10 people. He also needs access to court records.

3 Rushna wants to know what her fellow students think of mooting as a way of developing legal research skills. After one of the mooting sessions, all those involved in the university's internal competition have a social event at which Rushna asks people what they

think about mooting generally and whether it helps develop research skills. She makes a few notes on the day. She writes her dissertation based on those notes. She doesn't use people's names but refers to them as Senior Counsel A, Junior Counsel B, etc, which is the way mooting pairs are allocated in the university competition.

4 Jamie is writing a dissertation about international child abduction. It is a desk-based dissertation, but Jamie is finding it a bit boring and so decides to go and speak to his young cousins who are aged 4 and 7 to see what they think.

Scenario	Ethical issues	Suggested solution
1		
2		
3		
4		

Activity Is your proposed research likely to cause any ethical difficulties? If so, please make some notes in the space immediately below, and discuss these with your tutor as soon as possible.

....

....

....

....

....

....

....

4

Critical thinking

Learning outcomes

> To understand what 'critical thinking' is and how it can help to develop your legal skills
> To identify legal reasoning in the context of the law and to present your own legal thoughts
> To develop deep reflective skills and apply them to your legal studies

> To become aware of how analysis can greatly enhance your understanding of the law
> To learn how to successfully evaluate your own work and the work of others

When you study law, you are expected to demonstrate a whole host of new thinking skills. In order to achieve the highest marks in your course, you must categorise, analyse, criticise and evaluate the law. These complex cognitive skills are known as 'critical thinking skills', and this chapter will show you how to think about the law critically, and how to become a deeply reflective learner.

Your lecturers expect you to become better at critical thinking as you progress through your course. When you are constantly researching the law and reading a lot about the loopholes in various legal processes, you begin to form your own critical thoughts about the law. You will begin to ask deeper questions, such as: 'Why does it have to be this way?', 'Is there another way to do that?', or 'What if we tried this ...?'. This logical and reasoned questioning of the law is critical thinking.

Many students make the mistake of describing the law rather than analysing and criticising the law. This leaves little room for an analysis of the legal theories and principles in the field, which attracts the highest marks. Description should be kept to a minimum in a law assessment.

Being emotional can create barriers to effective critical thinking. Many people find it difficult to form a balanced and fair view of the law when they feel very strongly about a particular subject (for example, child abuse laws or abortion laws). You must now put your emotions to one side and think about the law with a rational mind. You must analyse both sides of the argument.

What is critical thinking?

Critical thinking is about exploring, evaluating and asking questions. It is about finding the hidden meaning when reading the law, identifying a line of reasoning (or, in other words, an 'argument') in a passage of text, and accurately constructing a conclusion based on the evidence provided. Some people are naturally more sceptical than others, but critical thinking is not based on your personality traits: any student can become a critical thinker of the law.

It is difficult, when first faced with a law textbook or a legal article, to understand what exactly you are reading. Is the writer simply providing you with unbiased information, or does the writer have a strong opinion about the area of law which has been cleverly integrated into the text? It is your job, as a student of law, to pick apart the piece of writing before you and to cast a shadow of doubt over the writer's opinion. Is what he or she is saying true? Where is the evidence? Has he or she only explained one side of the story? Has he or she ignored any other arguments?

Have you ever had the following comments on your work?

'Too descriptive.'
'Not enough analysis.'
'More critical analysis required.'
'You have merely stated the law rather than applied it.'
'Your lack of critical commentary has let you down.'
'Where is the conclusion?'

Below is a guide to help you distinguish a descriptive piece from a critical piece. These critical skills will take some practice to master, but they are very important to your studies of law. Refer to this guide when carrying out some of the activities below, and when you are writing your own assignment and assessing the work of others. The example below refers to a criminal law assignment but the principles are the same in all law topics.

Descriptive assignment	Critical assignment
✘ States the case study facts	✓ Analyses potential offences in the scenario
✘ Describes potential offences	✓ Dismantles specific offences
✘ Lists injuries/breaches	✓ Matches applicable areas of law to injuries
✘ States opinions of judges	✓ Examines the opinions of judges
✘ States the arguments	✓ Weighs and criticises the arguments
✘ Provides defence information	✓ Analyses and applies defences
✘ States a conclusion	✓ Draws a conclusion from the evidence
✘ Describes theories	✓ Critically assesses the theories

Descriptive or critical?

Activity Compare the two article abstracts below:

'The law in this area is varied. There are many cases, both old and recent. For example, in *R v Marley* (2005), the defendant entered into a verbal contract with the appellant because he was desperate and had nowhere to live. This was seen in the earlier case of *R v Winsher* (1956) where a tenant agreed with his landlord to only pay £5 per week to live in the flat above because the flat below had a vermin problem. The Lords do not know what to do with this area of law, as the case of *R v Littlewood* (2009) held that verbal agreements may not be binding when the appellant is desperate.'

'It is difficult to ascertain which way the law is going in this area. The older but well-regarded judgment by Lord Levy in *R v Winsher* (1956) had been applied consistently until the House of Lords allowed the defendant in *R v Littlewood* (2009) to escape from his contractual obligation. There appears to be a well-hidden clue in the judgment of *R v Marley* (2005) as to why this sudden change occurred: Lord Times stated obiter that had the defendant been under any serious pressure to find somewhere to live, this may have clouded his rational judgment. This seems sensible – a person should not be forced into a contract.'

Can you tell which piece is more descriptive and which piece uses critical thinking? In the space below, identify which piece you believe contains critical thinking, and pick out evidence in both pieces to illustrate your point:

....

....

....

....

....

Have you been guilty in the past of submitting mostly descriptive work? Do you feel that you could create a piece like the second one, which is a critical piece? Below is an analysis of the second piece:

'It is difficult to ascertain which way the law is going in this area. The older but well-regarded judgment by Lord Levy in *R v Winsher* (1956) <u>had been applied consistently until</u> the House of Lords allowed the defendant in *R v Littlewood* (2009) to escape from his contractual obligation. <u>There appears to be a well-hidden clue</u> in the judgment of *R v Marley* (2005) as to why this sudden change occurred: Lord Times stated obiter that had the defendant been under any serious pressure to find somewhere to live, this may have clouded his rational judgment. <u>This seems sensible</u> – a person should not be forced into a contract.'

The writer has identified and explained contradicting case law.

The writer has analysed the judgments closely.

The writer has formed his or her own view, drawn from the judgments.

Notice how there appears to be a flowing and logical structure to the critical piece. It successfully compares cases and forms a view when the analysis and comparison of the case law has been completed.

Many think of 'criticism' as a negative word. When critically thinking on an academic level, you must also look for the positive aspects of any theory, judgment, article, etc. If something works well, not only must you state that this is so, but you must state *why*. This is the analytical part of critical thinking. Question *why* a certain theory works well. Does it cover unforeseen scenarios that the other theories do not? Compare similar schools of thought in the same field, and, if possible, suggest your own theory using evidence and critical judgment. Forward thinking like this will demonstrate to your reader that you have fully understood the subject matter and have engaged with it and thought about it fully.

Critical thinking also prevents you from making common mistakes. You need to recognise when an article or theory is 'past its sell-by date'. Perhaps another writer in the field has disproved the theory that you would like to use, or the arguments made have been superseded by new case law or statutes. You need to read widely to avoid these pitfalls. Additionally, students are often not used to questioning academics and researchers and simply believe everything that writers say. It is OK to disagree with academics and have other opinions or a different view on a particular legal issue. You do, however, need to make sure that your differing opinion is based on a solid understanding of the subject and is fully informed. Remember to question whether an article or other material you are reading could now be too old or too heavily criticised to be authoritative. You must use your critical judgment to make these decisions.

Why should I develop critical thinking skills?

Below are reasons why developing your critical thinking skills will benefit both your educational and personal experiences.

- *Logical*. You will think logically and clearly about your work.

- *Reasonable*. You will not be emotional when presenting your view.

- *Attention*. You will notice small details and their implications.

- *Observation*. You will notice mistakes and see things in a fresh light.

- *Self-criticism*. Improvement occurs when you recognise your own errors.

- *Respond*. You will form a controlled response when you are questioned.

- *Knowledge*. You will learn a lot about the law when you critically think about it.

- *Argue*. You will be able to present your view calmly with evidence and authority.

- *Opinion*. You will be able to form an opinion about theories.

- *Sort*. You will recognise what is relevant and what is not necessary.

- *Balance*. You will be able to measure up alternative views and use them equally.

- *Fair*. You will notice when a bias appears in someone's opinion, and not be fooled.

- *Repetition*. You will re-read pieces to make sure nothing has been missed.

- *Objective*. You will learn to put your emotions to one side – an enviable skill.

- *Perspective*. You may see a situation from an unexpected point of view.

- *Reflection*. You will look at yourself and ponder your current practices.

How much easier would your academic and daily life be if you were able to think and respond more logically and clearly?

 How do you feel about your critical thinking skills in your daily life? Highlight any of the above skills you feel you are very good at, and any you need to improve on.

Can I be a critical thinker?

Students are expected to dig deep below the surface and investigate the many legal theories and schools of thought that surround the law. To engage in critical dialogue with well-regarded writers in the field shows a confidence and an ability in your subject that will lead to excellent marks at assessment time.

Self-assessment

How confident am I? Tick the statement that applies to you...	Very confident	Would like to be more confident
I can see both sides to any argument	☐	☐
I always investigate alternative ways to solve puzzles	☐	☐
I always find evidence to support my view	☐	☐
I can lead a team and run projects efficiently	☐	☐
I can separate the important from the irrelevant	☐	☐
I can think rationally	☐	☐
I don't need to become emotional to argue my view	☐	☐
I can wait patiently for other people to decide	☐	☐
I can offer criticism without feeling guilty	☐	☐

My biggest concern:

....

....

....

....

Critical thinking is not just a skill that you will use as part of your course. You will find that you can think more critically and accurately in other areas of life. You will see both sides to an argument, and you will be able argue and negotiate effectively. You will also be able to gain a much deeper understanding of current affairs and other issues affecting your daily life. Your legal research in turn will show a new depth when you seek out alternative arguments and views and analyse the direction of the law.

The higher the level of study you are engaged in, the more refined your critical thinking skills need to be. As an undergraduate or postgraduate, you are expected to display impressive and well-practised critical thinking skills to achieve the highest marks on your course. Many students make the mistake of researching and presenting a perfect history of case law in their assignments, but do not critically analyse the judgments in the cases using theoretical schools of thought. They then receive fairly low overall marks, and cannot understand why. *Stating* the law is only half the task: you must analyse and criticise the law to complete your assessment successfully.

How do I critically think about the law?

Some students find it easy to criticise the work of others. This may be logical and fair criticism, or it may be unfair criticism. Other students find it very hard to criticise the work of others. This is simply because 'criticism' generally provokes a negative feeling. Students often think of criticism as something unpleasant. If you were asked to criticise the work of your peer in your next seminar, what would you do? Would you be able to make reasoned and fair comments, would you shy away and say it was a good piece of work, or would you launch into criticism without being constructive? Remember, critical thinking in law is not emotional: it is reasoned, logical and unbiased.

Critical questions to ask...

- WHY?
- How far does this law/theory reach?
- How much of the law/theory is applied?
- How often does this result occur?
- To what extent?
- How do we know this is true?
- Where is the evidence to prove this?
- What reforms could be suggested?
- For what reasons?

- How reliable/authoritative is this source?
- What could be going on below the surface?
- What are the hidden problems?
- What are the implications of this rule/theory?
- What do we *not* know about this?
- Has enough research been done?
- Have assumptions been made?
- Which outcome/approach is preferable?

When you are ready to begin critically thinking, you may wonder what to select to critically think about! Here are some prime candidates for your criticism:

- Articles in well regarded law journals
- Judgments from leading cases
- Books written by leading academics

- Statutes/EU regulations etc
- Any other authoritative legal work

What are my lecturers looking for?

As a student at undergraduate or postgraduate level, you are expected to display critical thought processes in every task. You must examine, evaluate and draw conclusions – based on the evidence you have analysed – for every task you are given during your course, if you wish to leave your course with the highest possible mark.

Your lecturers want you to *ask questions* about the law. Read the lecturers' thoughts provided below. You *can* give your lecturer what he or she is looking for – it just takes practice.

Professor Chris Gale:

'Prepare properly for tutorials and seminars – read around the topic. If you disagree with your tutor's views, do so at the appropriate class. You may have misunderstood them, there may be alternative interpretations of the law, and (occasionally) they may just be wrong! Whichever it is, all staff enjoy informed discussion with students.'

Contract Law Lecturer Julia Cressey:

'In assessments, particularly in answers to problem questions, I am looking for students to not just explain and describe the relevant law, but to achieve a good mark they must also show how and why it will apply to the facts of the problem.'

Environmental Law Lecturer William Onzivu:

> 'Don't just describe the law, analyse it. Critically consider the various viewpoints in class, research, or exams, and appreciate these views in relation to the laws applicable. Be ready to justify your viewpoints and conclusions based on the law.'

Activity Can you think of any previous negative comments about your critical thinking skills? List them here. What are you going to do about them?

....

....

....

....

....

Critically thinking about the law

Self-assessment How good are your critical thinking skills when it comes to your subject of law? Below is an example of a controversial case judgment (*Airedale NHS Trust v Bland* [1993] AC 789 at 858–9). Read this extract and fill in the honesty checklist below:

Lord Keith of Kinkel: 'It was argued … that here the doctors in charge of Anthony Bland had a continuing duty to feed him by means of the nasogastric tube and that if they failed to carry out that duty they were guilty of manslaughter, if not murder. This was coupled with the argument that feeding by means of the nasogastric tube was not medical treatment at all, but simply feeding indistinguishable from feeding by normal means. As regards this latter argument, I am of opinion that regard should be had to the whole regime, including the artificial feeding, which at present keeps Anthony Bland alive. That regime amounts to medical treatment and care, and it is incorrect to direct attention exclusively to the fact that nourishment is being provided. In any event, the administration of nourishment by the means adopted involves the application of a medical technique. But it is, of course, true that in general it would not be lawful for a medical practitioner who assumed responsibility for the care of an unconscious patient simply to give up treatment in circumstances where continuance of it would confer some benefit on the patient. On the other hand a medical practitioner is under no duty to continue to treat such a patient where a large body of informed and responsible medical opinion is to the effect that no benefit at all would be conferred by continuance. Existence in a vegetative state with no prospect of recovery is by that opinion regarded as not being a benefit, and that, if not unarguably correct, at least forms a proper basis for the decision to discontinue treatment and care: *Bolam v. Friern Hospital Management Committee* [1957] 1 W.L.R. 582.'

Once you have read the extract from the judgment above, fill in the table below to measure your current critical thinking skills in law.

Honesty checklist Mark out of 10:

Tick the skills you have and give yourself a mark out of 10 if you feel you can successfully apply these skills to the legal theory piece above:

- *Select*. I can decide whether the piece is relevant to my current legal research. I know if the arguments and theories are applicable to my task. ☐
- *Identify*. I can identify the arguments in the text, as well as the evidence and the conclusion. ☐
- *Observe*. I can see whether the writer states his position at the beginning of his piece, or whether his argument is hidden away inside the text for the reader to fish out. ☐
- *Recognise*. I will recognise special tricks if the writer has used these to persuade the reader into taking a certain view. ☐
- *Reason*. I can use legal reasoning to decide whether the writer has constructed a fair argument. I can assess whether good evidence has been provided. ☐
- *Weigh up*. I can identify when opposing arguments have been provided, and I know when one side of the argument is over-represented. ☐
- *Reflect*. I can reflect on why the writer has said what he has. I will find and analyse an underlying motive to explain why the writer has taken a certain view. ☐
- *Read*. I can read between the lines and recognise any hidden assumptions. ☐
- *Analyse*. I can analyse the structure of arguments. I know what logical structure to look for. I will recognise the writer's theory if it has developed successfully through the piece. ☐
- *Judge*. I can judge whether the writer has succeeded in arguing his view with authority. I will be able to tell whether the piece adds to current discussions. ☐
- *Decide*. I can decide whether alternative arguments overwhelm the writer's theory. ☐
- *Conclude*. I will know if the piece provides valid evidence. I will be able to analyse and conclude whether the piece can stand up against other leading views in the field. ☐
- *Evaluate*. I can evaluate whether the conclusion draws together the earlier discussions in the piece. ☐

My total score: ☐

Refer back to this table after you have read this chapter and retake the test to see how much you have improved. New score: ☐

4.1 LEGAL REASONING

Whether you are reading the law or writing your own legal essay, you need to be familiar with legal reasoning.

When you 'reason' with someone, you try to explain something to him or her. You politely argue with that person and you try to make him or her see the situation from another perspective. Legal reasoning is just like this: it requires you to (a) formulate a legal view or theory, (b) put forward your legal arguments using evidence, and (c) persuade the reader (ie your lecturer) that you have an original idea that would work, or that you have found a flaw in a previous authority which means that it no longer makes sound legal sense.

This is a clever skill, and difficult to master. You will be expected to identify the line of reasoning in any law article, and you will also be expected to devise your own line of reasoning in your assessments. Would you be able to identify any writer's line of reasoning in any given law article? Would you know what to look for?

Below are some points to help you remember how to find a line of reasoning in a piece of legal text:

- Look for *assumptions*. Has the writer used a strange or odd example to make a point? Does the conclusion seem to spring from nowhere?
- What *proof* can you find in the piece? If there is any evidence, is the source identifiable? Is the evidence reliable, or is it the author's opinion?
- Can you identify the writer's *opinions* in the piece? How can you tell that they are mere opinions as opposed to statements of fact? How trustworthy are the statements?
- Can you spot any *originality* in the piece? Does the author make any unique and eye-catching statements that have the potential to change the school of thought in the field? How authoritive are the writer's unique ideas?

What is legal reasoning?

When your lecturer asks you to find and analyse the legal reasoning in a piece of writing, he or she is asking you to find the writer's arguments and analyse them. Sometimes a writer's argument or view can be difficult to find, and at other times there can be several arguments backed up by a huge pile of evidence which you will have to sift through and evaluate. This is all part of the critical thinking process, and it is a skill you must learn in order to achieve the highest marks on your law course.

'Reasoning' is another way of saying 'giving reasons' and using 'rational thought' to solve problems. When you are given an assignment question, you use your legal reasoning to determine which laws ought to be applied, decide whether the elements of the laws have been met, and evaluate the applicable area of law. You then form conclusions based on the facts and the evidence. This is legal reasoning.

Sometimes writers will make both positive and negative points about the law when they are presenting their legal reasoning. You must analyse both. If they have presented evidence to back up their views, you must also evaluate all the evidence. You will be shown how to do all this at **4.3** and **4.4** below.

Legal reasoning

In a legal piece	In your own work
• Select key words and phrases	• What is your view?
• Identify their argument	• Present your view logically
• Illustrate any tricks/assumptions	• Argue your position rationally
• Analyse their direction	• Is your view fair and unbiased?
• Observe the arguments' structure	• Use evidence to support your view
• Critically pull apart their theory	• Structure your argument
• Sceptically measure its authority	• Consider alternatives
• Reason with their commentary	• Identify flaws in other arguments
• Present alternative views/theories	• Analyse the theories of others
• Weigh up the conclusions	• Criticise popular/accepted views
• Examine their beliefs	• Query your direction
• Evaluate the evidence provided	• Construct an alternative way
	• Evaluate the evidence/outcome

How do I identify the legal reasoning?

Your first task when critically thinking about the law is to identify the arguments/theories in the text that you have chosen to include as part of your research. In law, this 'text' is most likely to be an article, a case judgment, the relevant chapter in a book, a Law Commission Report, or some other kind of authoritative legal document.

Would you know a theory if you read one?

'If a defendant does an act which he knows is blameworthy, he has caused that outcome. He has also caused that outcome if he did not know that his act was blameworthy. However, when a defendant does an act – blameworthy or not – and sits and awaits its consequences, he cannot be liable for the consequence if the consequence is totally unexpected and unplanned. The defendant may have set the wheels in motion, but to say that he caused an outcome which was totally unforeseen does not rest easily. A mistake, or an unforeseen mishap perhaps, but not a conviction, not a criminal record, and not a guilty person. Rather, a victim of fate. Let us assume you set out to do an act today, but for some unforeseen reason the consequence is the opposite to what you foresaw. Guilty? Or victim?'

 What is the writer arguing in this piece?

....

....

....

Notice that sometimes an everyday example will be used to illustrate the writer's point.

The author of the example above has presented his ideas based on his own legal reasoning. He is making predictions and providing critical thoughts, but these have not yet been conclusively proven. This is a theory, and as a law student you are expected to critically analyse the theories of others and present your own. The author's theory will add to the other perspectives in criminal law, and will develop a 'school of thought' in the field.

It is vital that you can identify a writer's theoretical perspectives if you are to criticise his or her line of reasoning and evaluate his or her conclusions.

(a) Hints to start

You must first decide whether the legal piece you have found is relevant to your research. There are specific places you can start in order to determine this. We have provided more detail on finding resources in your library, decoding this information and reading it effectively in **Chapters 2** and **3**, but the following hints should help you get started.

Books
- **Find** the chapter relevant to your assessment. For example, if your contract law assignment question is based on consideration in contract law, both the 'introductory' and 'consideration' chapters of contract law textbooks will be particularly helpful to you.
- **Skim** the whole chapter. This means 'surface-reading' it really quickly to see whether the chapter is relevant to your research.

- **Scan** the introduction to the chapter. Has the writer laid out his or her theories/arguments from the very beginning, or does he or she direct you to another part of the chapter for the theoretical perspectives? His or her legal reasoning will surely follow.
- **Scan** the conclusion. Has the writer drawn any conclusions? What are they? Are they based on earlier analysed evidence? Does the conclusion include any signs of legal reasoning?

Articles

- Does the article include an **abstract**? If it does, read it slowly. The writer's arguments, theories and perspectives will be outlined here. The conclusion or outcome may also be outlined, and if this is the case the writer may wish to use the entire article to present his or her legal reasoning as to why he or she came to this particular conclusion.
- If there is no abstract, scan the **introduction** to the article. These will be shorter in articles than they are in textbooks, and therefore more concise. The writer will lay out the current legal stance, his or her ideas/theories and arguments to support them, his or her legal reasoning and possibly an outline of the evidence found, and his or her conclusions (and possibly any proposals for reform).

Other

- If you are using a **statute** as part of your research, make sure you **read** the relevant sections in it thoroughly.
- If you have found relevant **newspaper** articles, use them to illustrate **facts** only – they are not authoritive sources of law.

A handful of chapters and articles is usually enough to allow you to begin the critical thinking process.

(b) Signals

Once you have scanned and skimmed your various chapters and articles and decided that they are relevant to your research, it is time to begin the first stage of critical thinking: identifying the legal reasoning in the text.

When we have face-to-face discussions in daily life, we use the tone of our voices to project how we feel. Sometimes we may also repeat phrases and raise our voices to make our point clear. These tactics are not available in legal writing. The writer must therefore use signals in the text to guide the reader. 'Signals' are leading words and phrases that drop hints and alert the reader that a theory, line of reasoning or conclusion is about to be presented or explained. They are giveaways that you are reading the writer's line of reasoning.

For example, if you were having a discussion with your friend about euthanasia and you disagreed with your friend's theory, you would indicate that you were about to present your own thoughts with a signal such as: 'however ...', or 'although ...'.

The following signals are sure signs of a line of reasoning in a law article or textbook.

Introducing a line of reasoning

'Firstly ...', 'Initially ...', 'To begin with ...', 'First of all ...', 'To start ...', 'In the year ...', 'It was once thought that ...'

Examples

'In the year 1943, the House of Lords held that this kind of action did not constitute consideration for the purposes of a contract ...'

'To begin with, the law was strict when it came to common law remedies for this kind of offence ...'

Activity Write your own: ....

....

....

A supportive line of reasoning

'Similarly ...', 'Equally ...', 'Likewise ...', 'Indeed ...', 'Furthermore ...', 'Moreover ...', 'What is more ...', 'Correspondingly ...', 'In the same line ...', Also ...', 'Again ...', 'In addition ...', 'As well as ...', 'Not only ...', 'Besides this ...'

Examples

'Furthermore, Jones believes that the tort of trespass needs a radical update ...'

'Equally, Lord Denning supported the previous case law, confirming that it was clear and relevant in today's application of public law principles.'

Activity Write your own: ....

....

....

....

A conflicting line of reasoning

'Either ...', 'Neither ...', 'Alternatively ...', 'A different perspective on this ...', 'Others argue that...', 'It might be argued that...', 'It can be said that ...', 'It could, however, be submitted that ...', However ...', 'On the other hand ...', 'Nonetheless ...', 'Nevertheless ...', 'Notwithstanding this ...', 'In any case ...', 'In spite of this ...', 'Despite this ...', 'Even though ...', 'By contrast ...', 'Although ...', 'In fact ...'

Examples

'Others have argued that the law on insanity is too embedded within the criminal law to be amended on a piecemeal basis.'

'On the other hand, Williams submits that only when the defendant has foreseen the consequence should he be considered as guilty. In fact, the House of Lords disagree completely.'

Activity Write your own: ....

....

....

....

Concluding the line of reasoning

'Therefore ...', 'This suggests that ...', 'This indicates ...', 'In conclusion ...', 'Thus ...', 'We can thus see that ...', 'As a result ...', 'As a consequence ...', 'Hence ...', 'Consequently ...', 'Because of this ...', 'From this we can infer that ...', 'From this we can deduce that ...'

Examples

'As a result of *R v Smith* (1958), the application of the European Building Regulations 2003 in UK courts has developed widely.'

'Consequently, a defendant must now have to prove that he had a reasonable belief in the victim's consent. We can deduce from this that he must as least ask the victim if he or she is consenting as opposed to merely assuming consent ...'

Activity Write your own: ....

....

....

....

Writers will use these signal words in their line of reasoning to support a theory, to reinforce a theory with their own views, to overshadow a theory with fresh evidence, to rebut alternative arguments, to contrast with previous ideas, and to introduce a new school of thought.

Critical versus emotional

A writer may wish to persuade a reader to take on board a certain view by using emotive language. This is a trick that writers use when their line of reasoning may not be strong enough to argue their viewpoint, but it is not a professional thing to do. Critical thinking is about being impartial and objective. Look out for the following emotive words when reading:

'cruel', 'unfair', 'nasty', 'abuse', 'natural', 'correct', 'normal', 'common sense', 'innocent', 'unique', 'extreme', 'radical', 'final', 'distraught', 'unfair', 'fantastic', 'useless', 'disappointment', 'worry', 'happy', 'surely', 'clearly', 'obviously'

Activity Write your own: ....

....

....

....

Legal reasoning guidance

Use the following table when reading pieces of legal writing to help you uncover everything about the piece that you need to critically think about in your assessment.

What to look for:	Done!
Identify the writer's main theory in the introduction	☐
Highlight the descriptive writing in the piece	☐
Find the main line of reasoning in the piece	☐
Highlight the signals used in the text	☐
Separate the individual arguments within the reasoning	☐

Identify any counter-arguments put forward by the writer ☐
Find all the evidence provided by the writer ☐
Highlight tricks: emotions, assumptions, misinterpretations, etc ☐
Find the writer's analysis of his or her own evidence ☐
Highlight the writer's support and rebuttal of other arguments ☐
Identify the writer's reasoning for his or her support and rebuttal ☐
Find the conclusion ☐
Identify the rationale behind the conclusion ☐
Identify the originality of the writer's piece ☐

What do I do with the legal reasoning?

Once you have identified a writer's legal reasoning, you need to criticise, analyse and evaluate it. This is the main part of critical thinking. Further guidance on analysis and evaluation is provided further on in this chapter, but as a general outline you should use the following structure when critically thinking about a writer's legal reasoning:

1 Identify and critically think about the line of reasoning:
   ● Question, analyse, criticise, research, argue, conclude, suggest, contradict
2 Identify and evaluate the evidence in the text:
   ● Up to date? Assumptions? Appropriate? Authoritative? Link to reasoning?
3 Identify and evaluate the conclusions:
   ● Linked to evidence? Sound? Original? Biased? Logical?

Activity Draw out a mind map, a flowchart or a brainstorm of how you usually like to structure your assignments and your arguments in your law assessments. What do you think of your current structure?

....
....
....
....

How do I put forward my own legal reasoning?

Critical thinking in a law assessment looks different to descriptive writing in a law assessment. A critical piece contains reasons, evidence, explanations, theories, arguments, judgments and conclusions. Descriptive writing merely describes the case law, the injuries, the outcome, the reforms, etc. This will not achieve the highest marks, but it is what most students do. Description should be kept to a minimum in law assessments.

When writing your own work based on your research and critical thinking, the rules to follow are similar to those when you read another's work:

● **Draft** – define your structure and what goes into each section of your piece before you start writing. It will flow better this way.

- *Pace* – use the 'legal reasoning guidance table' above to help you approach a legal piece logically. This staged approach can be mirrored in your own analysis and critique of the piece.
- *Introduction* – explain the legal issue, your theories and evidence, and conclusions you hope to draw.
- *Your line of reasoning* – establish your arguments, theories, alternative views and conclusions. These must run, intact, through your whole piece.
- *Signals* – when presenting your reasoning, use the signals listed above to guide the reader through your argument.
- *Structure* – make sure your reasoning is staged correctly – your argument and the evidence should build as the reader progresses through your piece.
- *Precision* – critical thinking in law presents reasoning with clarity and purpose. Make sure that only the important evidence/issues are selected for discussion.
- *Conclusion* – many students forget to write a conclusion. A conclusion allows the reader to decide whether you have successfully and clearly argued all your points.
- *Reading* – why don't you read your own work and critically think about it as you would with someone else's article/chapter?

When concluding ...

A word of advice when drawing conclusions in law. No outcome is *absolutely guaranteed* and, therefore, it is best not to use absolutes as signals, such as 'never', 'always', 'all' and 'proves'. Instead, use 'may', 'most', 'many', 'often', 'usually' and 'suggests'. Another writer may come along and disprove your theory, and theories are always evolving, so perhaps you could use some tentative conclusions instead.

 In the following fictional legal argument, find the following features:

- The theory in the introduction
- Main line of reasoning
- Arguments in support of reasoning
- Evidence
- Analysis of evidence
- Conclusion

- Descriptive writing
- Signals
- Counter-arguments
- Tricks
- Rebuttal of counter-arguments
- Rationale behind the conclusion

'Academic research has shown that defendants who seek to use the defence of provocation are most likely to be male. They have killed their partners or friends and are charged with murder, which they admit to committing, but they use the excuse that they were, in some way, provoked. This feeds a general public perception that men are unable to hold their temper, that they "fly off the handle" at the slightest thing. However, the law in this area is slowly turning. Women are now being recognised as having a "slow burn" reaction to circumstances or jibes. Is this appropriate? Must provocation be a defence to killing at all?

It appears that men and women are now afforded the same defence but on different grounds: men snap, women simmer. This is an indication that the criminal law is becoming decidedly more subjective and personal. One could argue that it does not matter whether a man or a woman snaps or simmers – they should *not* kill, and they should *definitely* not be afforded a defence to the murder simply because they could not control themselves emotionally. Emotional control is a part of everyday life – "if you can't take the heat, get out of the kitchen".

On the other hand, releasing emotions is part of human life too. A human who controls all emotions is akin to a robot. Therefore, perhaps the law should take account of "real life", no matter how idiotic some people's decisions may be? No, this would be wrong. It would justify the worst crime of all and it would impart little meaning to the lives of those who have passed, through no real fault of their own.

All in all, it seems like defendants can use any excuse they want as a defence to murder: "She laughed at my haircut …", "He called me fat …". Where does the law draw a line and restore common sense? We all have bad haircuts … that's no reason to kill.'

Once you have attempted this activity yourself, why not look at our suggested answer on our **Companion Website** at www.palgrave.com/law/legalskills.

4.2 REFLECTIVE LEARNING

The term 'reflective learning' it batted about quite often in further and higher education, but many students do not understand what exactly is expected of them when it comes to reflection. 'Do I keep a journal?', or 'Do I reflect in my assignments?' are questions which may have crossed your mind. Additionally, because the outcome of your course is reliant upon submitted assessments, the idea of keeping a reflective journal seems pointless if it's never going to be marked!

Well, you don't have to keep a journal if you don't want to. But there is something worth thinking about. Have you ever done something incorrectly and felt really embarrassed in front of everyone, or was told to not do it again? What did you do after the experience? Did you forget about it instantly and repeat the same mistake, or did you go away, reflect on the event, and realise that it would be a good idea to handle it differently next time? You probably did the latter. This is how reflection can help your learning in law. If you analyse and reflect on something that did not go according to plan, you are more likely to learn from the experience and be more successful with a second attempt. After all, being a critical thinker means reflecting on what is in front of you, and thinking about how it could be better.

You also need to reflect upon yourself as a learner and your current moods, skills, motivations and desires. Do you set goals for yourself? Do you devise plans of action to improve your performance? Do you reward yourself when you achieve something small? Why are you on your course? What would you like to achieve? It is important that you stay motivated during your studies, as it will get you through the periods of intense study and stress. You must also reflect upon your 'active learning' techniques. How well do you rate yourself as a student? Do you help yourself and display 'active' learning behaviour, such as conducting your own research in advance? Or do you simply study passively and wait for the answers to fall in to your lap?

In this box give yourself a score out of 10 for: (a) your current personal skills; (b) your current motivation levels; and (c) your current behaviour as an 'active' learner:

(a) ....

(b) ....

(c) ....

In this section, reflection will be tackled in three ways: reflecting on your own learning style; reflecting on your personal skills; and reflecting on your academic performance.

My learning style

Every person learns in a different way. Just because you cannot concentrate when trying to read a complex law book does not mean you are going to fail your course! It often helps students to know why they do not enjoy doing a certain activity. Your learning style may be more practical, and you may simply need to take a different approach, such as highlighting, rewriting or brainstorming. If you aware of *how* you learn, you will be more able to do your research in a way that suits you. No one learning style is better than any other.

Self-assessment Look at the activities below. Tick the boxes according to which activities benefit you most and which activities do not suit your personality:

Activity	Benefit most	Benefit least
Listening to lectures and watching the lecturer	☐	☐
Preparing answers for seminars	☐	☐
Preparing drafts for assignments	☐	☐
Using theories, structures and checklists	☐	☐
Getting feedback, receiving praise	☐	☐
Working independently to your own schedule	☐	☐
Peer-marking, discussing	☐	☐
Researching, searching, finding	☐	☐
Finding the sequence	☐	☐
Planning in advance/being ahead of everyone	☐	☐
Activities using feelings and emotions	☐	☐
Lots of practical examples	☐	☐
Working in groups/teams	☐	☐
Brainstorming	☐	☐
Open-ended exercises, eg interviews	☐	☐
Drawing, sketching, doodling	☐	☐
Taking part in role-plays and debates	☐	☐
Practising techniques, eg debating	☐	☐
Giving presentations, explaining your view	☐	☐

The activities become more practical the further down the list you go. Have you noticed a pattern in your ticks? Are you a mostly logical learner (towards the top) or a mostly practical learner (towards the bottom)?

....

....

....

....

There are many different learning styles, most of which are listed below. If you know your style, you can use it to your advantage and study the law in a way that suits you for optimum knowledge and understanding. Additionally, you will also become aware of the skills that you may need to improve on to make your learning experience more effective. Which style(s) describe you?

(a) Linguistic intelligence

This is the ability to use language in an advanced way. You will be very good at using languages and words, and you will be tuned into the power and influence of words, both spoken and written. The study of law will really suit you, and you should be able to order your thoughts and theories in a professional and legal way. You will be successful at:

- ☐ learning the complex Latin in the law;
- ☐ verbal debates about the law;
- ☐ writing legal letters;
- ☐ sorting your legal research;
- ☐ creative writing and developing theories;
- ☐ giving clear explanations of the law;
- ☐ essay writing.

If this is the basis for your learning style, you are likely to be wholly comfortable with studying the law. You probably greatly enjoy thinking about case judgments and reading articles, and you can hang on to the words and figure out an underlying meaning and structure to the text. There is still room for creativity and originality in your study of law. Perhaps you could try mind maps and creative revision methods – such as colourful cue cards – to add a new dimension to your studies.

(b) Logical intelligence

This is the ability to reason and calculate, and to think things through in a logical, systematic manner. You will be able to detect patterns, make connections and understand the relationships between actions. Law will really suit you because you enjoy the analytical thinking that is required of you, and you can pick theories to bits. You will be successful at:

- planning and structuring your legal arguments;
- writing a strategy for debates in law;
- structuring your law assessments;
- using logical thinking when criticising the law;
- managing your time effectively.

If this is the basis for your learning style, you are likely to enjoy the structured system of the law, and appreciate the clear legal and educational processes which come with studying the law. You are likely to have very good analytical and critical skills, and your revision plans are specially tailored to suit your love of structure and logic. There is, however, still room for creativity and flexibility in your studies. Perhaps you could try working with your peers to show you new ways of approaching the law and to pick up new ideas.

(c) Visual intelligence

This is the ability to visualise a result and to think in three-dimensional ways about problems and case studies. You can work with a range of tools and resources and you can see the 'big picture'. This is a very creative learning style. You will be successful at:

- designing unique revision methods in law;
- drawing mind maps of legal case studies;
- visualising the connections between offences;
- appreciating the distance between actions;
- creatively thinking about the law;
- finding imaginative solutions.

If this is the basis for your learning style, the law may seem really boring at times! But your creativity is your key to successful legal learning and assessments, and you have the ability to turn the law into something creative, magical and innovative. You will find an answer that nobody else had thought of. There is still room for structure and a logical approach to your studies. Perhaps you could try drafting a detailed structure of your assignment answers to help you to utilise your creative ideas more effectively.

(d) Physical intelligence

This is the ability to use your body and your manual skills to create something, or to solve physically-related problems. You should be able to put yourself in the position of the parties in a legal scenario and to feel their emotions, thoughts, motives and ideas. Well-developed physical intelligence leads to a highly physical learning style, and you enjoy field work and practical activities. You will be successful at:

- leading debates – playing the judge;
- manually solving a legal problem;
- visiting the library and building your research;
- building your craft of studying the law;
- diving into your work at any stage;
- devising practical methods of revision;
- appreciating court visits;
- showing others alternative approaches to law.

If this is the basis of your learning style, the law may seem frustrating at times – you feel the need to burst out of the lecture hall and jump into your work in your own practical and innovative way. You are likely to be able to work by yourself very effectively and you are very independent. You need to try to make the most of your strengths and use physical activities to recreate legal scenarios, build models or role-play certain situations which help you understand law, legal reasoning and theories. There is still room for rational thought and structure to your studies. Perhaps you could try sharing your ideas with your peers and drawing up a research timetable to add a new dimension to your studies.

(e) Personal intelligence

This is the ability to understand others, work very well with your peers, and honestly assess your achievements. You are able to manage a team because your personal skills are excellent, and you can work effectively in groups, cater for the needs of others, and reflect on your own practice. You will be successful at:

- teamwork and group work in law;
- leading and mentoring others;
- helping others to solve legal problems;
- planning your time effectively;
- appreciating the contributions of others;

- enjoying the process of development and reflection;
- reflecting on your motives, actions and goals;
- understanding the emotions of others.

If this is the basis for your learning style, you will find some aspects of studying law very enjoyable, such as working in groups, managing team projects, and listening to others. You are likely to be able to empathise with parties to legal proceedings as well as see legal theories from multiple angles. You are also very good at reflecting and thinking about your actions, and planning ahead. You are a very hard worker and your peers appreciate your sensitive and understanding approach. There is still room for independent learning skills and innovative ideas in your studies. Perhaps you could try turning one of your reflective ideas into a new way of working independently to add a new dimension to your studies.

(f) Left-brain learner

Left-brain learners prefer to use logic, order, sequence, calculation and reasoning in their study of law. You are able to write out information in structured lists, categorise the law into precise groups, work with intricate details and appreciate analysis and words. You will be successful at:

- structuring your answers;
- writing strategies and drafts;
- working independently;
- breaking down your law assignment into categories;

- using logical thinking when researching the law;
- thinking scientifically about the law;
- using lists, sequences and order in your studies.

If this is your learning style, the study of law suits you very well because of the logic, structure and order that comes with legal studies. You take a very organised approach to your learning, and you like to break everything down into small parts and deal with each one in a sequential order. You could perhaps inject some imagination into your studies – have you considered drawing mind maps to help you with your drafting process? Or, perhaps when you make detailed lists, you could use colour to organise them more clearly and make them more memorable.

(g) Right-brain learner

Right-brain learners prefer colour, drawings, images, emotions and imagination in their study of law. You are able to draw diagrams and mind maps to organise information, you can make connections through imaginative techniques, and you separate different topics by colour-coding. The study of law has to be livened up for a right-brained learner. You will be successful at:

- designing active and colourful research methods;
- drawing mind maps of legal case studies;
- visualising the connections between offences;
- jumping in and seeing the 'whole picture';
- creatively thinking about solutions;
- finding imaginative revision methods;
- working in groups and discussion;
- using a unique perspective.

If this is your learning style, use your imagination and create diverse and unique ways of making law accessible for you. You may still benefit from making lists and analysing your assignment questions more carefully to ensure that you include all the relevant material. Perhaps you could work with a friend and develop a more structured approach to writing assignments.

Now you know what your learning styles are, you know what may be missing from your approach. Do you need to be a little more original, structured, inventive, independent?

Activity Write down your learning style here: .... **Draw up an action plan of how you can change your approach to incorporate other learning style strategies into your own practice.**

....

....

....

....

Reflecting on your personal skills

This is a much more personal section, where you get to critically think about yourself. If you wish to develop as a learner and become a thriving law student, self-development requires self-assessment. This includes a knowledge of your learning style (above) and an honest analysis of your personal attributes (below).

Can you be positive?

Earlier in this chapter, critical thinking was defined as the analysis of both positive and negative factors. People find it difficult to be positive: when was the last time you praised somebody? How active are you as a learner? Do you feel that you are doing enough to get the best out of yourself and your course? How do you rate your current skills, both personal and professional?

As an adult learner, you now have complete control over your actions, your studies, your motivations and your attitudes. If something is not working out very well, or you are unhappy with something, you are the only person who can change it into something positive. Make changes – give yourself permission to succeed.

Fill in the questionnaire below to identify just how critical you can be.

Self-assessment Tick either 'yes' or 'no' below to measure your current attitude:

Attitude		Yes	No
1	When someone makes a mistake, I tell them: 'no – that's wrong'	☐	☐
2	I often tell people what to do	☐	☐
3	I notice and criticise small things about other people	☐	☐
4	I do not like being told what to do	☐	☐
5	I often accept rumour and hearsay as true	☐	☐
6	I often dive in without recognising the alternative course of action	☐	☐
7	I regularly miss the finer details	☐	☐
8	I forget to separate fact from fiction and get the wrong idea	☐	☐
9	I only ask questions if I can't do it	☐	☐
10	When I see somebody not responding, I want to answer for them	☐	☐
11	I tend to shout when I argue	☐	☐
12	I can be impatient	☐	☐
13	I have strong opinions which I often share with my peers	☐	☐
14	I wish I was able to figure out complex puzzles	☐	☐
15	When there is a heated debate, I am the loudest and proudest	☐	☐
16	If I am fooled by somebody, I become angry rather than intrigued	☐	☐
17	I don't often notice when I have been given the wrong information	☐	☐
18	If I have to arrange a trip away, I wait until the last minute	☐	☐
19	I am quite messy and think order and sequence is boring	☐	☐
20	When a crisis occurs, I run around and panic	☐	☐

If you answered 'yes' to 8 questions or more, you would greatly benefit from learning how to analyse, question, observe, plan, and to think logically and unemotionally. Your lecturers (and friends) will benefit little from hearing your views if you do not provide any evidence! Additionally, a lack of patience means that you may miss vital details and only end up with half the story. An analysis of the more negative traits in this questionnaire and a special action plan is provided for you on our **Companion Website**. If you answered 'yes' to 7 questions or less, your critical thinking skills are developing very well: you can think logically and sequentially and you can present your argument calmly and with rational clarity. However, unless you answered 'no' to all the questions, there is still room for improvement!

Activity Fill in the space below to address your main concerns:

I wish I did not: ....

....

I will fix this by: ....

....

Active learning

Excellent students take the initiative and find things out for themselves. They do not sabotage their own chances by making silly mistakes, or by being lazy etc. How are your current active learning skills?

> It's a waste of time.

> That's not logical. There's a right way and a wrong way.

> That's childish. I'm not doing that.

The following behaviours do not help your state of mind or your studies:

- Not turning up to lectures and not bothering to catch up
- Leaving work until the last minute and missing deadlines
- Filling your time with only social activities
- Trying to work when you can't concentrate
- Trying to study but letting your mind wonder
- Not asking for help when you really need it
- A negative attitude towards your course
- Copying notes, copying articles, copying textbooks
- Not caring about approaching exams or revision
- Never using the law library or using it only to meet with friends
- Reading without challenging what you have read
- Reciting the law without really understanding it
- Not making connections between law and real life
- Being totally unorganised and not setting goals or looking forward

How many negative traits do you display? Are there more than you thought? Are you happy with your current attitudes towards your course, or do you know that you could try harder to be more organised and more active in your approach? Below is an opportunity to analyse in detail just how positive or negative, active or passive, you really are when it comes to your legal studies. Do you have a basic expectation of the results of this questionnaire before you complete it? You never know, you may surprise yourself.

 **Self-assessment** How active are you? Plot your present position on the line with an X:

A passive learner:		An active learner:
I do no preparation for lectures	_ _ _ _ _	I prepare for my lectures
I do the research I am told to do	_ _ _ _ _	I do additional research
I study cases and units separately	_ _ _ _ _	I try to find links between cases and units
I wait for information to be given to me	_ _ _ _ _	I seek out information in advance
I don't talk about the law with my friends	_ _ _ _ _	I discuss my ideas and plans with my friends
I copy from textbooks at assignment time	_ _ _ _ _	I use the information from textbooks to construct my own understanding of the law
I don't reflect on what I have learnt	_ _ _ _ _	I use reflection at every stage of my studies and have a reflective journal
I don't analyse and criticise the law	_ _ _ _ _	I analyse and criticise cases, articles and theories
I get bored very easily	_ _ _ _ _	I liven up my studies according to my learning style
I write my assignment at the last minute	_ _ _ _ _	I plan my assessment answers well in advance
I hand my work in once printed	_ _ _ _ _	I evaluate my own work critically

I expect to be reminded about deadlines	_ _ _ _ _	I have my own diary/schedule and I never miss a deadline
My goal is to pass this module	_ _ _ _ _	My goal for this week is to draft my assignment.
My motivation is to finish my course	_ _ _ _ _	My motivation is to earn a legal qualification and to get a good job
I read feedback once	_ _ _ _ _	I use feedback constructively
I am jealous of my friends' successes and don't know how they do it	_ _ _ _ _	I help my friends to be as organised and as active as me.

How do you feel about your student skills now you have completed the questionnaire? Are there any areas in particular you feel need some real work?

Activity Fill in the space below to address your main concerns:

I need to improve: ....

....

I will do this by: ....

....

To help you get off to a good start, tips on how to revise actively during your exam period are contained on our **Companion Website**.

Below is a 'Good Study Skills' checklist. Tick the traits you feel most confident about, and fill in this checklist regularly to note your improvement.

'Good Study Skills'

- ☐ Reflect on your skills/experiences
- ☐ Think creatively
- ☐ Consider alternatives
- ☐ Listen to and work well with others
- ☐ Work according to your learning style
- ☐ Refine your timekeeping skills
- ☐ Sort your organisational skills
- ☐ Take responsibility for your actions
- ☐ Participate in everything
- ☐ Set yourself goals and priorities
- ☐ Be decisive
- ☐ Draw up imaginative revision methods
- ☐ Be assertive
- ☐ Take risks
- ☐ Use your imagination
- ☐ Be sensitive to the opinions of others
- ☐ Always plan ahead
- ☐ Manage your stress effectively

- ☐ Think critically about yourself/the law
- ☐ Enhance your problem-solving skills
- ☐ Learn from your mistakes
- ☐ Tailor your learning environment
- ☐ Make what you are learning enjoyable
- ☐ Make sure your IT skills are good
- ☐ Work hard at every task
- ☐ Evaluate every experience
- ☐ Be analytical of yourself/the law
- ☐ Select and categorise relevant material
- ☐ Pay attention to detail
- ☐ Break routine with new ideas
- ☐ Try something unique
- ☐ Think of other ways to do things
- ☐ Aim to soar above everybody else
- ☐ Improve written communication
- ☐ Work on your presentation skills
- ☐ Be aware of how you influence others

- [ ] Buy a diary and never miss a deadline
- [ ] Manage projects professionally
- [ ] Work with people from different faiths
- [ ] Understand other points of view
- [ ] Negotiate
- [ ] Be polite with difficult people
- [ ] Speak clearly and directly
- [ ] Take direction from others easily
- [ ] Develop your debating skills
- [ ] Ask for help when you need it
- [ ] Find your determination
- [ ] Trust in your own abilities
- [ ] Respect those in authority
- [ ] Stay calm in a crisis
- [ ] Reward your achievements
- [ ] Visualise your main goal

Reflecting on your academic performance

Most of us learn from our mistakes, no matter how big or small. However, sometimes we repeat mistakes when we find that our actions worked well in one context and failed spectacularly in another! The worse the incident, the longer we dwell on it afterwards and undertake a lengthy post-mortem to find out why it went so wrong. It is especially troubling when you were responsible for other people and you let them down too. This is where your reflective skills are really important.

Not only should you reflect on what went wrong in your studies, but you should reflect on your big achievements, and you should reward yourself when you develop a plan of action during your reflection and you implement it to great success. This self-development is not just about formulating new rules and shaping your future behaviour. It involves modifying or even eliminating some old behaviour patterns that are no longer useful or helpful to your development. This is difficult to do, as many of our attitudes stem from our upbringing, our beliefs and our experiences. But a flexible learner is a successful learner!

Below are some examples of common problems:

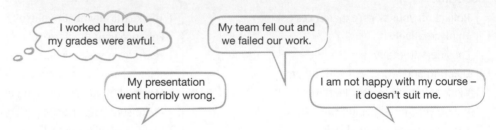

When these things happen – and be under no illusion, they happen to *everyone* – it is the perfect time to reflect on your experience and make a plan for the future. You will probably face a similar situation again in the near future, and you will feel much more confident if you have a plan of action which takes into account everything that went wrong the first time.

If you are going to reflect on your experiences, you need to follow some kind of structure. An excellent structure to follow is set out below:

- *Incident*: An event or problem that excites, confuses, angers or upsets you.
- *Ponder*: In order to make sense of the event, you need to analyse and examine the event, including the feelings and attitudes you felt at the time.
- *Design*: You develop new ideas and perspectives, and begin to design an action plan, detailing how you would deal with the same problem again, should it recur.

- *Experiment*: Your new plan is ready for experimentation, and at the next available opportunity you put it into action and monitor the results. Were they better than last time?

INCIDENT
Live through an event or incident.

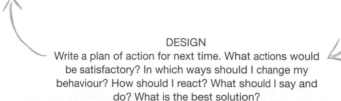

EXPERIMENT
Put your plan into action! 'I put my new plan into practice today, and …'

PONDER
Ask yourself: what was I doing? Why did I do it? What was I thinking at the time? How did I feel? What were my goals when I acted that way? What should I have done?

DESIGN
Write a plan of action for next time. What actions would be satisfactory? In which ways should I change my behaviour? How should I react? What should I say and do? What is the best solution?

You must complete the whole cycle before you can truly benefit from your reflection, as there is no point in reflecting on an experience and then reacting in the exact same way the next time it happens! You may have to go through the cycle a few times before you deal with a difficult situation in a way with which you are completely happy, but the cycle works, and it makes you a much better learner. You will respond better, you will think more logically, and you will feel much more confident in yourself that you have dealt with the situation to the best of your ability.

When you find yourself in a professional situation after your studies, surrounded by people with knowledge and qualifications in law, excellent reflective skills will be expected of you. Your employer will be pleased with you if you reflect on a problematic event and improve your performance as a result.

Below is an example of a law student reflecting on a bad experience using the structure provided above, and how she overcame her experience through reflection.

Incident. 'We did our contract law presentation an hour ago, which was formally assessed by our lecturer and watched by our whole tutorial group. The four of us had allocated slides to explain, and I read through the slides a few times beforehand. The presentation started well, but I was very panicky. When my turn came, I could feel myself shaking and turning red and sweating. I couldn't speak properly and everyone was staring at me. When we finished, the lecturer asked me a question about contract law which I should have known the answer to, but Andy – one of my group members – answered it for me instead. The lecturer gave me a look before writing some notes, and I was so angry at both myself and at Andy. I hadn't rehearsed enough, I was not confident, and Andy should have given me a chance to respond.'

Ponder. 'I knew what I was doing, but only on a superficial level. I had been so concerned with building the presentation perfectly that I hadn't given any thought to the delivery. At the time I was simply panicking because I had not rehearsed. I should have practised my presentation skills for days beforehand. I wasn't confident about what I was saying because my knowledge was not deep enough. I did not do thorough research and I should have because it would have made me more confident. As well as that, I was feeling shaky because everyone was staring at me. I thought they were thinking 'what an idiot – look at her shaking' and that made me even worse. I should have talked more slowly and looked out the window at points to distract me from the staring eyes. They probably weren't thinking anything malicious at all … I was angry with Andy because he made me look stupid by responding for me which made the lecturer look at me as if I hadn't done any work. I should have either asked Andy if I could have responded, or supplemented his point with an explanation of my own.'

Design. 'Next time, there are several things I can do to make sure that it goes better. First, I should pay equal attention, not only to the development of the presentation, but to my delivery and presentation skills. I can do this by practising speaking techniques and pacing myself, and by doing it in front of my family. Secondly, my research should illustrate much more depth. How can I stand in front of an audience and talk about the law if I have not done my work properly? I will then be more confident that I can answer all the questions thrown at me. Thirdly, I should not panic so much when presenting. The audience mean me no malice – they look at me every day – and genuinely want to hear what I have to say. My main problem is shaking and talking too fast. I will slow down next time and concentrate on every word! Fourthly, I cannot control Andy's actions but I can stand up for myself, and the lecturer should have given me another chance to respond. Next time, I will add to Andy's comments with my own answer, and, additionally, I could ask the lecturer if I could respond to her question myself.'

Experiment. 'Two weeks ago I had a terrible presentation experience with Andy, Paul and Abdul in contract law. Today I had the chance to do it again with a public law presentation. Although it was not formally assessed, it was the same set-up – my lecturer and *the same tutorial group* were watching! I read this journal a week ago to remind myself of what went wrong last time, and I prepared my research in advance and practised my delivery faithfully every night for a whole week. This time I was much more confident in front of the class, and I made myself speak slowly by keeping myself in check. I also observed how my other peers presented, and they looked more nervous than me – I mustn't have noticed it last time. I kept looking out the window at the people outside to remind myself that my task was actually pretty small. Luckily Andy did not answer for me this time because I answered the lecturer's question so quickly that he didn't have the chance, and I looked really clever! I am really pleased with myself – I'm going out now to buy that album I've wanted for ages.'

Activity List an incident in this box that you wished you had reflected upon, or think you should reflect upon today:

....

....

....

....

....

Journals

If your learning style means that you enjoy processing your experiences, jotting them down, putting an order to them, and reflecting on them and analysing them, then some kind of reflective journal or book is an excellent idea. This can include good *and* bad experiences.

You will probably not write in your journal every day like a diary. It is there for reflective emergencies, such as when a terrible thing happens to you and you wish it had worked out differently, or when you achieve a great success and you want to brag about it for hours and read about it all over again the next day! You could also make a list in your journal about current issues that concern you, and take your journal to a tutorial with your personal tutor.

Top three reflections

1 A bad assignment grade
2 Arguments with peers
3 Struggling with a current topic

The following events may find themselves working their way into your reflective journal:

- I was totally confused by the lecture I just had
- My group had a big argument today
- I don't like my lecturer
- I fell out with my friend when we were researching together
- I don't understand this topic and I am struggling
- My presentation was really rushed and I went all red
- My friends are getting better marks than me
- I can't seem to start my research
- I worked really hard but I failed my assignment
- I received a fantastic grade for my essay

- My new research plan was a huge success
- My friends talked to me about their assignment ideas
- My presentation was cool, calm and collected
- I am really enjoying this current topic
- My lecturer helped me a lot
- My group project is going very well
- I just had an amazing lecture
- I have a million research plans
- My revision table is working well

When you wish to reflect on a bad experience in your journal, below are some excellent questions to ask:

Reflective questions

- Your feelings about the course and your progress overall
- What do you find difficult and why do you think this is?
- Have there been changes in your attitude or motivation?
- Illustrate how different areas of your course connect
- Why are you good/bad at a certain skill/task?
- What have you achieved?
- What strategy did you take when a difficult situation arose?
- Have you asked for support?
- What was significant or meaningful about your achievement?
- What can you do to build upon your success? How could you fine-tune your skills further?
- What would you do differently if the same event happened tomorrow?
- Note down any ideas that arise
- Have your goals for the future changed?
- Write a detailed account of your bad experience and review it

- What discoveries have you made about the way you learn best?
- What conclusions have you reached as a result of your bad experience?
- Plan out your next steps after your experience: what are you going to do?
- What is going well?
- What could have gone better?
- Are you happy with the way you dealt with the difficult situation?
- What are your current challenges?
- Did your feelings affect the outcome of a difficult situation in any way?
- Describe how your studies and experiences can be applied to daily situations
- What are your strategies for tackling tasks and problematic people?
- Describe new things you have found out about yourself
- Did you reflect on your performance?

Below is an example of a reflective conversation that you may have with yourself straight after an event:

> 'I tried to work with my group today because our deadline is approaching. Alex was missing again, which makes me really mad because his part of the presentation is falling behind. I don't think he's even done any work towards the report. I showed them all my first draft, but they told me that we were going to do it a different way and would not listen to my ideas. We ended up arguing for the rest of the hour and I couldn't understand how they could make a decision without me. They haven't even given me any guidance as to how to write my report in their "new style". I hate them all!'

If you were to write all of this down in a journal/book, by the time you were finished writing you would have calmed down significantly! Some logical solutions may even begin to creep into your mind. It will make you feel much better when you break the experience down into small pieces and clarify your thoughts and emotions. You can also keep it for future reference, and not only use it as a reference book in case the incident happens again, but to see yourself develop as a professional worker and an independent learner.

Goals

If you are studying law, you are probably in post-compulsory education (aged 16+). This means you are now responsible for your own learning, your own time-keeping, and your own goals and motivations. You can probably choose to leave your course voluntarily if you want to, and so there has never been a more important time to reflect on your goals and motivations. What do you want to achieve? Why are you here? What is keeping you on your course?

It is important to clarify your motivations because you will need to refer back to them when times get hard. There will be days when you will feel frustrated, bored, stressed, and think about giving up completely. Don't! You will also need to create goals to aim towards during your studies, and then reward yourself when you achieve them!

Activity State in this box your main motivations for being on your course:

....
....
....
....
....
....
....
....
....
....

I want to:	Yes!	Maybe ...	No
Improve my career opportunities	☐	☐	☐
Get a better job	☐	☐	☐
Earn a better salary	☐	☐	☐
Prove to myself that i can do it	☐	☐	☐
Prove to my family/friends that i can do it	☐	☐	☐
Get more self-confidence	☐	☐	☐
Broaden my horizons	☐	☐	☐
Get my life out of a rut!	☐	☐	☐
Experience university life	☐	☐	☐
Make up for my bad education earlier in life	☐	☐	☐
Gain an FE/HE qualification	☐	☐	☐
Learn about a subject that interests me	☐	☐	☐
Have the opportunity to study	☐	☐	☐
Get a good grade	☐	☐	☐
Just get through	☐	☐	☐
Learn 'people skills'	☐	☐	☐
Improve myself	☐	☐	☐
Earn respect for myself/from others	☐	☐	☐
Hear someone say that I can achieve good things	☐	☐	☐

What do your answers say about your real motivations for being on your course? Have your responses surprised you?

Put your motivations somewhere safe and refer to them when times get tough. You may need to focus on them to get you through the tough assessment times.

Setting yourself short-term and long-term goals to aim for is very important – it gives your hard work a purpose, and you will develop drive and enthusiasm for your studies.

Below are examples of goals you can set yourself:

'I want to achieve at least 50% for the next assignment.'

'I want to finish my Legal Skills assignment by the end of the week.'

'I am going to draw up a revision plan and stick to it this year!'

'I want to develop my personal skills this semester and be kind to my peers.'

'I need to finish the highlighting for my contract law assignment by Friday, and the writing up by the Friday after that.'

What are *your* short-term goals? Do you have something to finish by the end of the week?

Use the table below to plan out your goals:

Goal table		
	Goal 1:	Goal 2:
Positive outcomes:		
Potential obstacles:		
Ways to overcome the obstacles:		
Targets along the way:		
Any sacrifices?		
How I will celebrate?		

4.3 ANALYTICAL THINKING

Analytical thinking takes up the bulk of critical thinking. Once you have described the law and identified the line of reasoning, you must analyse the law and the evidence in order to get to the evaluation stage.

What does analysis entail?

- *Objectivity*: stand back from the information given.
- *Check* for accuracy, flaws, tricks, inconsistent reasoning, etc.
- *Flaws*: are the conclusions based on the evidence? Does the legal reasoning follow through?
- *Compare* the same issue against other writers/ theories in the field.
- *Assumptions*: are any hidden in the reasoning?
- *Argue*: can you find a loophole in the evidence or theory?

- *Examine* in detail every angle of the piece.
- *Accuracy*: check all the facts and statements closely.
- *Logic*: does the structure flow succinctly?
- *Observe* why certain conclusions have been met and why others differ.
- *Explain* why different views contrast and why some are more preferable than others.
- *Tricks*: writers can lure and persuade the reader in several ways.

In addition to analysing the evidence and research you have collected, it may also help to analyse something closer to home – your assessment question!

Assessment question

The title

Many students do not read their assessment question properly, whether it be in an exam or an assignment. This leads to an inaccurate research focus and, inevitably, an incorrect answer. Additionally, if the question is in two parts, students find themselves answering the first question rather than the second, missing out on a lot of marks.

Here is an example of a law assessment question:

'Critically assess the current standard of care applied to medical professionals in the law of tort, and how this differs from the test applied to the average man.'

In order to narrow your focus, a really good trick is to rewrite the question:

 Rewrite the question here:

....

....

....

Another really useful trick is to highlight the key words in the question and ask yourself: (a) what you are being asked to do, and (b) what area of law do you have to research/analyse:

(a) *'critically assess'* and (b) *'the standard of care to medical professionals'*

This narrows your legal research significantly. You will now know to search for articles and chapters about the duty of care applied to medical professionals, rather than a duty of care in general. Notice that there is more to the question:

(a) *'critically assess how this differs'* and (b) *'from the average man test'*

Make sure you pay attention to *both* tasks in the question. You will only be marked for the parts of your answer that are directly relevant to the question. To make sure that you do not deviate from this, refer back to the question throughout your research and your writing, so as not to lose your focus. You can always consult with your friends if you are still unsure about exactly what the question is asking.

 Reword the following assessment questions:

Contract law: 'Describe the laws relating to the formation of a contract, and analyse their effectiveness.'

Legal skills: 'Reflect on your own presentation skills and draw up an action plan of how you would like to improve during your degree.'

European law: 'Critically analyse the laws regarding the free movement of persons within the European Union. Do you think they are adequate?'

Criminal law: 'Identify the instances in which a defendant can use the defence of intoxication and evaluate the current limits of the defence.'

....

....

....

If you receive a case study question – a question which contains people and an incident – you may wish to draw out who did what to whom. For example:

'Jason drank too much alcohol and assaulted Wendy. Wendy's brother Fred observed this incident and pounced on Jason, stabbing him twice.

Discuss who is liable for which non-fatal offences and if any defences are available.'

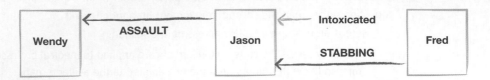

It will also help to identify and break down the applicable offences at this stage, which will focus your research even more:

- **Jason:** common law assault and battery: *actus reus* and *mens rea*; *R v Ireland* (1997) and *Fagan v Metropolitan Police Comm*issioner (1968).
- **Fred:** section 20 definition OAPA 1861: malicious wounding; *R v Mowatt* (1967) and *R v Parmenter* (1991).
- **Jason**: defence of intoxication; *DPP v Majewski* (1976) and *R v Kingston* (1994).

Now you will know to look for chapters and articles relating to assault and battery, s 20 of the Offences Against the Person Act 1861, and the defence of intoxication. If your research was to spill over into other areas, it is very unlikely you would pick up marks for it, no matter how good the work. This is why a word count is provided – to keep your work relevant and focused. Explain one party at a time – this is a more logical approach. Defences can be explained after you have established whether any offences have been committed. Sometimes, your lecturer may include two topics in one question. This is common in more practical subjects, like criminal law, employment law, etc. It is your task to identify what these two topics are, yet to successfully differentiate and apply them in your answer.

If you fail to identify the important issues at the very beginning of your research, your work will begin on a slightly different foundation to that which your law lecturer was hoping for, and throughout your assessment your line of reasoning will move further and further away from the original question. If you are still stuck, check your course syllabus and read what you have covered in lectures so far. Which topic links most closely to your case study scenario? You can always ask for guidance, but a fraction of your marks are allocated to your ability to be an independent learner, so make sure you try to find the answer for yourself first.

Don't forget! Refer back to the title in your conclusion, to show the reader that you have answered the question set.

Activity Below is a contract law assignment question. Reword the question, break it down into separate issues, and note down some key words for your article search:

'Describe how a contract is formed in law, and evaluate whether the laws of consideration are appropriate.'

....

....

Notice how you are asked to show two skills: *description* and *evaluation*.

Additionally, you are asked to look at two things: the formation of a contract, and to focus in on consideration in contract law. This is all the information you need to begin your research.

Analysing the writer's position

It is now time now to turn to your analytical thinking of the law. Let us assume that you have received your assignment question, you have broken it down and identified what you need to research, and you go to the library and find all the articles, textbooks and case judgments that you need. You identify the line of reasoning in each text successfully, and are now ready to think analytically about the pieces. A really good place to start is with the writer of the article/chapter. Can you capture his or her position? What is his or her theory? What does he or she believe?

Activity Skim the abstracts below and then read them critically. Can you identify the writer's position in any of them? (Suggested answers can be found on our Companion Website.)

'Everybody knows that this was an Act to enable people to walk along without being molested or solicited by common prostitutes ... it can matter little whether the prostitute is standing in the doorway or on a balcony ...

Lord Parker, *Smith v Hughes* [1960] 1 WLR 830

'It is to be noted that the couple never bound themselves to pay the instalments to the building society, and I see no reason why any such obligation should be implied. It is clear law that the court is not to imply a term unless it is necessary, and I do not see that it is necessary here.'

Denning LJ, *Errington v Errington* [1952] 1 KB 290

'Why is this apparently basic and underlying condition of seaworthiness not treated as a condition? It is for the simple reason that the seaworthiness clause is breached by the slightest failure to be fitted "in every way" for service. Thus ... if a nail is missing from one of the timbers of a wooden vessel ... at the time of sailing, the owners are in breach of the seaworthiness stipulation.'

Upjohn LJ, *Hong Kong Fir Shipping Co Ltd v Kawasaki Kisen Kaisha Ltd* [1962] 2 QB 26

'The reasonable man is a person having the power of self-control to be expected of an ordinary person of the same sex and age of the accused, but in other respects sharing such of the accused's characteristics as they think would affect the gravity of the provocation to him; and that the question is not merely whether such a person would in like circumstances be provoked to lose his self-control but whether he would react to the provocation as the accused did.'

Lord Diplock, *DPP v Camplin* [1978] AC 705

Here are some further questions you can ask yourself when getting a feel for the writer's standpoint:

1 How well does the introduction present the writer's theory?
2 Is it clear what message the writer is trying get across to the reader?
3 How well does the evidence reveal the writer's position?
4 Does the conclusion confirm what you thought the writer was trying to argue?

It might be useful to be aware that writers sometimes use theories as arguments. They believe that by putting forward a theoretical position, the theory 'speaks for itself' and there is no longer any need for the writer to go into his or her own reasoning. This is a clever trick as it means that the writer is using other theorists to argue his or her point, but it also means that the writer is unable to build upon current research with his or her own ideas.

 An example is given below of a writer using other theories to argue his point for him. Can you identify where the other theories kick in?

> 'Smith writes in 1976 that "there is little point in reforming the area of negligence through Parliament as this would stagnate the law and turn negligence into an immoveable rock." Williams in 1988 agreed, who also submitted that "the law of negligence is unique in that it is flexible and can move with the times." The law of negligence should remain as case law. This "gives the judges as much freedom as they like to cater for the needs of the people" – a thought by Roberts in 2001.'

Notice how the writer of the piece has not explained his own position. He is making an assumption that by reading the work of other theorists, the reader will also recognise that this is the writer's position. This is laziness on the part of the writer. The other theorists are now highlighted below:

> 'Smith writes in 1976 that <u>"there is little point in reforming the area of negligence through Parliament as this would stagnate the law and turn negligence into an immoveable rock."</u> Williams in 1988 agreed, who also submitted that <u>"the law of negligence is unique in that it is flexible and can move with the times."</u> The law of negligence should remain as case law. This <u>"gives the judges as much freedom as they like to cater for the needs of the people"</u> – a thought by Roberts in 2001.'

The writer has used their words to explain himself, and has not taken the time to let the reader know what his own view is. Other views are meant to be used as support when writing, not as your own voice.

Analysing the arguments

Academics may put forward many different views in their work, and judges may list several different reasons why they have come to a particular outcome in a case. These arguments need to be identified in the text, as this helps you to analyse the line of reasoning. The arguments will most likely take the form of propositions: this is where something is assumed or predicted but it could be true or false.

 Look at the extract from the case judgment in *Paris v Stepney Borough Council* [1951] AC 367 below. Can you find Lord Oaksey's proposition?

'The duty of an employer towards his servant is to take reasonable care for the servant's safety in all the circumstances of the case. The fact that the servant has only one eye if that fact is known to the employer, and that if he loses it he will be blind, is one of the circumstances which must be considered by the employer in determining what precautions if any shall be taken for the servant's safety. The standard of care which the law demands is the care which an ordinary prudent employer would take in all the circumstances. As the circumstances may vary indefinitely it is often impossible to adduce evidence of what care an ordinarily prudent employer would take. In some cases, of course, it is possible to prove that it is the ordinary practice for employers to take or not to take a certain precaution, but in such a case as the present, where a one-eyed man has been injured, it is unlikely that such evidence can be adduced. The court has, therefore, to form its own opinion of what precautions the notional prudent employer would take …'

Propositions usually lead to a conclusion, so be on the lookout for signals (above). If propositions are used by the writer as the basis of his or her argument, and the propositions turn out to be false, the whole argument is based on *false premises*. This means that if the reasons underlying the writer's argument are not true, his or her whole theory and line of reasoning are meaningless.

Conclusion: based on arguments and evidence

Reasons, arguments, support, evidence

Underlying beliefs, assumptions, foundation

If you can find weak propositions in your research, you will probably find weak arguments too.

Note. An argument is different from a disagreement. A disagreement simply means two sides believe something different. An argument presents reasons for the disagreement.

Additionally, you have to search for the argument in amongst other text, such as descriptive writing, conclusions, supportive reasons and other research. It can be difficult to separate everything – a highlighter pen is very useful.

 Read the article abstract below and make a note of the descriptive writing, the background information, propositions, the supportive reasons, the argument, the theory and the conclusion. Do you think the piece is built on false premises?

'It is important to keep "wife battering" in its correct perspective and realise that this loose term is applied to incidents ranging from a very minor domestic fracas where no Police action is really justified, to the more serious incidents of assaults occasioning grievous bodily harm (which include scratches and bruising) and unlawful woundings (such as stab wounds). These more major incidents do not occur very often, and take up less time than the minor incidents, such as common law assault. Additionally, it is assumed that the private individuals who are involved in these incidents do not wish for police intervention and prefer to sort their family disputes out for themselves. Many of the "victims" drop all charges, realising that family life must go on. Whilst such domestic problems take up considerable Police time during, say, 12 months, in the majority of cases the role of the Police is a negative one. We are, after all, dealing with persons "bound in marriage", and it is important for a host of reasons, to maintain the unity of the spouses.'

Association of Chief Police Officers, Select Committee Report, 1975.

Theory:	
Argument:	
Descriptive writing:	
Background information:	
Proposition 1:	
Proposition 2:	
Supportive reasons:	
Conclusion:	

Tricks

Be aware! When it comes to analytical thinking, you need to pick up on the large number of underhand tactics that writers use to lure or persuade their reader to believe their theory or agree with their views.

Writers need to do this when they cannot find any appropriate evidence to illustrate their point, and it is a sign that they are desperately trying to win over their readers. A correctly written legal piece would not have to resort to such measures: if the writer has been objective and fair – and presented both sides of the argument – then the evidence should speak for itself and the reader should be free to make his or her own decision.

(a) Assumptions

An assumption is where a writer takes something for granted, or expects something to happen, when there is no proof that this will be the case. We make assumptions in our daily lives all the time:

It is acceptable for a writer to make certain assumptions. For example, a judge who delivers a judgment in a contract law case assumes that the recipient of the judgment knows the basics of formation of a contract, and so sees no reason to repeat the rules of offer, acceptance, etc. However, writers can make implicit (unclear) assumptions which are not easy to spot. If an argument is based on an implicit assumption, the whole argument may be built on a misconception. There are four ways in which you can identify implicit assumptions:

1 Statements or facts in the text appear not to be explained or supported by any evidence, thus not linking to the conclusion.
2 There appear to be gaps in the argument.
3 You are left with the feeling that more evidence could have been presented.
4 Conclusions seem to jump out of nowhere, indicating that a hidden assumption has been made. There is no logical sequence from argument to conclusion.

 Can you spot the assumptions and the loose conclusion in the text below?

> 'The amount of youth offenders on our streets is at its highest in 30 years. Many of them skip school, many more do not hold down stable jobs. The NHS is overwhelmed with incidents of underage drinking every weekend, and as a result there are more youths signing on for welfare than ever before. Therefore, the tagging system should be banned.'

What follows is an illustration of the assumptions and the unconnected conclusion in the above example:

> 'The amount of youth offenders on our streets is at its highest in 30 years. <u>Many of them skip school, many more do not hold down stable jobs.</u> The NHS is overwhelmed with incidents of underage drinking every weekend, and <u>as a result there are more youths signing on for welfare than ever before</u>. Therefore, <u>the tagging system should be banned</u>.'

Notice how the writer has assumed that youth offenders skip school and do not hold down stable jobs. How does he know that? He has also drawn from these assumptions that more youths are on welfare than ever before. He has assumed this fact without presenting any evidence. At the bottom of the statement, a completely unrelated conclusion jumps out of nowhere. The writer should not assume that, simply because we have a youth offender problem, the tagging system has failed. Where is the evidence for this?

(b) Implicit arguments

Implicit arguments fool the reader into thinking they have come to their own conclusion and made their own decision, when, really, the writer has planned all along to make a hidden point to persuade the reader into thinking that his or her theory is correct. This is a clever trick, as obvious and clearly structured arguments are more likely to be subject to criticism, analysis and evaluation, whereas implicit arguments are not obvious to the human eye, and so escape the usual scrutiny.

These are very difficult to spot, but if you find yourself forming an opinion whilst reading, reflect on whether you have come to that conclusion yourself, or whether you have been unknowingly lured into your conclusion by a cleverly structured argument.

This trick is often seen in advertising:

> 'Mystical Mya is on the line now. Are you looking for that special someone? Mya has led over 1 million callers to their destiny. Call now. Make your dreams come true.'
> 'Congratulations!! Over £1 million to be won! Call now to claim your prize!'

In these messages, the reader is being led to believe something which is not actually stated (and will probably not happen). For example, Mystical Mya is claimed to have led callers to their destiny and readers are urged to call her, leading them to believe that they too will be lucky. Readers will believe that they have come to their own conclusion, but they have really been persuaded by a hidden message.

(c) Connoted meanings

A connoted meaning is a hidden meaning lurking behind the obvious meaning. People are often accused of 'insinuating' something when they pass a comment, meaning that their comment has a hidden message. If you can find such meanings in a legal piece, you are more likely to be able to identify the structure of the argument, the reasons behind the arguments, the rationale behind the legal reasoning, and the premise of the conclusion.

Below is a statement with an obvious (denoted) meaning. Can you spot three connoted meanings?

> 'The law cannot continue to allow smokers to put non-smokers at risk.'

Denoted (obvious) meaning:
The law allows smokers to put non-smokers at risk.

Connoted meanings:
1 Smokers currently put non-smokers at risk.
2 The law currently puts non-smokers at risk.
3 If the law continues to allow smokers to smoke, non-smokers will be at risk.
4 If the law forbids smokers to smoke, non-smokers will be at no risk.

(d) False correlations

When things correlate, they are related and connected to each other. Arguments in a piece of text or a judgment must correlate, as must theories, evidence and conclusions. They must link together and follow on from each other. A false correlation happens when a writer presents an idea, argument or theory, and then writes a conclusion that is not linked in any way to what went before. The writer has assumed a correlation when there was none – this is a false correlation.

For example:

'The Legal Skills module is important in year 1. This is where our law students learn how to read and write in a legal context. They learn how to analyse and criticise the law in Legal Skills. Out of our 50 third year law students, only five did not graduate. It serves them right – they must not have attended the Legal Skills module.'

Notice how the writer argues that if a student does not attend his Legal Skills lectures, he or she will not graduate. How has the writer proved this link? Perhaps the five third year students did not graduate because they failed their third year modules, or were struck down by illness?

(e) False analogies

An analogy is another word for a comparison. Analogies can be drawn between similar things to help the reader to understand something, but analogies cannot be drawn between two different things. This will only confuse the reader, and it may be the writer's way of introducing something into his or her argument which does not really fit. If during your critical analysis of a piece you find a false analogy, you will suddenly be doubtful about the line of reasoning and the arguments in the whole piece. You will probably ask yourself: 'why has the writer made a comparison between two completely different things?' and you will not be as confident about the authority of the piece as you were before.

Unfortunately, false analogies occur in law quite often. This is because people have very different ideas about what the law is and what is right and wrong. When a writer compares his or her new theory to an old theory, some readers may agree with him or her and appreciate the comparison as it has made things clearer for them, but other readers may think: 'they are nothing like each other!' These kinds of false analogies are not malicious or intended, but sometimes a writer will intend to compare his or her idea to another idea with is clearly different to try to make his or her idea seem to 'fit'. As a reader you will be able to tell when a writer is trying to fit a square peg into a round hole, and you should instantly question why the writer has done this.

For example:

'It is submitted that the constitutional rules and regulations in the UK are out of date and need radical reform. As Smith contended, back in 1973, the cultural regulations governing Europe were out of tune with the many beliefs in Europe.'

Notice how the writer has compared his own theory to that of another, which is completely different. How can the constitutional rules of the UK be compared to the cultural regulations governing Europe?

(f) Signal tricks

Signals are an effective way of indicating to the reader that a new argument is about to be presented, or that a certain piece of evidence or research is being analysed. However, signals can also be used maliciously to fool the reader or to force the reader to go along with an idea that might not be supported by everyone.

For example, the writer may suggest with a signal that the argument is already proved and does not need to be dissected:

'... obviously there can be no arguing that Lord Denning misread the facts of the case. Clearly this has been an injustice and highlights the ambiguity of the law.'

The writer may also entice the reader into agreeing with him or her by stating that everybody believes the same thing:

'... as we all know, this area of the law is in dire need of reform. We all know that the case of *Smith v Chester* (1945) was a rare but significant oversight of the House of Lords ... surely there is a consensus that reform should be on the way ...'

Writers may also put people into categories:

'All decent people know that the abolishment of the death penalty was for the good of the people ... as intelligent people we believe that to be a part of the European Union, we must abolish all forms of inhuman treatment towards humans.'

These tricks are often used in law when a writer believes that a point is obvious. When you find these signal tricks during your analysis, highlight them and tease out the point that the writer is trying to make. Why do you think he or she needed to use a signal trick? Is he or she not confident that his or her point will be understood by the majority of readers?

(g) Emotive language

This trick is seen as unprofessional in law, which is a subject that values objectivity, rational thought, structure and clarity. There should not be any reason to provoke an emotional reaction from the reader if the writer puts forward his or her argument fairly and with substantial research and a clear line of reasoning. A credible article or chapter would put forward counter-arguments in a fair way and would not personally attack the other academics in the field to undermine them. If you are researching an emotive issue – many occur in criminal law, tort and medical law – be on the outlook for strong views from writers. Where the topic is emotive, readers are less likely to use critical thinking.

Below is a good example about 'battered women's syndrome' from criminal law:

'... these poor women are being held against their frustrated will, at the helpless mercy of the cruel and heartless men who drag them through their violent and demeaning marriage, only to find that society, and the law, turns its back on their desperate pleas for help.'

Notice how the words 'poor', 'frustrated', 'helpless', 'mercy', 'cruel', 'heartless', 'drag', 'violent', 'demeaning' and 'desperate' have been used to really bring home the writer's opinion that this area of the law does little to help women who suffer from domestic abuse. A published article of this nature would not attract much respect for the simple reason that the writer cannot show objectivity and has clearly not looked at any alternative viewpoints. If the writer has, there is a fair chance that his or her view is biased and the writer has interpreted the alternative views in his or her own way.

(h) Tautology

This is where a writer says the same thing twice, but uses different words. This can be infuriating for the reader, who is hoping to follow a clear and developing line of reasoning through to a conclusion, but instead finds that the piece does not make any progress or does not move any further forward.

For example:

'If the previous theory of Roberts was applied to this problematic contract, Timmy and Alexis would find that they could not enforce the agreement.'

'According to Roberts, this contract between Timmy and Alexis could not be enforced.'

Inconsistency

Analytical thinking at its best will highlight inconsistencies in even the most highly regarded work. It is vital when a writer presents a line of reasoning – and evidence to support it – that everything links coherently and logically. Nothing must contradict or detract from the main message, which must flow succinctly throughout the article, chapter or judgment. Your reader will become doubtful if he or she cannot follow your line of reasoning easily.

A very clever piece will consider alternative and opposing points of view, but will still revert back to the main argument, cleverly using the other views as evidence that the main argument is still the preferable view to take.

A consistent line of reasoning will do the following:

- Make it clear throughout the line of reasoning what position the writer takes and what he or she is trying to get across.
- Use signals to guide the reader through the writer's arguments, counter-arguments and evidence.
- Present counter-arguments and opposing theories in an objective and fair light, but present evidence to show why these are less convincing than the writer's main theory.
- Conclude using all the previously analysed evidence and research, and prove that his or her line of reasoning is correct.

The writer's conclusion *must* draw from the evidence if it is to be consistent. All of the reasons given throughout the text must be there to support the overall conclusion; otherwise the reader will feel that the author is including irrelevant material, which takes away from a logical structure.

Wording is also very important when it comes to consistency. A writer must be precise and critical of his or her chosen words if the writer is to present evidence to support his or her line of reasoning. A strong argument will be very hard to argue against, but a weak argument will fall down at the slightest criticism.

 Which one of the two quotes below are you, as the reader, most likely to argue with and find evidence to contradict?

'It is more beneficial to place young offenders on to rehabilitation programmes. Evidence has shown that they are less likely to re-offend.'

'The Offences Against The Person Act 1861 is out of date. It does not work in the courts anymore. Everybody is committing malicious wounding offences because they know they can get away with them.'

Meeting conditions

This criterion requires strong analytical skills and is at the heart of critical thinking. Every argument is a condition that must be met for the argument to be proved correct. If a writer argues that his or her theory is better than all the others, he or she must prove it. This is the condition the writer has set for him- of herself, and if he or she can't prove it, the condition has not been met, and the writer's argument loses all meaning.

For example:

'It is submitted that if the death penalty was reinstated, there would be a significant reduction in the murder and manslaughter rates.'

This writer has claimed in the introduction that if we brought back the death penalty in the UK, this would lead to lower rates of murder and manslaughter. This is a condition which the writer must now prove in the remainder of his or her article. The conclusion should draw on all the evidence and confirm that the writer has met this condition. If the conclusion does not correlate to the writer's evidence, or is based on false premises, his or her evidence has led to nothing and the piece is worthless.

To think analytically about whether a legal piece has met its conditions or not requires you to read the whole piece – from start to finish – and to focus in on what the introduction promises and what the conclusion confirms. If they match up, does the line of reasoning and evidence in between link them both together? Below are some critical questions you can ask about a piece when analysing conditions:

- Not necessarily – what if ...?
- If X doesn't happen, then Z won't occur.
- If X isn't true, then Z can't be true either.
- If it doesn't have that, then it can't have this.
- If it doesn't do X, then it won't do Z either.
- If X is true, then Z must always be true.
- If X is present, then that proves Z.

Misrepresentation

This is another element of critical thinking that requires strong analytical skills. When a person or a theory is misrepresented, they are put forward in an unfair or biased way. This is like bullying in the academic world: one academic will insinuate that another academic proposed something different to what he actually wrote, or that a theory is useless when it is highly regarded. Unfortunately, this does happen in law. To submit that he or she has something original, a writer has probably shown another popular view or argument in a negative light in his or her article or chapter. Judges may even do it when talking about a previous case and distinguishing it from the case facts in front of them (perhaps they did not like the argument of the leading counsel, etc). There are two common ways in which a writer can misrepresent the work of others: ignorance and trivialisation.

- *Ignorance*. Writers can choose to ignore the most successful facets of a theory, and simply put forward the minor points instead, which are easier to criticise. This makes the earlier theorist look weak. In addition, the writer may attribute certain beliefs and motivations to the earlier theorist which are untrue and unfair.
- *Trivialisation*. A writer may consider the chief argument of another academic, but make light of his or her view by using emotive language or signal tricks. For example, a writer could say of an earlier theorist's argument: 'they clearly want us to believe that ...' or 'clearly, this would not actually apply to the majority of us ...'.

Activity Look at the earlier theory below and then at the more recent article abstract. Highlight and explain the misrepresentation.

Old theory by Professor Smith: 'Let us say that a man has dug a hole and left it unguarded. He has a feeling that his enemy may come along and fall into the hole, but he is not sure. He leaves for home. Sure enough, the enemy walks along and falls into the hole. He is injured and is left alone all night. It would be difficult to say that the first man who dug the hole is guilty of assault. There should be an application of force to the body for there to be an assault. The act of digging the hole not only happened earlier, but it was not directed towards a certain individual at the time. At the time of the injury, the first man was not doing anything blameworthy.'

New abstract by different writer: 'It has been said in the past that if a man commits an act, he must do that act at the time of the harm. Thus, to do the act hours before does not count. This is incorrect. Let us take Professor Smith's example of a hole in the ground dug by A, which injures B hours later. It was said that this could never be an assault, but this is wrong. B has been injured by A's act. Professor Smith contends that A is not blameworthy, but he is. The digging of the hole happened with B's injury in mind, but this is denied by Professor Smith.'

Misinterpretation that I could identify:

....

....

....

Analysing the conclusion

Conclusions are vital to research. They allow the writer to draw together all the evidence, arguments, theories and contradictions in his or her piece into an overall evaluation. This is where the writer can interpret the area of law in his or her own way and may offer suggestions for the future.

A conclusion:

- will bring all the supporting evidence together;
- can present the writer's theory concisely and with conviction;
- will sum up all the disproved evidence and distinguish it;
- can illustrate the significance of the writer's theory;
- will present to the reader a way forward that is original.

Many students forget to add their own conclusions to their law assessments. This gives the lecturer the impression that the piece is not finished, and marks suffer as a result. Academics who publish in the field of law cannot make this mistake – they always add a conclusion at the end of their chapter or article, and judges always conclude at the very end of their judgment what they wish the outcome of the case to be and why. As a student of law you must find these conclusions and critically analyse them.

Finding a conclusion is harder than it sounds. They can be scattered everywhere as summary conclusions, they can appear at the beginnings of paragraphs to affirm the writer's position before he or she presents evidence to support it, or they can appear at the end in one large paragraph. Below are two examples.

In this example, the writer has placed a summary conclusion in the middle of his text before his evidence is presented:

'The law is in disrepute. Consideration in contract law has been unstable ever since *Balfour v Balfour*. The following modern cases illustrate this clearly …'

In this example, the writer has used signals to illustrate a rather wide conclusion at the end of his piece:

'The case of *R v Watershed* confirms Walter's view, above, that the provisions in this area of medical law are confusing and based on unstable grounds. This ought to affirm the belief that the malpractice area of medicine needs reform. It was highlighted earlier that Lord Viscount disagreed with the law of malpractice, and this indicates that more judicial unrest is on the way. Consequently, patients may have to suffer further delays whilst the Lords decide what avenue they would like to take.'

Notice how both pieces use signals to show the reader that a conclusion – however large or summative – is approaching. Good ones to look for include:

'Therefore …', 'So …', 'As a consequence …', 'Finally …', 'This ought to …', 'As a result …', 'This will …', 'This should have …', 'This must …', 'This means that …', 'In effect …', 'This suggests that …', 'This indicates …', 'Thus …', 'We can thus see that …', 'Consequently …', 'Because of this …', 'From this we can infer that …', 'From this we can deduce that …'

Look out! When you find a conclusion – large or summative – you will also find a group or a cluster of similar arguments/theories/reasonings to support it in the same place. Usually, writers will clump together conflicting arguments and supportive arguments, and they will almost always appear just before a conclusion which ties them all together, or just after the conclusion to illustrate how the writer reached that particular outcome.

 Below is a table containing all the guidance from this section to provide assistance when analysing legal articles, textbook chapters and cases. Use the table to help you analyse the following two legal extracts:

Extract 1: *R v Brown* [1994] 1 AC 212, per Lord Templeman

'In *Rex v. Donovan* [1934] 2 K.B. 498 the appellant was charged with indecent and common assault upon a girl whom he had beaten with her consent for his own sexual gratification. In delivering the judgment of the Court of Criminal Appeal Swift J. said [1934] 2 K.B. 498, 507:

"If an act is unlawful in the sense of being in itself a criminal act, it is plain that it cannot be rendered lawful because the person to whose detriment it is done consents to it. No person can license another to commit a crime. So far as the criminal law is concerned, therefore, where the act charged is in itself unlawful, it can never be necessary to prove absence of consent on the part of the person wronged in order to obtain the conviction of the wrongdoer. As a general rule, although it is a rule to which there are well established exceptions, it is an unlawful act to beat another person with such a degree of violence that the infliction of bodily harm is a probable consequence, and when such an act is proved, consent is immaterial."

The assertion was made on behalf of the appellants that the sexual appetites of sadists and masochists can only be satisfied by the infliction of bodily harm and that the law should not punish the consensual achievement of sexual satisfaction. There was no evidence to support the assertion that sadomasochist activities are essential to the happiness of the appellants or any other participants but the argument would be acceptable if sadomasochism were only concerned with sex, as the appellants contend. In my opinion … sadomasochism is concerned with violence. The evidence discloses that the practices of the appellants were unpredictably dangerous and degrading to body and mind and were developed with increasing barbarity and taught to persons whose consents were dubious or worthless. In my view the line properly falls to be drawn between assault at common law and the offence of assault occasioning actual bodily harm created by section 47 of the Offences against the Person Act 1861, with the result that consent of the victim is no answer to anyone charged with the latter offence or with a contravention of section 20 unless the circumstances fall within one of the well known exceptions such as organized sporting contests and games, parental chastisement or reasonable surgery.'

Extract 2: Ewan McKendrick (2008) *Contract Law: Text, Cases and Materials*, 3rd edn, Oxford University Press, at p 201

'*Selectmove* establishes, as a matter of authority, that *Foakes v Beer* remains good law and that it has not been undermined by *Williams v Roffey Bros*. That said, *Foakes* received a distinctly lukewarm reception in *Selectmove*. Had the matter not been governed by authority it seems clear that Peter Gibson LJ would have reached a contrary conclusion to that reached by the House of Lords in *Foakes*. But he does make one very significant point in relation to the extension of the "practical benefit" test to a promise to pay part of a debt and that is that its effect will be to leave the principle in *Foakes* "without any application". The reason for this is that payment of money will always constitute a "practical benefit" to the creditor. Thus the consequence of extending *Williams v Roffey Bros* to the case of part payment of a debt will not be to limit or confine *Foakes* but to undermine it.'

Use the table below to analyse the above abstracts.

Making critical analytical notes	
Name(s) of writer(s):	
Title of article/case:	
Title of journal/vol:	
Year published:	

Full reference:	
What does the title imply?	
What position does the writer take?	
What are the main arguments in the piece?	
Could you find any assumptions, implicit arguments, connoted meanings, false correlations, false analogies, signal tricks, emotive language or tautology?	
Are the arguments and reasons consistent with the evidence?	
Have the conditions of the piece been met?	
Can you find any misrepresentation of other views/theories?	
Do the conclusions draw logically from the evidence?	
Are alternative views provided along with the main line of reasoning?	
Are any theoretical perspectives included/challenged?	
Does the writer make recommendations?	

4.4 EVALUATING

The highest skill of all – above analysis, description, criticism and reflection – is evaluation. This is where the highest marks are found, and yet this is the element that many students forget to include. Critical thinking involves evaluating evidence, arguments, theories, facts, and everything in between. All law lecturers consider evaluation to be a vital skill in law assessments, but it must build upon previous description, analysis and criticism in your assessment before it will make any sense and add anything to your argument. You must demonstrate the full spectrum of skills – not just evaluation – to get top marks.

Bloom's taxonomy

Educational psychologist Benjamin Bloom developed a famous taxonomy of skills which students must display to perform at their best. Simple skills such as 'knowledge' feature at the bottom of the taxonomy, and high order skills such as 'evaluation' feature at the top. For example:

Skill	Importance
Evaluation	☆ ☆ ☆ ☆ ☆ ☆
Synthesis	☆ ☆ ☆ ☆ ☆
Analysis	→ ☆ ☆ ☆ ☆
Application	☆ ☆ ☆
Comprehension	☆ ☆
Knowledge	☆

Bloom believed that each level complements the next, and that an excellent assessment includes all six skills in their order of importance. As far as law assessments are concerned, Bloom is a good approach to take. You must have knowledge of the law certainly, but the laws that you claim to have knowledge of must be applied, analysed and then evaluated.

'Critical thinking' is a high order skill because it includes analysis and evaluation. Many students are very good at displaying knowledge and comprehension in a law assessment, but once it comes to application, the work appears to stop. Very few law assessments achieve over 70%, and it is usually because analysis, synthesis and evaluation are missing from the answer. This section will show you how to evaluate the work of others (during your research as part of your critical thinking), and how to utilise the skill of evaluation in your own work.

If you wish to use Bloom's taxonomy when structuring your critical thinking, here is a breakdown of the taxonomy into the individual skills that you will need to show for each level.

Skill	Indicated by	Example
Knowledge ☆	Words that invite a factual or descriptive response or a straightforward statement of law	Describe, define, outline, state, identify, list, what, how, when, which
Comprehension ☆ ☆	Words that require an explanation of the law, interpretation, or the ability to extrapolate key information	Explain, use examples, summarise, paraphrase, interpret
Application ☆ ☆ ☆	Words that suggest the need to apply the law to different circumstances or predict how the law would react to a new situation	Apply, demonstrate, advise, predict
Analysis ☆ ☆ ☆ ☆	Words that indicate that a case or a legal principle should be broken down into its component parts and subjected to close scrutiny	Analyse, assess, consider, measure, quantify, how far
Synthesis ☆ ☆ ☆ ☆ ☆	Words that indicate the ability to draw together strands of an argument and to identify similarities and differences	Justify, compare, contrast, distinguish
Evaluation ☆ ☆ ☆ ☆ ☆ ☆	Words that indicate that the law should be measured to determine whether it is effective, consistent, moral, desirable, better than before, or a useful solution to a particular problem	Appraise, criticise, evaluate, comment, reflect, discuss, how effective

(For further information on Bloom's taxonomy, see DR Krathwohl and LW Anderson (2001) 'A Taxonomy for Learning, Teaching, and Assessing: A Revision of Bloom's Taxonomy of Educational Objectives', New York, USA: Addison-Wesley Longman, 2001)

Notice how the skills become more and more complex and difficult.

At the beginning of this chapter, it was stated that evaluation was part of the critical thinking process. It is just as important that you form your own evaluations as it is for you to evaluate the theories of others. You can thus 'evaluate' in two ways – you can integrate your evaluation of the law into your assessment, and you can evaluate your own work when it is finished.

Evaluating the work of others

This is one of the most important skills that your lecturers expect you to demonstrate on your law course. Unless your assessment question specifically asks you merely to 'describe' the law, if you cannot evaluate the law, the theories of other writers and the articles and other works in the field, it is likely that you have only half-answered your assessment question.

Once you have successfully found and analysed the writer's line of reasoning, you must evaluate it. Many questions must be asked at this final stage, to show that you have taken a thorough and detailed approach to the law.

(a) Evidence and sources

The first place you should look is at the evidence provided by the writer. Just because you can see a lot of previous publications listed in an article's footnotes, this does not mean that the evidence is valid or useful. Additionally, an article or a book may use relevant evidence to illustrate a point, but the evidence does nothing to further the debate.

Activity Look at the three examples below. Which one uses the best evidence to support the main line of reasoning? Why? Which one uses relevant evidence that does not further the argument? Suggested answers are provided on our Companion Website.

Example 1: 'This contract is void. Sam and Jo have not provided the appropriate consideration to constitute a valid contract. This was held in *Williams v Williams* [1957] 1 WLR 148 by Denning LJ when he stated that unless any new circumstances arose throughout their temporary break-up, the husband should honour his promise to provide financial support to his estranged wife.'

Example 2: 'It is submitted that Hart is incorrect when he states that punishment is based upon the fault of the individual and should be measured against the gravity of the offence committed. This does not correlate with the historically accepted theories of punishment which purport that punishment is a tool of the people, to express their hatred and revenge towards the wrongdoer for hurting one of them. The work of Harris states: "punishment has well been considered an instrument of the harmed group in society, who, as a cohort, feel they are entitled to take their feelings of rage and injustice out on the perpetrator and to restore a feeling of balance and equity amongst the people." Harris has found much support over the years for his theory …'

Example 3: 'I believe that the laws on adoption should be changed. The current regulations are too complicated and ambiguous for anybody to understand them. There was a survey done back in 1996 in Birmingham which stated that 65% of the population would adopt. There should be a reform immediately.'

Notice how the third example has provided evidence in the form of a general public survey, but its results do not add to the argument that adoption laws are too complicated. The first two examples use good sources of evidence to support their argument: Example 1 uses a case authority, and Example 2 analyses an old but well-respected theory about punishment.

 Would you know how to choose relevant evidence? It will need to support your line of reasoning and further your argument. Below is a criminal law assignment question and a list of articles in the field. Tick the articles you think are relevant to the question:

Question: 'Critically assess the current state of the defence of provocation.'

☐ A Ashworth, 'The Doctrine of Provocation' [1976] Cambridge Law Journal, 292

☐ J Chalmers, 'Merging Provocation and Diminished Responsibility: Some Reasons for Scepticism' [2004] Criminal Law Review 198

☐ DW Elliott, 'Necessity, Duress and Self-Defence' [1989] Criminal Law Review 611

☐ RD Mackay and G Kearns, 'The Continued Underuse of Unfitness to Plead and the Insanity Defence' [1994] Criminal Law Review 546

☐ JC Smith, 'Liability for Omissions in Criminal Law' (1984) 4 LS 88

☐ RD Mackay and B Mitchell, 'Replacing Provocation: More on A Combined Plea' [2004] Criminal Law Review 219

Notice that sometimes you cannot tell by reading the title alone ... you may find yourself searching out these articles and scanning them briefly before you decide whether they are relevant to your research or not.

(b) Representation

The evidence provided must represent the group or circumstances it is standing for.

 Imagine you are doing a study into the nation's views on euthanasia. Which sample below would best represent the nations views?

'This sample is taken from a random selection of 25 shoppers in Oxford's High Street in November 2006. 72% said they were in favour of euthanasia being legalised in the UK, 8% said they did not know how they felt, and 20% said no to euthanasia.'

'A survey was conducted by the National Statistics Office in December 2007, which received responses from over 12,000 recipients all over the UK. 68% were in favour of euthanasia in the UK, 4% said they had no preference, and 28% were not in favour.'

Notice how the size of the group in the second example is larger and thus more likely to represent the country's views. It also comes from a more reliable source.

(c) Certainty

In law, not many things are certain. Theories can be updated, facts can be disproved, and outcomes cannot be predicted. However, when reading a law article or a textbook, writers can increase their certainty by making sure that their evidence is authentic, valid, and by applying critical analysis to the old evidence and theories.

For example, let us say that you wanted to prove that ASBOs did not have any effect on young offenders. In order to make your theory more certain, you would:

- find all the current authoritive evidence on the topic;
- critically analyse the evidence and look for flaws in their rationale;
- compare your theory to the current beliefs and present evidence for support;
- reflect on any other issues which might have been missed in past research;
- evaluate how your theory would be a better way forward.

(d) Facts versus opinions

When you are evaluating a legal piece written by another academic, you must look out for tricks in the text which are meant to persuade the reader to believe the writer's arguments. Sometimes, the writer may even state opinions as facts.

Facts can be proved with evidence. For example, a defendant may argue that he did not shoot his friend, but the prosecution may be able to prove through finger-printing, DNA evidence and eye-witness testimony that the defendant did in fact shoot his friend. Taking a simpler example, it can be proved that it is raining outside by walking outside and standing in the rain.

Opinions are personal views which are not based on proof or evidence. The majority may have the same view, but it is not a fact until it can be proven.

Activity Look at the quotes below. Which ones are merely opinions?

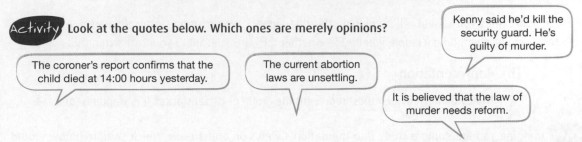

The coroner's report confirms that the child died at 14:00 hours yesterday.

The current abortion laws are unsettling.

Kenny said he'd kill the security guard. He's guilty of murder.

It is believed that the law of murder needs reform.

Notice how the first speech bubble contains a statement which is based on fact: a coroner's report is considered as authoritive evidence. The rest of the quotes are simply personal opinions, which are not based on fact or are yet to be proved.

You will often find well-regarded academics putting their own views across (two typical examples are provided in the bubbles above). But no matter how influential the academic, his or her view is only an opinion, and must be treated as such. This does, of course, mean that the academic's opinion is open to critical scrutiny, and this is how theories in law evolve.

(e) Eye-witnesses and interviews

In law, you may deal with a lot of eye-witness testimony, especially in criminal law. However, if this kind of evidence features in an article or any other legal work, be critical. Eye-witness testimony is, after all, somebody's *opinion*. There is no way of proving eye-witness testimony unless actual footage of the event is found. Additionally, if you are carrying out your own research and would like to interview people, the results you attain are also mere opinions, and the law cannot be measured against opinions, so be careful how you use such evidence.

Look out for:

- Memory mistakes – what was seen and heard may be misinterpreted.
- Interpretation mistakes – have things been explained to the interviewer properly?
- Forgetfulness.
- Recall problems – hearing other accounts may distort the memory.
- The blending of several experiences into one.
- The witness may enjoy being interviewed.
- Helpfulness – the witness may tell the interviewer what he or she wants to hear.

- The witness may benefit in some way from concealing the truth.
- Bullying, duress or intimidation – was the witness forced?
- The witness may not like the interviewer.
- Protection – is the witness shielding somebody?
- Promises – what if the witness has promised to keep secrets?

(f) Triangulation

This is a highly critical skill – it means comparing a set of evidence against another set of evidence to find an outcome – one which may be different to what the writer is suggesting. It requires you as the reader to do further research into the writer's theory. Triangulation is only undertaken by the really ambitious student, but your lecturer will be extremely impressed if you can show that you have undertaken further research to disprove a popular theory.

 Read the statement below. What kinds of evidence would need to be compared against it in order to triangulate what the writer is suggesting?

'The study of law has become increasingly popular in recent years. Many more females are taking part and are overwhelming their male counterparts. Universities nationwide are finding that they now have many law graduates and fewer training contracts. As a result, law students are able to investigate new and innovative careers with the police, in education, and in social services. There is so much choice that many law graduates cannot decide what route to take after graduation.'

Evidence I would triangulate

....

....

....

....

....

Did you think of: the other side of the story, evidence of the outcome, alternative explanations, published records, comparing statistics with other similar sources?

This further investigation of the law takes time but, if done properly, it will guarantee the highest marks. Make sure that you select your evidence and sources correctly, devise a clear line of reasoning, and put forward an original idea which is explained thoroughly in your conclusion.

Putting it all together

Activity Read the article abstract below, and then answer the evaluative questions underneath, presenting your answers in an essay-type format. If your answer flows well and is properly structured, you will achieve higher marks.

Christopher McCrudden, 'Human Dignity and Judicial Interpretation of Human Rights' (2008) *European Journal of International Law*, 19(4), p 655

'Despite its relative prominence in the history of ideas, it was not until the first half of the 20th century that dignity began to enter legal, and particularly constitutional and international legal, discourse in any particularly sustained way (but see Decree of 27 Apr. 1848 of the French Republic abolishing slavery in all French colonies and possessions, referring to slavery as an "affront to human dignity".) Several countries in Europe and the Americas incorporated the concept of dignity in their constitutions (Iglesias, 'Bedrock Truths and the Dignity of the Individual', 4 Logos: A Journal of Catholic Thought and Culture (2001) 114): in 1917 Mexico (Art. 3c.); in 1919 Weimar Germany (Reich Constitution of 11 Aug. 1919, Art. 151); and Finland (Pt I; General Provisions); in 1933 Portugal (Constitution of Portugal, 1933, Art. 45); in 1937 Ireland (Preamble); and in 1940 Cuba (Art. 32). It seems clear that the combination of the Enlightenment, republican, socialist/ social democratic, and Catholic uses of dignity together contributed significantly to these developments, with each being more or less influential in different countries. So, for example, in Finland the socialist influence was clear. In the Central and South American context, the social democratic/ socialist and Catholic influences were both significantly present (Constitution of the Republic of Costa Rica, 1949, Arts 33 and 56). Though growing, this constitutional use of dignity remained pretty marginal, however, until the end of the Second World War. It was not surprising, perhaps, that of the new national constitutions which incorporated dignity between 1945 and 1950, three of the most prominent (Japan, Italy, and Germany) were of defeated nations of the Second World War responsible for a substantial part of the horrors that the human rights movement was aiming to eradicate. In 1946 Japan (Art. 24), in 1948 Italy (the Constitution of the Italian Republic, 1948, Arts 3, 27, and 41); and in 1949 West Germany (Chap. 1, Art. 1(1)) incorporated dignity in the constitutional documents. In his 1950 assessment of post-War constitutionalism, Carl Friedrich identified "the stress laid upon the dignity of man" as its core value (Freidrich, 'The Political Theory of the New Democratic Constitutions', 12 *Rev of Politics* (1950) 215, at 217).'

Evaluative questions to ask...

- What does the writer believe?
- How far does his theory reach?
- Is it relevant to the topic?
- What are the implications of his theory?
- How do we know that what he is saying is true? Is there certainty?
- Where is the evidence to prove his theory?
- Is his evidence reliable?
- Are the sources of evidence credible?
- What reforms/alternatives have been suggested?
- Are the reforms up to date and relevant?
- Have any issues been overlooked?
- Are there any doubts that the evidence has not been reported accurately?
- Has enough research been done?
- Is thorough research indicated?
- Is anything irrelevant included?

- Could there be assumptions below the surface? Are there opinions?
- Have any tricks been used in the text to lead the reader?
- Are all avenues considered? Is the writer's view objective?
- What do we *not* know about this area?

- Does the writer contradict what is already known?
- Does the writer reflect upon the issues?
- Does the conclusion stem from the evidence presented?
- Is the piece original to the field?
- Is the line of reasoning consistent?
- How reliable/authoritative is this piece?

Notice that you are evaluating not only the sources used by the writer but how they are used by the writer and how the sources supplement the piece.

Evaluating your finished work

Students do not often evaluate their own work, which is a shame as it can help to enhance the quality of the work by some way. There are two vital elements of your assessment that need to be evaluated *during* the research stage:

- *Your sources*: Browse, select, compare and contrast potential articles and chapters, etc before you embark on your writing. Evaluate your sources carefully: there may be flaws in the evidence, gaps in the theories, or they may simply add nothing to your argument.
- *Selection*: Pick the sources that closely link to your own line of reasoning, and those that completely contradict it. Also pick sources that have contributed significantly to the field; challenge all previous theories; deserve a main mention as opposed to a passing reference.
- *Authenticity*: Are your sources likely to contain accurate information and are they recognised in law as a leading authority? Are they written by someone with relative expertise in law? Have they been recommended in leading textbooks or by your lecturer?
- *Contribution*: Have your sources contributed to the field of law? Do they contain original ideas? Do they list many other leading sources, indicating thorough research? Have new and more contemporary pieces overtaken the influence of your sources? Are the arguments too old to be applied to today's law?
- *Your evidence*: Is your evidence authentic? How did you find it? If you have used the writings of others (ie articles), you must evaluate these sources (as above). Is your evidence valid? Have you included irrelevant material or theories which are outdated and do not support your argument? Does your evidence support your line of reasoning, or do you need to change your approach? Have you found any contradicting pieces?
- *Currency*: Is your evidence applicable to the current legal climate? Have you checked very recent publications to see if there has been a new theory in the field, or a fresh perspective, which throws doubt on all the other arguments? Can your evidence stand the test of time?
- *Reliability*: Check your evidence for bias, subjectivity, assumptions and other writers' tricks if your source has been written by an academic. Additionally, there is no point in relying on a leading article if it does not support your own conclusion.

Case judgments are a more reliable source when supporting your legal reasoning. They are devised by judges who have a highly regarded legal authority, as opposed to academics who may exert bias, be subjective, raise assumptions and use other writing tricks. However, case judgments are still subject to critical analysis and evaluation, as sometimes judges can get it wrong too.

 Activity **Can you identify the leading journals and theories/writers in your different law modules? Write a list of them and show them to your lecturer, who may add his or her favourites to your list.**

Word counts

Evaluating your own work can also help you to reduce your word count. Students often submit assignments that exceed the allocated word count by some way, and this is an indication that some irrelevant material has been left in the piece. Most of your word count should be allocated to analysis and evaluation, not description.

Ask yourself the following questions when evaluating your piece:

- Is this word/sentence/paragraph relevant to the overall piece?
- If it is, how concise can I make it?

Buy a red pen ...

Why don't you mark your own work? This is a highly effective way of improving your chances of getting a better grade, because you notice errors in your punctuation and grammar, you can identify whether your legal reasoning is consistent throughout the text, and you can measure whether your arguments and evidence weigh up. This also contributes to your reflective learning capabilities, explained earlier in this chapter.

A badly presented submission will make a bad impression, even if the work itself answers the question perfectly. You will be surprised how often lecturers receive law assignments written in different fonts and sizes. If the difference between a 2:2 and a 2:1 is only 1%, it is well worth going through your final print-out with a fine-toothed comb before submission to give your work the best chance possible of achieving a high mark. Never think 'this is good enough...' or 'that will do ...' because you could be improving a good assignment with a little extra work. You will not suddenly become a first class student in your final year – these skills take time to build.

Self-assessment **Use the guide below to evaluate your own work:**

How should I evaluate my own work?	Tick when happy
Have I understood the law?	☐
Is my written style and presentation professional?	☐
Has my introduction set the tone correctly and made my aims clear?	☐
Have I made my underlying rationale clear?	☐
How are my spelling, punctuation and grammar?	☐
Have I organised the material in a logical way?	☐
Does my work illustrate a strong structure?	☐
Have I linked all of my separate arguments successfully?	☐

Is it clear that I have incorporated wider reading into the piece? ☐

Do I make good use of other writers' perspectives? ☐

Does my line of reasoning flow throughout the piece? ☐

Have I used appropriate signals to guide the reader through my line of reasoning? ☐

Do my main points clearly stand out? ☐

Have I included something that is irrelevant? ☐

Is the evidence that I have provided applicable? ☐

Have I provided accurate referencing? ☐

Are the arguments I have put forward relevant to the question? ☐

Have I shown that I can analyse the law? ☐

Have I shown objectivity and introduced other views? ☐

Do any of my personal thoughts and beliefs distort my arguments? ☐

Do I fairly evaluate the theories of others, even when they contradict my own? ☐

Is my conclusion based on the evidence? ☐

Is the balance of description to analysis and evaluation appropriate? ☐

Have I met the word count successfully? ☐

Have I included a bibliography and full referencing? ☐

5

Written and oral communication

Learning outcomes

> To appreciate the importance and relevance of communication skills in the study and practice of law
> To identify the similarities and differences between effective written and oral communication

> To improve your own performance when communicating legal information
> To evaluate and improve your communication skills
> To understand how to reference and avoid plagiarism in your written work

In the world of law, there is a unique way of communicating information. Whether you are studying law or practising law, you are expected to communicate with your peers, tutors and colleagues using specific legal language.

As a law student, you will notice in your textbooks that certain new words or phrases are used. There are many strange Latin phrases in law that are used regularly, and as a law student you will be expected to incorporate these into your research projects, reports, assignments, exams and dissertations.

When researching and writing your law assessments, you will need to reference your research properly. You need to do this in order to avoid passing off others' work as your own (plagiarising) and to show that you are putting forward a well researched and reasoned argument which is backed up by legal and academic authority. Correct referencing will also show your tutor that you understand how to find the law and how to use it correctly when communicating in a legal piece of writing. Many students lose vital marks through poor referencing, but, if done correctly, referencing can aid production of a polished and professional piece of work.

Many students are also unsure about their writing skills. How effectively can you communicate the law? Are your assignments and exams presented as well as they could be? Are you able to control your word counts? Can you cut down or enlarge the size of your introductions and evaluations? These small tricks lead to big marks if practised and presented effectively.

Finally, presentation skills are vital on any course. One day, you may need to stand in front of a judge and a jury in a court room and present a legal argument. Could you do it? How effectively can you present both yourself and your legal work? Do you get nervous? Presentation skills are, however, vital in everyday situations, you will have to attend job interviews, give presentations in class, speak at meetings in front of your peers, colleagues or strangers and present ideas or concepts to your boss, clients, family or friends. Many students have not had much experience of presenting in front of large (or even small) audiences and the more practice you can get the better.

5.1 LEGAL LANGUAGE

You may have noticed, when reading cases and textbooks, that the law uses special Latin phrases to convey a legal point. In addition, the use of the English language is complex and carefully expressed. This is also expected of you as a student! Your tutors will no doubt tell you what certain Latin phrases mean, but for the most part you are expected to learn them for yourself.

There will be ample help available in your law library, and a good law dictionary is a very helpful addition to any law course. But this is not all you need to do. Once you know what the Latin phrases mean, can you use them correctly in an assignment or in an exam? Reading the law also helps you to become acquainted with how and when these phrases are used. Leading textbooks are a good place to start.

Self-assessment At the bullet points below, list your thoughts about your current legal language standards. Do you think you write and speak like a lawyer yet?

* ....
* ....
* ....

The importance of communication skills

Whilst excellent communication skills are extremely important for all students in all subjects and professions, they are essential for any law student or legal professional. Communication is 'the tool of the trade' of any lawyer or aspiring lawyer. Legal language and legal words are the 'nuts and bolts' of any legal document, whether it is your law assignment, or a barrister's brief. Legal documents are usually of great importance – they establish contracts, create property deeds, confirm a marriage or a divorce, and report legal developments, amongst many other purposes. As a result, any legal documents that you create must be professional, set out appropriately, and free from grammatical errors. If you received a legal letter through the post which was messily handwritten on crumpled-up paper with spelling errors, would you trust it? Realistically, your writing will improve slowly throughout your course, but you must start as you mean to go on!

Legal communication can be written or oral. Your tutor will ask you to produce a number of legal arguments in many different forms throughout your course. Most will be written, but there will almost certainly be an oral presentation along the way!

Communication is something we all do and have practised since birth. As students you may already have significant experience in formal written and oral communication, for example: exams and coursework; job applications; UCAS personal statements; presentations; job and university interviews, and so on. Communication is an essential skill for lawyers and law students, and it is something that can often be greatly improved to enable you to achieve good marks in assessments as a student, and to satisfy clients, colleagues, employers and employees as a professional. One of the big advantages of a studying law at any level is the emphasis on communication skills. You can take these skills with you and continue to use them in your everyday life and in your employment, whatever the nature of the work.

All students should learn to:

- communicate effectively both orally and in writing;
- communicate appropriately to the needs of a variety of audiences;
- use the English language and legal terminology with care and accuracy.

For students on a quailfying law degree or undertaking a graduate diploma, mastering these skills is a professional requirement, and the Solicitors Regulation Authority and the Bar Standards Board – who regulate solicitors and barristers – also publish specific standards relating to the communication skills required of their trainees.

Student vs professional

Activity In the space below, list the types of written and oral communication you think you may be required to create or prepare as a law student or as a professional:

As a student:

....
....
....
....
....
....
....

As a professional:

....
....
....
....
....
....
....

Take a moment to look at your responses. Have you listed mainly assessments for 'students' and mainly letters for 'professionals'? This is a common misconception! Students may secure work experience during the summer months, meaning they may get the opportunity to draft letters and communicate professionally with clients. Additionally, professionals are required to present their ideas clearly before varying audiences, and they often need to write legible notes whilst listening to clients (almost like being in a lecture!). As a student, you have more in common with professionals than you think, and so your communication skills must measure up.

Legal communication as a student:

- Coursework
- Exams
- Presentations
- Debates and moots
- Feedback from tutors
- Notes from lectures and tutorials

Legal communication as a professional:

- Letters and emails
- Telephone calls
- Legal documents of all kinds
- Meetings with clients and other professionals
- In a court room

Effective communication

The key to effective communication is to understand and use language and legal words appropriately. When you are communicating the law, you need to ensure that your legal language has the 'WOW' factor!

(a) WHO is your communication addressed to?

As identified from the list above, you will see that you could be communicating with several different audiences. You will need to adjust the language, style and tone of your writing or speech to take this into account.

Activity List all the possible audiences you anticipate you will come into contact with as a student and as a (legal) professional in the space below:

....

....

....

....

(b) OUTCOME – why are you communicating and what outcome are you seeking?

You need to bear in mind the purpose of your communication. Again this will affect the language, style and tone of your writing or speech.

Activity List all the possible reasons for your legal communications as a student, and then as a (legal) professional, in the space below. Think about your potential audiences as you consider this:

....

....

....

....

(c) WHAT message are you communicating and what words, style and tone should you use?

What are you trying to say and how should this be worded and structured? The same language will not be suitable for writing an essay in an academic setting and for writing a letter explaining the legal position to a client.

Can you think of any significant differences between student legal writing and legal professional writing? Why do these differences occur? Do you think you would find it difficult to write a professional legal letter after writing numerous law assignments? Fill in the space below:

Differences between student writing and legal writing:

....

....

....

Thoughts about my current ability:

....

....

....

How do you feel about your current legal communication abilities? Are you confident that your law assignments and exams can convey a legal message that is not only appropriate to your audience but is written in the correct legal style? Do you feel that your presentation skills can illustrate, in an honest light, the legal view you would like to get across?

Activity Below is a good example and a bad example of legal writing in an exam answer.

Bad example	Good example
'The man who cleaned the windows didn't ask for any money beforehand. He had done it in the past for the same guy so he expected to be paid the same amount as last time. The man tried to get some compo but the courts wouldn't let him.'	'The claimant completed his consideration by cleaning the windows. The defendant's form of consideration was not discussed before the action was carried out. The claimant assumed that his past dealings with the defendant would imply payment. The claimant unsuccessfully brought an action for damages for breach of contract.'

Can you identify the main differences between the two examples? Below is another example of a bad piece of legal writing in an exam. Can you turn it into a good example in the empty box below? See a completed example on our Companion Website.

Bad example
'The drunk man stole some DVDs from the corner shop. He was arrested under theft. He went to court and his excuse was that he was drunk. They said in the court room that the drunk man needed to intend to steal the DVDs. He said he was so drunk he didn't know what he was doing.'

What factors went through your mind when turning the bad example into a good piece of legal writing? The following may help:

- the audience;
- being professional;
- appropriate tone and style;
- the space and size available;
- the point you need to make;
- any legal support to incorporate;
- length of legal explanations;
- special legal words and phrases.

Ordinary words having legal meanings

We have identified the importance of effective legal communication. The correct language and words are essential to presenting professional documents as a student and as a lawyer.

You will often find during your study of law that a normal, everyday word develops a legal meaning, and suddenly a whole case can turn on the meaning of that particular word and whether the parties and their actions have satisfied the meaning of that word. Indeed, the resolution of many legal disputes hinges on the interpretation of the language found in legislation and legal documents. For example, in *Stevenson v Rogers* [1999] 1 All ER 613 the case turned on the meaning of the seemingly straightforward phrase, 'in the course of a business', which is found in the Sale of Goods Act 1979. When these discussions occur, the case will often rule that the particular phrase has a separate legal meaning which must be applied in all further similar cases. *Stevenson v Rogers* was in fact distinguished (ie 'set apart') from *R&B Customs Brokers v UDT* [1988] 1 WLR 321, in which the exact same phrase had been interpreted completely differently for the purposes of the Unfair Contract Terms Act 1977. As a law student, you are expected to learn that identical words and phrases sometimes have varying meanings in different fields of law. This can confuse matters at times, but it is vital that law students learn just how important the seemingly plain meanings of everyday words are when interpreting cases and legislation.

'The nuts and bolts'

As with other disciplines, law has its own specialist language. It is important that you are familiar with and can use specialist legal language appropriately and that you can explain it to others. As a law student you will have to become aware that not only do Latin words exist in law, but many ordinary words have a specialist meaning when used in a particular legal context. Consider the following:

Word	*Res ipsa loquitur*	Consideration
Meaning	Specialist Latin phrase	Ordinary word with a special legal meaning

Regarding the words above, if you have already studied tort and contract law you should know the answers already! *Res ipsa loquitur* means 'the thing speaks for itself', and consideration is another word for 'payment' in contract law. As a new law student, you will be learning the meanings of these and many other strange words and phrases during your studies. If in doubt, or if the words are new to you, do not panic! This is simply one of the challenges of being on a law course, and it is a research skill you will need to master as a law student. Remember, you can refer to the relevant textbooks in a particular topic; sometimes they contain glossaries with helpful definitions. There are also specialist legal dictionaries – a law dictionary will be invaluable for new law students.

When is it appropriate to use a phrase?

You will notice that many specialist and technical terms in law are of Latin (or sometimes French) origin and appear more frequently in older law reports and documents. In recent years there has been a deliberate push to replace these with English phrases to help demystify the legal process and improve accessibility. For example, an 'ex parte' application to court is now a 'without notice' application, and the 'plaintiff' is now known as the 'claimant'. These developments are meant to help simplify the law for the lay person (ie the general public). They also help law students immensely! However, certain phrases have a specialist legal meaning and are regarded as terms of art and continue to be used. *Res ipsa loquitur* is an example of such a phrase.

When communicating to your tutor in an academic situation (for example, in an essay), if you use a phrase with a specific legal meaning, you will normally be expected to explain that term in detail. This will illustrate your legal understanding as well as your ability to use the appropriate legal word or phrase in the right context. When communicating the phrase to a fellow legal professional in practice, an explanation will not be required, although an explanation will always be essential when communicating to a client. In fact, the use of a Latin or specialist phrase should really be avoided altogether when communicating with a client to avoid confusion!

 Consider the following words and phrases. What do they mean and when is it appropriate to use them? The first one has been done for you. A law dictionary would be an excellent aid for this activity.

Word or phrase	Meaning?	In use today?	Appropriate to a legal professional?	Appropriate to a student or a tutor?	Appropriate to a client?
Res ipsa loquitur	'The thing speaks for itself.'	Yes	Yes	Both – but you may need to explain the meaning	No
Plaintiff					
Consideration					
Caveat emptor					
Obiter dictum					
Ratio decidendi					
Appropriation					
Mens rea					
Guardian ad litem					

How often do you use the above phrases in your legal writing? You will notice that some legal words and phrases appear only occasionally, but that some words and phrases carry such a significant legal meaning that they crop up frequently (such as *mens rea*). You will get used to these words and phrases very quickly. When you embark on your course reading, you will learn more about which legal words are still in use and where in a sentence they should be placed. Perhaps you could draw your own table and stick it on your wall: legal phrases on one side, and their meanings on the other. Remember, practice makes perfect!

Goal table!

- I will learn Latin phrases in my module!
- I will use them in my assignment and in my exam, with appropriate explanation!

5.2 NOTE WRITING

The skill of writing efficient notes may not seem particularly important at first glance. Surely all students know how to take notes in a lecture? Actually, it is surprising how many students do not record information effectively in their lectures and tutorials. Months later during the exam revision period, when rummaging around in the bedroom for old lecture notes, most students will stumble across old, tatty lecture scribbles that are illegible and make no sense.

Think about this: you only receive each lecture once. Unless you video record your lecture, or it appears on your virtual learning environment (most establishments use either Blackboard or WebCT), you will not be able to see or hear your lecturer explain that aspect of the law ever again! In the next week, your lecturer will move on to more complex issues, and if you do not understand your notes from your previous lecture, your knowledge progression will become stuck and you will reach a dead end. You will begin to fall behind, and you will need to do more work than everyone else just to catch up. In this section we will consider how to make effective notes, which are the foundation to your legal research for assessments. In order to do this, it is important to consider the 'when, why, and how' of note writing and the distinction between note taking and note making.

Self-assessment

My note-writing skills Tick the statement that applies to you...	I like to do this	I should do this more
I buy brand new stationery before my new academic term starts	☐	☐
I take notes in lectures	☐	☐
I take notes in tutorials/seminars	☐	☐
I make mental notes when I am talking to lecturers when they say something valuable	☐	☐
I use my notes later for revision or assignments	☐	☐
My notes have many pictures in them	☐	☐
I listen better when I take notes	☐	☐
I remember better when I take notes	☐	☐
I order my notes in a specific way, ie with colour coordination	☐	☐

Improvements I will make to my current practice:

....

....

....

....

When and why?

As a law student, you will have different reasons for making notes. Sometimes you may be receiving feedback. At other times, you may suddenly think of a very clever idea that you need to jot down before it disappears. Consider the occasions when you may need to make notes and why. In particular, think of the outcome you wish to achieve when writing a certain note.

Self-assessment In the box below list the occasions you can think of when you may need to make notes. Explain why you may need to make notes in these particular situations.

When?	Why?
Lectures	
Tutorials	
Other	

The diagram below illustrates some reasons why writing notes is a really good idea. You will find that making effective notes aids your legal studies in the following ways:

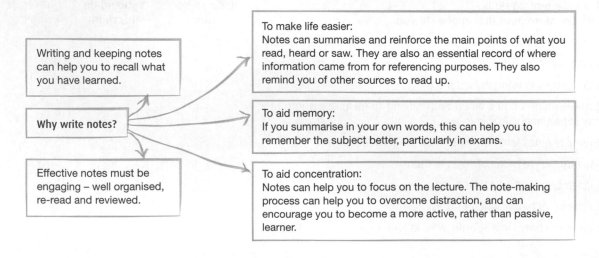

Writing and keeping notes can help you to recall what you have learned.

Why write notes?

Effective notes must be engaging – well organised, re-read and reviewed.

To make life easier:
Notes can summarise and reinforce the main points of what you read, heard or saw. They are also an essential record of where information came from for referencing purposes. They also remind you of other sources to read up.

To aid memory:
If you summarise in your own words, this can help you to remember the subject better, particularly in exams.

To aid concentration:
Notes can help you to focus on the lecture. The note-making process can help you to overcome distraction, and can encourage you to become a more active, rather than passive, learner.

From the listed advantages above, it is apparent that it is not just the process of writing notes that can help you learn; it is what type of notes you make, and what you do with them afterwards that is important.

Note taking or note making?

There can be a distinction made between note *taking* and note *making*, although both should feature in note-writing strategies. One leads to the other:

Note *taking* is the robotic process of simply writing exactly what you hear or read. For example, in lectures or printed texts, if the subject is an unfamiliar one, most students will find themselves repeating in their notes the exact same phrases they see or hear because they are struggling to understand the new and unfamiliar information. This style of note writing is often inevitable in lectures, particularly when students are trying hard to understand, follow, and keep up with what is said or written. It should be regarded as the first stage of the process and should lead on to note *making*.

Note *making* follows on from note *taking*. It happens largely when you leave the lecture and find some private study time in the library or in your room. You begin to review your notes, and start to reorganise them in a way that makes more sense. You make connections between points, and rewrite certain parts which were not explained clearly earlier. You may supplement your note making with a textbook to gather more legal information about that day's topic, and you will then supplement your notes with further research from the book. Your notes will then be in an appropriate form for revision at a later date.

Note *taking* is often inevitable in lectures, particularly when students are faced with new and difficult material. Lectures are often delivered at a fast pace, so most students concentrate on taking notes and recording accurately what the lecturer has said. However, taking notes should just be the first stage of the note-writing process. Note *making* happens when you engage more actively and creatively with the notes you have taken after the lecture. Note making can also lead to further research to expand and explain your lecture notes or prepare an answer to an assignment or tutorial question. You have more time in this situation to organise, synthesise and present your notes in a way that makes sense to you. You can change them to suit your own learning style! It also gives you an opportunity to be creative: why write dull notes when they can be interesting to look at?

- use colour;
- buy cue cards;
- reorganise your notes with your friends;
- create giant posters;
- record yourself reading your notes;
- draw pictures on your notes to emphasise a point.

Almost all students engage in note *taking*, but not as many then follow it up with note *making*. Why do you think this is? Note making is actually a very effective way to study the law, as students can engage in ongoing research and build their legal knowledge as they progress through their course.

 Look at the notes made below. What do you think the notes looked like before they were organised properly? Fill in the 'lecture notes' box to illustrate what the notes could have looked like before. It may help to recall what your own lecture notes look like straight after leaving a lecture!

Lecture notes	**Contract law week 4**
	Offer can be unilateral or bilateral.
	Unilateral offer made to the world: Carlill v Carbolic Smoke Ball Case.
	Offer made by the customer, offers not on shelves: Boots Case.
	Counter-offer cancels original offer: Stevenson v McLean
	Offer is terminated by death, time lapse and counter-offer.

How do I write notes effectively?

There are many ways to write effective notes. The 'best' method is the one that works best for you and your learning style.

- Visual learners: use colour!
- Audio learners: take in a Dictaphone!
- Kinaesthetic learners: draw doodles and mind maps!

Remember, note writing is a form of communication to yourself, so do not forget the 'WOW' factor, as suggested by J Maughan and C Webb (2005) *Lawyering Skills and the Legal Process,* 2nd edn, Cambridge University Press:

- **WHO** are you writing to? Even though you are writing notes for yourself, you still need to be able to read and understand them! Could you decipher your own exam script easily?
- **OUTCOME** What do you want from the notes and why are you making them? Consider whether you really want or need the information that you are about to record and, if so, which parts. Will it be useful in the future? How?
- **WHAT** Consider what information or bits of information you require, whether you have already got the information elsewhere, and what questions you want to answer from the information.

Working out how you prefer to revise and research will actually help you to decide how to write lecture notes. For example, if you like to use lecture notes as a foundation to exam revision, it would be a good idea at the start of your course to develop your lecture notes thoroughly in a way that works with your learning style. If you prefer to use your notes as a foundation to your assignments, make sure you highlight key points in your notes, so you know where to begin your research. Sometimes the odd off-the-cuff comment from a lecturer can point you in the right direction. Keep your ears open at all times!

 Describe in this box what your notes usually look like. Are you proud of your notes, or could they be improved?

....
....
....
....

Notes in style!

Essentially, note-writing styles fall into three main types:

- *Linear notes* – traditional recording information as it is presented using phrases, abbreviations, headings.
- *Visual or pattern notes* – using diagrams to present and link information and ideas.
- *Voice notes* – using a voice recorder or Dictaphone to summarise and record information in your own words.

There is no reason why visual elements cannot be integrated into linear notes. Many students doodle when they are listening – it helps them keep their minds awake and on the job! Making notes is a study technique that is open to new, creative and imaginative ideas. Having a wild and exciting way of taking notes will transform your lecture experiences.

(a) Linear notes

These are notes that summarise the law by using phrases, sentences, half-sentences and abbreviations, and they repeat the main points heard or read. To be effective, there needs to be effective engagement with linear notes.

Tips for effective linear notes
- summarise the main points from a lecture or other source;
- review and reorganise notes;
- connect and synthesise ideas;
- add your own personal comments and reflections on the ideas summarised;
- full sentences not necessary – use shorthand and abbreviations you can understand;
- leave space to add notes later;
- use headings;
- number points;
- link points with arrows, boxes, maps, by colour coordination etc;
- note sources (ie reference quotes and cases);
- use your own words;
- jot down main ideas, key words and sudden moments of genius;
- aim to have just one set of notes.

Do not
- copy chunks of text or attempt to write everything said in a lecture;
- rewrite notes just to make them neater: reviewing, organising and inserting additional information is the key.

Shorthand is another useful way of making linear notes, although symbols in particular can be complex to master. Perhaps it may be easier to start with the legal abbreviations first. Many textbooks shorten 'House of Lords' to 'HL' and so on.

Useful symbols, abbreviations, and shorthand			
Symbols		**Abbreviations**	
&	and	eg	for example
<	less than/smaller than	ie	that is
>	more than/greater than	p	page
=	equals	para	paragraph
≠	not the same as	ch	chapter
w/	with	D	defendant
w/out	without	C	claimant
∴	therefore	e/er	employer
∵	because	e/ee	employee
		t/ee	trustee
		HL	House of Lords
		a/p	Act of Parliament
		CA	Court of Appeal

If you want to be really creative, you can devise your own shorthand symbols and abbreviations, as long as you remember what they stand for! A common method is to write the first part of the word and then the last letter(s), for example 'dept' is short for 'department'.

You can use the space to below to keep a key of your own symbols and abbreviations to make your note taking easier:

Key to my abbreviations	
Symbol/abbreviation	**Meaning**

Note-writing records

It is an excellent idea to go into a lecture or a tutorial with a note template to write on. This instantly provides your notes with some structure and helps with note making later. An example of a template is provided below. Perhaps you could tailor a template to suit your own note-taking needs?

Lecture Notes	
Date:	
Time:	
Venue:	
Subject/session:	

Topic(s):	Main points:

Other important points:

(b) Visual and pattern notes

Visual learners in particular can struggle with traditional lectures and the traditional study of law which consists mainly of reading large amounts of text. You therefore need to tailor your note writing to suit your personality. Be creative in your note writing and try different techniques and formats.

Look at the mind map below. You can create something like this in a lecture to help you to link up ideas and theories. As long as *you* understand it, go for it!

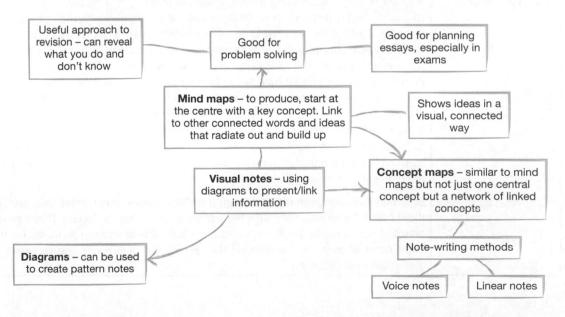

(c) Voice notes

Recording your own notes in your own voice using a voice-recorder or a Dictaphone to summarise key ideas can work well for some students, as it can help you to concentrate on your reading skills, and it allows you to summarise in your own words what you have read. The process of summarising what you have read, heard or seen into your own words can help you to focus on the main points and select the right words to express a particular idea. Some students think better when they are talking out loud. Listening to your own voice summarising the notes that you have made is actually a very powerful memory aid, and can be a particularly effective tool for revision. The tapes (or files) can also be replayed in many locations away from the library or allocated reading areas, for example you can listen while you exercise, drive or travel on public transport.

You can also record lectures, as long as you don't distract other students and ask permission from your lecturer first. This may seem like a good idea, and it can be helpful, but as with other methods of recording notes, you will need to make sure that you engage with the information, review it, and incorporate it into your own notes afterwards. Will you want to listen to the whole lecture all over again later on that same day? Recording the information may also be a disincentive to engage with the lecture at the time. If you want to record lectures you should check the policy of your institution and always approach each individual lecturer and ask their permission first. You may even discover that some lecturers create podcasts or videos of their lectures or summaries of them and put them on Blackboard or WebCT for students to access.

Trouble shooting!

Below are some common problems experienced by students when taking or making notes. If they have ever happened to you, fill in the self-help boxes below to take positive action.

Issue:	Solution:
'I don't understand.'	If whilst reading a textbook, a journal, a case, or listening to a lecture, you find yourself confused about a particular point, make a note of it either on your materials or in your diary. Read around the area first to see if any further research can clarify the point. Some writers explain principles in a very complicated way and others may provide simpler explanations. If you are still struggling, you can see your lecturer, but this is a last resort. Remember, you are probably deemed to be an independent learner if you are a university student, and you are therefore expected to research the law yourself. Sometimes you can ask your lecturer for help in the lecture if the principle you are struggling with is on the lecture slides, but some lecturers like to deal with questions at the end, so be sure of the rules before you put your hand up. Your lecturer will usually be happy to see you out of teaching hours, particularly if it is clear that you have already used your notes to research the problem before going to see him or her.

Sometimes you are given material in advance, for example lecture notes, or a case. Read them *before* the lecture, not during the lecture, and not after the lecture. They have been provided early for particular reasons – so you will be able to research them, discuss them, make notes on them, and understand the relevant law before your session begins. This aids active legal discussion. |

What I will do:

Issue:	Solution:
'I didn't hear.'	This may often occur in a lecture, and because one of the main aims of any lecture is to transmit information, lecturers will be happy for you to ask politely for repetition. However, if you are sitting in the back row of the lecture hall when there is plenty of room at the front, think more practically next time!

What I will do:

Issue:	Solution:
'I can't keep up.'	This is a common issue in lectures, especially if the lecturer is covering new material and it is complex law. If the lecturer is speaking too fast, a polite request for him or her to slow down will be welcomed. There is no need to write down every single word that your lecturer says, because lecturers often re-explain the points on the PowerPoint slides in their own words with several different interpretations to consolidate the legal point. Perhaps you could note down your own understanding of the principle rather than simply copying what the slide or the lecturer says?

What I will do:

Issue:	Solution:
'Do I need to take any notes if there is a handout or a PowerPoint presentation I can print out?'	What is the purpose of writing notes in lecturers and tutorials in the first place? Is it to simply repeat every word the lecturer says, or is it to jot down your lecturer's pointers when he or she expands on the material provided? Usually, even if there is additional material to print out etc, the lecturer will expand on it, highlight particular parts, re-interpret it, place it into a more understandable context, and use daily examples to illustrate how the principle is applied to everyday situations. Making additional notes will help you to engage with the material on a deeper level, link related points or issues to each other, or highlight points or questions for further research. The key issue is that students take the opportunity to help themselves to learn on a deeper level. Mechanically noting down everything that is said is usually a sign that you are not thinking about what is being lectured, and are not making the most of the opportunity to develop your own knowledge and understanding of the subject. Use any additional materials to help you to create your own set of personal notes.

What I will do:

Organising your notes

This is where you can be at your most organised and creative and tailor your notes to your own learning style and personality. There is no 'best' way to organise lecture notes, but a good start would be to keep them all in the same place, or at least write dates on them! Put simply, your notes need to be organised so you can easily find and refer back to them for legal information and research pointers for assignments, tutorials or exam preparation. It is a good idea to devise a system that works for you, and here are some suggestions:

- use a separate file for each subject;
- use loose-leaf, hole-punched paper so you can easily add and remove information (plastic wallets may be tidier but they create a barrier to updating notes);
- hole-punch additional material such as handouts and additional research on cases that you wish to keep;
- use dividers to separate topics;
- start a separate page for each minor topic;
- colour coordinate your subjects, topics or cases;
- number and label pages so you can find them easily and cross-reference them;
- aim to have only one set of notes per subject;
- consider creating an electronic set of notes. Many institutions use Blackboard or WebCT, which both enable you to access electronic versions of lecture notes, slides, recordings and any other materials which will enable you to create your own electronic database. Ask the ICT department in your institution about your options.

Self-assessment Why don't you swap lecture notes with a friend? How helpful are they and how do they compare with yours for accuracy, clarity and organisation?

....

....

....

....

5.3 PLANNING AND DRAFTING COURSEWORK

Whilst some subjects may be assessed by way of presentation or may require you to write a report or devise your own essay title, the majority will be assessed by way of essays and/or problem questions. You may be required to produce an essay or answer to a problem question in either an exam or coursework setting. In this section we will focus on writing answers in a coursework setting, although much of what is said applies to exams and other forms of writing as well. There are also many similarities in effective preparation and production of essays and answers to problem questions. In this section we will identify common principles that apply and highlight any differences to help you produce effective essays and answers to problem questions.

Note. Whilst essays are not often phrased as questions, the titles are often referred to as questions. In this section 'question' covers both essays and problem questions.

Self-assessment

Planning and drafting coursework Tick the statement that applies to you...	This is me!	I can't say that this is me...
I plan my work in advance	☐	☐
I have a favourite assignment structure that I have used for years	☐	☐

I never miss anything out ☐ ☐

I cover not only the important issues, but original and hidden issues ☐ ☐

I do my coursework well in advance ☐ ☐

I gather relevant information well in advance ☐ ☐

I mark my assignments with a red pen like a lecturer ☐ ☐

I am proud of myself when I submit an assignment ☐ ☐

I have never missed a deadline ☐ ☐

My biggest concern:

....

....

....

....

....

When an assignment question first lands on your desk in your lecture, whether it is an essay question or a problem question, the task ahead seems overwhelming. How do you start? Once you break up the sequence of work, however, it is not that bad! It is possible to identify six main stages of planning and drafting coursework:

1 Identifying deadlines and managing your time

2 Analysing the question

3 Gathering relevant information

4 Planning your structure

5 Writing and rewriting

6 Referencing

Once you have these stages clearly separated, the task ahead is not so overwhelming after all. In addition, your work will seem better structured, well thought-out, and rather more professional.

(1) Identifying deadlines

At the start of a semester, the submission dates seem a long way off – but they are not!

You may find that you have to write five or six assignments in any one semester, and that the submission dates for these are very close together – and also close to the dates of examinations.

If you have done little work to prepare for the assignments, the result is likely to be panic, as you rush to complete the work in time.

It is advisable to have a timetable for each semester, taking in both exam dates and dates for assignments. You need to think, too, in terms of stages of completion of work needed to write each assignment.

You can set yourself a strict time limit for:

- research and gathering information;
- writing first draft;
- rewriting.

The research and information gathering stages take the longest, but you need to have a cut-off date for these. So you really need to start the research and information gathering early in the semester – once you have the questions.

See also the section on 'Time Management' in **Chapter 6** for further helpful tips.

(2) Analysing the question

To produce a good answer you need to be clear as to what is required. Generally a good answer focuses on the question or issues raised, and demonstrates a range of written and analytical skills. It is also likely that you will be given an indication as to what is required by way of assessment criteria which may be handed out with the assignment. See the example of assessment criteria in 'Feedback' at **5.9** below.

You may also be given more specific information by your lecturer and will probably have been given the opportunity to practise the necessary skills formally or informally in tutorial or seminars. Ensure you take advantage of all the information and opportunities provided to help you achieve the best results you can!

As you can see from the sample assessment criteria, assignment questions usually require you both to explain the law and to demonstrate you understand it by applying it to the questions/issues raised by the essay title or facts of the problem question, and also subject the law to detailed analysis with reference to the appropriate authorities. See also **Chapter 4** for detail on analysis.

Tips for analysing the question

- pick the question to bits and identify key words by highlighting or underlining;
- reformulate the question into your own key questions but be careful not to change it into a completely different question;
- discuss the question and your thoughts on it with others;
- identify how many sections there are to the question;
- ensure you understand the common academic keywords used in questions (see the examples below);
- identify how the question relates to your lecture/tutorial material;
- make notes on your analysis of the question – visual or pattern notes may be useful at this stage;
- use the question to guide both your research and your writing – put it where you can easily see it and keep checking the wording.

Common Academic Keywords in Essays	
Word:	Meaning:
Analyse	Examine in very close detail; identify important points and chief features.
Comment on	Identify and write about the main issues. Avoid giving purely personal opinion.
Compare	Show how two or more things are similar. Indicate the relevance or consequences of these similarities.
Contrast	Set apart two or more items or arguments to draw out differences. Indicate whether the differences are significant.

Criticise or critically evaluate	Weigh arguments for and against something, assessing the strength of the evidence on both sides. Use criteria to guide your assessment of which opinions, theories, models or items are preferable.
Define	Give the exact meaning of something. Where relevant, show that you understand why trying to define something is problematic (eg 'poverty' is a notoriously difficult term to define). You need to look closely at the essay topic or question and analyse significant words.
Demonstrate	Show clearly by providing evidence.
Describe	Give the main characteristics or features of something, or outline the main events.
Discuss	Write about the most important aspects of the topic in question; give arguments for and against a topic; consider the implications of (a topic).
Distinguish	Bring out the differences between two items or topics.
Evaluate	Assess the worth, importance or usefulness of something, using evidence. There will probably be cases to be made both for and against.
Examine	Put the subject 'under the microscope', looking at it in detail. If appropriate, 'critically evaluate' it as well.
Explain	Make clear why something happens, or why something is the way it is.
Illustrate	Make something clear and explicit, giving examples or evidence.
Interpret	Give the meaning and relevance of data or other material presented.
Justify	Give evidence that supports an argument or idea; show why a decision or conclusions were made, considering objections that others might make.
Narrate	Concentrate on saying what happened, in the sequence that it happened.
Outline	Give only the main points, showing the main structure.
Relate	Show similarities and connections between two or more things.
State	Give the main features, in very clear English (almost like a simple list but written in full sentences).
Summarise	Draw out the main points only, omitting details or examples.
To what extent ...	Consider how far something contributes to a final outcome.
Trace	Follow the order of different stages in an event or process.

(Cottrell, S (2003) *The Study Skills Handbook*, 3rd edn, Palgrave Macmillan)

Key words in problem questions

In problem questions, the key word is usually 'advise', and you will be required to advise one or more of the parties involved in the facts of the problem. In an academic setting, the word 'advise' is normally used to indicate that you should both explain the law with reference to the relevant authorities as well as explain how the law would apply to the facts of the particular problem. When advising a client in a professional setting, you would not normally refer to the legal authorities and explain the law in the same way. In some problem questions, you may be asked to advise in relation to a particular aspect which may give you an indication as to what area(s) of the subject you need to focus on. In others, you will just be given the facts and asked to advise. You then have to analyse the facts of the problem to work out which particular aspect of that area of law you need to focus on.

Sometimes, keywords may be combined, and even those questions which appear to be mainly descriptive may require some analysis in order to achieve good marks. **Chapter 4** can help you to master this skill.

(3) Gathering relevant information

The information gathering stage is an important one, as it builds on the work you did in analysing the essay or problem question. Selecting relevant information is an essential skill in higher education and for assignment writing. You should take at least as much time with this stage as you do writing the answer.

As most assignments are fairly short in length, eg 2,000 words, you must ensure that the information you gather is *relevant* to the question – don't get sidetracked – keep *focused* on the question.

Ask yourself:

- *What do I need to know?* Be guided by your analysis. Remember, research is not the first stage.
- *What do I know already?* Make a note of what you already know about the issues from your lectures/tutorials.
- *What additional information do I need and where will I find it?* **Chapter 2** sets out the detail on researching a range of legal sources that you should refer to. The starting point will usually be lecture notes and the relevant chapter(s) in a good textbook, but do not limit yourself to just one book. Ensure you understand the basics and build on that by reading relevant cases and journal articles.
- *Is my recording of the information useful and well organised?* Refer back to the section on note writing and consider: Do I really need this information? How will I use this information in my answer? Remember to note your sources and organise your notes by referring back to your analysis and the specific questions you wish to answer. Try writing the questions/issues you have identified on a separate sheet of paper and note the source and location of any information relevant to that question or issue.

Make sure you give yourself a deadline for collecting the information. Most students enjoy this aspect of learning – but don't make information gathering a delaying tactic for writing.

Self-assessment

Look at the tasks below. Now that you have come this far in this book, are you able to do these before the planning and drafting of your coursework?

- [ ] I know where all the relevant resources are in the law library and how to use them.
- [ ] I can gather all the resources I need and all the resources that would take my mark higher.
- [ ] I can plan my time effectively and draw up a timetable for my coursework.

- [ ] My notes from my lectures are really useful – I can use them when planning my answers.
- [ ] I know how to critically analyse the law and I know what is required of me to get a really high mark.
- [ ] I am able to plan my structure in a way that enables my answer to flow better.

Things I have left to do:

....

....

....

(4) Planning your structure

Your answer should have a clear structure:

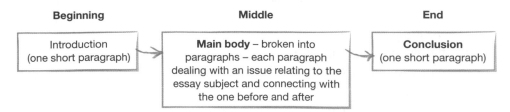

Beginning	Middle	End
Introduction (one short paragraph)	**Main body** – broken into paragraphs – each paragraph dealing with an issue relating to the essay subject and connecting with the one before and after	**Conclusion** (one short paragraph)

This sounds simple enough, and you are probably already aware of this. The important thing is to make sure to adopt this approach which can be applied to both problem and essay questions. The difference is that what you put in the sections will be slightly different. Although this structure sounds simple, problems can occur if you do not link the sections together or fail to have a proper structure to the main body of your answer.

Your structure should also be adapted to the structure of the question. As a general rule, if the question is in separate parts, your answer should be as well. See much more detailed guidance in **Chapter 4** about analysis and evaluation – key skills to show in your assignments.

Activity Below are some examples of essay and problem questions. Write your own definition of an essay question and a problem question from what you see below. List the differences between the two.

> 1 'Whilst certainty is an essential requirement for a legally binding contract, ironically, the legal principles regarding certainty are extremely vague.' Discuss with reference to case law.
>
> 2 Dragon Retail Ltd imports and sells toys from China. Dragon contracted to buy 50,000 at £5 each from China Link Ltd, the UK agents. Dragon had £100,000 worth of orders for the toy before Christmas. Due to production problems in China, China Link said the price had to be increased to £7.50 each to ensure delivery before Christmas. Dragon agreed as it did not want to be unable to fill its orders. In addition, Dragon agreed to Trade Union demands just before Christmas to increase staff wages and holidays to avoid a threatened strike that would have prevented delivery of the Christmas orders and put it in breach of contract with its customers. Advise Dragon as to whether it can avoid the contracts with its employees and China Link and recover the extra money paid.

Essay: ....

....

Problem Question: ....

....

....

Key Differences: ....

....

....

(a) Essays

These are the serious, one-line assignment questions which ask you to do some deep thinking, such as 'discuss', 'analyse' or 'evaluate'.

The essay introduction

The introduction will introduce the topic and set a direction for the essay. In the introduction, set out your interpretation of the essay and the questions you have identified and will be addressing in your essay following your analysis.

The introduction to the essay is important for two main reasons:

- to gain the reader's attention;
- to set yourself a purpose, clear direction and structure to the essay.

Two ways to get started ...

(a) The 'tell them what you are going to tell them' approach:
Example

> This essay will look at the following issues ... It will also be asked whether ... Finally the reform in this field will be investigated, and a new way forward will be suggested.

(b) The 'quote on quote' approach (but you also need to set the direction and structure):
Example

> 'The law of consideration in contract law is in disrepute. Discuss.' This essay will look at the law of consideration, and it will analyse the current case law in addition to recent developments in the area of past consideration ...

Your introduction should be short, ideally one paragraph and about 1/10th of your total essay.

The essay main body

Having set the direction and structure for your essay in your introduction, you then need to examine the ideas and issues raised in detail, referring to relevant supporting material, law and cases where appropriate. You need to structure your points and ideas in a readable, coherent form. This involves putting your points and ideas into paragraphs in a clear, logical order.

- Each paragraph in the essay should contain *one* main idea, perspective or point of view.
- There is no 'golden rule' about how long a paragraph should be. However, avoid very short paragraphs of just one or two sentences.
- One consistently effective approach is to have an opening sentence in each paragraph that introduces the topic. Move on then to give the relevant supporting material and legal authorities or evidence to support this opening statement, and think about how you are going to make a link with the paragraph that follows.
- The aim is to try to ensure a coherent and sequential flow of ideas. Key to a good structure and answer is ensuring that your paragraphs are linked in some way to create a logical progression.
- Words such as 'but', 'however', 'on the other hand', can be used to move on to a different point or idea.

- Words such as 'in addition', 'furthermore', 'similarly', 'likewise', can be used to extend a point or argument.

The essay conclusion

It is important to end an essay well. The concluding paragraph will be fairly short, again about 1/10th of the essay, and will remind the reader of the main points raised in your essay. It will leave the reader with a sense of completion and a sense that you, the writer, have explored the topic as far as was possible on this occasion.

The concluding paragraph will remind the reader of how your essay has answered the question. You do not always have to have come to a definite position on one side or the other, as in the more descriptive style of essay you may have simply been required to summarise the main theories of a topic. But you need to show that your essay has highlighted the main issues on both sides in a clear and unambiguous way.

There also needs to be a sense that you have reached the end of the essay. Sentences you could use in your concluding paragraph to signal the end of the essay include:

- 'In conclusion then, the main point is that ...'
- 'Finally, it can be argued that ...'
- 'The balance of the arguments suggests that ...'
- 'Despite the evidence to the contrary, it could be argued ...'
- Quotations, if relevant to the topic, can also be an excellent way of ending an essay, as they can make the reader think.

Remember to link your conclusion to the title and never introduce new ideas in your conclusion.

(b) Problem questions

Look back at your definition of an essay and problem question and the differences you identified. Do they both require the same things from you and, if the topic is the same, will the content and structure of an essay and answer to a problem question be the same?

In general terms, they both require you to be able to demonstrate knowledge and understanding of the law and apply and use the law, but there are key differences:

- An essay requires you to explore and analyse a particular topic which is normally readily identified in the essay title.
- A problem question requires you to analyse a set of facts to identify the relevant law and apply it to the facts. Usually, people will be injured, contracts will be breached, or someone's property will be damaged, etc. In a problem question the relevant legal topic(s) are not as readily apparent.

Demonstrating the ability to apply the law is key to achieving a good mark in a problem question as well as being a crucial skill for any lawyer. Your own institution may have a preference or its own guidelines. However, they all require you to go through four key steps:

- *Identify the legal issues.* You need to identify what aspects of the law you need to discuss in order to provide a solution to the problem. This means identifying the relevant legal issues, not just repeating the facts of the problem. Spotting the legal issues is a key legal skill.

- *Explain the relevant law*. You need to describe the relevant legal rules and principles with reference to the relevant authorities, ie case law or statute. Only describe those rules and principles that you need to help you solve the problem. Avoid including irrelevant material. In an academic situation, you need to be able to show that you know the law and where it is found.
- *Apply the relevant law to the facts of the problem*. You need to show how the relevant law applies to the facts of the problem, distinguishing or relating the problem situation to legal authorities as appropriate. This is another key legal skill.
- *Reach a justified conclusion*. Provide a conclusion that answers the question, ie summarises your advice.

Essentially, the structure for a problem question is the same for an essay and a problem question:

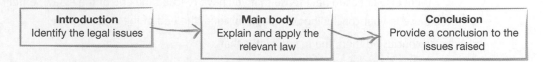

Introduction
Identify the legal issues

Main body
Explain and apply the relevant law

Conclusion
Provide a conclusion to the issues raised

Example of an introduction to a problem question answer

In some instances, even though all the essential elements required for formation of a contract may be present, it may be possible to avoid the contract if there was no true consent by one of the parties. In line with the principles of freedom of contract and the requirement for intention, if someone is forced to enter into a contract and does not enter it of their own free will, the law will step in and allow the unwilling party to avoid the contract. This is achieved through the application by the courts of the common law doctrine of duress.

Identifies the legal issue

To advise Dragon it is necessary to establish whether the conduct of China Link and the Trade Union is sufficient to amount to duress and allow Dragon to avoid the contract. To do so, it is necessary to establish the nature of duress and what requirements have to be met.

Tells the reader what you are going to discuss

Example of parts of the main body of a problem question answer

Duress is a common law doctrine that allows contracts induced by unlawful pressure to be rescinded by the innocent party. Essentially there are two main requirements for duress. Firstly a threat or compulsion overriding someone's free will and, secondly, the threat or compulsion must be unlawful. Originally the only type of duress that was recognised was physical duress ie violence or threats of violence to the person. This has clearly not happened here. However, because of the limits of duress and dissatisfaction with the rule in *Skeate v Beale* (1840) 11 A&E 983 that threats to property cannot amount to duress, the courts have developed the doctrine of economic duress.

Explains what duress is and the development of economic duress is introduced. Note the use of the linking word 'however' to move on to a different idea.

In *Occidental Worldwide Investment Corp v Skibs A/S Avanti, The Sibeon & The Sibotine* [1976] 1 Lloyd's Rep 293, the hirers of a ship renegotiated the contract price with the ship owners who accepted because the hirers said they would go out of business if a lower price was not accepted and that they had no assets and were not worth suing. The ship owner's claim for duress failed but Kerr J rejected the idea that duress was limited to physical violence to the person. He considered that if economic pressure went beyond normal commercial pressure resulting in a coercion of will depriving the other party of their ability to freely consent, English law would allow a plea of coercion and the agreement would not be upheld. In addition, he considered that the party alleging coercion should protest immediately and not accept or affirm the contract.

These principles were applied in the case of *Atlas v Kafco* [1989] QB 833. There the defendant's Christmas deliveries and ability to fulfil its orders would have been jeopardized had it not agreed to the carrier's demands to pay extra; otherwise the carrier threatened not to carry out their previously agreed contract to deliver the defendant's goods. The court held that the agreement to pay extra was voidable for economic duress.

Whilst there is nothing to suggest that either contract in this case was induced by physical duress, there is evidence of economic pressure because Dragon needed to ensure the Christmas deliveries were fulfilled and orders not lost. The question is whether this pressure was sufficient in either case to amount to economic duress. To establish whether there has been economic duress, the following requirements have to be fulfilled. ...

Example of application of the law to the facts of the problem.

Also introduces a new issue, ie whether the pressure is sufficient, for examination in later paragraphs.

Example of a conclusion to a problem question answer

In conclusion, the advice to Dragon would be that there is a very good case for arguing both contracts are voidable for economic duress given the nature of the pressure applied and the similarities to the *Atlas* and *Universe Sentinel* and *Evia Luck* cases in particular. However, it is important to note that this is still a developing area of law and the distinction between legitimate and illegitimate pressure is sometimes a fine one and is to some extent dependent on the facts. Even though the absence of illegitimate pressure may not be fatal, it would make Dragon's case very much more difficult to argue, as this is also a commercial case as in the *CTN* case where duress was not established on the facts and the court identified the difficulties of maintaining such an argument in a commercial situation. It will also be necessary to ensure that the contracts have not been affirmed and that Dragon has acted quickly, otherwise it may be deprived of a remedy as in the *North Ocean Shipping* case.

Activity What do you think of this example? Is it similar to your own work, or completely different?

....

....

....

....

....

....

....

(5) Write and rewrite

When relevant information has been gathered, the time comes to begin to plan the shape of your answer and to write a first draft. The hardest part is over; all you have to do now is write up your answers! The main points to bear in mind are these:

- The answer will need a clear structure, which will include an introduction, the main body and a conclusion.
- Some people just 'dive in' and start writing – but they usually have a rough idea about structure in their minds; the structure begins to take shape as they write.

- Others work out a rough plan of the structure, then start to write the first draft. If you are relatively new to essay writing, this often proves the best approach.
- The first draft should be written quickly, not worrying too much about style, spelling or grammar at this stage.
- Once the first draft has been written, leave it to one side for a few hours or preferably longer.
- Come back to the draft at regular intervals and ask yourself *'have I really answered the question?'* The answer will probably be 'no' or 'only partially', at this stage.
- Develop your first draft – you may need to do this two or three times before you are happy with it.
- Go over it for spelling and grammatical errors and correct these.
- Be ruthless and cut out irrelevant points.
- Make sure you have included evidence and examples to support your points and arguments.

Normally your supporting evidence will be legal authorities, ie statute, case law or academic opinion expressed in leading textbooks or journals. See **Chapters 2**, **3** and the referencing guide on the **Companion Website** for how to use and reference these materials:

- Make proper use of legal and supporting authorities. You need to relate it clearly to the points you are making in your answer. Just listing cases is not enough.
- Ensure you get the balance right between description/explanation of the law and application and analysis, as most questions require you to do both in order to achieve a good mark. Refer back to the **Chapter 4**, 'Critical Thinking'.

Problems when writing

Check out these frequently asked questions below from law students when planning and drafting essays and problem questions. Do any of them seem familiar?

'Where should I start?'

You do not necessarily have to start with the beginning, and you could start with the part you find easiest first, which may be a particular section or a more descriptive part. As you will be using a word processor at some stage, it is easy to reorder and move text around. However, remember your plan and stick to your structure.

'How should I start?'

For the 'tell them' approach try:

'This essay will firstly look at ... Secondly, it will be asked whether ...'
'To advise Freddie, it will be necessary to examine the rules relating to ...'

'How many cases should I use?'

The short answer is 'it depends'. In some subjects you will be using more case law than in others, but it is always a question of quality rather than quantity. If you are making a statement as to what the law is, you will have to refer to the relevant legal authority which may well be case law. Cases may also illustrate how legal principles apply and provide authority for the interpretation and meaning of legislation. The key thing is to ensure that the case is relevant and contributes to your answer and that you explain how the case supports the point you are making.

> *'How much detail on the cases must I put in?'*

Again it depends. The key thing is the legal principle or rule the case establishes or relates to, and putting in sufficient information in your answer to link the case to the point you are making. Just putting the case name in brackets or in a footnote, or setting out the full facts in detail without explaining how the case is relevant, is not an effective use of the case. To achieve a good mark, you need to explain how the case is relevant and how it impacts on the point you are making.

> *'What do I do if I do not know all the facts in a problem question?'*

Often facts may have been left out deliberately, and this allows you to briefly comment on this and mention the alternatives, but take care. Your answer should not invent new facts but answer the question on the facts presented. If you speculate too far, you will create another question and may fail to answer fully the question set.

> *'In an answer to a problem question, where there are several issues, do I have to explain all the relevant law first before applying it?'*

It is advisable to avoid including a large section of legal detail and then applying the law at the end. You will make your answer more focused and be able to explain the relevance of the law more clearly if you explain and apply the law to the different issues separately as you go along. This will also help your answer flow better and could save you words by having to repeatedly refer back to the law and authorities you have already mentioned.

Rewrite

If you have edited your first draft on at least one occasion, you should be ready to write the final draft. Do not submit a first draft unless you want also to submit spelling and grammatical mistakes, a bad structure and unclear referencing! Would you give a high mark for that if you were your lecturer?

- The assignment should be prepared on a word processor.
- As a guideline, it should have a margin of at least one inch to the left to allow comments by the tutor and 1.5 spacing between lines, unless instructed otherwise by your tutor. Find out if your institution and/or subject tutor have any particular requirements regarding presentation and follow any guidelines given. If there are no guidelines, consider our general pointers at **5.5** below.
- Before you hand it in, you could ask someone to read it for you, particularly to check for spelling or grammatical errors and to get feedback on how convincing or persuasive it is.
- Read you essay out loud. Listen to check if the meaning is clear and punctuation correct.

(6) Referencing

You need to ensure that your assignment is fully and properly referenced and the references and bibliography incorporated as appropriate. See **5.5** below for further referencing advice. Our guide on the **Companion Website** also shows you how to reference the law correctly.

Planning and drafting coursework: the key steps
● Manage your time
● Analyse the question
● Gather relevant information
● Plan your structure
● Write and rewrite
● Reference

5.4 WRITING EFFECTIVELY

We have considered the importance of written communication to lawyers and law students and identified strategies for producing and structuring certain types of writing you will need as a law student. Now we are going to look at some particular writing skills you need to master in order to write effectively. Bad English can lead to poor results. This is true in both academic and professional legal environments. We focus on coursework and exams but the same principles apply to other forms of written communication.

To achieve a good mark in written assessments, particularly coursework, your assignment must be well written. Spelling mistakes, grammatical errors and confusing sentences can interrupt the process of communication between you and your tutor. If an assignment is hard to follow or understand, it makes it difficult for a tutor to connect with your line of thought. This can cost you marks. To write effectively, you need to adopt an appropriate style.

 **My current written style is ...**

....

....

....

Style is about the way a writer chooses to express him- or herself. When we read something, we should hear the authentic voice of the writer. Unfortunately, this is where many people go wrong.

The best style of writing is that which is close to formal, correct speech. Imagine, for example, you were explaining an idea to a tutor, or making a presentation to a group of people. It is likely that you would speak in a formal way. You would not use slang, but instead make an effort to put your ideas clearly in good English. You might use jargon if there was a shared understanding of this between you and the tutor or audience. However, it is unlikely you would use words you did not understand, or words you regarded as pompous or pretentious.

The same rule applies to good writing

The test of good writing is to read it aloud. If it sounds formal but still natural, you have probably got the style and tone right, although you will need to check the accuracy of the grammar and spelling. But, if it sounds convoluted and pretentious and difficult to read aloud, it is likely to be all of those things; how it sounds is how it is likely to look and read.

Audience: your tutor and the invisible reader!

Remembering the 'WOW' factor, you need to consider your audience. Who are you writing to and what tone should you adopt? When you write an answer to a written assessment, bear in mind two readers. The first reader is your tutor who will mark it. The tutor understands all the law, theories and ideas relating to the subject. However, there is another reader – an imaginary one.

This is a bright, intelligent, imaginary person; one who is quite capable of understanding unfamiliar, complex ideas if they are explained in a simple, straightforward way. Write your assessment with this person in mind. Write as if you were explaining things aloud to this second reader. This means you will explain the background of the subject to this person, briefly define legal terms and concepts with reference to relevant authorities, sum up arguments for and against issues – using simple language – and ensure this invisible reader understands all the main issues. This invisible reader should be in no doubt at the end of your assignment what your main argument or point of view is. If you do this, you will not go wrong as far as writing style is concerned.

Adopt an objective style

One way to present ideas in a detached, objective way is to remove the term 'I', 'We' and 'You' from your writing. This is the style that is normally preferred in academic writing.

Alternatives can include:

'It can be argued ...'
'Arguably ...'
'This assignment will present the following point of view ...'
'Some commentators, notably Bloggs (1990) and Jones (1992), have argued ...'
'It may be that ...'
'This assignment will attempt to show that ...'
'One point of view is that ...'
'Another point of view suggests, however, that ...'
'There are two sides to this question. First, ...
'However, ...
'In conclusion, it can be argued that ...

Note. There may be occasions when a personal view is required or appropriate, and note any preferences indicated by your tutors.

- *Avoid abbreviations* such as 'they're'; 'didn't'; 'would've'. While these abbreviations are acceptable when communicating in a relatively informal way, they should not be used in formal or professional communication.
- *Write in continuous prose*. Use full sentences. Avoid lists and headings in essays and problem questions. They may be appropriate in dissertations and reports.
- *Be clear.* A golden rule in all forms of writing is 'good English is plain English'.

Tips for writing clearly

- *Use familiar words*. Keep it simple. M O'Connor (1991) *Writing Successfully in Science*, Taylor & Francis, gives an example of a student who once wrote in a science report:

'Although solitary under normal prevailing circumstances, racoons may congregate simultaneously in certain situations of artificially enhanced nutrient resource availability.'

This means that racoons normally feed alone but will group together if food is left especially for them. So why not simply say this?

- *Use specialist legal language appropriately* (see **5.1** above).
- *Do not include language you yourself do not understand.*
- *Write in your own words.*
- *Avoid old fashioned language*, eg 'aforesaid', 'hereinbefore mentioned', 'heretofore', 'inter alia', 'pursuant to'.
- *Be precise.* Avoid phrases such as 'Some academics argue ...' (specify which ones); 'It was stated in a case' (specify which case and by whom); 'The court may or may not decide that the defendant is liable' (specify what you consider will be the outcome and why. Why is there some doubt?).
- *Prefer the active to the passive voice.*

Active	Passive
The dog *bit* the man	The man was *bitten* by the dog

An **active voice** is where the subject (dog) performs the action of the verb (bit the man).	The **passive voice** is where the subject (the man) is on the receiving end (is bitten).

The active voice is more direct, closer to the way we speak; it gets straight to the point. It can help you save on words when writing within tight word-count requirements for assignments.

The passive voice can be and is recognised by the way the verb is formulated in two parts. Overuse of the passive voice can add unnecessary words.

Be concise

Use short sentences as far as possible. A sentence is more likely to be clear if it is short. Another good reason for shorter sentences in assessed coursework is to avoid exceeding the word limit and losing marks as a result.

There are four kinds of sentence:

Type	Construction	Example
The simple sentence	One sentence and one predicate or statement	'Two thieves robbed a bank yesterday'
The compound sentence	Two simple sentences joined by a conjunction	'Two thieves robbed a bank yesterday and stole £80,000'
The complex sentence	One principal statement and one or more subordinate statement or clause which modifies the main statement	'Two thieves, one armed with a handgun, the other with a knife, robbed a bank yesterday and stole £80,000'
The compound-complex sentence	All the statements have one or more modifying statements or clauses	'Two thieves, one male, armed with a handgun, the other female, armed with a knife, at 10am, on Peckham High Street, South London, audaciously robbed a bank yesterday and stole £80,000'

All the above sentences are clear, and any effective piece of writing will contain a mixture of sentence types and sentence lengths. This gives rhythm, pace and variety to writing.

However, compound-complex type sentences risk confusing the reader, as they present a mass of information that has to be navigated. To write effective 30+ word sentences requires a firm grasp of grammar, so that the main idea and modifying clauses in the sentence are clear, connected and coherent.

Long sentences can confuse readers; and the risk increases or declines in proportion to the writer's ability to punctuate sentences correctly. Use of the active voice also often produces shorter sentences.

Avoid redundant words

Why use four or five if one will do? Why use a longer word if a shorter one will do?

Activity Look at the table of words below. Redundant words are on the left, and more useful words are on the right. In the empty space to the side, there is room for two short paragraphs. Write a short paragraph about your current essay writing skills. How well are your essays progressing and how happy are you with your structures and references? Now repeat your paragraph again. In the first paragraph, use the redundant words to describe your experiences. In your second paragraph, repeat the same message using the shorter words. Can you see a significant difference in your word count?

Redundant phrases	Useful short words
ahead of schedule	early
a large proportion of	many
ascertain	learn
attempt	try
demonstrate	show
despite the fact that ...	although
give consideration to	consider
in many cases	often
made an approach to	approached
one of the purposes	one purpose
terminate	end
draw conclusions	conclude
take into consideration	consider

Grammar

This refers to rules of language that are generally considered appropriate. However, these rules often change over time, and so it can be difficult to know what is and is not appropriate. For example, you may have been told that the word 'different' should be followed by the word 'from' and not 'to'. Modern usage often replaces 'from' with 'to', and so this may now be appropriate. The word 'hopefully' is also considered by some as ungrammatical but is in common usage.

If in doubt, refer to one of the many reference books available and take advantage of the grammar checker on your computer.

Write in complete sentences

A common problem is failing to write in complete sentences. Additionally, do not start a sentence with a conjunction such as 'but', 'and' 'because' and 'or'.

Spelling

There is really no excuse for bad spelling. Whilst it may not obscure the meaning of your writing, it may make your reader think you are, at the very least, incompetent and lazy! This may not crucially affect your grade in an assessment, but could send out all the wrong messages in both an academic and a professional environment, and accurate spelling usually attracts some marks in assignments. If you are uncertain, you can use a dictionary, and when word-processing your coursework use the spellchecker to help you. You could also ask a friend! However, remember that the spellchecker will not identify incorrect spelling of homophones. Failure to correct these mistakes could impair the actual meaning of your writing and show a lack of understanding.

Activity Distinguish between the following commonly confused words below and insert their meanings. The first one has been done for you.

their: *belonging to them*   there: *in, at or to that place*

principal...

principle...

advise...

advice...

practice...

practise...

cause of action...

course of action...

precedence...

precedent...

affect...

effect...

Punctuation

There are many books written on English punctuation. One of the best in recent years is *Eats, Shoots & Leaves* by Lynne Truss. The extent of the success of this book surprised the publishing world, but highlighted the concerns many people have about punctuation. There are two particular areas of concern: misuse of the comma, and misuse of the apostrophe.

Comma confusion

The use or misuse of the comma is a particular problem. Misuse of the comma, for example, is a cause of misunderstanding in student assignments. Commas separate words, phrases and clauses. They usually indicate pauses in the spoken language. It is such an insignificant mark on the page, but a lack of a comma in the right place can change the meaning of a sentence. Take the following, for example:

'The solicitor said the client was entirely to blame for the failure of the case.'

This sentence suggests that the solicitor was putting the blame on the client; the emphasis is put on what the solicitor said: that the client was entirely to blame. However, the addition of two commas can completely change the meaning:

'The solicitor, said the client, was entirely to blame for the failure of the case.'

The commas now change the emphasis to what the client said about the solicitor: that the solicitor was to blame, not him!

Awful apostrophes!

The apostrophe is used in the following situations:

(1) To show where a letter, letters or figures have been left out

- 'It is' can be merged to 'it's'
- 'You will' can be merged to 'you'll'
- 'He is' can be merged to 'he's'
- 'Do not' can be merged to 'don't'
- '2006' can be merged, if appropriate, to "06'

Note that using an apostrophe in these situations is acceptable in informal writing, but should be avoided in formal writing for assessment purposes.

(2) To indicate possession

This is when the apostrophe shows ownership or possession of something by someone or something:

- The company's articles
- The companies' articles
- The judge's aims
- The case's outcomes
- Women's rights
- The system's complexity

For singular nouns and plural nouns *not* ending in 's', put the apostrophe *before* the 's'.
For plural nouns *ending* in 's', put the apostrophe *after* the 's'.
For singular nouns *ending* in 's', put the apostrophe *after* the 's' and you can *add another* 's'.

Some common problems

- *It's* – only use 'it's' when a letter has been left out and 'it's' is short for 'it is', eg 'It's an open and shut case'.
- *Its* – with no apostrophe, 'its' is used to denote possession, eg 'The Landlord is responsible for the exterior of the building and the Tenant for its interior.'

Plural problems

Apostrophes are not used to denote plurals and are not added to verb endings.

- So 'barrister's only' is a mistake, as it is referring to barristers in the plural.
- So 'CD's', 'Video's', 'Book's' and 'Gift's' are all common mistakes, as they all refer to these items in the plural.
- Another common mistake is to add an apostrophe to CV's. It should be CVs, if denoting plural.

 **Identify what is wrong with these sentences:**

1 The University is holding it's first 'Plagiarism Awareness Week' in February (13th–17th).
2 Its estimated that more than a thousand people were affected by the radiation leak.
3 The CV's were'nt particularly impressive I'm afraid.
4 The report was logical short, and reading it was easy.
5 The decision to introduce computers has already been made by the director's.
6 I decided not to take out the insurance policy on principle as its too expensive.
7 The BBCs response to the MPs criticism was to invite the MPs to take part in a televised broadcast on the topic.

....
....
....
....

5.5 REFERENCING AND STYLE GUIDES

It is important that you learn how to write academic essays and answers to tutorial and assignment questions early on, and one important aspect of academic writing is referencing. This sections sets out what is meant by referencing and why it is important in academic writing. It also gives an example of a referencing guide used in our law school.

Self-assessment You may hear your lecturers go on about it all the time, but correct referencing is vital on a law course. Describe in this box how you feel about your current referencing technique.

....
....
....

Definitions

'Citation'	A piece of information (usually a number or details about a source) that can direct the reader to a reference, eg Lockton (2011).
'Reference'	A reference lists all the information a reader needs in order to identify and locate the source that you have referred to in a citation, eg Lockton, D, *Employment Law*, 8th edn (Basingstoke: Palgrave Macmillan, 2011).
'Bibliography' or 'reference list'	The complete list of all the works that you have cited in your essay.

Why reference?

In your academic writing you are going to be thinking about other people's work, assessing it, criticising it and using it to formulate your own ideas. You will use academic and legal sources to help you build up your argument and get your point across. You will not be able to score highly without referring to legal sources and the work of others, and the best examples of academic writing incorporate sources into the text in such a way that clearly demonstrates your knowledge and understanding of the subject area you are writing about. When writing, it is crucial that you distinguish between your *own* work, ideas, criticisms and arguments and those of the author(s) that you have come across in your reading. This is vital because, by failing to reference correctly, you are presenting work someone else has produced as your own. This is plagiarism and all universities have very strict policies on plagiarism (see **5.6** 'Plagiarism' below).

There are a number of ways in which you might use legal sources or the work of others in your academic writing. You might paraphrase what someone has written, you might summarise someone else's writing or you might quote him or her directly. In all three cases you need to acknowledge that the ideas you are presenting are not your own. When you are using quotations, it will be obvious which part of the work is someone else's idea or argument. It is less obvious when you are summarising or paraphrasing, and it is therefore important that you make that clear in your work and reference the relevant sections fully.

Referencing systems

Referencing systems can seem confusing because there are a number of them and some are very similar. We do not intend to give a full explanation of different systems here, but you should be aware that there are a number of systems that you may come across in your reading:

- The MLA Referencing System (or 'Author-Date' System) – languages/linguistic and social sciences
- The MHRA Referencing System (or 'Footnotes' System) – humanities
- The Numeric Referencing System – science
- The Harvard Referencing System (or 'Parentheses' System) – used widely
- The Oxford Standard for Citation of Legal Authorities ('OSCOLA') – often used in law

Your department is likely to have its own referencing guidelines, and you should follow these meticulously to avoid losing marks for poor referencing.

Footnoting

Where do I put the footnote?

Straight after the source! Consider the following examples:

After a **direct quote** from another:

'To help with the provision of local legal advice, *"there are currently 66 Law Centres in England and Wales staffed by salaried solicitors, trainee solicitors, and non-lawyer experts in other areas like debt management."*[1] The money to run these comes from central government, from local authorities, and from various charities ...'

After mentioning the **work** of another:

'Malleson[2] gives an account of the various stages of parliamentary legislation ...'

After mentioning the **findings** of another:

'The output of Parliament is enormous, with 55 general public acts being passed in 2006 and 3,509 statutory instruments being made.'[3]

Notice how the footnote appears after the quote, after the name, and after the facts.

---

1   Slapper, G and Kelly, D (2009) *The English Legal System*, 9th edn, Abingdon: Routledge-Cavendish, at p 585.
2   Malleson, K (2007) *The Legal System*, 3rd edn, Oxford: Oxford University Press, at pp 49–54.
3   See note 1, at p 96.

Repeating footnotes

This is an issue which students find difficult. There is no need to repeat the exact same foot-note. Legal writing is more advanced than that (and the repetition looks unprofessional as well). So, you can type the following:

1 Slapper, G and Kelly, D (2009) *The English Legal System*, 9th edn, Abingdon: Routledge-Cavendish, at p. 96.
2 See note 1, at p. 98.

Notice that you can repeat 'see note 1' throughout a particular section. This is fine – the source you are using may occur more than once in your piece. Footnoting is designed to make things easier for the writer too.

> **Don't forget!**
> If you combine accurate referencing with excellent legal research, your assignment will look polished and professional.

Books

Author surname, initials (Year of publication) *Title of book*, Place of publication: Publisher.
For example:

Jowell, JL and Oliver, D (eds) (2007) *The changing constitution*, 6th edn, Oxford: Oxford University Press.

Journals

Author surname, initials (Year of publication) 'Title of article', Title of journal, volume and part number / month / season, page numbers.
For example:

Cherkassky, L (2007) 'Intoxication and diminished responsibility', Journal of Criminal Law, vol 71, no 3, pp 203–8.

Alternatively, the journal title, volume and issue numbers, and page references can be abbreviated as follows:

Connor, T (2005) 'Accentuating the positive: the "selling arrangement", the first decade and beyond' ICLQ 54(1), 127–60.

Cases

Party v party [Year] Case reference.

In your assignment:
'In the case of *Pepper v Hart** it was the opinion of Lord Oliver at page 53 that ...'

In your footnote:
[1993] 1 All ER 42.

Statutes

Short title and Year, Section (subsection)

In your assignment:
'It is an offence to place an embryo in a woman that has been created otherwise than by fertilisation.'*

In your footnote:
Human Reproductive Cloning Act 2001, s 1(1).

The Consequences

By placing the focus on the commission of the discriminatory act in preference to the condition of the employee, *Coleman* represents a fundamental development in EC equality law. In *Coleman*, the actionable discrimination by association was founded on the disability of a third party. However the general framework Directive providing for equal treatment in employment is expressed to apply to an arena wider than discrimination in the context of disability. 'The Directive' removes completely 'religion or belief, age, and sexual orientation' as grounds on which the employer is permitted to act.

Further, the employer may now find it more difficult to justify refusal of requests for flexible working from an employee caring for a disabled or dependant relative. Flexible working requests from carers must be carefully handled by the employer. There must be an equality of treatment in the response given to all those whose circumstances are not materially different; the carer must receive an equality of treatment in the employer's response as that given for example when the request concerns flexibility for child care. Further, employers may also have to take more care not to discriminate against employees on the grounds of the sexual orientation or religion or belief of close associates.

The ramifications of *Coleman* are huge, not only for the carer but for employees connected to people covered by other anti-discrimination legislation, such as sexual orientation, religion and race. An employee for example who is denied certain benefits because of marriage to a much older partner should be protected under age discrimination legislation, as should employees subject to harassment or bulling because of the sexual orientation of their close associates.

The case of *Coleman* refocused attention on the condition of the employee and thus offers a different way of looking at discrimination in EC law. EC law traditionally covers discrimination on a number of grounds and the *Coleman* case dealt with disability discrimination by association.

The consequences of the case are that employers are likely to find it more difficult to refuse flexible working requests and that they must handle such requests carefully. Equality of treatment must be ensured not only in relation to disability but also in relation to the other grounds such as sexual orientation and religion.

As Connor has noted, the ramifications of *Coleman* are huge. ...

Where would you add a reference and why?

Reference   Reason

1 ....

2 ....

3 ....

Students often worry that avoiding plagiarism means they have to come up with completely original thoughts and ideas which no one has ever thought of. This is not necessary (and may in fact be impossible!). You need to demonstrate your engagement with the task you have been set, and you need to demonstrate that you have understood and thought about the topic you are writing about. In doing so you will draw on previous knowledge and writings as well as on primary sources of law. If you present your own response to the questions set in sentences you have constructed, and reference fully any quotations and summarised or paraphrased sections, you will have nothing to worry about.

Locate your department's referencing guide and note down below where you can find it again if you need it:

The type of guide:	Location/web address:
Referencing guide hard copy – my copy	
Referencing guide online	

It is good practice to familiarise yourself with both the referencing guidelines and style guides as soon as possible, and get into the habit of writing and formatting your work in the way required from the outset. This will save you a lot of time in the long run and reduces the risk of losing marks for poor referencing or sloppy presentation.

For an example of a comprehensive footnoting referencing guide, see the **Companion Website**. Check with your own institution too.

Self-assessment

Referencing Tick the statement that applies to you...	Very confident	Would like to be more confident
I know how to reference in my assignments	☐	☐
I know how to reference law	☐	☐
I know how to reference books, journals and cases	☐	☐
I know where to place a reference in a piece of writing	☐	☐
My own referencing makes sense to me	☐	☐
I can see how referencing tidies up a document	☐	☐

My action plan:

....

....

....

....

....

Style guides

Style guides are broader in scope than referencing guidelines and include matters such as how to format your documents and present your work.

Activity Compare the two extracts below. Which one do you think is presented better and why? What advice would you give the author of the first piece? Record your points in the space below.

Extract A

The issues which this essay intends to discuss are central themes pertaining to the aims of the European Union and their objective of establishing an internal market within which free movement of goods can operate. The contentious statement under discussion relates to the European Court of Justice's jurisprudence and effectively considers the supposed problems which the distinction in the case of Keck and Mithouard [1993] caused. The ECJ functioning on the basis of the Directive 70/50 article 2EC (which provides examples of the measures that could be considered discriminatory against goods), wish to prevent any barrier that would hinder free movement of goods, which means they consider customs duties imposed by member states, and measures having the effect of a customs duty (MEE), internal taxation which affects products in competition and similar products. In addition the article bans quantitative restrictions and any measure having the equivalent effect of quantitative restrictions (MEQR); therefore if the measure is a ban on import or a quota which restricts the amount of goods that can enter that member state, then it is unlawful due to its inherently discriminatory nature.

Extract B

The issues which this essay intends to discuss are central themes pertaining to the aims of the European Union and their objective of establishing an internal market within which free movement of goods can operate. The contentious statement under discussion relates to the European Court of Justice's jurisprudence and effectively considers the supposed problems which the distinction in the case of *Keck and Mithouard* [1993] caused.

The ECJ functioning on the basis of the **Directive 70/50 article 2EC** (which provides examples of the measures that could be considered discriminatory against goods), wish to prevent any barrier that would hinder free movement of goods, which means they consider customs duties imposed by member states, and measures having the effect of a customs duty (MEE), internal taxation which affects products in competition and similar products.

In addition the article bans quantitative restrictions and any measure having the equivalent effect of quantitative restrictions (MEQR); therefore if the measure is a ban on import or a quota which restricts the amount of goods that can enter that member state, then it is unlawful due to its inherently discriminatory nature.

Advice for improving the presentation of Extract A:

1
....

....

2
....

....

3
....

....

Some universities have very strict guidelines about font size, line spacing and margins for example, whereas others do not. In any event you should check carefully, and if in doubt ask your tutor to ensure that you meet your department's expectations. If there is no style guidance available to you, bear the following points in mind:

- Small fonts are harder to read, especially when the reader is tired or is reading a large volume of material.
- 1.5 line spacing or double line spacing can make the text easier on the eye.
- Generous margins allow for comments and corrections.
- Number your pages.
- Include the question at the start or on a front sheet, especially where you are given a choice of questions.

- Using *italics* for quotations or <u>underlining</u> for highlighting primary sources of law can be useful to draw attention to key points but can also be off-putting and encourage skim-reading – check with your tutors what they prefer.
- Do not use colours in your documents; anything other than black ink can be very tiring to read and there are better ways to highlight key issues. You could use a quotation (properly referenced of course) or you could use italics or bold. Do not do this too often or for large amounts of text though – it should only be for emphasis where it is absolutely necessary;
- Think carefully about how you are going to hold your work together. Most tutors do not like plastic wallets because they have to remove your essay to mark it and put it back in when they are finished. That's fine once or twice but gets a bit much after 150! For most undergraduate work, a simple staple in the top left corner will do fine.
- Check carefully if you are required to list the word count and/or any information on the title page.
- Consider whether using sub-headings is going to make your work more readable and user-friendly, but check expectations as some tutors will expect you to write your essay without using sub-headings. Either way you should make good use of paragraphs.
- If your work is being marked anonymously (ie blindly), do not put your name on it!

5.6   PLAGIARISM

Plagiarism is another word for 'unreferenced work' or 'copying'. Many students are tempted to copy the work of others, whether it comes from a textbook, an article, a case judgment or from a friend. If a student deliberately takes another person's work and that student then declares that work as his or her own, he or she is stealing it.

What is plagiarism?

- copying an idea;
- copying a statement/sentence/paragraph;
- copying a theory or an idea;
- copying another person's explanation of the law(s), principle(s) in the case;
- copying a conclusion ...

... without referencing the other person's work, to pass it off as your own.

It takes academics and authors many months or years to write legal articles and textbooks, and to copy their work without their permission is considered to be morally wrong in all UK universities. Plagiarism is a very serious offence in UK universities, and students can be ejected from their course if they are caught plagiarising. In the academic world, plagiarism is equivalent to theft, and the plagiarising work is disregarded as worthless. Students will certainly have to resubmit the assessment that was found to have been copied or badly referenced.

You will be caught!

What plagiarising, students do not realise that it is very easy for a lecturer to detect a copied sentence or paragraph in their assignment or exam. Your lecturer is probably an active researcher in the field that he or she is teaching in, and is thus completely acquainted with all the academic material in that field. If a student takes a particular quote from a leading article in, for example, contract law, the lecturer will instantly recognise it in the assignment and will immediately search for the correct reference in the appropriate textbook. Even if your lecturer is not actively researching in the area of law upon which your assignment is based, he or she will have seen so many assignments on that topic that even the hint of a familiar sentence or paragraph will grab his or her attention. If referenced properly, however, the academic quote will attract high marks.

In addition to your lecturer being clued up about legal sources, the submitted plagiarised work appears 'patchy' when read. Many lecturers will notice that a badly written assignment will suddenly flow seamlessly and make perfect sense for a few lines, before returning to a badly written assignment again a few lines later. This is a dead giveaway that a copied sentence or paragraph has been slotted into the student's work without being acknowledged by a reference. Many UK universities also use electronic detection to identify plagiarism.

So why do students do it? There are a few reasons, all of which can be avoided if the student simply asks for help.

- **Reason 1:** The student is completely stuck and has no idea what to write when faced with an assignment question.
  Solution: It is best to go to your lecturer at the earliest stage of your course if you are so stuck that you feel that the only way you can get good marks is to copy from books and journals.
- **Reason 2:** The student has basic knowledge of the subject but is worried that his or her submission is not good enough to attract high marks.
  Solution: More research and revision is required throughout the course. This will build knowledge and confidence. Ask your lecturer if you can see an example of an excellent assignment to give you an idea of what is required.
- **Reason 3:** The student has no idea how to reference legal resources or has simply not correctly applied the footnoting system to his or her submission.
  Solution: Ask your law library for a referencing guide. Additionally, your lecturers expect you to pick up the basic rules on referencing once you have begun to read textbooks and journals as part of your course. Open any law journal and look at the footnoting system used.
- **Reason 4:** The student is simply lazy and does not want to write the submission him- or herself, and so uses other materials instead.
  Solution: This is an example of low motivation levels and a lack of dedication and respect for the course. If this student does not begin to pull his or her weight, the university will quickly ask him or her to leave.

Additionally, international students may not be fully aware of UK university policies relating to plagiarism, as the practices may be different in their home country. The UK considers academic research to be highly esteemed and something to be respected, but different countries may have different rules. The law library in each university will provide information about its current plagiarism policy.

 **Have you ever been tempted to plagiarise? Why?**

....

....

....

....

Types of plagiarism

There are four main types of plagiarism:

1 Straight-forward copying of another person's work, including the work of other students (with or without their consent), and claiming that it is your own or pretending that it is your own:

> **Legal source:** 'There is no case directly in point, but the prisoner was under a moral obligation to the deceased from which arose a legal duty towards her, that legal duty the prisoner has wilfully and deliberately left unperformed, with the consequence that there has been an acceleration of the death of the deceased.'
>
> *(R v Instan* [1893] 1 QB 450, per Darling J)

> **Plagiarised version:** 'The prisoner in *Instan* was under a moral obligation to the deceased from which arose a legal duty towards her, that legal duty the prisoner has wilfully and deliberately left unperformed, with the consequence that there has been an acceleration of the death of the deceased.'

> **Correct version:** 'Darling J agreed with Lord Coleridge CJ in *Instan* (1893) who stated: 'there is no case directly in point, but the prisoner was under a moral obligation to the deceased from which arose a legal duty towards her, that legal duty the prisoner has wilfully and deliberately left unperformed, with the consequence that there has been an acceleration of the death of the deceased.'*
>
> **R v Instan* [1893] 1 QB 450, per Darling J.

2 Presenting arguments that blend your work with another person's work, but not acknowledging the other person's work and passing it off as your own:

> **Source:** 'Critical thinking when writing includes most of the elements of critical thinking when reading. It can be more difficult to analyse your own work critically, however, and to recognize and admit to your own opinion and bias.'
>
> (Cottrell, S, *The Study Skills Handbook* (Palgrave Macmillan, 2008) at p 285)

> **Plagiarised version:** 'Critical thinking when writing includes all of the elements of critical thinking when reading. However, it is very difficult to analyse your own work critically. Students find it difficult to recognize and admit to their own opinions and views.'

> **Correct version:** 'Cottrell has highlighted a common problem encountered by students when incorporating critical thinking into university assignments. She notes that students find it difficult to analyse their own work critically and to recognize their own opinions.'*
>
> *Cottrell, S, The Study Skills Handbook (Palgrave Macmillan, 2008) at p 285.

3 Paraphrasing (rewording) another person's work and not acknowledging the original writer of the work:

> **Legal source:** 'Was it intended that the 100L should, if the conditions were fulfilled, be paid? The advertisement says that 1000L is lodged at the bank for the purpose. Therefore,

it cannot be said that the statement that 100L would be paid was intended to be a mere puff. I think it was intended to be understood by the public as an offer which was to be acted upon.'

(Carlill v Carbolic Smoke Ball Company [1893] 1 QB 256, per Bowen LJ)

Plagiarised version: 'Was it intended that the 100L should be paid if the conditions were fulfilled? The advertisement stated that 1000L was lodged at the bank for that exact purpose. Therefore, it cannot be said that the statement that 100L would be paid was intended to be a mere puff. It is submitted that it was intended to be understood by the public as an offer which was to be acted upon. This makes the advert an unilateral offer.'

Correct version: 'Bowen LJ in *Carlill v Carbolic Smoke Ball* (1893) noted that the deposit in the bank was an intention to be bound: 'the advertisement says that 1000L is lodged at the bank for the purpose. Therefore, it cannot be said that the statement that 100L would be paid was intended to be a mere puff. I think it was intended to be understood by the public as an offer which was to be acted upon.'* Thus *Carlill* represents a unilateral offer to the whole world.'

*Carlill v Carbolic Smoke Ball Company [1893] 1 QB 256, per Bowen LJ.

4 Colluding (working with) other students and submitting either identical or very similar work:

Jamilia's work: 'Lord Smith in *Peters v Coombs* (1945) stated that if a defendant does not see the consequences of his actions, he cannot be liable.* This is controversial as the earlier decision in *R v Holley* (1935)** perpetuated that a defendant who does not see the consequences of his actions but is reckless towards a dangerous consequence will find liability for his actions.'

*[1945] 1 All ER 879, per Lord Smith.
**[1935] 2 QB 445.

Beebi's work: 'Lord Smith in *Peters v Coombs* (1945) stated that a defendant cannot be liable if he does not see the consequence of his actions.* This would mean that a defendant would need to see the outcome of his act to be liable. This contrasts with the earlier decision in *R v Holley* (1935),** which stated that a defendant who does not see the consequences of his actions but is reckless towards a dangerous consequence will be held liable for his actions.

*[1945] 1 All ER 879, per Lord Smith.
**[1935] 2 QB 445.

Do not let the whole concept of plagiarism put you off using academic references in your law submissions. It is vital that you quote the work of leading academics in your law assessments. This is how you attract the highest marks. When you find an authoritative piece of legal research that you feel will really add something special to your assignment, as long as you reference the work of the other author correctly, you can include the piece in your assignment to analyse, critically think about, and evaluate as you wish. This practice is expected of legal researchers and will attract very positive comments from your lecturer. However, when you do use external legal resources to support your own work, they *must* be referenced correctly; otherwise they will simply be plagiarised. As noted above, many social science subjects use the Harvard referencing system, but law commonly uses the footnoting system. Check with your law school.

Plagiarism or sharing?

Below are some tips to help you differentiate between 'unacceptable plagiarism' and 'acceptable sharing'. This is often a difficult line to draw, particularly if you enjoy working with your friends.

- If you are discussing your work with a group of friends, do not write down their thoughts and ideas word for word. Your friends might later decide to incorporate their ideas into their assignment, and if you do the same thing from your notes, it looks like you have all colluded and there is no way of telling who the original author was.
- There are, however, certain things that student study groups can do without facing plagiarism accusations. Friends can share ideas, discuss assessment questions and lectures, search websites together, revise together, find cases and articles together in the library and analyse them, encourage each other, and test each other.
- If you are working on a group project, do not write anything jointly. Put all data, ideas and results into your own words. This way, your friends will not type out the same sentences as you.
- Group project writing tasks sometimes end up being split between group members to make the workload easier, and then shared out between all group members at the end. This often results in everybody submitting almost identical projects. Students are usually required to submit any individual reports or projects in their own words, regardless of whether they have been placed in a group or not.
- If you do find yourself working in a group project – which are popular on law courses – then there are many activities that you can share together. You can all decide on a title, a methodology, a research plan, a timetable for meetings, a writing strategy (ie style and format of individual reports), collecting cases and articles, taking notes, and analysing your findings.
- Do not share your assignment with friends, even if they are desperately stuck and you feel that you have done a good job of yours and want to give them a helping hand. If a single sentence is copied from your submission, the lecturer has no way of telling who cheated, and so you *and* your friends will face tough regulations.
- If it is you who is desperately stuck on your assignment question, do not 'borrow' words from your friends' submissions and put them in a different order or combine them with your own words. This is still plagiarism.

Fighting temptation!

If you are stuck for words and sick of reading the same sentence in your textbook, you will be tempted simply to copy from the textbook. Do not do it! If you cannot put the idea/theory/sentence into your own words, you may simply not understand the legal principle. Re-read the area and develop your *own* ideas.

- When you find a quote you'd like to use, copy it *exactly*.
- Use *speech marks* to show that it is the work of another.
- Make a note of *exactly* where you found the quote.
- Can you *recite* the principle in your own words without the book?
- Put the quotes of others in *different colours*.
- *Reference the quote immediately in a footnote.*

You are more likely to plagiarise if you do your assessment at the last minute. You would not have had time to form your own ideas and thoughts if you simply snatched the last book out of the library two days before the submission date in the hope that you would find the answer. When you plan in advance, find several sources, and read around the area for at least two weeks, you will form so many thoughts, theories and views that you will never, ever feel the need to plagiarise.

Why should I reference the work of others?

When you use your own words to explain a point of law rather than plagiarising the work of another, your lecturer can see that:

- you are able to think deeply and clearly about the law;
- you understand the topic and can form opinions and theories based on the evidence you have found;
- you have strong legal reasoning and critical thinking skills;
- you can apply original thinking, which in turn produces work of publishable quality;
- you can link new information to what you have studied previously;
- you are able to question and reflect upon the law and ask yourself whether what you have read is really true.

Activity Imagine that the abstract below is published in a popular law journal. You need to use it in your assignment. In the empty box below, use the research in your own paragraph to show how you feel about the death penalty in criminal law, but *do not* plagiarise it. Reference it properly. A suggested answer is provided on our Companion Website at www.palgrave.com/law/legalskills.

'Research from the state penitentiary in Texas found that defendants on death row live longer than those in the cells for life. Additionally, those on death row have a chance to think about their impending death, and repent for their sins. Two wrongs do not make a right. The victims' families will never be able to accept their loss anyway – why then kill the perpetrator when it does not bring the victim back?'

5.7 PRESENTATIONS

Presentations are popular on law courses. Many people who work in the legal field need excellent advocacy skills, because one day they may need to stand in front of a judge in a court of law and present their client's argument. To be a good advocate, you need to present yourself well. You need to be able to project your voice clearly, present your view succinctly, and reason professionally.

Why presentations?

Presentations have many uses in education, no matter what level of law you are studying. A few reasons for creating and delivering presentations are provided below:

- Presentations can make an area of law more exciting and accessible to students.
- They can encourage students to research an area of law in depth.
- Presentations make students actively engage with the law and how it works.
- They develop many vital skills, from communication skills to research skills.
- They mix together different views, beliefs, concerns, learning styles and experiences.
- They build individual confidence and group comradeship.
- They encourage students to take control of their own learning.
- They are good practice for the real world – your future career and interviews.
- They help you to project your thoughts clearly in everyday life.
- It is good practice for when you are a solicitor, a barrister, a legal executive, etc.

 **Fill in the table below to identify the factors you believe contribute towards a good presentation and a bad presentation:**

Good presentation	Bad presentation
✓	✗
✓	✗
✓	✗
✓	✗
✓	✗
✓	✗
✓	✗
✓	✗

Students can sometimes have a bad experience when presenting, which then puts them off presenting ever again!

 **Can you think of a presentation you took part in which did not leave a positive lasting memory? Make a note below of the topic, the length, whether you presented alone or as part of a group, what went wrong, and why.**

It is rare for the first presentation you ever do to go well, because you have never stood in front of your peers and presented before. You do not know what looks right, what sounds right, and you do not know how the audience is feeling. You simply have to work this out for yourself in the heat of the moment, and this is hard to do when you are so busy worrying about what the audience is thinking of you.

Self-assessment Have you delivered a successful presentation? What happened? How did you feel about yourself afterwards? If not, have you seen an excellent presentation by someone else? Why was it memorable?

....

....

....

....

....

Presentation skills

How do you feel about your current presentation skills? How much experience have you had of creating and delivering presentations? Perhaps you remember seeing a really bad presentation and think you would perform just as badly. Do you feel confident that you could deliver a perfect presentation, or do you not know where to start?

Self-assessment How confident are you about your presentation skills? Tick the boxes below to measure your current confidence levels.

Presentation skill:	Not confident	Reasonably confident	Very confident
I work very well independently	☐	☐	☐
I am creative and I can implement new and unique ideas	☐	☐	☐
I can transfer my imaginative ideas over into a solid piece of work	☐	☐	☐
I can make logical and practical decisions	☐	☐	☐
I can successfully execute a project from start to finish	☐	☐	☐
I can speak in front of large crowds of people	☐	☐	☐
I do extra research to feel more authoritative in front of the audience	☐	☐	☐
I can answer unexpected audience questions	☐	☐	☐
I can let go of good ideas if they do not work in practice	☐	☐	☐
I can listen to others and I can appreciate their views	☐	☐	☐
I can take on board new and exciting methods of presenting	☐	☐	☐
I can put my view across clearly in group situations	☐	☐	☐
I can lead a team efficiently	☐	☐	☐
I can plan ahead and I take group meetings seriously	☐	☐	☐
I can think rationally and can separate relevant content from irrelevant material	☐	☐	☐
I can offer balance, fairness and compromise	☐	☐	☐
I know how to overcome my nerves and I can offer support to my peers	☐	☐	☐

Are there any particular skills above which you feel you would never be confident enough to do? Make an action plan today to enhance this skill. This may be something as simple as practising in front of our mirror or in front of your family, or you may like to take a student support course at your university which develops general presentation skills.

Below is an example of a presentation observation by a lecturer. Do you feel you would attract similar comments?

Perhaps you could get together with some of your friends and create a mini-presentation for one of your lecturers to watch? Develop a feedback form similar to the one below, and choose some particular presentation skills that you would like to work on. Even basic feedback will be useful to you and will help your confidence.

Presentation observation

Date: *15th February 2009*

Venue: *Room 34, University Building, Main campus*

Time: *13:00pm.*

Group members: *Charlene, Neelah, Ahmed, Mike.*

Topic: *"How students can use critical thinking in their law course"*

Duration: *20 minutes*

Positive observations:
- *"Frequent eye contact and scanning of the room – good."*
- *"Clear ideas that are well expressed and easy to understand."*
- *"Gestures begin to open up as presentation progresses…"*
- *"Voice pace and articulation appropriate to audience level and understanding."*

Needs improving:
- *"Distractions – hands in pockets, fiddling with keys."*
- *"More smiling and a more friendly approach at the beginning would have enhanced presentation – put down to nerves."*
- *"Lack of preparation when changing speakers at one point – lack of rehearsal perhaps?"*

General comments: *"Connection to the audience improved towards the end – confidence to ask the audience questions. Preparation showed, good share of roles. Further subject knowledge required."*

Presentation observation

Date:

Venue:

Time:

Group members:

Topic:

Duration:

Positive observations:
-
-
-
-

Needs improving:
-
-
-

General comments:

Working with others

Creating presentations with your peers is one of the most interactive tasks you will do on your law course. You will have to work directly and closely with other members of your course, and you will get to know them personally. Law degree courses like to use this method of assessment in the first year, because if there are any problems with group members or content (ie lost USB sticks, failing technology, etc), the final grade will probably not count towards your final degree. Additionally, it encourages students to get to know each other at an early stage of the course, making sure that, by the second year, support groups and connections are up and running between you and your peers.

Are you nervous about working with your peers on a presentation? Students often worry that they will be put into a presentation group with people who are completely different to them, and so anticipate that their presentation experience will be a disaster and they will receive bad marks. These fears are very common when a lecturer first utters the dreaded words 'group presentation'. Perhaps you are usually a quiet student, who prefers to take a back seat and listen rather than talk? Equally, perhaps you are an outspoken student who always has something to contribute and has a clear idea of how to do things? You will find that you will have to compromise a great deal, but this is the very reason why your lecturers plan presentations into your course. You learn all the professional skills you need – in double quick time – when you take part in creating and delivering a group presentation.

Below are lists of all the new skills you learn when working on a group presentation. *All* of the skills below are considered to be of vital importance by employers, no matter what job you aim for, and no matter which field you work in.

Presentation skills

New skills
- Putting forward your view
- Breaking routine with new ideas
- Trying something unique
- Re-addressing your priorities
- Improving oral communication
- Developing competitive skills
- Becoming aware of how you influence others
- Managing projects professionally
- Working with people from different faiths
- Negotiating with difficult people
- Being polite and courteous
- Learning to share
- Encouraging each other
- Learning to assist others
- Testing your learning style

New skills
- Using your creativity
- Listening to others
- Enhancing your timekeeping skills
- Developing your organisational skills
- Making authoritative decisions
- Being assertive
- Using your imagination
- Showing sensitivity to the opinions of others
- Considering new ideas
- Taking responsibility for your actions
- Sharing a large pool of experience
- Learning how to handle criticism

How many of the skills above do you believe you are highly competent in? Many law students have never experienced a full-time professional job before, and so have never had to use many of these skills in practice. You will experience and enhance them all when you develop your group presentation.

Going it alone

Look at the list below, which highlights some common fears when a lone student is faced with doing a presentation by him- or herself. Have any of the factors below affected you when you have performed on your own?

- lack of preparation;
- lack of support if presenting alone;
- not getting on with your audience;
- being formally assessed;
- strong accent/low level of English;
- being judged by others;
- being the centre of attention; 'not getting it right';
- letting yourself, your lecturer, and your audience down;
- worried about being worried;
- showing vulnerability.

These happen to everybody! Don't worry – your peers will not be able to tell how you are feeling on the inside if you stay composed on the outside.

Presentation time!

Write your presentation task/title here, even if it is only a practice presentation:

....

....

....

....

....

....

....

....

....

....

There follows below guidance when planning and building your presentation, including ways in which you can combat your nerves, whether you are presenting alone or in a group.

(a) Building your presentation

This is the most important stage of your entire presentation: if you do not plan and build your presentation correctly, you will have nothing to show for your work on presentation day.

One of the main considerations you (and any co-presenters) must take into account is the make-up of your audience. Ideally, your entire presentation should be totally geared towards their needs.

• Who will be in the audience? • What is the audience's role in your presentation? • What age/ethnicity is the audience? Are there any special considerations to make? • How much background information would the audience appreciate? • How does the audience feel about the topic itself? If they are negative, how would this be dealt with in a way that suits them?	• What will the audience already know about the subject/topic? • Why should the audience be interested in your presentation? • Will the audience have any expectations? • Is the audience knowledgeable in the topic, experts, or new to it? • What will the audience know/need to know about the presenter(s)?

Whether you are going out there alone or working in a group, the guidance below is key to building a successful presentation:

- Build your presentation as soon as you get the green light from your lecturer. Once you receive your topic, you are ready to prepare. If you are working in a group, email your group members on the same day as you get the go-ahead and do not wait around for their responses. Begin your research as soon as you have a free hour in your timetable.

- If your presentation is a formal assessment (ie it is graded and that grade contributes towards the official result of your course), your lecturer will tell you clearly what is expected of you. Find out how much time you will have for your presentation so that you can plan ahead.

- Meet up with your group members often. Exchange mobile numbers and chase up any non-attendees. Most planning and building decisions cannot be made in group presentations if somebody is missing from the meeting. There arises a risk that the missing person feels left out, and he or she might have a valid reason for their non-attendance, such as illness.

- Be strict with yourself and set aside some time every day or every week to work on your presentation. Remember, slow and steady progress is solid progress.

- During the building stage, there are three main questions which you must ask yourself before embarking on research: (1) What is the aim of our presentation and how does it contribute to the module? Is our main point/idea/topic clear? (2) Who is our audience? Are we building upon our audience's current base knowledge? (3) How much time have we been allotted for our presentation? Once you have pinpointed the scope of your presentation, start planning your research.

- Make sure that, during the building stages, you stick to your topic and do not deviate from your aim, which should be clearly placed in the introduction to your presentation. By simply sticking to one specific topic/idea/theory throughout the whole presentation, your audience is able to pick up on the common thread that runs all the way through your work.

- Make sure your content is relevant and applicable to the needs and interests of your audience. Who will be watching you on the day? What is their experience and knowledge of your topic? Make sure that, during the building stages, you build and plan according to your audience's needs.

- Make sure everybody plays a part in building the presentation, and everybody has a chance to speak during the presentation. These roles are allocated during the building stage. Your lecturer will not be impressed if only half of you in the group speak – he or she will be left with the impression that not all of you did the work.
- Research, research, research. You will stand with confidence and will speak with authority if you know in your mind that you have all the knowledge that you need to answer unexpected questions. When you do find and incorporate your research, make sure it is all *relevant* to your main aim.
- Include daily, familiar examples to support your points. Formal legal research is always a good bet, but practical everyday examples are also very useful and illustrative, and provide your audience with a strong connection to their own lives and gives them something to think about.
- If you would like to do any experimenting with your delivery, this is the stage to consider it. If you are using PowerPoint, supplement it with other aids so you do not bore your audience. You can also consider a whiteboard (interactive or traditional), flipcharts, posters, acetates and overhead projectors, handouts or group exercises. If you decide that you would like to use several methods of delivery (be careful not to overload yourself) then take a note of it for now and complete your research first.
- This may sound obvious but, somehow, most students forget the following advice: make sure your presentation has a clear structure: a beginning, a middle and an ending. The beginning is your introduction complete with your aim, the middle is the bulk of the presentation and explores your findings, and the ending sums up what you have found and proves your aim. Once you have established these three parts, make sure they link together well. Does your presentation flow easily? Is the sequence easy to follow?

Self-assessment

Building and planning tasks to do...	Tick when complete
Start planning and emailing when lecturer gives green light	☐
Find marking scheme and time allocation for presentation	☐
Meet with group members often	☐
Strictly set aside presentation time every day or every week	☐
Stick to topic – choose one thread and do not go off on a tangent	☐
Is the main aim clear? Is the gathered research directly relevant?	☐
Make sure all group members play a part in building and delivery	☐
Conduct plenty of research	☐
Include daily examples	☐
Make sure needs of the audience are met	☐
Think up ways to experiment with delivery	☐
Make sure the presentation has a clear structure which flows easily	☐

(b) PowerPoint guidance

Students (and, sometimes, lecturers) make the mistake of using PowerPoint as a method of delivering a whole presentation or lecture. That is not what PowerPoint is for. PowerPoint slides are simply a *base* from which to spring from, or a *guide* to help the presenter along during his *own* vocal presentation. The slides are meant to be referred to only every now and again to remind the presenter where he or she is and what point comes next. They should really be called 'reminder slides'.

Students make the mistake of relying heavily on the slides to do the presenting for them. This does not impress the audience. It is obvious when this happens because the slides are overloaded with information (see example below) and the student simply reads from the slides themselves and does not turn to the audience to present any further information.

See below for an example of a bad slide:

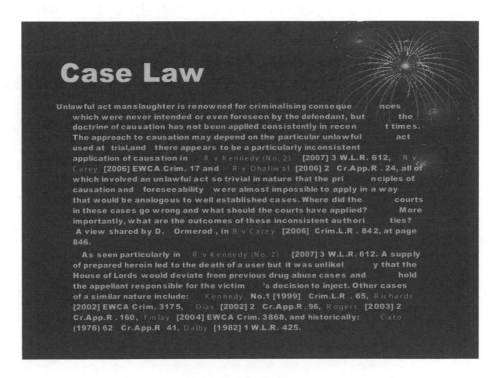

There are many things wrong with the above slide:

1 The colours are not audience-friendly. Dark colours are too strong for a background and contrast wildly with the lighter text (causing eye-strain). Pastel and neutral colours are best as they suit most types of eyes. Some students will be overwhelmed by this slide and will get a headache.

2 There is text overload on this slide. The audience members cannot read all of this text and listen to you at the same time, so they will simply give up on the slide and wait for you to explain why you have placed all of your legal knowledge into a PowerPoint slide rather than explained the law face-to-face to the audience.

3 The text is too small. How is the audience supposed to read the slide?

4 The slide presents information in paragraphs. This automatically means that there is too much text on the slide. Bullet points work much better, as they appear more like *guides* for the presenter, rather than an obvious crutch for his or her lack of legal knowledge.

5 The presenter will clearly have to read from this slide, because it contains so much information. This will be boring and monotonous for the audience, who at this point become passive listeners and lose their engagement with the presenter and the presentation as a whole.

Follow the guidance below if using PowerPoint to avoid the mistakes listed above:

- Keep slides simple. No strong colours, no overwhelming paragraphs, no silly pictures, no ambiguous structure.
- Don't crowd every slide with text. This puts the audience off and gives the impression that the presenter has not remembered anything. How would you view your lecturer if he or she overcrowded every one of their PowerPoint slides and simply read from them – and did nothing else – for the duration of the lecture?
- Use bullet points, *not* long paragraphs. You should type enough information in one bullet point to keep you on track during your talk, but that should be enough. Any more information than that, and you are relying on your slides too much. Six bullet points on each slide is an absolute maximum.
- You can use supplements, such as handouts, to help the audience along and to keep them engaged. Do not rely solely on PowerPoint for the entire presentation.
- Size 28 font is an absolute minimum for PowerPoint slides. You must ensure that audience members at the back of the room can see all the text on your slides, and there may be other students at the front of the audience who have visual impairments.
- One new slide should only be used every few minutes, depending on the length of the presentation. Remember, they are guides only, and the presenter is expected to talk *independently* of his or her PowerPoint slides.
- Have you considered putting a picture in? Animations, videos, posters, sound effects and flashy graphics can be really useful and imaginative, provided they are used correctly and are *directly relevant* to what you are trying to say. For example, if you are presenting about study skills, a small picture of a pile of law books in the top left corner of your slide would add a playful touch to the presentation without looking unprofessional or out of place.

Look at the example of a good slide below:

Notice how:

1 The colours are audience-friendly. Pastel/pale colours are easier on the audience's eyes.
2 There is no text overload on this slide. The audience members will be able to read the points provided and listen to you explain them in more detail at the same time.
3 The text is large enough for all of the audience members to see, even those who are sitting at the back.
4 The slide presents information in bullet points. This automatically means that there is further information to come from the speaker, and the bullet points appear as simple *guides* for the presenter.

Presentations

Good things about presentations:

1. An opportunity to do some research
2. Working with others
3. Learn about yourself
4. Improve your verbal communication skills
5. Career preparation

In the templates below, sketch some of your planned PowerPoint slides. Do you think they are appropriate for your audience?

(c) Conquering nerves

All students worry about presentations. Even the most confident students – who seem to be completely unaffected – will be wondering about a certain element of their presentation and whether it is 'good enough'. What are you most likely to worry about?

> 'I don't know what my lecturer is looking for in relation to skills, knowledge, style and content. I'm going to fail because I don't know what to put in to the presentation.'

Find out from your lecturer what the marking criteria will be. This way, you can build into your presentation the skills that your lecturer is looking for.

> 'Should I deliver my presentation in the same way as my lecturer presents his lectures every week? They seem boring, but would this please him? Can I use notes to help me? I can't do it without my notes!'

Be original. Think about your law lectures for a moment. Some of them may be boring, but they are professional methods of communicating knowledge to an audience. Yours must achieve this too, but you can also be original and interesting. Try not to rely on your notes. If your lecturer simply read incoherently from scribbled notes for a whole hour and made no sense, what would you think of his or her lecture?

> 'I'm so nervous I can't do the work. I'm going to do a terrible job.'

Nerves take up a lot of time during the preparation stages. Worries about content, delivery, and being watched by your lecturer and all your friends, will plague your mind. Students sometimes worry so much that they cannot face the rehearsal stage and simply leave their presentation well alone once it has been finished! Rehearsal is the biggest antidote (ie the biggest cure) for nerves, so if you are nervous, or have any doubts, do plenty of research on your topic, and rehearse many, many times.

> 'I get so nervous when I present in front of people that I freeze up and I feel sick and I just want to run away. I know I'll ruin it – I don't want to do it.'

Anxiety is not only normal but it is good for your performance – it helps you to concentrate, focus on your task and stay alert. Look at the 'Top Six Nerve Aggravators' listed below. Do you suffer from any of these?

1. Worried about losing marks and being laughed at by friends.	2. Not happy with your level of preparation.	3. Worried about the audience and what they think of you.	4. You don't like the venue for the presentation.
	5. You don't feel technically competent.	6. Your bad past experience is affecting you.	

The aggravators above affect most presenters, so you are not alone. Check out the stress signals below. Do any of these effect you too?

What are the cures? There are many, which are listed below. But there is one fail-safe way of combating the nerves ... research and rehearse, research and rehearse, research and rehearse ...

- practise, practise, practise, practise, practise, practise;
- be well prepared – start your planning early;
- have a back-up at hand, or a plan B for an emergency;
- research your topic so thoroughly that you can answer every conceivable question;

- tell yourself you'll be alright;
- tell yourself that it will go well;
- know that the audience is on *your* side;
- think about something different five minutes beforehand.

Inner stress signals	Outer stress signals
Dry throat	Sleeplessness the night before
Heart beating very fast	Voice trembling or raising a pitch
Stomach churning	Shaking hands and legs
Feeling sick	Sweating
Headache	Avoiding eye contact
Negative thoughts/premonitions	Blushing
	Turning away from audience
	Not being able to breathe
	Sweaty hands
	Stumbling over (or imagining doing so)
	Jumbling up words
	Total freeze-up
	Passing out!

If you are a student presenter and you are being watched by your peers, 100% of the audience is on *your* side! They support you!

Stress relief!

Try some positive affirmations (ie positive thinking). For example, imagine yourself standing in front of a large audience delivering a successful presentation. Imagine that the audience is nodding along to your points, and they are asking you questions at the end that you answer with ease. Imagine that your lecturer smiles at you as if to say that he or she is very impressed. Imagine feeling good, looking good, and receiving positive feedback from your audience at the end. Hold on to that feeling, and believe that it will happen to you. There is no reason why not if you have put the work in!

(d) Practice makes perfect

Many students believe that building the presentation is the only work that needs to be done. This is only 60% of the workload. The other 40% is rehearsal and practice and, without it, your presentation will not be the best it can be when it comes to delivery.

- Practise in front of your family. If you can be serious in front of them, you can be serious in front of all your peers on the day of your presentation. Your family will also be honest with you, and tell you that you are speaking too fast, etc without offending you. Additionally, they will be really proud of you, and will give you a big round of applause!
- You will become so engrossed in your presentation by the end of the building stage that you will become totally subjective and you will no longer be able to identify its flaws. Make sure you plan time in your building schedule to take a step back before the rehearsal stage to look at your presentation through objective (indifferent) eyes. How will the audience see it?
- Time yourself in a vital draft run-through with your friends. You are guaranteed not to finish your presentation the first time. Students always include far too much information

because they fear that they have missed out something important, and do not realise how quickly the time passes during a presentation until they do it for real, but by then it is too late.

- International students are often worried about their English presentation skills. This is common and all universities cater for this. Any student can seek extra guidance from his or her university's student support services. Look out for courses or counsellors who can offer advice. Additionally, ask your peers to give you *constructive* feedback. They will be supportive of you because they are working *with* you and would like to achieve good marks too.

- Rehearsal stage is a good time for yourself or your group members to step back and analyse your work on a big screen. Book up a lecture hall for 30 minutes and ask yourself: Does the presentation get to the point? Is it clear? Is the scope just right or is it too wide? Is the amount of detail appropriate, or has too much information been placed on the PowerPoint slides? At this point you can identify small formatting mistakes and delete some slides, because it will probably be too long at first instance. The test is simple: *'if it doesn't add anything, take it out.'* Make it a dress rehearsal too, so it feels more formal.

- Index cards are an excellent presentation aid, and the rehearsal stage will highlight those parts of your presentation you find hard to remember. Put some extra points on your index cards and keep them to your chest during your presentation for an emergency. Do not rely on them too heavily – your audience will notice if you are reading from your cards instead of speaking to them directly.

- Are you or your group brave enough to record yourselves during rehearsal stage? It will highlight all the small fidgety habits you don't realise you have, and you will be able to see your presentation from your audience's point of view. It can be uncomfortable viewing, but nothing will highlight the problems with your presentation quite like a recording.

- Non-attendees in your group should be shopped at this point. If you and your other members have built the presentation from scratch and you have come to the rehearsal stage with no sign or effort from another group member, tell your lecturer quickly before it becomes a problem within the group.

Self-assessment

Rehearsal and practice tasks to do...	Tick when complete
Make sure 40% of the work is allocated to practice and rehearsal	☐
Practise in front of your family	☐
Step back objectively and analyse from the audience's view	☐
Time yourself in a draft run-through with friends	☐
Seek advice from your university student support services	☐
Book out a lecture hall for rehearsal	☐
Use index cards for presentation guidance	☐
Record a rehearsal and watch it back	☐
Alert your lecturer of non-attendees at rehearsal stage	☐

(e) Delivery

This is the part that every student dreads – the presentation itself! Actually, it is the anticipation of doing the presentation that makes presenters nervous. All the nervous symptoms listed above are a result of the student's mind worrying about the impending presentation, not the actual presentation itself, which is actually harmless.

Perfect delivery	
Use the guide below to ensure presentation success	
• Arrive *early* at your presentation venue. Check out the room, the resources, the technology, the audience layout, and any other problems (such as missing resources or broken computers). Give yourself plenty of time to set everything up and deal with trivial problems.	• Show some authority when you begin by asking your audience to be quiet (in polite terms of course), but wait until everybody is settled before you actually begin. Let your audience know when you will welcome questions on your topic – either throughout the presentation or (better) at the end.
• Never apologise to the audience for an 'ill-prepared' or 'not up to standard' presentation. This is one of the worst things you can do; it is the equivalent of saying 'don't bother listening to what I am about to say'. Students do this because they believe that it is what the audience is thinking, but it is *not* and *never* is. The audience is eager to see what you have prepared and what you have to say. Even your peers will be interested to see what you or your group have created as there will be competitiveness in the air.	• Your introduction is vital. Tell the audience what is about to happen in the next 10 or 20 minutes. A few essential points will do. Include one (or two) main aim(s) in your introduction: What is your presentation going to show or prove? How have you or your group gone about proving your aim(s)? How will your results be presented and what will they show? The audience will then make themselves comfortable and will be ready for your main presentation.
• The structure of your presentation is also very important. Break it into three (a maximum of five) pieces, two of which should always be 'introduction' and 'conclusion'. It depends of the length of the presentation, but if it contains too many sections your audience will not take very long to get lost.	• A group presentation will get off to a good start if the first speaker introduces all the members of the group and outlines the main aim(s) of the presentation. This shows the audience that the group has worked well together, that the members are professional and take their work seriously, and that the work has been sewn together tightly.
• Use language that is acceptable and appropriate to your audience and their level of ability and understanding of the topic. If they are students or your friends, it is tempting to make jokes to make them laugh. Humour is acceptable during presentations depending on the way it is used. Simply being silly in front of your audience will see your professionalism (and any good marks you may have achieved) slip away.	• Eye contact is a sign of honesty. It seems impossible when you are nervous, but make eye contact with your audience so they know that you mean what you say. A presenter who never looks at his audience puts up a barrier between himself and the audience as if they are both in different zones and cannot connect to each other. The audience will not be engaging with your words if you do not look at them.
• Make each point clearly. Additionally, give your audience the chance to absorb each point. They will be actively thinking about the points you are making, but if you rush through and do not give them time to think, they will stop thinking about your topic and will simply passively listen for the rest of your presentation.	• Be enthusiastic about your topic. It is your creation and you will want to share it with the world. Show people what you have created with a smile because you are proud of your work.
• Is it clear to your audience how the different pieces of your presentation link up? Make sure you explain – either at the beginning or as you are going through – how your presentation has been structured and which part comes when. If your audience knows what to expect, they can concentrate on what you are saying much better.	• Don't forget the golden rule when using PowerPoint slides: too many slides equals a lost and bored audience. Remember, the slides are simply your foundation from which to spring from, and they should only be used as a background tool every once in a while (ie one slide every few minutes).

● You need to speak slowly during your presentation. Almost every student falls at this hurdle because it is a difficult thing to do when you are nervous. You do not need to be in such a hurry to tell your audience what you have to say because you have an allocated time slot. A student who speaks perfectly coherently during a formal presentation will impress the lecturer significantly.	● Over-preparation is good for the nerves, but save any extra information for emergencies only (ie if you run out of time). Remember, the audience does not know that you have done the extra work, so they will not know if you miss it out. Do not overwhelm your audience by giving them any unnecessary detail – it will throw them off their train of thought.
● If you are using index cards as props or guides, make sure you only glance at them once in a while. Do not read directly from them, and do not read directly from your PowerPoint slides either, unless you want to give your audience the impression that you have nothing else to offer them in terms of content and research.	● You need to be confident about what you are saying. This requires extra research and sound knowledge of the area of law that you are presenting, but it will be worth it. When you complete your extra research, you will be able to stand with your head high in front of your audience and explain the law in an authoritative manner.
● Presenters can have distracting habits: fiddling with keys, coins, pens, hands in the pockets, shuffling from one foot to the other when other group members are talking, even talking to each other when another group member is talking. This is unprofessional, and all of these things will distract the audience and your fellow presenters. The overall impression will be one of thoughtlessness, carelessness and unprofessionalism, so deal with these habits at rehearsal stage.	● Sum up what you and your group have said at the end of the presentation. It will prove to both your audience and your lecturer that you have followed through with your aim at the very beginning of your presentation by using evidence and research to prove and support your view, before coming to your own conclusions.
● It is okay to run out of time, as long as you sum up what you have covered so far. This way, you can at least provide a professional ending for the audience.	● *Any past lessons I have learned:*

Taking it a step further

If you are a confident speaker, enjoy presentations and have spoken in front of a large audience many times, you may like to push the boundaries a little. This does *not* mean turning your presentation into a circus of imaginative delivery techniques, but simply engaging your audience with more original methods of speaking. A very professional and engaging beginning means you can relax slightly during the rest of the presentation.

1 *Ask a challenging question at the very beginning.* This will grab the audience's attention and make them think hard about what you are saying. It also shows that you have done some creative thinking about your topic.

2 *Use a story to open your presentation.* Perhaps you have some interesting personal experience? This enables your audience to connect your topic to everyday life, and it pulls them into your presentation as they imagine themselves experiencing the same thing.

3 *Make a startling statement at the beginning of your presentation.* Perhaps a judge said something in a case judgment that makes no sense? Perhaps an academic has published a theory that is confusing? This gives your audience something to think about.

4 *Use props.* This is an unexpected addition to any presentation, and grasps the attention of the audience. These can include role plays (short), models, videos (short), quizzes (short), physical objects/examples, handouts, flipcharts and overhead projectors, discussion and question slots.

The top 13 'further guidance' tips	
1 Appear confident even if you're *dying*	9 Do not overshadow or neglect your group members
2 Use appropriate language for your audience	10 Do not recite from a script or slides from start to finish
3 Smile at the audience and look happy to be there	11 Do not go over the time limit
4 Dress smartly, stand straight, and *look up*	12 Do not look like you don't care
5 Get to the point quickly and succinctly	13 *Mini-presentation structure* (for use in mini-presentations of nine slides or less): Introduction; Situation; Problem; Solution; Summary; End
6 Add interesting visual aids to engage your audience	
7 Aid your simple slides with authoritative and confident commentary	
8 Do not distract the audience from the message	

5.8 RESEARCH PROJECTS, REPORTS AND DISSERTATIONS

Earlier in the chapter we talked about effective assignment writing, and much of what was discussed applies to any sort of academic and professional writing. However, in relation to writing up research project reports and dissertations, there are a few additional issues to tackle. Research projects which you will carry out as a student are likely to be written up in one of two ways, either as a dissertation or as a research report. While they are similar in many ways, there are some differences and this section offers some advice on both.

Structuring your dissertation

You need to pick a project topic that is feasible, which means 'do-able' in the short time that you have. Many student project proposals are initially over-ambitious. They are often very wide-ranging in their focus and/or rely on the collection of information or even primary data which is not achievable in the time available.

The best projects are those where:

- the topic is of particular interest to you;
- you can easily collect information – the information is readily available, or you can collect and analyse it easily, and within a short time period;
- the aim of the project is *focused* on a particular aspect of a chosen topic.

See 'Project Management' in **Chapter 6** for further guidance and tips regarding choosing topics and managing your dissertations and projects.

Self-assessment In the space below, make a list of four topics on your law course that you find fascinating and would like to do further research on:

1 ....

2 ....

3 ....

4 ....

When it comes to writing up your dissertation, you should seek guidance from your dissertation tutor about how to structure your work, but it helps if you are clear in your own mind on the purpose of each of your dissertation chapters. You should also be clear about your word limit. Undergraduate dissertations can vary from 7,000 words to 12,000 words, and postgraduate dissertations are typically between 12,000 and 15,000 words in length. The main body of your dissertation will be sub-divided into sections or chapters. Each will have an introduction, a main body and a conclusion that leads the reader easily on to the next. The sections you might typically find in dissertation are as follows:

- Introduction
- Background
- Literature Review
- Methodology
- Results
- Discussions
- Conclusions

Although all dissertations will include engagement with all the broad sections described above, the sub-headings chosen will vary from one dissertation to the next. Law dissertations also tend to place less emphasis on the literature review and methodology sections.

What should be included in these sections?

Section	Suggested content
Introduction	The introduction to your report is very important – don't be tempted to leave it to last. If you make this the first writing item, you immediately begin to focus on what you need to say and how you need to say it. Indeed, you should be thinking about what you want to say in your introduction at an early stage of your research. The introduction should shape the remainder of the report, not vice versa. A good introduction sets the tone and direction of the report. It informs the reader what the research is about, presents the overall research objective and specific research questions – and why these have been selected and pursued. In particular, you need to make it clear what specific business-related problem or issue is being addressed. What does your project contribute to address this particular problem or issue? The introduction may also present and summarise the contents of the remaining sections to the reader.
Background	The background information puts your work into a particular legal, social, commercial, theoretical or historical context and helps to *explain* the research. For example, if your project is centred on the analysis of a particular area of company law, your background section should briefly explain the law in that area to ensure your readers are familiar with the legal provisions you are looking at.
Literature review	A main aim of the literature review is to inform the reader what previous research has been done on the topic and how it has guided or informed your own research. For example, you may want to test or challenge findings from previous research, or approach your study from a different perspective. Or you may want to explore how relevant today are the conclusions reached from earlier studies both generally and for your own research?
Methodology	The methodology section informs the reader of the overall research methodology you have adopted – *and why* – and what research tools (or methods) you have adopted to gain and analyse your result. It also describes the participants involved in any empirical work you did (how many/how they were selected/their characteristics, etc). It is also an opportunity for you to present an objective reflection on the limitations of the methodology and methods used. This is important, as all research has its limitations and there is no shame in admitting this; indeed, it will be expected of you.
Results	The results section presents a summary of the data or other information you have gathered. This section presents the data information without discussion of the implications of your findings – this goes into the next 'Discussion' section.
Discussion	This section presents *analysis* and discussions of the result, including implications, consequences and issues raised. It will also compare and contrast results with previous research findings, identified and discussed earlier in the Literature Review. If it is a project, it may also include recommendations, although these could go into a separate 'Recommendations' section if there are a significant number to be made.
Conclusion	It is the end of your dissertation but, hopefully, the beginning of a positive contribution to knowledge. The conclusion reminds the reader of the main aim of your research, your methodology, the findings and what this *means* for the topic studied. You are also likely to point out the limitations of your research findings and how future researchers might take your work a stage further. Finish well – leave the reader with something significant to think about.

Activity Use the table below to map out the sections of your dissertation. If a section is not relevant, say so and give an indication as to why you don't think you need the section. If you don't feel that this structure works for you, map out an alternative. The important thing is that you cover everything in a way that makes sense to you and your readers.

My Dissertation	
Section	**Suggested content**
Introduction	
Background	
Literature review	
Methodology	
Results	
Discussion	
Conclusion	

Report writing

A dissertation may take the form of a long academic essay or it may take the form of a report. You already know quite a lot about assignments and effective writing generally, but it is worth considering how reports are different and how you can write effective reports throughout your studies and professional life.

A report is a form of *communication* that will do one or more of the following:

- Describe
- Analyse
- Summarise
- Criticise or praise
- Make predictions

Reports are based on an analysis of current or past events or identifiable phenomena.

If you are studying on an undergraduate or postgraduate law course, you will be expected to write reports and to present findings in written and verbal and/or audio/visual forms. You will, for example, write reports:

- for module assignments, eg case study reports;
- presenting the results of an individual research project;
- summarising the result of a group project and presentation;
- reflecting on a work experience or other placement you were involved in.

What's the difference between a report and an essay?

There are two main differences: aim and presentation.

Aim

Essays give you more opportunity to expand on possibilities, ideas or concepts. Reports deal with describing and/or analysing *actual past events*. Reports can be written that make predictions or recommendations for the future, but these are usually the result of an analysis of past events or of current or past social, cultural or economic phenomena.

The English statesman, Sir Thomas More, wrote an essay titled *Utopia*, which visualised an ideal state or 'perfect world'. He couldn't have written a report on the same topic!

Presentation

Reports are also usually broken up into sections, each section with a relevant sub-heading. Bullet points, illustrations, diagrams, charts, tables can also be used in reports. Essays at Bradford University School of Management, for example, can be presented in a traditional form (no sub-headings; very limited use of tables, charts, etc) or non-traditional form (with sub-headings grouping a cluster of related paragraphs and discrete use of bullet points, graphs, tables etc). In terms of presentation, the distinctions between reports and essays are beginning to disappear, although you should always check with your tutor what presentational style is required.

A summary of the differences and similarities between report and essay writing is presented below.

Similarities	Differences
• Both should have one or more central points to make – and these central points should be given emphasis in both.	• Reports can be presented orally, but essays are usually submitted in written form only for marking purposes.
• Both can include references (essays usually *will* include them, although reports *might*, depending on the report).	• Essays can explore hypothetical situations – but reports are almost always concerned with actual past events.
• Both should include an introduction and a conclusion.	• Essays are usually written in the 'third person', ie as if detached from the subject. Reports can adopt either the first person or third person depending on the context.
• Both should be well structured and have a logical progression of ideas.	
• Well-structured reports or essays have text broken up into readable 'chunks'. In reports, sub-headings are used to label each 'chunk', whilst traditional essays would use paragraphs to the same end.	• Reports can selectively include illustrations, charts, diagrams in the main text, but in traditional essays these will be usually be included as appendices.
• Usually only *one key point or main idea* will be found in any single report section or essay paragraph.	• Bullet points can be used in reports, but they are *not common* in essays.
• Both will have a particular readership in mind and will therefore use language appropriate for that readership.	• Reports can include a *'Recommendations for Action'* section, but this will be very unusual in an essay.
• The best essays and reports are written in a simple, direct and unpretentious way.	

Bad reports are often written in ways that obscure their message. Look again at the following sentence (see **5.4**).

'Although solitary under normal prevailing circumstances, racoons may congregate simultaneously in certain situations of artificially enhanced nutrient resource availability.'

Activity What do you think the sentence means? Can you rewrite the sentence so it makes more sense?

....

....

....

....

....

An effective report

A good report is like telling a good story. In a report you are telling the reader what happened, why it happened and in a way that holds his or her interest. Like any good story, you will also set the scene first, making the reader aware, for example, of the history, background and overall context of the report topic. The contents of any written report should be organised into a well-structured form. Unless it is a short, eg one page, it will be usually be necessary to divide the information contained into sections, each section with its own sub-heading. You should choose sub-headings that are *appropriate for the report*. Most reports will contain a five-point structure, which present five broad areas and sections 2–5 are likely to have sub-sections (each with relevant sub-headings). The five broad areas are:

1 Introduction
2 Background information
3 Development

4 Discussion
5 Conclusion

As you can see, these categories are broadly in line with the general structure of a dissertation and could easily be adapted by including an additional section on literature review and methodology or by integrating the literature review into the Background section.

Your report structure	
Introduction	In the introduction you can introduce the aim and subject of the report. You can tell the reader what to expect: what issue is being explored or evaluated and, if necessary, why. It is often helpful to summarise very briefly the main finding of the report at this point, as this can stimulate the interest of the reader.
Background information and context	In this area you present an overview of the historic, economic, political or social influences and/or the micro factors that enable the reader to put the report issues (see below) into context or perspective.
Development	In this broad area of the report, you present key issues, ideas, and practices, etc that are the main focus of the report. You might also present relevant data or information to help build a picture for the reader of what has happened. You might include, for example, the way a certain law is currently being applied by the courts.
Discussion	The discussion section is the heart of the report – and is usually the most important in terms of the mark you receive! This is where you present your analysis of the issues presented earlier in the report. This is where you *interpret, explain and discuss* the issues you have outlined.

Conclusions, summary, or recommendations	This section should bring the report to a close by pulling together the main points emerging from the report and by giving a relatively brief resume of the main or overall conclusions or recommendations reached.
Additional features	
Contents page	In a lengthy report you will normally include a contents page, to include main chapter headings, any sub-divisions within these and page numbers.
Appendix or appendices	An appendix is the place for lengthy and detailed material that would interfere with the easy flow of reading in the main report. An appendix may well contain the key information that you refer to in your report – but the main body of the report should be used to *summarise this key information*. The appendix items are there for readers to look at if they wish, particularly if they want to check the accuracy and validity of your report discussion or conclusions. The appendix might, for example, contain detailed statistical data or examples of questionnaires used in any research project. Appendices should be used sparingly – and not included as a device to avoid the word-count limits of an assignment!
References	In a report written for academic purposes, you will normally cite evidence throughout the report and provide a full list of references.
Abstract or summary	In longer reports it is common to have an abstract or summary page. This is a brief summary of the project, research, experiment, etc and the results or conclusions reached. An abstract or summary will normally be no more than half a page in length. Check with your tutor to see if you need to include this with your report.

My ideas:

....

....

....

....

Activity Here is your chance to write your own report. Pick a legal issue that you have strong feelings about, such as abortion, capital punishment, terrorism, family law, etc, and write a mini-report of 200 words. Make sure you follow the structure above. What are you trying to tell your reader?

....

....

....

....

....

Writing tips for dissertations and project reports

- Good writers continually revise and rewrite until they are satisfied with the final result. Don't underestimate the time this takes.
- Talk to people about your research and explain it to them. By explaining it to others, you will explain it to yourself.
- Always keep in mind your original research aims and research questions and *remind the reader of these at regular intervals*.

- Always keep in mind the *central point or findings* of your report and emphasise these in your writing. Emphasise them in the results section and emphasise them again in the conclusion.
- *Start writing early*. Write a section at a time as you complete your preparation for that section. Ideas evolve as you write, and your final dissertation will be much stronger as a result.
- Don't try writing the dissertation all at once. Give yourself plenty of time for revision, correcting and formatting the document – this can be very time-consuming. Discuss and agree with your supervisor arrangements for sending and returning completed materials to each other.
- In a long dissertation, it is necessary to remind the reader of the main points in each section. Summarise the main points made at the end of each section and build the anticipation of the reader for what is to come next.
- Write with the ear. A sentence may look correct on paper, but often sounds jumbled or rambling if read aloud. Listen to your sentences in your head as you write, and do not write anything that sounds false or uncomfortable to say aloud.
- Write for the eye as well. Make the document visually appealing, using plenty of white space in margins, between sections and paragraphs.
- Keep your writing clear and simple. Avoid long, convoluted sentences – and don't fill them with jargon or pretentious waffle.
- Don't use 20 words, if 10 will do; good writing in reports is plain, clear and succinct. Be ruthless with your pruning of redundant words and sentences.

5.9 FEEDBACK

A vital component of your law course is the feedback you receive from your lecturers. Whether it is verbal feedback at the end of a tutorial, or formal feedback as part of an assignment, any kind of feedback will provide you with a valuable insight into your current academic abilities and legal skills. Students do not pay enough attention to the feedback they receive from their law lecturers. This may be because students are unsure when they are receiving feedback, or do not know what to do with the feedback once they receive it.

Activity At the bullet points below, write what you would consider to be 'feedback' from your lecturer:

- ....
- ....
- ....

What is considered 'feedback'?

In both further and higher education, 'feedback' can occur at any time and at any place. If you approach your lecturer at the end of a lecture and ask about your assignment question, your lecturer's guidance will be considered as informal feedback. If you are in a tutorial and you and your friends ask your lecturer what is meant by 'critical analysis', your lecturer's answer will again be considered as informal feedback.

Other types of informal feedback include:

- meetings with your lecturer in his or her office;
- emails between you and your lecturer;
- general assignment guidance in a lecture to all students;
- tutorial question-answer sessions with your lecturer and friends;
- help and guidance from your lecturer with your tutorial work in your tutorial sessions;
- discussion about general legal principles in tutorials with your lecturer and friends;
- informal conversations with your lecturer whilst passing in the corridor relating to the law or your assessment;
- discussions about the law whilst working in the library with a group of friends;
- feedback from your friends on an assignment draft or presentation rehearsal;
- group work with peers;
- self-assessment of your own work and/or practices;
- assessing the work of others.

As you can see, any interaction with your law lecturers and peers can be considered as beneficial to your studies.

When your formal assignments are returned, with a sheet on the front containing marking criteria, your lecturer's comments and a final grade, this is considered formal feedback. You will not receive formal feedback very often on your law course as it only occurs during your formal assessments. However, it is the most valuable type of feedback, because it measures your present performance and your current level of understanding. This is the real opportunity for law students to look at their current study strategy and work out where they are going wrong and what they are doing right. Action plans can be built off the back of formal feedback, and your lecturer will help you to do this.

The form of feedback you receive will be different depending on the task completed. For example, if you are working with a group of friends on a group assignment or presentation, their comments about your ideas will be 'peer feedback'. If you are receiving assignment feedback from your lecturer in his or her office, this is 'informal' or 'formal feedback'. If you have completed an exam and your lecturer is telling the whole class of 200 students that the level of analysis in the exam answers was disappointing, this is 'exam feedback'. Notice how the quality of the feedback differs between exams and assignments. Usually, you do not receive your exam scripts back or any detailed feedback on your exam answer, and so it is harder to gauge your current ability and performance in law exams. However, you can always arrange a meeting with your lecturer, who may still have your script or a copy of his or her comments on your exam paper, and he or she will be able to tell you the main factors that determined your exam mark.

As a law student, it is up to *you* to incorporate all of this formal and informal feedback into your work and studies and improve your submissions as a result. Your lecturer will not tell you: 'You are about to receive feedback from me ...', and your peers will not tell you: 'I am about to give you some informal feedback on your ideas ...'. You will be expected to recognise when you are given good advice. If students do not use the feedback that comes their way, they have only themselves to blame.

What is the purpose of feedback?

The main purpose of feedback in education is 'improvement'. Feedback improves performance, research, dedication, quality and marks. If you have goals and aspirations, your feedback will tell you how to get there. If you plan to achieve 60% in your next assignment, the feedback on your current 54% grade will tell you what else you need to do to pull your mark up. For example, if your assignment was missing 'critical analysis', your lecturer can tell you what it is and how to successfully incorporate it into your next assessment. You will receive more detailed feedback on an assignment than you will on an exam.

Many students make the mistake of simply looking at their grade, and disregarding the written comments made by the lecturer. This is a big mistake! The comments from your lecturer are written specifically with you and your academic style in mind. The comments are tailored to help *you* to improve your research, performance, presentation, analysis, evaluation and marks. This personal guidance is invaluable if you are trying to increase your grades – as most students are – so why ignore the best academic advice you may ever be given?

Ask yourself the following questions:

- Do I understand the comments?
- What is my lecturer trying to say?
- Are there any recurring themes on my feedback forms?
- Do I agree with the comments?
- What are the positive aspects in my submissions?
- How do I feel about my feedback?
- What do I do with my feedback now?
- How do I use my feedback?

Here are some common feedback comments in law assignments:

> 'You have not answered the question set.'
> 'The promises made in the introduction have not been met.'
> 'Your writing has diverted into a different area of law.'
> 'The evidence you provide in the piece is not used appropriately.'
> 'Arguments are not backed up by appropriate legal sources.'
> 'The legal authorities are not referenced properly.'
> 'The writing style and/or layout is not appropriate.'
> 'More precision and/or clarity is required.'
> 'The points/arguments you make are too vague.'
> 'The conclusion does not correspond to the arguments put forward in the piece.'
> 'Your structure is all over the place.'
> 'Spelling, punctuation and grammar are an issue.'
> 'Too descriptive – explain why the law is inappropriate.'

Here are the underlying reasons behind these comments:

- Read the question properly and identify the relevant area of law.

- Make sure your arguments flow clearly throughout the piece.
- Your scope has been too wide and you have included irrelevant material.
- Link your evidence and sources to your answer. Use them as your support.
- Wikipedia is not a legal source! Cases are a primary source of law.
- Become familiar with the referencing system of your law school.
- Good presentation adds marks, as do introductions and conclusions.
- Have you made your position clear? Have you simply skimmed the surface?
- Depth on a particular point of law is much better than a broad sweep of the whole area.
- Have you followed your arguments through or did you change your mind half way through the piece?
- The parts of your assignment do not link up properly.
- Proof-read, and show more dedication to presentation detail.
- Not enough analysis, synthesis, criticism and evaluation.

It can be disheartening when you receive negative feedback. Students often feel that their assignment mark does not represent the work and effort they put into their piece. Lecturers have several good reasons for giving you your allocated mark and feedback – you may have done all the research required, but did you actually answer the question?

'I feel as though I need to be a naturally clever student to get high marks. All my friends seem to be getting better marks than me. I work just as hard as them and we all work together when doing our research, but I still don't seem to be getting the results that I deserve.'

Many students feel this disappointment when receiving assignment feedback. Try not to compare your performance against that of your friends – they are completely different learners to you, and you have your own unique learning and writing style. When you get to this point, the best advice you will receive will come directly from your lecturer.

Take a look at the table below. Which categories have you fallen into in the past?

Low marks (40–50%)	Medium marks (51–60%)	High marks (61–70%)
<ul><li>little structure</li><li>scarce legal research</li><li>no reflection or thought</li><li>mostly describes the law</li><li>no analysis of the law</li><li>no criticism of the law</li><li>few legal arguments</li></ul>	<ul><li>some background research and analysis</li><li>some legal understanding</li><li>answers the question</li><li>develops a legal argument</li><li>links different ideas</li><li>some thought and reflection</li></ul>	<ul><li>in-depth legal research</li><li>significant legal points raised</li><li>original/unique issues investigated</li><li>academic commentary used for support</li><li>deep critical analysis of the law</li><li>strong conclusion</li></ul>

Typical lecturer comments are provided below for each of the categories above. Do any of them seem familiar?

42% 'This piece contains hardly any legal research. You only answer the question vaguely – what about the reforms? More case law could have been used to supplement the answer, and significant critical analysis of the law is missing.'

55% 'This piece displays some good legal research. You answer the question well using appropriate case law. Some analysis is present. More discussion could have been provided on the topic of reforms, and more critical commentary would have helped your arguments.'

68% 'This is a very good piece of work. You answer the question correctly using the main legal authorities. You criticise the reforms in the area very well and you provide further research to present your own ideas. However, further analysis would be required to support your argument.'

72% 'This is an excellent piece of work. You present an original answer and use an impressive amount of academic commentary to support your strong line of reasoning. The presentation of your work is excellent and you highlight the underlying legal issues. Well done.'

What is my lecturer asking for?

What is required of you really depends on your level of study and the question set. If you are studying at A-level, you need a good degree of critical analysis complete with case law and perhaps some academic journal references to support your answer. At LLB level, you are expected to take these references further by critically analysing them and introducing relevant theories and legal principles into your answer. Additionally, the level of synthesis and evaluation required depends on the level you are currently studying at on your LLB. For example, if you are in your first year, the lecturers are aware that you are still finding your feet when it comes to critical analysis and evaluation of the law. You will be required to use additional research, but your evaluation skills and legal reasoning are still developing. However, in the third year of the LLB, it is assumed that all students know how important criticism, analysis, synthesis and evaluation are to a legal argument, and these factors are expected to be professionally woven into a solid, well-researched, and thought-provoking legal answer. How do third year students know this? Their feedback from their previous two years of study tells them so!

Don't forget! Description is only a lower-level skill and does not attract high marks, no matter what level of law you are studying. You need to show some level of application, understanding and analysis in order to show your examiner or marker that you know and understand the law. The grid below can be used as a rough guide:

Skill illustrated:	Grade it will achieve:	Example of skill:
Knowledge	20% (fail)	Describe, define, outline, state, identify, list, what, how, when, which
Comprehension	30% (fail)	Explain, use examples, summarise, paraphrase, interpret
Application	40% (3rd class)	Apply, demonstrate, advise, predict
Analysis	50% (2:2)	Analyse, assess, consider, measure, quantify, how far?
Synthesis	60% (2:1)	Justify, compare, contrast, distinguish
Evaluation	70% (1st class)	Appraise, criticise, evaluate, comment, reflect, discuss, how effective?

What do my lecturer's comments mean?

Sometimes lecturers may write all over your assignment, and you may feel offended, disappointed or let down by their comments:

No! No! No! This is wrong.

This makes no sense.

It is common to feel that the grade you receive does not represent the work that you put in, but there is a simple explanation for this. Students seem to forget that the lecturer does not see how much research, time and effort you put in to your assessment before submission: your lecturer will only see the final submission. If your tireless work and extra effort is not represented in your final piece properly, or does not come through in the right way, ie through quality of research or appropriate structure, you will not receive any marks for it because the lecturer cannot identify it.

The trick is to decipher what your lecturer is trying to say through his or her feedback. Is he or she telling you how to improve, or how you have gone wrong? Can you pick out the reasons for your mark? For example, if the lecturer writes 'what does this mean?' more than three times on your assignment, it may be a sign that you are not explaining your point very well or that you are not adequately supporting your argument with legal authority. If you lecturer simply writes 'this is wrong' or 'no' on your assignment, it is a good idea to arrange a feedback meeting with your lecturer to clear up why your answer attracted these comments. It is likely that your lecturer was expecting more up-to-date research or clearer explanations. Every lecturer has a different way of feeding back to students. This can become quite complicated. As the student, it is your job to work out what lecturers mean when they write comments on your work, and to do this you must untangle and translate their comments to identify how they are trying to help you. Your lecturers do not mean to criticise on purpose – they want as many of their students to succeed as possible. All the comments they make are meant to show you where you went wrong so that you can improve next time.

Take this example from Legal Skills lecturer, Lisa Cherkassky:

'I like to include positive comments in my assignment feedback so that the students know which skills to take through to their next year, and which aspects of their regime are not working for them. I'll likely write: 'research could have greatly supplemented your answer' as my way of saying 'you didn't do enough research and your marks suffered as a result'. Whether students pick up what I'm trying to say – or in fact read the comments at all – remains to be seen when they submit again a year later at a higher level.'

Feedback is for improvement. Students cannot improve their performance if they do not understand why they are stuck at their current grade. Once you have read and understood the feedback from your lecturer and arranged a personal appointment with him or her to receive your detailed feedback, it is time to make an action plan for your next piece of work based on the feedback you have received. Your lecturer will be very pleased to help you with this, as it means that one of their students shows great signs of improving in the next assessment.

If your formal feedback clearly states that you did not present enough research in your last piece, or that your punctuation and grammar needs to be improved, you are now able to build in some study time before your next assignment to enhance these skills. The students who take this process seriously will notice a greater improvement in their grades in their next formal assessment. Hopefully, by using this strategy, your assignments will gradually get better and better throughout your course.

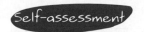

Plan of action! Done!

Read your lecturer's comments carefully. Are there any comments that you do not understand? Make an appointment to see him or her. ☐

Are there any comments which appear more than once? Highlight them. ☐

Separate the comments into 'big issues' and 'small issues'. ☐

Prioritise your 'big issues'. Which issue would you like to tackle first? Are there any student development courses ongoing at your university? ☐

Set realistic targets. Students cannot normally jump from 43% to 73% in one attempt. Pace yourself – gradual development is stronger development. ☐

Deal with each issue on your list separately. Think of a constructive and inventive way to improve rather than panicking with heavy revision. ☐

Ask your friends about their thoughts on your feedback or share your feedback with each other. Try not to be competitive! ☐

If you are struggling for ideas on how to improve your marks or enhance a certain skill (such as critical analysis or evaluation) then ask your lecturer. ☐

If possible, ask your lecturer to see examples of excellent pieces of work, to illustrate how the lecturer would like his or her questions answered in the future. ☐

My small issues ....

....

....

....

My big issues ....

....

....

....

What I need to do now: ....

....

....

....

How well would you say you currently use your lecturer's feedback? Give yourself a mark out of 10: .... /10

Assessment criteria

If you are not sure what your lecturers are looking for, check the module guides for your course. The aims, objectives and learning outcomes of the course will be listed inside your guides. These are the 'assessment criteria' which you must meet in your submission, and your lecturer will be marking your ability against these criteria.

Sometimes you may find that the assessment criteria feedback form at your law school will be vague, and not give you a detailed indication of the level or quality of work that is required or an adequate explanation of why you achieved your particular mark. For example, look at the marking scheme below for Bradford University's Law School:

	Fail – 40%	3rd 40–49%	2:2 50–59%	2:1 60–69%	1st 70% +
UB No:_____ Module Name_____ Course_____					
Knowledge & Understanding Appropriate explanation of legal issues at this level	Insufficient details of relevant law	Some basic detail of relevant law	Clear statement of most of relevant law	Clear statement of all relevant law	Excellent statement of all relevant law
a) Discipline Skills Appropriate identification, application and analysis of legal issues at this level	Fails to identify key issues, poor or no attempt at application	Identifies obvious issues only, weak application of law	Good coverage of obvious issues, reasonable application of law	Obvious and subtle issues dealt with, good application of law	Excellent coverage of all issues, excellent application of law to all issues
b) Discipline Skills Appropriate problem-solving, criticism and evaluation at this level	Poor/no attempt at evaluation, critical judgment, or problem solving	Weak evaluation, critical judgment and problem solving	Reasonable evaluation, critical judgment, and problem solving	Good evaluation, critical judgment, and problem solving	Excellent evaluation, critical judgment, and problem solving
c) Discipline Skills Appropriate research, referencing and legal terminology	Very poor referencing, no research apparent	Weak referencing, evidence of basic research only	Adequate referencing, evidence of some further research	Clear referencing, evidence of some detailed research	Excellent footnote referencing, bibliography, and research
Personal Transferable Skills Appropriate written communication and overall presentation	Inadequate spelling, grammar, messy and careless presentation	Significant errors in spelling, grammar, careless structure	Reasonable spelling and grammar, satisfactory presentation	Good spelling and grammar, well organised structure	Excellent spelling, grammar, structure, and presentation
Grade (subject to approval):	Other general comments:				

This tick-box style feedback form – in which the lecturer must tick one box on each level – tells the student very little about his or her current ability. It only shows the student that his or her critical skills may have been judged as 'reasonable', or that his or her evaluation skills are considered to be 'weak', but it provides little further explanation as to why this is. Many law schools use tick-box feedback forms: it is the lecturer's way of measuring which academic and legal skills the student has displayed, and whether the student has displayed them to an appropriate level. Other law schools may use large comment boxes, which provide more detailed explanations.

However, the lecturers who use these comment-style feedback forms find that their long, flowing comments cannot be measured against a particular level or percentage, and so the student cannot link the comments to a particular skill. In general, assessment criteria feedback forms often leave a lot to be desired at further and higher education level, and they do very little for the student who is hoping to use formal feedback to improve their performance. This is why it is vital to read your lecturer's comments and arrange an appointment to see him or her in person, as the written comments and verbal feedback can add meaning and context to why the particular tick-boxes on your feedback sheet have been ticked and why your particular grade has been given. Additionally, lecturers welcome the opportunity to help their students to succeed and are always very encouraged to see individual students querying their grade and how they can improve.

6

Study skills

Learning outcomes

> To understand and appreciate basic study skills and the way they can be used to advance your knowledge of law

> To engage in activities that will help you explore the practical aspects of these skills and use them to enhance your learning experience at university

> To reflect upon your ability to work with others in a constructive way to help you to acquire or disseminate legal knowledge and skills

> To become aware of methods of managing your time and university projects in ways that ensure efficient use of available time and resources and optimal achievement of learning objectives

> To develop effective strategies for dealing with revision and exams

Studying in a higher education institution has never been a simple process. There are a number of critical steps that you need to take and skills to develop to ensure that your university journey will reach its final destination. A number of students will not be able to reach this destination, whereas others, whilst successful, will go through a lot of stress before achieving their goal.

However, university is not meant to be a negative experience dominated by fears of failure in exams, a struggle to meet deadlines, or frustration fuelled by disappointing grades. University is meant to be a positive experience, helping students to acquire skills and knowledge that will lay the foundations for a successful career and a bright future.

In this chapter you will learn to work with others in groups. Group work helps to develop a number of skills which employers value highly, such as interpersonal skills, problem-solving and decision-making skills, and collaborative learning is particularly useful for advancing student knowledge.

This chapter will also show you methods of managing your time efficiently so as to ensure that all course tasks will be completed according to your expectations and within the prescribed time limits. Guidance on the management of course projects will also be provided. Finally, the chapter provides detailed advice and guidance on two critical areas of student activity: revision and exams.

Self-assessment

Study skills Tick the statement that applies to you...	I can do this	I would like to practise this more
I can identify the basic study skills that I use on my course	☐	☐
I am aware of which basic study skills I need to improve	☐	☐
I can put my basic study skills into practice	☐	☐
I can work with other students on my course effectively	☐	☐
I can manage my time successfully	☐	☐
I can use resources efficiently and get the best out of them	☐	☐
I set myself learning objectives	☐	☐
I can develop a unique revision and exam strategy that suits me	☐	☐

My action plan:

....

....

....

6.1 GROUP WORK

Studying with others as a group can take place in a variety of contexts in your law course. Groups of students may be created by tutors in tutorials, seminars or workshops to accomplish small tasks. They may also be created for formative or summative assessment purposes. In the latter case the work of the group will be assessed by the tutor. Law students will be allocated into groups to handle real cases in law clinics, to work on research projects, or to take part in moots.

Usually these groups are small and the allocation of students into groups is made by the tutor, who also sets the ground rules and monitors their work. Students may form their own groups for study, support or other purposes. In these cases the students themselves are responsible for the operation of the groups.

What are the advantages of teamwork? It presents an opportunity to:

• share your ideas and find solutions to problems;

• work closely with students from a range of different cultural and social backgrounds;

• develop your key skills, eg teamworking and time management, which are essential for most jobs today;

- discover your specific strengths in group or teamworking;
- learn how to deal with challenge and conflict;
- gain new, additional, and even creative perspectives on study topics;
- get to know socially a small group of students;
- make new friends;
- develop your communication skills.

Self-assessment

Teamwork Tick the statement that applies to you...	I have done this	I have not yet experienced this
I have been part of a social team	☐	☐
I have been part of an academic team on my course	☐	☐
I feel that I am a team member even when I am not doing group work	☐	☐
I have led a team before, either social or academic	☐	☐
I have seen how teams can contribute to society/education	☐	☐
I have seen how teams can isolate people	☐	☐
I have had a bad experience in a team of people	☐	☐
I turned my difficult team experience into a good one	☐	☐

My biggest area for improvement:

....

....

....

....

Working in groups with other students offers a number of learning advantages, including opportunities to transfer personal knowledge to others, to receive feedback on that knowledge, to learn from the experiences of the other group members, to adopt new perspectives on study topics, to develop critical thinking and evaluation skills, and to synthesise a collective response to the topic of study.

Additionally, working with others helps students to acquire or improve a number of transferable skills, such as teamworking, leadership, communication and time management. These skills are in high demand by employers and essential for developing a successful career as a lawyer.

Lastly, group work offers students the opportunity to make new friends and mix with new cultures. This is particularly important in a university environment. The UK demonstrates an increasing ethnic, cultural, age and social mix in student populations. Bringing students from diverse backgrounds to work together in groups constitutes valuable experience for them by enhancing their learning experience and social awareness, and it also harmonises student relationships on campus.

The increasing student populations in universities, coupled with employers' demands, mean that group activities have greatly increased in all courses during the last three decades.

Today it is a standard practice in all university courses that some elements of group work will be included in the curriculum.

Details regarding leadership can be found in **Chapter 8**. In this chapter the focus will be on group work related to the study of law.

Self-assessment **In the space below, make a note of your initial feelings when a lecturer tells you that you will be working in groups. Why do you think you react in this way?**

....
....
....
....
....

How to form a group

Most students have had experience of being a member of a group before they come to university. This is likely to be as a member of a social grouping of some sort: family, neighbourhood or community group, or member of a small or extended group for a particular interest, or vocational or educational purpose. Study groups may be formed by the tutor or by the students. They are usually formed by the tutor when the group work will be assessed, whereas there is more flexibility when the groups are formed for other, smaller student activities. In the latter case, students may be allowed to form the group.

Self-assessment **In the space below, make a note about how you feel about your own group working skills. How do they differ from your peers? If your skills do not stand out, how could you make them truly excellent?**

....
....
....
....

The selection of the group members is very important since the overall performance of the group depends on the individual contributions of the group members, which in turn depends on the level of knowledge and skills possessed by them as well as the relationships between them. Factors such as:

- culture;
- age;
- language;
- gender;
- academic performance;
- learning styles;
- and personality profile,

may be taken into account by the tutor when allocating students into groups. Many studies on group work have concluded that working in groups can enhance group performance, improve learning and encourage a diversity of views, experiences and learning needs which could be used as a source of learning. However, if a group mix is too broad or not exploited in a constructive way by group members, it may lead to the formation of dysfunctional groups by giving rise to operational difficulties, mistrust and conflict between group members.

Sometimes the selection of group members, if made by the tutor, is random or follows an alphabetical order. When students make the selection, they tend to choose students they get on well with, share similar interests with, or who are acquainted with the topic of the group task. Students usually create their own groups simply to share knowledge or promote the study of law through study-buddy groups, for example. Working in a group in university will bring with it for most students a mixture of the familiar and the unfamiliar. Familiar, in the sense that it is another social situation in the life of that person that has to be negotiated and navigated. But unfamiliar too, in that the 'rules of the game' are unknown, and the student's previous education experience may not have included any previous opportunity to work closely in a group for assessment purposes – and particularly with a culturally diverse group of unknown strangers.

Some believe that the selection of the group members as well as the group size must be closely related to the goals set for the group. Group size can be small, for example 4–6 students, but it can also be much larger, with up to 15 or more students involved. If the goal is to help students acquire transferable skills such as group working, communication and problem-solving skills (which are usually emphasised by law firms), then tutors should make the selection because they are more impartial and better positioned to create groups whose composition will help to create or improve such skills. If students are allowed to make the selection in such cases, a group of friends is usually subject to informality, inadequate control, task-sharing and a high level of social interaction, which is not what employers would want to see in their employees when dealing with important cases.

Self-assessment Have you experienced a negative group project in the past, or have you made excellent connections? How would you study differently tomorrow if you were to be put back in the same group?

....

....

....

....

The tutor should ensure that the selection process does not favour certain students at the expense of others. The learning needs of disabled students or of students belonging to minorities or lacking adequate interpersonal skills (ie very quiet students) should not be ignored. The overall aim of the selection should be to offer equal learning opportunities to all students.

Key points about group formation

- Groups can be formed by tutors or students.
- The group goal is an important factor that should be taken into account when making the selection of group members.

- The size of the group depends on the group goals and on the student group experience.
- Factors such as culture, age, language, gender, academic performance, learning styles and personality profile must be taken into account in the selection.
- Heterogeneity (mixing) in groups usually enhances group performance.
- The needs of disabled or other disadvantaged students should not be ignored.

How to make it work

A very important first step after the group formation is to explain to group members the purpose of the group. This will help members to understand what is expected of them and most importantly how their involvement in the group work will enhance their learning experience.

Groups formed and controlled by tutors may be serving a variety of purposes:

- to help students acquire and develop teamworking skills;
- to carry out a large project which cannot be carried out individually;
- to achieve the learning objectives of the module;
- to manage the class more efficiently;
- to promote collaborative learning and assessment.

The purpose for the creation of a group must be clearly identified and communicated by the tutor to the group members. This will help to reduce confusion between the members and increase the group's chances of achievement.

Group tasks will then be set, as well as the deadline for the completion of the tasks. The tasks and the deadlines, if they are the responsibility of the group, could be negotiated and agreed by group members, but if they have been set by the tutor they may not be negotiable. For example, if the group task is an assessed presentation on a law topic for which a specific date has been fixed, the group members cannot change that. They have to be ready for the presentation on the fixed date; otherwise they will fail the assessment.

After setting out the tasks and the deadlines, ground rules must be laid down. These are to bring some order to team tasks, scheduling issues and group leadership. The group members have to agree on the ground rules upon which the operation of the group and the conduct of its members will be based. The roles of people in the group can be formalised and explicit – complete with titles – or implicit and informal. For example, in the latter case, the dominant role of an older family member may be implicitly acknowledged and accepted by others. In a study context these rules could be agreed with or without the involvement of the tutor. The tutor may intervene if the group members are unable to reach an agreement or if he or she wishes to advise them on the rules or monitor student performance within the group.

Making a group work effectively and efficiently is not always an easy task, and many groups fail to exploit their full potential. It is important to stress some personal and group attributes that are essential for setting up and running a successful group.

First stages

There are a number of things you can do to help move quickly through the first stages of teamworking and get on with the job in hand.

(a) Contact list

You could start by all team members providing their names and contact details. This should be circulated to all members of the team.

(b) Introductions

Team members should introduce themselves and say a little about their backgrounds. Even if team members know each other already, it can be useful to do this, as it gets everyone speaking.

(c) Clarify aim and purpose of the task

For the first meeting, someone should volunteer to lead the discussion and another to take notes. However, it is a good idea for the leadership and recording of meetings to be rotated around group members so everyone gets the chance to do it. This could feature in the 'ground rules' discussion (see below). The group should also clarify the aim and purpose of the set task. This can involve, for example, looking closely at the wording of any question or project and making sure everyone is clear on broadly what is involved, when the task as a whole must be completed and who is going to do what. It can be helpful if a written summary is made of this discussion. Copies should be made for all members.

> The aim of our meeting today is:

(d) Ground rules

Groups should formulate their own ground rules on the expected conduct of meetings and members. Ground rules are simple written statements on agreed conduct. All group members should receive a copy of these.

Ground rules could include:

- punctuality;
- attendance;
- leadership of meetings (who does it);
- recording the discussion (who does it);
- commitment;
- contribution to the group (everyone should contribute something to its success, but individuals need to commit in writing to this);
- confidentiality;
- mobile phones, eg switch off at meetings;
- the importance of *listening* to each other;
- respect (eg not allowing, for example, sexist or racist comments, and not accepting abusive or aggressive remarks, etc);
- decision-making procedures.

Reviewing progress

Once your group has been formed and has been running for a while, it is a good idea to review its progress, particularly if members feel there are problems in the group to overcome. The evaluation form below can help your group to review its progress.

 Rank your experience of working in the team from 1–10. 10 indicates 'excellent', 5 indicates 'needs improvement' and 1 indicates 'terrible'!

	10	9	8	7	6	5	4	3	2	1	
Group committed to tasks											Lack of commitment by significant number of group members
Challenging, rewarding, enjoying atmosphere											Flat, lifeless atmosphere
Time used efficiently											Time wasted
Systematic approach to discussion											Lack of systematic approach to tasks
People present on time or send apologies if unavailable											Unpunctuality a significant feature
Leadership skills demonstrated											Drifting or dominating by individuals
Consensus decisions											Authoritarian decisions
Respect shown for each other											No or little respect shown by or for other group members
Opinions could be questioned without resentment											Opinions 'untouchable' and could not easily be challenged
All able to express opinions											No opportunity to express opinions
Open and trusting atmosphere											Distrust and defensiveness
We listen to each other											Listening skills weak
Everyone participating											Significant number not participating
Tasks completed as agreed											Agreed tasks not completed
Agreement reached at most meetings											Disagreement a feature of most meetings
Group goals clearly defined											Goals unclear

(NIMBAS, 2005: adapted from a group evaluation questionnaire produced by NIMBAS, Utrecht, Netherlands)

Some teams work well together from the word 'go', but others struggle through to the end of the task, not really working effectively or efficiently.

Personal attributes

How do you behave when you join a group? Would *you* work with you? When joining a group you must be prepared to:

- demonstrate good faith and genuine interest in the group goals;
- work with people that you do not know or who you dislike;
- assist and encourage other group members;
- compromise when disagreements erupt;
- demonstrate patience especially in the early period of the group formation and operation;
- make sure that you understand the reasons for your participation in the group and role allocated to you;
- listen to the views of others even if you do not agree with these views;

- speak out with your views on group matters;
- accept criticism and even rejection of your positions;
- take into account the views or interests of other group members;
- be honest to other group members about your intentions and your level of commitment to the group's goals;
- intervene when intense agreements threaten to completely derail the group from its goals.

In general, when joining a group you must be flexible and have an open mind. Both will help you to overcome obstacles and address challenges which commonly occur in group tasks.

Group attributes

Groups can have amazing chemistry from the beginning, or they can be confrontational and divided from the start. However, groups can be effective if they demonstrate at least some of the following attributes:

- All members share the group goals.
- All members have detailed knowledge of the group's goals and of the necessary tasks for achieving these goals.
- Clear and realistic deadlines have been set for completing the group tasks.
- Each member knows his or her role within the group.
- The group has clear and comprehensive ground rules (eg all members know what types of behaviour are unacceptable).
- Tasks are allocated to members equally and fairly.
- There is mutual respect between all members.
- There is a regular review of group activities.
- There is genuine commitment of all members to the group goals.

Disputes

Imagine you have joined a group of relative strangers to work on a project for your course. There are 10 of you. From the start, things go badly wrong – and get worse! Group members fail to get on with each other and fail to work together successfully on the project. This is a nightmare scenario. So, what do you think would cause this to happen? Try to separate out the reasons into two types: *process-related reasons* (the procedures for running the group don't work) and *people-related reasons* (there are problems among the group members themselves). Write in the spaces provided the reasons why a group would fail.

Process-related reasons for failure

....
....
....
....

People-related reasons for failure

....
....
....
....

Many problems in groups stem from the individual members themselves. Specific problems, particularly talking too much – or not at all – often arise from anxiety and misunderstanding. But we all have strengths to contribute to the success of any group – and weaknesses that we need to be aware of. There are a variety of personality type tests which can help you and your team members understand those strengths and weaknesses better and enable you to work more effectively in a team.

For now try the following activities which are designed to make you think about how you work within a team:

What I like about teamwork

....
....
....
....
....

What I don't like about teamwork

....
....
....
....
....

What do I bring to a team; what are my strengths?

....
....
....
....
....

What are my weaknesses in relation to teamwork?

....

....

....

....

....

It might be useful to complete the activities above on your own and then discuss your responses with team members. This will help you understand each other better and should help you work more effectively as a team because you will be able to draw on each other's strengths and compensate for weaknesses.

Some general strategies of conflict resolution will be mentioned here. According to Appelbaum, there are at least nine strategies which could be used for conflict resolution:

- *Dominate*. Using power and pressure. This may be useful when the conflict is minor or when there is need for speedy action or to resist abusive use of power.
- *Smooth*. Gaining others' approval by accentuating the benefits and smoothing over disadvantages that would fuel opposition.
- *Maintain*. Keeping to the status quo until the collection of sufficient information is completed or to let emotions cool down.
- *Bargain*. Offering something the other party wants in exchange for something you want. This is useful when collaboration is difficult.
- *Coexist*. When no agreement can be reached, following more than one option until it becomes clear which of them is the most appropriate.
- *Decide by rule*. Using an objective rule, such as a vote, lottery, seniority system or arbitration, when there is need for taking decisive steps.
- *Collaborate*. Making joint efforts to reach a compromise and adopt a solution satisfying all group members, especially when the issue discussed is very important.
- *Release*. Letting others solve the matter.
- *Yield*. Supporting the other members' views when you become convinced it is more appropriate, or when the issue is much more important to them than to you.

(S Appelbaum, B Shapiro and D Elbaz, 'The Management of Multicultural Group Conflict' (1998) *Team Performance Management*, 4(5) at p 228)

Some of these strategies may be less relevant in student groups. For example, using power or pressure to resolve disputes, even if successful in achieving a specific goal, could aggravate personal differences within the group and endanger the achievement of other, more important, group goals. Conversely, collaboration is always an effective way of solving disputes without sowing the seeds of further conflicts.

For deciding which is the appropriate strategy to take, factors such as the nature of the dispute or the reaction of the other group members should be taken into account. Additionally, the strategy should be appropriate to help resolve genuine disputes and support the achievement of group goals. In either case, mediation or advice from the tutor could be requested.

How confident am I in groups?

Tick the statement that applies to you...

	Very confident	Would like to be more confident
I can help to diffuse arguments	☐	☐
I can motivate my group to find alternative ways of doing things	☐	☐
I can encourage my group to search for supporting evidence when we do research	☐	☐
I can lead a group and run group projects efficiently	☐	☐
In group tasks I can separate the important information from the irrelevant	☐	☐
I can think rationally in a group when emotions become high	☐	☐
I can argue my view logically when my group does not agree with me	☐	☐
I have patience when working in groups	☐	☐
I can offer and receive criticism to and from my group members	☐	☐

How my behaviour will change in my next group task on my course:

....

....

....

Troubleshooting

Below are some typical problems which can hamper progress in the team and suggested solutions or ways of dealing with the problems.

(a) Someone gets upset if his or her ideas are challenged or rejected
This problem usually arises because of the way an idea gets challenged in the group. The person who puts forward the idea may feel personally rejected or insulted if his or her suggestions are scorned or insensitively rejected. If someone puts forward an idea, and others don't accept it, the objectors need to make clear that it is the idea that they want to challenge, and not the intelligence or integrity of the person proposing the idea.

(b) Problems from outside being brought into the group
If group members are experiencing problems outside the group, they may find it difficult to ignore these. Worries from the outside can cause group members to be angry or aggressive to others without too much obvious provocation. It can be helpful if group meetings start with members saying what has happened to them generally since the last meeting. This may bring worrying issues up to the surface. The group may also want to build in a ground rule about not accepting abusive or aggressive behaviour.

Since last week, I've started my assignment. I don't have much spare time.

Ok. Let's design a timetable that we can all stick to.

Since last week, I've finished all the tasks we were given. I'm ready to move on.

(c) Group imbalances, eg one or two people tend to dominate the discussion; a few people do all the work; some members opt out of most discussion/work

If these issues are coming up to the surface, they need to be openly discussed; otherwise resentment will start to destroy group cohesion. The chairperson needs to lead discussion on to the topic of group dynamics by inviting group members to say openly, candidly, but not abusively or aggressively, how they feel the group is working. The chairperson should invite someone to start the discussion, and once someone has raised a sensitive issue, others will usually follow with their comments. The chairperson should ensure all group members get a chance to say what they think. This can lead to a difficult and tense meeting, particularly if a lot of resentment is below the surface. However, an honest discussion can clear the air and lead to a much more open and committed group. Some group members, for example, may be completely unaware that their opinions and actions have been causing problems. The meeting should try to close on a positive action point for the future.

(d) Silences: sometimes a group will not have much if anything to say on a particular topic or occasion

This can be perceived as embarrassing in some cultural groupings, and often someone will jump in with a superfluous comment or joke to fill what they think is a void. However, silence is often a good thing, particularly when the group is considering an important point. The chairperson could, indeed, encourage group members to sit in silence for a minute or two to mentally weigh up important issues before commenting on them.

(e) Sexist, racist or other stereotyping or abusive remarks

Such remarks should not be allowed, accepted or tolerated in the group, and there should be a ground rule to this effect. It should not be left to the chairperson to have to challenge these remarks; all members have a moral responsibility to intervene.

(f) Not listening to others in the group

It can take a lot of courage and encouragement before some members voice their opinions in a group. They may be a variety of reasons for this. The group member concerned may be a quiet, reserved person, and/or unsure what is expected of them, and/or a person who prefers to march to the beat of his or her own drum, rather than the synchronised rhythm of the group. Whatever the reasons, if the ideas or opinions of any member are not genuinely listened to, the speaker may retreat emotionally from further group discussion.

A ground rule about the importance of listening to others and paying attention when others are talking is a good idea, as at least this will raise this often unacknowledged issue to the surface. Group members should find ways of encouraging quiet members to contribute to the discussion, and the chairperson has an important role to play in ensuring everyone is given the opportunity to speak – and be listened to.

(g) Someone allocated a group task does not complete it, or completes it poorly

This is a fairly common problem, unfortunately, and is a situation that can cause considerable frustration and resentment among group members who are willing to work to the best of their ability. The problem can be avoided by members discussing who does what at an early stage of group formation, and what results are expected.

Individual group tasks should be identified, delegated, and the expected outcome clarified.

If all members have entered into a contract on expectations, the group is then justified in asking the group member concerned to complete his or her part of the contract in the way previously agreed. However, in extreme and irresolvable cases, group members, particularly if marks or grades are involved, should discuss the matter with the module leader. Tutors are increasingly asking group members to identify and summarise their role and contribution in a group, or using peer assessment to decide whether or not individual members are *entitled* to share a group mark or grade.

(h) The leader or chairperson of the group is proving to be unsuitable and unacceptable to the majority of the group. He or she may be, for example, too directive, dogmatic or aggressive or, by contrast, indecisive and ineffective

It is unusual in any group for the leader or chairperson to be completely isolated and without some partial support from one or two group members. So if there is a consensus among group members about the problem, it is best approached via those individuals who are most likely to be listened to by the leader. The leader should be given a chance to discuss the issues with all the group members, and make changes, if necessary. Sometimes, the leader simply does not understand the negative impact of his or her leadership style on others. It may have been fine in situation X, but not in the new Y or Z context. The real problem can occur if the group divides into two, or even three factions, because of leadership-related issues. Often in this situation, the real problems are not aired and discussed, and a general mood of disagreement, hostility and non-cooperation prevails. The answer is to discuss the problem, no matter how painful, awkward or difficult it is for a group.

If I was a team leader accused of being ineffective, I would ...

....

....

....

....

(i) The group has discussed a subject honestly and democratically, but no agreement or decision can be reached

There are likely to be two or more positions within the group, and the role of the chairperson is to summarise these and then allow group members to vote on which option on balance they prefer. This can be done publicly, but is often best done privately and in writing, as the voting preferences of some members might be influenced by the dominant personalities of others in the group. One approach would be to briefly adjourn the meeting to give everyone a chance to think the issues over, but then ask group members to return after a break and to vote to reach a majority view. In the case of three options, an initial vote can identify the two strongest positions, which can then be voted on. If the three options all receive equal votes, the chairperson may have to decide which two options should be voted on. This may make him or her temporarily unpopular with some, but at least not for being indecisive.

Activity Think about your ideal team. Who would be in your team, and what would you do? How would you all achieve your end goal? Your ideas can be as fantastical as you like.

....

....

....

....

....

....

....

....

Group work and plagiarism

An important issue which students participating in group work should consider carefully is plagiarism. Plagiarism can become an issue when the groups are set up by students and the aims of their creation are not set or approved by their tutors. Such study groups may be created, for example, to help students prepare for exams, to exchange lecture notes or to discuss ideas on a law topic.

While collaborative learning is actively promoted by universities, most areas of student activity are still governed by the requirements of individual knowledge and assessment. For example, written exams, individual coursework or dissertations are used to test individual knowledge and skills. In these cases collaboration between students, while allowed, should not go too far because issues of plagiarism could arise. For this reason, before deciding to work together on a university project, students should read the university rules on plagiarism first to ensure that their group activities do not violate the rules. Plagiarism is discussed in detail in **Chapter 5**.

Self-assessment Identify an occasion when you *successfully* worked in a group with other students and you had to submit a joint piece of work where you all contributed. Describe the operation of the group and how successful it was in the achievement of each goal. How was the work of each team member combined? Has the group participation enhanced your learning and skills?

....

....

....

....

....

....

....

....

....

6.2 TIME MANAGEMENT

Law students engage in numerous daily activities which require an appropriate allocation of time. They have to prepare for and attend classes at university, work on projects or essays and prepare for exams. In addition to university activities, students need to maintain normal life off campus. An increasing number of students in UK universities are mature students, many of whom also manage their own families and jobs. Other students, due to the increasing costs of education, have to take paid work to cover part or the whole of their university fees and expenses.

Self-assessment Time management

Tick the statement that applies to you...	This is me!	I have this under control
I can't get out of bed in the morning!	☐	☐
I have walked into a lecture after it has started	☐	☐
I have missed an appointment because I totally forgot about it	☐	☐
I have lost some of my belongings because I was rushing around	☐	☐
I miss deadlines without good excuses	☐	☐
I start my assignments way too late	☐	☐
I lose track of the time easily	☐	☐
I often get distracted onto other matters	☐	☐

My action plan:

....

....

....

....

Self-assessment Write in the space below how good your time management skills are on your law course. How do you feel about them? Have you experienced any loss as a result of poor timekeeping? How much can they be improved, and how?

....

....

....

....

....

Students who work part time find that the penalty for not turning up for work or not completing special tasks in the workplace may be getting into trouble or not being paid (or getting fired!). Such strict punishments are not a threat when completing university work, although the consequence can be more severe in the long run. What if you leave university with a much lower qualification than you are capable of simply because you could not organise your time? When students work outside of university (or, in fact, have any other responsibility, such as raising a family), allocating adequate time to study and remaining focused on the curriculum activities becomes a difficult task. On the other hand, if you enrol on a full-time course, this is what you are expected, and required, to give: your *full* time. Failure to allocate appropriate time to study is associated with negative consequences, and some of the following may occur:

- failure to complete the course;
- completion of the course, but failure to achieve a satisfactory degree grade;
- reduced career potential;
- loss of self-confidence;
- tensions with family;
- adverse financial consequences;
- increased stress levels;
- adverse health consequences (illnesses).

On the other hand, successful on-time completion of study activities has various benefits including:

- completion of the course;
- higher course grade;
- improved career prospects;
- increased self-confidence and happiness;
- peace at home;
- better health.

All law students wish to achieve their course aims and at the same time maintain normal life outside of their studies. This though does not always happen. A significant number of students find it hard to maintain a healthy balance between activities within the university and outside of it, the result being in most cases that time available to study and to ensure successful completion of the degree or course is severely limited.

One of the causes of the problem is the inability of many law students to manage their time in an efficient way. This may be because students are unable to prioritise and schedule their various activities, allocate sufficient time to each of them, and adopt an effective action plan for the completion of these activities. As a result, many important deadlines pass without the tasks having been completed or, if completed, without having met the required standard of quality.

Time management is a process which helps students to manage their time in an efficient way. Time management can help students to identify and assess their curriculum tasks, to ensure that appropriate time is allocated to them without excessively restricting their other activities, and to ensure that their hard efforts are not wasted. Using minimum effort in this context does not mean compromising the quality or quantity of study but completing tasks at the desirable level of quality and quantity without using more effort and time than is necessary.

Daily challenges

Jamie, a law student, has to accomplish the following activities and tasks within the next 30 days:

- Complete two summative essays in land law and criminal law respectively.
- Attend the scheduled classes at the university and complete successfully the prescribed tasks and exercises in the tutorials and seminars.

- Complete the scheduled part-time work in the local Starbucks where he works three 8-hour shifts weekly.
- Spend a weekend in Glasgow to attend his cousin's wedding.
- Complete his gym programme which involves four 2-hour sessions weekly.
- Secure adequate free time to engage in social activity, which includes visiting family and friends, going to cinema, bar etc.
- Cope with any uncertain or unpredictable events that may appear in the course of these 30 days (eg sudden illness, unexpected visits by friends, or other unexpected but unavoidable social commitments, etc).

For many of the above activities and tasks, there are specific deadlines attached. For example, there are fixed deadlines for handing in essays, fixed times for classes and the part-time job, fixed dates for weddings and fixed times for classes at the gym. Jamie knows exactly what amount of time he will have to spend at work: he knows that for his part-time job he needs to spend 24 hours weekly divided into three 8-hour shifts scheduled for specific days of the week, and he also knows that to attend his course classes he needs to spend a specific amount of time on specific days according to the programme set by the university. However, for other activities (eg social activities and research) there are no strict deadlines. Jamie cannot say, for example, how many hours of research, study and writing he will need to successfully complete the two essays for each of which he seeks at least a 2:1 grade. He only knows that he needs to allocate adequate time to complete the essays.

Many students like Jamie, facing numerous tasks and activities that need to be accomplished within a relatively short period of time, run into panic and feel a mounting sense of frustration. They lose confidence in their ability to cope with the situation and react by removing some tasks and activities from their schedule. Other students have more confidence in their ability to accomplish everything, but the modes of action they use are insufficient, the result being that at the end of the 30-day period some of the tasks and activities will not be properly started or even completed.

 **Self-assessment** Time management checklist

List the tasks below that you have to complete in the next seven days, and in the column to the right, write the day and time that you will complete them (and the treat you will give yourself!)

Task	Date and time of completion

Common mistakes

Some of the common mistakes that students make when they seek to accomplish tasks and activities include the following.

(a) Procrastination

Students procrastinate (ie they postpone decisions or the commencement of study until another day for no good reason). Reasons for procrastination include the following:

- when students are faced with decisions or tasks which they perceive as difficult (eg *'This topic on constructive trusts in the land law essay is difficult and I do not know how to plan my research and study of it. I will postpone my decision until next week.'*);
- when students perceive the topic to be too easy and therefore to require no serious consideration (eg *'The tutorial questions on English Legal System for next week are too easy so there is no need to work on the answers now.'*);
- when students perceive the subject of study as boring or uninteresting (eg *'I am not interested in the law of trusts so I will not commence the essay work on secret trusts until next week.'*);
- when students feel the environment is not appropriate (eg *'I can't study in the library because there are too many distractions from other students.'*);
- when students feel tired, anxious or stressed (eg *'I cannot work on my essay today because I spent many hours at the university attending classes.'*);
- when students are engaged in some other tasks or activities (eg *'I will start work on the land law topic next week because this week I have to complete my criminal law assignment.'*);
- when students exhibit a general tendency to procrastinate (eg *'I always complete my tasks at the last minute.'*).

Procrastination is common to all students, and as long as it remains under control it does not cause problems. However, a significant proportion of students procrastinate constantly and in ways that deter them from completing essential course tasks and activities which, in turn, has serious adverse consequences including failure to complete the course. This occurs because procrastinators are generally disorganised and tend to underestimate the time and effort required to complete a task. As a result, they allocate an inappropriate amount of time and effort to the task, which increases the chances of failure. Generally, procrastinating students are also less competitive than non-procrastinating ones and are bad performers too. Additionally, as a result of their disorganised activities and consequent failures and the sense of guilt they feel, they suffer from a variety of health problems including anxiety, stress, forgetfulness and various illnesses.

Self-assessment 'This is me!' Make notes in this box about how you will tackle your occasional procrastination:

....

....

....

....

....

(b) Inflated personal abilities and perfectionism

Some students believe that they are always in a position to cope with any task, whatever its level or complexity. Some seek 'perfect' outcomes for their activities. Others believe that they can work better under pressure and with looming deadlines hanging over their heads. There are also students who believe that they are smart and capable of accomplishing the tasks by spending less time and effort on them than other students.

> No worries – I'll do it later. I always perform best with a deadline over my head.

While a high level of confidence in personal skills and abilities can be an advantage and can help students to overcome the fear of failure and to achieve higher grades in the course, it may become a disadvantage if not kept in check. Excessive self-confidence may lead to procrastination and a failure to complete tasks in a timely manner.

By focusing on personal strengths and positive experiences, perfectionism could increase motivation to work harder and improve university performance, but it could also inhibit performance by setting unrealistic goals and increasing anxiety and stress. Perfectionists must also bear decreased levels of self-confidence and self-esteem when their inability to achieve their unrealistic grades transpires on results day. Perfectionists can also place unreasonably high demands on their classmates and their tutors which may aggravate their relationships, offering little personal benefit and happiness.

Self-assessment 'This is me!' Make notes in this box about how you will tackle your over-confidence in your studies:

....

....

....

....

....

(c) Inadequate planning and time scheduling

Many students do not make an advance plan or schedule for the commencement and management of their studies. Other students do not use their timetables adequately. Students often base their study plans on vague or unrealistic assumptions and estimates. The result in both cases is failure to achieve the desired outcome for the task, and increased levels of anxiety and stress.

The lack of advance planning and time scheduling in many younger students is the result of a lack of experience. Young students join the university from secondary education where their school activities were more closely supervised and controlled by their teachers, who could help them with numerous planning and scheduling activities. At university level, students enjoy more freedom and their study is self-directed, meaning that it is their responsibility to plan and schedule their study.

'This is me!' Make notes in this box about how you will schedule your studies from now on:

....

....

....

....

(d) Existence of distractions

Some students do have a realistic plan of action but are unable to implement it due to the existence of distractions which hinder their efforts. There are various sources of distractions:

- friends;
- social activities;
- sports activities;
- music;
- video games;
- Internet chat;
- television.

Sometimes the distraction may come from another less relevant task, from the mind of the student when he or she faces concentration problems, or when the task that he or she is dealing with is difficult. Also, some students engage in multi-tasking, ie they try to perform several tasks simultaneously believing that they can successfully complete all the tasks together and save time. For example, they write their law essay while listening to music on the radio or iPod, or when in the library they chat with other students whilst studying.

The ability to multitask may be an advantage in certain cases (eg you can read your lecture notes while commuting, ensuring that the commuting time is not wasted). However, in other cases multi-tasking may mean doing badly in the tasks involved – if you chat on the Internet with friends while writing your law essay, it is likely that the quality of your work will not be good, and neither will you be able to enjoy the chat with your friends due to the distraction caused by the essay writing. This could happen because, by hopping back and forth between tasks, the student loses his or her concentration and none of the simultaneous tasks receives the student's full attention. Additionally, by constantly switching between tasks, the mind gets tired faster and its overall performance decreases because each time a person switches from one task to another the mind needs time to adjust.

Generally, distractions may be needed to give the mind a break, especially after prolonged study. They become a problem when they are deflecting students from starting or completing their tasks. Distractions are closely related to procrastination.

Have you recognised your own behaviour in this section? Note here what you think of your current attitude to distractions:

....

....

....

....

How time management can help

Time management helps students to manage their time more efficiently by allowing them to complete their tasks properly and save time and energy. Time management is a continuous process which to be effective needs to be regularly revised and updated to adapt to changing conditions, needs and improved capabilities.

The process is complex, reflecting the intricacy of the tasks involved and the number of factors that need to be taken into account. Also, it has several stages which need to be tailored to the individual needs of the student.

(a) Getting to know yourself

An essential preliminary step that students need to take before deciding how to manage their time is to get to know themselves and to identify the personal attributes and needs that must be taken into account when planning and implementing study tasks and activities. The process should also identify factors in the surrounding environment that exert an influence on the student's ability to cope with tasks. The process will also help to identify areas where improvements will be needed.

Consider the following questions:

- When is the best time for you to study (morning, afternoon, evening)?
- How well organised are you? (Do you have a diary? Do you have box files for storing materials for the modules and courses you are attending? Do you take notes in the lectures and seminars? Do you have a dedicated working space?)
- What is the best place for you to study? (At the library? At home?)
- Do you usually complete the tasks allocated to you?
- Do you usually meet the deadlines?
- How much time do you usually need to complete a university task (eg to write a 2,000-word essay, prepare the answers for the weekly tutorials, etc)?
- What are your other main responsibilities outside of the university? (Do you run your own family? Do you look after your parents?)
- Do you have paid work during your student period?
- Are there any factors personal to you that could affect your ability to study? (Concentration problems? Stress sufferer? Disability?)
- Are you a perfectionist?
- Do you have a career plan?

By answering the questions above, it will be possible to identify your key personal attributes and assess your current needs, which will then be used to design your time management programme.

	My response or action	Done!
My organisation skills are terrible!		☐
My notes, files, books and assignments are everywhere!		☐
I cannot find my favourite place to study or my favourite time of day to study.		☐
I miss deadlines quite often – it depends on the nature of the task.		☐
I have other responsibilities I cannot get out of!		☐
I need to write a weekly, monthly or annual plan.		☐

Knowing yourself is a very important stage in the process. If you are not sure about how well you currently cope with tasks, you could keep records of your activities for a couple of weeks and then assess your performance on the basis of the collected evidence.

The process of knowing yourself will be successful if at the end of it you are able to answer the following questions:

- What are my main strengths?
- What are my main weaknesses?
- What are the environmental factors that currently influence my ability to study?
- What are the areas where improvements are needed?
- What are my current needs?

Strengths and *weaknesses* How well or badly do you cope with tasks? Questions for identifying your own strengths and weaknesses could be as follows: In the last two weeks did you complete all the required tasks within the deadlines? Were there any tasks which took longer than expected? How well did you manage to deal with distractions or unexpected events? How well organised were you?

Regarding *environmental factors*, you should look to identify those factors external to you which influence your ability to study. Do you live in a noisy environment? What were the main external sources of distraction in the last two weeks (friends? family?).

Regarding *improvements*, you should look into your weaknesses and identify those which could be eliminated or at least limited.

Current needs concern objectives you want to achieve (complete an essay in public law, install an Internet connection at home so you can study at home, etc).

Self-assessment Write your answers to each of the five bullet-pointed questions (above) in this space:

....
....
....
....
....
....
....

(b) Planning and scheduling

Having identified your own needs and attributes, you can now proceed to planning, scheduling and implementing your activities. Planning and scheduling can be effective if you can predict with reasonable accuracy the duration of the activities and schedule them in a way that allows for their realistic accomplishment within the set timeframe.

There are a number of things that a law student can do to ensure effective planning and scheduling, which are considered below:

(i) Goal setting

Before starting any activity, you should determine the goals you expect to achieve by undertaking that activity. Goals may be short or long term depending on the nature and significance of the activity. Achieving a first-class university degree, for example, is a long-term goal for first-year undergraduate students. Achieving a first-class grade in a land law assignment is a short-term goal. Sometimes successful completion of an activity helps to achieve multiple goals (for example, achieving a first-class LLB degree will also improve career prospects, secure entry to a postgraduate university programme and greatly increase self-confidence and self-esteem). In other cases, the accomplishment of a long-term goal can depend on the completion of numerous short-term goals. The overall grade of your LLB degree, for example, depends on your performance in the individual modules forming it.

When setting goals, priority should be given to long-term goals. Shorter-term goals will then fit into place. By way of example, becoming a solicitor is a long-term goal that an undergraduate student can set. To achieve this goal, he or she must successfully pass a number of compulsory stages:

(a) obtain a qualifying law degree;

(b) complete the legal practice course (LPC);

(c) complete a two-year training contract;

(d) complete a professional skills course.

The meaning of 'long term' and 'short term' depends on the overall picture. It is the choice of the person setting the goals. For example, for a first-year law student, a long-term goal is to successfully complete the LLB course and short-term goals to pass all the modules of the course.

Self-assessment Identify a long-term goal you set yourself and the shorter-term goals you designed to help you achieve your long-term goal. Explain the reasons for the selection of these goals and how successful you have been so far in accomplishing them.

....

....

....

....

....

....

....

....

....

The nature of the goal determines the amount of time and effort you have to dedicate towards that goal. Seeking a first-class degree requires you to study more and with greater intensity than seeking merely to pass.

Successful goal-setting includes goals which are realistic and attainable within the set time limit. You could make a list of strengths and weaknesses in relation to your current study skills and what is realistic for you.

By way of example, if the activity concerns writing coursework on family law, the strengths/weaknesses list of a law student might look something like this:

Strengths	Weaknesses
• I have completed assessments for other law modules, so I possess relevant experience and knowledge of what I have to do to achieve the grade I need. • I have good notes from lectures and tutorials. • I have good experience of legal research, so collecting and analysing the materials for the coursework will not be a lengthy process for me.	• I have no prior knowledge of the coursework topic. • I have missed many classes. • Family law is not my favourite subject. I find it boring and have little personal interest in it. I only want to pass. • I have to complete two more assignments on criminal law and land law during the same period, so I may not have the time I need to complete this one.

Make one of your own!

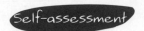
Self-assessment

Module: Course:	
My strengths	**My weaknesses**

You could use evidence of your own experience and take into account your current level of preparation when predicting how much time you will need to complete all your tasks. If you have no prior experience, you should allow as much time as possible for the activity so that you will be able to deal with unforeseen difficulties and complications. Personal tendencies to procrastinate should be taken into account, and you should avoid making unreasonable demands on yourself. Being realistic in your goals increases the chances of success.

Goals checklist
- Specific goals
- Realistic goals
- Attainable goals

Lastly, your goals must be as specific as possible by setting clear dates and times for their completion.

Very often, the achievement of a goal does not depend solely on the efforts of the student. For example, when working with other students as a group, the achievement of group goals depends on the efforts of the other group members. Also, student performance at university is assessed by lecturers whose views about the quality of a student's work may differ from the student's own. For these reasons, when setting a goal which includes factors beyond your control, you should focus more on the realistic nature of your goal and on the efforts required to achieve it, rather than on the final outcome. However, it is usually the case that the final outcome of an activity is reflective of the quality and quantity of the work done by the student (although some students disagree when results are published!). Your 'goal table' and further reflective learning information can be found in **Chapter 4**.

(ii) Action planning

Having set realistic and attainable goals, the student can now proceed to the planning of the necessary study activities that will help him or her achieve these goals. Effective planning is a key element in the accomplishment of short- and long-term goals. Sometimes it may be useful to break down the big goals into smaller ones and design relevant smaller tasks to achieve them.

For example, the goal of writing law coursework can be broken down into a number of smaller goals supported by appropriate tasks as follows:

Goals	Activities
Collection of materials	Research the available resources (eg databases, textbooks etc)
Study	Study the materials attained from the research
Identify the answers	Prepare a plan of your answers
Put the ideas on paper	Write a draft of the coursework
Complete the coursework	Write the final draft
Is there anything else you have to do in the foreseeable future?	

Breaking down a big goal into a number of smaller ones helps you monitor more effectively the progress of your work. It is even more effective when supported by specific timetables for the accomplishment of each of the smaller goals.

Effective planning also requires you to take unpredictable events into account. Even though unpredictable events are not known in advance and therefore their impact on planning cannot be assessed before they occur, it is nevertheless useful to take some precautionary steps to enable you to mitigate such events if they occur. One such step would be to ensure that provision for free time is always included in your plans. This free time could then be used to cover delays or disruptions to your planned activities.

(iii) Prioritising

This is closely related to planning. Sometimes it is not possible to complete all of your tasks within the set timeframe. In this case you need to decide which activities should be given priority and which should be pushed to the background or abandoned altogether. There are different ways of prioritising tasks. The task significance or task urgency are two possible criteria. More significant tasks should be given priority over less significant ones. For example, finishing a summative essay is more important than going to the cinema. If you cannot achieve both, you should give priority to the essay. Similarly, if the deadline of the submission of your land law essay is earlier than that of the criminal law one, priority should be given to the former.

Below is an organiser that will help you to organise your course priorities. In the first column, place your list of tasks. In the second column, number each task according to its significance (1: least significant – 5: most significant). In the third column number each task according to its urgency (1: least urgent – 5: most urgent). The fourth column contains the sum of both columns added together. The task with the highest overall score could be given priority over the others. The other tasks could follow in order of their overall score.

Tasks	Significance (1–5)	Urgency (1–5)	Overall score
eg start my assignment research	5	3	8/10

(iv) Time allocation and scheduling

After prioritising your tasks, the next stage in the process concerns allocating time to these tasks.

The aim is to ensure that all set tasks will be completed within the prescribed timeframe. For some tasks the time required to complete them is fixed and pre-determined. For example, students know that they have to spend a specific amount of hours per week attending lectures and tutorials. For other tasks the amount of time that needs to be allocated to them is harder to predict. For example, it is difficult to predict how many hours of study you will need to be ready for your exams.

Prior experience of similar tasks may help you to make a realistic allocation of time. In the absence of such experience you may have to make an initial prediction and then make adjustments according to the development of your course. Being flexible and adaptive is often essential for accomplishing tasks which you have no prior knowledge or experience of.

In all cases, knowing the way you work and making a realistic assessment of your existing personal skills and capabilities can help you to make a reliable and efficient allocation of time. You could test the accuracy of your decisions by using planners or diaries to schedule your tasks and record the progress of their completion, and by reassessing the situation on a weekly basis.

Task scheduling should be realistic. Failure to do so could increase your stress levels and mess up your entire schedule. For example, if you are unable to finish your family law assignment by the end of the week as planned, you will have to use extra time in the next week which will be at the expense of activities planned for that week. It is therefore important not to use stringently tight schedules and to allow yourself some flexibility so you are able to deal with unexpected events.

A problem commonly experienced in time management is that students fail to complete their tasks on time. Keeping to the schedule proves an impossible task for some students and they end up quitting their tasks early. Various methods have been proposed for addressing these problems, including the following:

● *Be organised!*

Have specific and detailed plans, keep planners or diaries to record your activities, use an effective note-taking method or devise a filing system. These are some of the steps you can take to help you stay committed to the task. Well-organised students can complete tasks in a more timely and efficient way than students lacking adequate organisation.

● *Stay motivated!*

A task can be completed faster if the student stays motivated throughout the process. Students can stay motivated if they see that the task is interesting or is serving an important purpose. However, not all tasks undertaken at university are interesting. Some tasks are boring or difficult for many students. Staying motivated in such cases is hard. One of the best ways to stay motivated is by keeping in mind the ultimate goal that has to be achieved through the task. For example, passing the assessment in a difficult law module helps you to progress to the next level of your course. Another way to stay motivated is by looking into other potential benefits, such as financial or social benefits. Lastly, students can stay motivated if they have an exciting reward in place for the completion of the task. This increases their levels of enthusiasm and increases the chances that the task will be completed.

(v) Resist procrastination and distractions

This is enormously difficult on a law course! Sometimes, *anything* seems more interesting than the assignment you are doing! Procrastination and distractions are closely related to each other. Procrastination prevents students from getting started on work whereas distractions prevent them from completing it. They could be the result of a variety of factors. Addressing these factors could help reduce distractions and procrastination.

Self-assessment **My biggest distractions!**

In the space below, write a list of your biggest study distractions. Compare them to those of your friends – you will notice that sometimes really strange things can take a student's mind off his or her studies!

....

....

....

....

Anxiety and stress begin to arise when students turn a blind eye to their course responsibilities. Students fear that they will not be able to accomplish the course tasks so they delay starting them. This fear is often unjustified and is caused by false perceptions about the level of difficulty of the task or the personal ability to cope with it. If you don't have a plan for accomplishing the task then it is likely that you will suffer from stress and procrastinate as a result.

Drawing up a plan is the solution in these cases. Even if your plan is not perfect, it is always better than no plan at all. Drawing up a plan helps you to address false perceptions and increase your self-confidence.

Consider the following situation:

> You were recently given your coursework questions for contract law. They are a series of problem questions and rumours are spread by some students who say they are confusing and difficult to answer. After a quick reading of these questions you agree with the rumours. You become anxious and postpone the commencement of the work until next week in the hope that you will be able by then to find a solution.

Adopting such an approach is not helpful. The confusing and difficult questions will still be there next week. Acting now would help to find an early solution and reduce anxiety.

Draw up a plan for solving the problem. In this case, a plan of action might be as follows:

- Collect the materials
- Study the materials
- Make a plan of your answers
- Write a draft
- Write your final answers

Act immediately. In many cases, the process of collecting and studying the materials will gradually dispel your fears. The questions will not prove as difficult as you had initially thought. The initial reaction might have been the result of inadequate knowledge of the topics or the influence of the rumours spread by other students. A question that is difficult to one student may not be to another. Research of the topics and a study of the materials will increase your knowledge and produce better answers. If, after a lot of research and study, you still cannot find the answers to the questions, you could then contact your tutor for clarification. Experience shows, though, that in most cases students will eventually find the answers themselves alone.

Other students procrastinate because they cannot concentrate or because they demonstrate a general tendency to procrastinate. Try this strategy:

> Set yourself small, relatively easy tasks (eg to read the lecture notes, a journal article, etc) for a duration of no more than 10–15 minutes. At the end of that period, set another small task. The accomplishment of these small tasks will help you to build a momentum that will allow you to continue.

Some students do not delay commencement of work but cannot complete it due to distractions from various sources (eg interference of friends, TV, Internet, family, etc). In these cases the student needs to find a quiet place where people cannot distract him or her. Switching off mobile phones and other communication means (email, Facebook, etc) will be required too. Starting with the unpleasant tasks first and getting them out of the way early can help reduce anxiety and stress and avoid distractions. If you find a particular textbook hard to understand, try another one and then another until you find the textbook that suits your needs. Always make notes of the book's key points or your flowing ideas.

While procrastination and distractions cannot be completely avoided, it is possible to limit their harmful impact.

In the box below, write about recent personal procrastination experiences that caused you trouble (made you miss a deadline, forced you to stay awake until the early hours to complete a delayed university project, etc). Explain what the cause of the procrastination was, and if after the event you took any action to avoid similar problems in the future. If your answer is 'yes', did it work? If your answer is 'no', or if the action you took did not prevent repetition of procrastination, explain the reasons for the failure and outline any further steps you intend to take in the future to address the problem. Present your answer to your peers – can they relate to your issue?

....

....

....

....

....

....

....

....

....

....

Maintain a normal life

Accomplishing university tasks is necessary for the successful completion of the course, but students also need to allow time for maintaining a normal social and family life. Visiting friends, having fun and doing physical exercise all help to maintain a good mood and a healthy life which in turn facilitates the accomplishment of study goals. Living a hectic lifestyle has a negative impact on health and motivation, which in turn affects performance at university too. Students should avoid overloading themselves with excessive tasks that could restrict their life. Allocating sufficient time for sports and recreation should be included in the weekly plans as well.

Resist perfectionism

Perfectionism increases motivation but it also increases stress. Students setting very high performance standards for themselves face frustration and a drop in self-confidence and self-esteem when they do not meet these standards.

Setting realistic and attainable goals is the solution to perfectionism. When carrying out a task, the focus of the student should be on doing his or her best in the circumstances. Failures should be treated as lessons for improving performance rather than as sources of criticism and frustration.

Students already seeing themselves as perfectionists will have to abandon their personal perceptions and adopt a more realistic approach to life. Otherwise perfectionism could take away their peace of mind, hinder future chances of success and turn student life into a disappointing nightmare.

Time management offers solutions

Managing time effectively can save time and energy which can then be allocated to other activities.

However, for the process to be effective, it needs to be regularly assessed and updated, taking into account changing course and study conditions. Also, it needs to be used on a permanent basis and become part of the daily student routine. Only if the student remains committed to time management and implements it consistently can he or she enjoy its beneficial effects.

Self-assessment List all the treats you want to buy for yourself below and, next to them, list the task you have to complete first in order to attain them!

....
....
....
....
....
....

6.3 PROJECT MANAGEMENT

If you:

- miss deadlines;
- have to rush essays, assignment and tutorial work;
- feel like you often waste time;
- would like to work more efficiently;
- would like to get better marks;
- would like to be more organised and on top of your work,

then you need to master the skills of project management.

What is project management?

Project management is a set of skills and processes that helps you complete set tasks efficiently, effectively and on time. Projects can be managed in phases, with each phase including specific, well-defined activities.

Project management phases include:

1 *Defining* the project, including clearly defining project objectives, constraints, schedule expectations, criteria for completion, and measures for success.
2 *Planning* the project, including work breakdowns and task lists, schedule and time requirements, materials required, and charts to highlight deadlines and milestones.
3 *Executing* the project, including all required tasks, performance against the planned schedule, and management of changes to the project objectives.
4 *Analysing* the results of the project to help you learn from mistakes and improve your skills for the next project.

The table below summarises what happens in the different phases of project management. Note that not every box will apply to every project. For example, there is no need to define the team if you are working on an individual assignment.

	(1) DEFINITION	(2) PLANNING	(3) EXECUTION	(4) ANALYSIS
WHAT HAPPENS?	Define the team	Work breakdown	Actual work	Review project success
	Define requirements	Task list	Completed tasks	Understand changes required
	Define objectives	Project schedule	Changes to objectives, tasks or schedules	What went well and not so well
	Define completion criteria	Preliminary research	Prepare output: essay, tutorial work, etc	
		Timetable		
DOCUMENTS TO HELP YOU	Clarification of project	Task list, including who does what in group work	Project schedule and task list to tick off	Record of comments, issues, problems

Why is project management important?

In the workplace, project management is a critical skill. It can help you ensure you complete what is required of you and should give you the flexibility to deal with life's little surprises. Successful projects are very well planned and completed within budget and on time. Poor planning leads to extra work because tasks are not done on time or in the right order. Therefore, deadlines are missed, quality suffers, and you will feel stressed, unsuccessful and frustrated. As a student you have a fantastic opportunity to practise your project management skills.

You can see your whole law course as a 'project' to be managed, but this may be quite ambitious and the management of that overall project will develop in stages. Alternatively, you can view each subject or module you are studying as a project, and it is sensible to split that up further into very manageable chunks, mini-projects if you like. For example, each tutorial that you have to prepare for may be viewed as a project, your exam preparation could form another, as could your assessed essay. You could also view your tutorial preparation for all tutorials for a given week as your project.

So why should you develop project management skills? They will help you to:

- structure your workload and help you keep tabs on what you need to do by when;
- organise work into structured phases. This makes it easier to measure progress and keep an eye on your overall workload;
- prioritise your work;
- complete your work on time without last minute panics;
- maximise your results;
- give you experience of a skill which is essential for your future professional life.

Project management essentials

In this section we look at the four phases of project management in a little more detail to enable you to effectively manage the projects you have to complete during your studies.

(a) Defining the project

Your first step is to clearly define the scope of your project. Think about what your project is and whether you are being too ambitious and should consider smaller chunks of work as separate projects.

Self-assessment **In the space below, list three examples of projects you think you will have to deal with over the next few months:**

1 ....

....

2 ....

....

3 ....

....

Once you have decided that a particular piece of work is a project, clearly define the project objectives. What do you hope to achieve; what are your goals? If your project relates to an assignment or exam preparation, make sure you are aware of any assessment criteria. In any project it is always worth considering expectations others, such as tutors or peers, may have from the outset.

From your list above, pick one project, and in the table below list your own objectives and what you think others' expectations might be in relation to that project:

My objectives	The expectations of others

Once you have a clearly defined project and are clear about what you hope to get out of it, you need to think about how much time you have overall and about any resource constraints or other issues which you will have to take into account in the planning stages.

In relation to your chosen project, fill in the information in the table below:

My Project Table		
Project start date:		Project finish date:
Total duration:		
Resource constraints:		Library opening hours:
Other issues:		

Once you have a clearly defined project and are clear in your own mind about any constraints and issues you will have to deal with and the time you have to complete the project, it is time to start planning!

(b) Planning the project

Project planning gets easier with practice as you gain experience of how long certain tasks take to complete. Be prepared to revise your plan as you go along, and learn from mistakes – it's all part of the process.

When planning your project, the easiest starting point is to make a list of all the things you will have to do to complete the project. This is known as a task list. Your task list should include everything you need to do even if it seems obvious. Once you have a task list, try putting the individual tasks into a chronology so that you can see what you need to do first and which tasks are interdependent. The exercise below should help.

Self-assessment **In the table below, list and organise the tasks you will have to do in order to complete your project:**

My Task Table			
	Task:	Before I can do this, I need to complete the following action:	Deadline:
(1)			
(2)			

(3)		
(4)		
(5)		
(6)		
(7)		
(8)		

You should now have a table that lists the tasks you need to complete roughly in the order they will be completed. Now think about what materials and other resources you need and where you will find them. Again listing these in a table can be useful. Try it below:

Resource:	Location:	Time needed to get it:
(1)		
(2)		
(3)		
(4)		

If you need resources or materials that are more difficult to get hold of, you may need to return to your task list and consider whether to add acquiring certain resources as individual tasks and how that impacts on the chronology of your project. Further help with finding legal resources is included in **Chapter 2**.

You can now seriously begin to think about timing. Go back to your original task list and think about how long each task will take you. Jot that down and then add it up and see if you have enough time to complete your project. You might well find that you need to revise those timings. Once you have a rough idea of how long things will take, you can work on a schedule. It is often easier to work backwards from the deadline. Remember to leave enough time for surprises and dealing with issues or problems you had not anticipated, and try to set your project deadline a little before your deadline for submission or project delivery so that you don't end up in a last minute panic. Also, remember that it is unlikely that you will be dealing with only one project at a time and that your schedule may have to take account of you juggling multiple projects at the same time.

Use the table on pp 273–4 to add deadlines for each task on your list. Perhaps highlight those deadlines which you think are suitable milestones at which you can review your progress so far and revise your plan if necessary. Guidance on effective time management is provided at **6.2**.

(c) Executing the project

Executing the project refers to the phase where you are actually carrying out the work you have planned to do in (b). Try to stick to your plan as much as possible, but remember it is a tool for you to use to get the best out of your project so you do need to keep it under revision. You might find that some tasks do not take as long as you thought while others take a little longer. If this is the case, there is nothing wrong with amending your schedule to reflect those changes as long as you keep your overall deadline in mind.

You might also find that once you start your project, your goals and objectives change. Research can take you in a new direction, for example, or you might have misunderstood a tutorial or assignment question which you realise once you start working on the project. In such cases you need to go back and redefine your project, its scope and its objectives. You then need to check that the tasks you identified are still appropriate and add any missing ones, as well as remove any you no longer need. In other words, managing projects, however large or small, is a fairly fluid process and you have to learn to be flexible and adapt. If you have spent time on the defining and planning stages, you should find this much easier than if you just jump straight in.

(d) Analysing the project

Analysing the project is an important part of project management and is something that you should do throughout. If you have to adapt your project definition or plan, think about why you have to do this and whether this is something you can learn from for future projects.

At the end of the project, or if it is a larger project, whenever you reach a milestone, think about what went well, what you found easy, what was hard and what did not go too well. Make a note of what you could do differently next time and what you could do in the same way or build on next time.

Taking this phase as seriously as the other phases will really help develop your project management skills.

Self-assessment

Once you have finished your project (or as you go along if you like) complete the following boxes.

What went well?

....

....

....

....

....

What didn't go so well?

....

....

....

....

....

It is most useful to evaluate and analyse the project as you go along. If you consider how well or otherwise you have done in identifying and gathering your background and preparatory material, you can build on your experience and make appropriate changes when gathering primary and secondary sources later on. If you consider your experience of completing one draft chapter before starting the next, you can learn from mistakes and make the whole process more efficient and effective.

Also, remember that your supervisor or tutor is there to help guide you, and you can learn a lot from feedback you receive as well as from the mistakes you make!

Self-assessment In the space below, write a mini-self-assessment about your performance when managing your own project (this can be anything from a mini-assignment to a full dissertation). Give yourself a score out of 100. Did you do better than you thought? If not, why not?

....

....

....

....

....

....

....
....
....
....

6.4 REVISION

Revision is much more involved and active than many students real-
ise. Excellent revision requires a number of smart study skills: time
management, creativity, imagination, motivation, interactivity, writing
skills, thought skills, dedication, critical thinking, and memory. Simply
re-reading your lecture notes for a month will have almost no effect.
Many students also make the mistake of simply revising (or 're-reading') only a week before their exams. This is almost always totally
ineffective. In order to remember all the law that you have learnt during one or two full semesters, you quite simply need to implement
your revision strategy throughout the entire duration of the semester(s). If your exams are
in May, you should at the very least begin revising once you return to university or college in
January after the Christmas break.

It is difficult for students during revision time not to feel resentful, or fed up, by the whole
revision process. Negative attitudes such as *'I know I can't do it so what's the point?'*, or *'I
never perform well in exams – they don't work for me'* will not improve your chances of success. You simply need to find a revision method that suits you.

A handful of students find exams exhilarating – a chance to test knowledge, work to strict
deadlines, and taste the fear of failure. However, most students simply dread revision and
exams because they are boring and stressful. Rather than looking at exams in a negative
light, look at their positive aspects. Your lecturer has chosen to examine you in order to test
your knowledge in a certain area of law. This is a good thing – it shows you the best of what
you can achieve when put in a stressful situation. What will you get out of the examination?
A treat? Relaxation for the rest of the summer? A graduation with all your friends? The job
you've always wanted? If you have a strong incentive or a long-term goal, your drive to do
well in your exams will be even stronger.

Exams seem to be more difficult for students than assignments. This is probably because
of three main factors:

Stress   Time restraint   Memory

Exams are stressful. Your legal qualification could literally depend on how your few hours in
an exam hall go. The limited time you have during your exam puts an extra stress onto your
shoulders – will you have enough time to write all that you need to write to achieve a good
mark? In addition to this, you may panic that you won't be able to remember even the most
basic facts. Exam time is a difficult time for all students.

	I have never done this	This makes me nervous	I am good at this	This is my priority
I can use my learning style to design a revision strategy	☐	☐	☐	☐
I use my own motivation to develop a revision plan	☐	☐	☐	☐
I can organise my time, work and management skills	☐	☐	☐	☐
I use new research strategies when faced with revision	☐	☐	☐	☐
I have confident and unique revision skills	☐	☐	☐	☐
I am able to make, use and store my notes effectively	☐	☐	☐	☐
I can get the best out of my lecture notes	☐	☐	☐	☐
I can manage a number of tasks at the same time	☐	☐	☐	☐
I have a good memory and know how to improve it	☐	☐	☐	☐
I have a number of revision strategies which suit me	☐	☐	☐	☐
I know how to limit my stress levels	☐	☐	☐	☐
I can make strict schedules and stick to them	☐	☐	☐	☐
I like to plan in advance to achieve the highest marks	☐	☐	☐	☐

How do your answers look? Are they mostly in the *'I have never done this'* column? It may be time for a complete overhaul of your revision strategies if this is the case. If you can develop your revision strategy in a way that suits you, you will give yourself the best chance of success. One method that works for everybody is to allocate plenty of time and to start revising either well in advance or during your ongoing studies.

How to begin your revision

Below are some original ideas for revising law. Some will work for you, and some will not benefit you. Experimenting is part of the learning process. Make it fun!

(a) Organise your notes

The first thing you must do is to find and organise your lecture notes. If your time-keeping skills are excellent and you have planned for revision in advance, your lecture notes should be perfectly legible because you have been revising from them since day one! However, if this is not the case, you may need to rewrite some notes, catch up on lessons missed, and generally tidy your writing style by both highlighting the main points of law that were explained in the lecture, and outlining the authoritative cases and articles that were mentioned during tutorial discussions. Re-read your lecture and tutorial notes often if this method works for you, or you can turn them into more colourful and memorable revision notes and use them as a foundation to build your revision program. Tutorial work will also significantly add to your lecture notes, as tutorials or seminars often explore the law in much more depth and talk about application and analysis of legal principles to everyday scenarios.

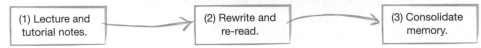

(1) Lecture and tutorial notes. → (2) Rewrite and re-read. → (3) Consolidate memory.

(b) Select and prioritise

If you have had an indication from your lecturer as to which areas of the law will examined, then begin to select the areas of law that you wish to revise, and line them up in order of priority. Perhaps you would like to revise cases before statutes? At this stage, index cards are useful. These are small lined cards that people sometimes use to jot down ideas when delivering a speech. You can buy them in different colours, which is ideal for revising cases. Simply write the case name on the top of the card, two lines of case facts, and three lines for the *ratio* of the case from the relevant judge. Read through these 'case cards' before bed every night or every evening after dinner. They will stick in your mind after only a short time. To get the best use out of your case cards, create them on the same day as your lecture and read them every few days after that for the rest of the semester. Stick them on a big mind map on your bedroom wall to illustrate where they relate to each other in the particular field of law. An example has been created below:

R v Smith [1976] 1 QB 567
Facts: Defendant stabbed victim whilst drunk. Argued intoxication as a defence.
Held: Lord Smith stated that if the defendant could not form the intention, he could not have the mental element of the offence. Intoxication was a defence.

In addition to selecting areas of law for revision, it is important that you select the most important evidence in that particular field. For example, what are the 10 most important cases in that area of law? Which statutes will your lecturer want to see in your exam answer? Do you have a list of well-regarded theories in the area that you can use for revision? If not, it is time to do some research to supplement your lecture notes, as all of these things show further research and attract very high marks. An example has been created below:

Criminal Law – Intention – Cases
- *R v Robinson* (1967) – Lord Jones – definition of intention
- *R v Gerraint* (1969) – Lord Oxley – oblique intention
- *R v Howells* (1974) – Lord Finlay – restriction on definition
- *R v Andrews* (1986) – Lord McGarry – oblique abolished
- *R v Perry and McKay* (1996) – Lord Floyd – oblique back
- *R v Solesbury* (2003) – Lord Beeston – direct intention definition

Some students cope quite well when doing some new research at revision time. It can refresh an old area of your notes and add a new perspective to your understanding of a certain theory or doctrine. However, taking something new on board just before an exam may only add to your stress, so if you feel you have enough research and revision on your hands before branching out into new areas of law then simply stick to the notes that you have already got.

(c) Draw up a revision schedule

Time keeping is one of the most important skills when it comes to revision. Students do not pay much attention to time-keeping skills in the early days of their course, and it is only when the exam is a week away that students suddenly realise that they've left everything too late. Excellent revision takes a lot of time. The longer you dedicate to revision, the stronger the facts and cases are in your mind. You must start revision as early as possible, preferably from the very beginning of your course. Buy a diary or an organiser – or simply draw up a weekly timetable on a scrap piece of paper – and begin to sketch in weekly slots to go over what you have learnt in lectures that week. As you get closer to your exams, you can develop a more intense revision period.

Revision timetables can be hard to stick to at first, particularly if they are overwhelming from week one. Pace yourself. Students become easily distracted if reading or revising for long stretches of time, and often find themselves attending to other 'very important' matters (ie watching TV). Short bursts of reading lasting 40 or 60 minutes will be enough time to read over a major point of law without your mind digressing onto other things.

Below is a one-week revision plan. Use this as a guide to create your own weekly revision plan that you can stick to.

	Monday	Tuesday	Wednesday	Thursday	Friday	Saturday	Sunday
Morning							
Lunchtime							
Evening							

	Monday	Tuesday	Wednesday	Thursday	Friday	Saturday	Sunday
Morning		Contract		Group – tort			Mock
Lunchtime	Equity		Land Law	Tort		Friends!	Mock
Evening	Equity	Contract	Group – land law		Friends!	Friends!	

Build in breaks, mornings and afternoons off, and treats for completed tasks. This way, your revision plan will be more enjoyable and you will be more likely to settle into a routine. You will also appreciate the study breaks.

There are a few things that you could build into your personal revision plan. You could sort your revision by subject, for example: *'contract law: offer'*, or *'criminal law: murder'*. Additionally, you can place a *'mini mock exam'* in every fourth afternoon, or a *'group revision session'* every third evening.

(d) Revise according to your learning style

Revising in a way that suits your personal learning style is the most effective method of revision. In **Chapter 4** you were introduced to different learning styles, which illustrated how students of all ages and backgrounds learn in different ways. Some students prefer to learn using lists, logic, bullet points, order, sequence and organisation, whilst other students prefer to learn using colour, activities, communication, imagination and thoughts. The revision strategy that works for you will depend on your learning style. By finding out how you prefer to learn, you are more likely to enjoy your revision activities because you can tailor your revision strategy to match your personal preferences. Which one of the above methods are you already drawn to?

'Pyramids' and 'mind maps' are very practical methods and will mostly suit learners who like to see the 'big picture'. However, law students need to be aware of how one area of law connects and interlinks with another, and sometimes the law can be very complex with many different principles overlapping with other ideas and doctrines in separate legal fields, so this revision method may be advantageous for everyone who studies law.

More 'logical learners' may prefer simple lists to show how one area of law links to another:

Contract law – formation of contract
- *Invitation to treat* (from seller…)
- *Offer* (from buyer…)
- *Acceptance* (from seller…)
- *Consideration* (from buyer & seller)
- *Legal relations* (from buyer & seller)

However, more 'imaginative learners' may like to personalise their pyramids with colour, shapes and pictures:

Formation of contract

Invitation to treat
↳ Offer
↳ Acceptance
↳ Consideration
↳ Legal relations

You can use bright, bold patterns, clusters, connectors, pictures, personal touches and imagination. Don't forget to leave plenty of space for later additions, either as you progress through your course, or during your intense revision at the end when you do some further research. Your imagination can go wild when it comes to using pyramids and mind maps for revision. Cases, research, articles, facts, evidence, statistics and any other type of information that you may need for an exam can be placed on a mind map. The best way to ensure that the information sticks in your mind is to put a giant copy of your mind map somewhere where you can see it every day. Buy a roll of wallpaper, design your mind map on the back of the paper, and stick it up on your bedroom wall with sticky tape or pins so you can see it constantly. You will remember your drawings when you enter the exam hall.

(e) Improve your memory

We all remember the words to our favourite songs, and we all remember really special things that were said to us. It might seem impossible at the beginning of your intense revision period, but you can remember the law off by heart too. Below are some ideas which you could use to improve your memory, no matter what your learning style.

- *Self-awareness.* What strategy currently works for you?
- *Repetition.* Over-learn the law from early on.
- *Association.* Relate the law to your everyday life.
- *Listen.* Some students like to listen to themselves.
- *Write.* Rewrite your notes to remember a point.
- *Play.* Make your revision time fun and engaging.

People remember facts and figures in different ways. Some have quite a photographic memory and can remember images and pictures with remarkable accuracy. Most of us are not this lucky, and so you will need to be creative. Recording your own voice whilst you are reciting cases and facts may be uncomfortable, but some students find it very helpful! 'Case cards' and mind maps are usually the most memorable methods of revision for more active and imaginative learners, although more logical learners will find it beneficial to make colourful lists and categories too. Start small: revise only case names and *ratios* first, before moving on to the facts of each case at a later stage (which do not often pick up a lot of marks in exams or assignments unless the facts of the case have a direct relevance to the question).

(f) Past exam papers

Ask your lecturer for past exam papers in your law subjects. Reading the questions will help you to become familiar with the style and type of question that are likely to face you in the exam hall. In addition, completing your own mock exam is an excellent method of revision – it will highlight in an instant the areas where your knowledge of the law is below par. If you can't handle writing out a whole exam answer, draw a brainstorm for your answer instead, which will place that particular area of law into context on one piece of paper, linking up cases and theories in a clear and imaginative way.

With past exam papers comes a warning: read the question thoroughly before you proceed. Each question will ask you to write about several legal issues, but some will be subtle (ie 'hidden'). This is good practice for the real thing – many students divert in their exams because they have misread the question. If you find that your mind goes blank when you are faced with a mock exam question, get together with your friends in a study group and answer it together. They will point things out to you that you never thought of. Additionally, your lecturer can help you too. Ask him or her how law exams differ from assignments. Be clear how much research and referencing is expected of you in an exam answer, and – just as importantly – what you need to leave out.

Past exam questions to use	
Contract law	'Explain the ways in which consideration can be provided to form a contract.'

Land law	'Discuss the law relating to landlords and tenants and evaluate the common law developments since 1997.'
Criminal law	'Describe the rules relating to intention and critically discuss the latest attempts to bring clarity to the law.'
European law	'Evaluate the developments since 2001 relating to the movement of people in the EU.'
Tort law	'Discuss the common law liability of policemen in the law of tort.'
Employment law	'Assess the laws relating to unfair discrimination against women in full-time employment.'

(g) Your friends can help!

A really good way to keep your motivation levels up is to set up a revision group with your friends. Make sure the revision group is not too big and does not include less motivated members of your circle of friends; otherwise you will not achieve much work in an afternoon. Small groups of three to five in a small room or in the law library will provide stimulating group discussion, competitiveness and a supportive atmosphere. You will be learning about the law without realising it.

My four study-buddies

....

....

....

....

When you get together with your friends, go over your tutorial questions, questions in text-books and mock exams. Try to find solutions and write up an answer together. Many heads will cover more avenues and possibilities and will show you things you never even considered. Perhaps you could also make a brainstorm of possible impending exam questions and the answers you might give.

(h) Handwriting

How is your handwriting? In the exam hall you will be getting back to basics – writing with a pen and paper. If your writing is messy or too small, your exam marker will not be able to pick out the points you are trying to make. Try completing a mock exam to get back into the practice of writing long essay answers using a pen and paper. Remember, in your exam it is not the *amount* of writing you can present which picks up marks, it is the *quality* of your submission that is important.

(i) Anxiety and stress

Stress levels are significantly worse just before an exam. Waiting outside the exam hall can be the most stressful few minutes of your semester, because the anticipation of seeing the unknown exam question and worrying about your performance tends to cause the most panic. However, during your whole revision period, your stress levels can be significantly heightened. You may worry that you'll never be able to achieve the grade that you want, and that the mountain of work you need to tackle is simply too high. The secret to overcoming this can be to take bite-size chunks, and deal with them one at a time. For example, in week one of your intense revision plan, deal only with 'offer' in contract law. In week two, deal only with 'acceptance'. Then in week three, combine them both and set yourself small tests. It may become clear at this point why you need to start revising *well* in advance. You need plenty of time to take this thorough approach, but it will pay off significantly during your exam.

Additionally, do not forget to take care of yourself during the revision period. It sounds boring, but make sure you get plenty of sleep and eat well. This will give you more energy and longer periods of concentration. Enjoy your breaks from revision and seek a balance: if you revise too much, your motivation will fall away, you will become frustrated and exhausted, and you may end up feeling so overwhelmed that you will want to give up entirely.

 **Revision troubleshooting!**

Below is a list of the most common problems when it comes to revising law. Helpful solutions have been provided, and in the spaces below write what you can do about your current revision issues.

Issue:	Solution:
'How do I plan ahead?'	<ul><li>Make a revision plan at the beginning of your course/semester/term.</li><li>As you go through your course, make your lecture notes lively and easy to read – it will help you to revise them.</li><li>Every evening, revise everything you learnt that day. Rewrite your notes if this helps.</li></ul>
What I will do:	
Issue: *'How can past exam papers help?'*	Solution: <ul><li>You will be reading through your notes over and over again and becoming familiar with the law.</li><li>You may need to undertake some extra research to complete the question.</li><li>It will highlight the areas of law that you are struggling with.</li></ul>
What I will do:	
Issue: *'How can I enhance my memory?'*	Solution: <ul><li>Rewrite your notes a few times to consolidate the facts of the law.</li><li>Use index cards to revise case law if you prefer to remember your notes in their current format.</li><li>Personalise your studies to make them more relevant and interesting to you. For example, imagine that it is you who has purchased a defective item and that it is you who now needs to take it back under the Sale of Goods Act 1979.</li></ul>
What I will do:	

Issue:	Solution:
'I get distracted from my timetable.'	• Put your distractions into your revision plan as rewards for completing a revision task. • Ask yourself if the 'emergency' is really important. You can watch TV or go shopping later. • Don't put your revision off – it will build up. Revising with your friends may make things much more fun.
What I will do:	
Issue:	Solution:
'I keep putting my revision off. It's so hard to start it.'	• Make a note of your motivations for completing your course. What are your career goals? • Look to the future – the exam period is small compared to the rest of your life. Put things into perspective. • Encourage and entice yourself to return to your study. Book rewards into your timetable.
What I will do:	
Issue:	Solution:
'I get really bored. I would rather do anything else but revision.'	• If you are bored, you are not working to your preferred learning style. It is now time to personalise your revision method to suit you. • Introduce variety and creativity into your revision sessions. Use colours, index cards, pictures, tables, memory games, mock exams, etc. Do it with your friends. • Take your revision to the next level – read some new material in the area and challenge yourself.
What I will do:	
Issue:	Solution:
'I haven't got time to revise.'	• Allocate time to yourself every day – even just 30 minutes a day – to make some 'case cards' or read a few pages. • Prioritise. If people can find time to eat, watch TV, and take a shower, they can also find time to read or write a case. • Break the work into small pieces, or choose a smaller number of areas of law to focus on in depth.
What I will do:	
Issue:	Solution:
I'm not remembering anything – it's not working.'	• Make sure you are revising in a way that suits your learning style. If you are not remembering anything, you are not revising in a way that suits you. • Set tests for yourself, or try a completely different strategy from what you're normally used to. • Revise with your friends to see what methods they're using.
What I will do:	

Revision makes the world of difference

When you have been revising for an exam for weeks or months, you feel much more confident as your exam approaches. The feeling that you have genuinely done your part, and pulled your weight, and made an effort to give yourself the best chance, will calm your nerves and fears significantly and you will perform much better. You will remember more facts and cases, and you may even feel confident enough to include some articles or academic debate into your answers for the very high marks.

6.5 EXAMS

Exams are a big part of studying law. It is likely that you will experience an exam as part of your law course. Most students dread them, and many law lecturers dislike marking them, but they are an excellent way of testing a student's legal knowledge and understanding, and so they are usually incorporated into A-level law courses, LLB law courses, and most other professional legal qualifications.

There are several types of law exam, and many different styles of questions which will confront you in an exam hall. It is best to have a strategy ready to deal with these different types of questions, and some ideas are provided in this section. A student without an exam strategy is a student who will not do as well as he or she could. Give yourself the best chance!

Why exams?

Practical subjects – such as plumbing or teacher training – are assessed in other ways because of the characteristics of the subject. A plumbing course may require a practical exam to show that the student can successfully fix a broken pipe, and teacher training usually requires formal observations in a classroom to show that the student will make a competent teacher. Law is a traditionally intellectual subject. Legal professionals are expected to know many different types of facts and are required to advise members of the public on a wide range of legal issues. The best way to test this retention of knowledge is through a closed-book examination which puts the student under pressure and shows the examiner how much of the law the student can remember.

With this aim in mind, exams are not designed to catch you out. They are quite straightforward. They simply want to measure (a) how much law you can remember; and (b) your application, critical, analytical and evaluation skills. The examiner does not simply want you to state the facts; he or she wants to see you use the law effectively to advise a client, or to academically assess legal principles.

There are advantages to exams which students do not often consider:

- Some students perform brilliantly under pressure.
- The adrenaline and high energy pushes you to succeed even more.
- You know when your exam will be from day one of your course.
- You can plan a revision schedule for an exam.
- Not as much rigorous research is expected in an exam answer.
- The exam only lasts a short amount of time before it is over for ever.

- You will not need to compile a bibliography at the end of your exam answer.
- You will learn new skills whilst preparing for your exam, such as time management.
- Examiners may be slightly sympathetic towards questionable grammar in exams.
- You will become more self-disciplined.
- You will learn a lot about the law during the revision and exam period.
- You will welcome the challenge of being tested on your knowledge.
- You will affirm your belief in yourself when you perform well.
- You will understand how you prefer to learn during your revision.
- You will look to your future, and your aspiring career will be a step closer.
- You will enjoy a free summer with your friends when you pass your exams.

'I can't do it!'

It is well known that students do not perform as well in exams as they do in assignments. This is mainly because in an exam you have no materials to hand and so must rely solely on the knowledge in your head. Additionally, many students only revise for their exam a week or a fortnight beforehand, meaning that their knowledge does not really increase at all between their last lecture and their first exam.

 **Below are the top six reasons why students fail exams. Are you guilty of any of the following?**

Common reason for failing:	Guilty!
Missing out key cases, legal theories, key legal principles and evaluations	☐
Poor time management: running out of time and not allocating sufficient time to each question	☐
Over-descriptive answers: not enough analysis or deep exploration of the key issues	☐
Not answering the question: misreading the task and jumping in without thinking	☐
Bad presentation: poor grammar and spelling and illegible handwriting. Structure inappropriate	☐
Panicking that your performance will fail you because you know the law but can't explain yourself properly on paper	☐
Over-reliance on a statute book in an open-book exam: no further information provided by student	☐

Many of the simple mistakes above can be rectified by proper planning and clever strategy. Why give yourself a harder time than is necessary? Why waste opportunities to gain better marks? You will know from the very beginning of your course that an exam is on the horizon, so you have no excuse for bad performance and silly mistakes. To make sure you get the best start, you really need to understand your course content, and this means attending all of your lectures and tutorials from the very beginning of your course. If you have made a solid effort in your studies all year, it will be worth achieving good marks in your exam to represent all your hard work. It will feel like it has all been worth it. Time management is key to successful examinations.

In the box below, make notes about your past exam experiences. Are they positive or negative? How have they affected your attitude towards exams today?

Course/topic:	Type of exam/question:
Describe what happened:	**How did I feel?**
Positive aspects:	**Negative aspects:**
Lesson learned:	**Influence on future performance:**

If you have had a negative experience in the past, you can turn it into a positive lesson to change your experience in your next exam. If you achieved lower marks than you hoped for, then improve your exam strategy with the help of this chapter. If you had a positive experience in the past, build on it and improve even more next time.

Bad habits:	I do this	I never do this	Plan of action:
Failing to read the whole exam paper	☐	☐	☐
Not checking my answers at the end	☐	☐	☐
Not following instructions	☐	☐	☐
Not staying focused during the exam	☐	☐	☐
Not answering all the questions I need to	☐	☐	☐
Forgetting an introduction and conclusion	☐	☐	☐
Never planning my time appropriately	☐	☐	☐
Taking too long to get to the point	☐	☐	☐
Not reading the questions thoroughly	☐	☐	☐
Not jotting down notes/planning answers in advance	☐	☐	☐
Not revising enough topics	☐	☐	☐
Not taking the exams seriously	☐	☐	☐
Not feeling confident in my own ability	☐	☐	☐
Having no idea what a 'good' answer looks like	☐	☐	☐
Not using my legal research appropriately	☐	☐	☐
Not developing a clear and authoritative argument	☐	☐	☐
Including material which is not relevant to the question	☐	☐	☐

Types of exam

Law exams come in many forms, but at A-level, LLB level and LLM level you will probably meet with the following two types of exam:

(a) Open book exams

Open book exams occur frequently on law courses. These are where you may take some materials into your exam to supplement your answer. Usually they are legal materials, such as a statute book, which you would have to hand in real life if you were a practising solicitor advising a client. The rules for open book exams are very strict – statute books must not usually be annotated with your own notes – and any other materials are still thoroughly checked for hidden messages or answers. The reason for using open book exams as a method of assessment is simple: your lecturers need to measure your ability to advise a client with the help of a simple legal resource. Can you turn the statute into a source of help for your client? How will you apply the statute to your client's situation? Can you read the law properly? Can you decipher which sections of the Act will help your client, and which sections provide a defence for the other party? Sometimes you may be allowed to take legal regulations into a law exam (for example, in family law or social services), but the examiner will be looking for the exact same skills of application and advising.

Sometimes, students are allowed to take their notes into an exam. These must be clear and tidy, and may be checked by an invigilator for any hidden messages or answers. This is your opportunity to really deliver a good exam answer as you can take notes of legal theories and principles into the exam with you and use them to supplement your work. However, a warning comes with open book exams which allow lecture or course notes. Many students fall into the trap of believing that if they can take their lecture notes in with them, they do not need to revise. This is not true. Your lecture notes are there for *additional* help on top of your usual case law, statute law and legal theory revision. Consider them a *'memory aid'* or your *'critical analysis reminder'* to achieve some extra marks on top of your regular answer. To rely simply on your lecture notes to achieve a good mark in an exam will lead to certain disappointment unless you have greatly supplemented your notes with additional research and revision. You are only given the bare bones of a subject in your lectures. Your exam answers requires evidence of further research and reading.

Advice for open book exams

- Don't fool yourself! Just as much revision and preparation is required for an open book exam as for a closed book exam.
- Consider any materials you take in to the exam hall to be 'additional help' to supplement your answer – do not rely solely on your material to help you pass your exam. There will probably not be enough.
- If you can take a statute book or legal regulations into your exam, revise the case law under those provisions too. Additionally, what do academics in the field think of the provisions? Revise legal theories too.
- If you can take your notes into your exam, make them tidy, legible and pack them full of legal principles and theories. You will still have to revise your case law separately.
- It may be a good idea to refresh your notes before your exam, using up-to-date *ratios* and finding new publications in journals in the field. Complete a search on *LexisLibrary* or *Westlaw* to find any recent developments. These are good pieces of information to include in your exam notes, as you may not have time to revise them in addition to everything else.

(b) Closed book exams

Closed book exams are the most popular type of exam on law courses. No material *at all* is permitted in the exam hall. These exams tend to cause law students the most stress, putting immense pressure on the student to remember what seems like hundreds of case names, numerous legal principles, countless legal theories and complicated offence structures – which are prone to merge into other areas of law – simply leading to further confusion.

In reality, closed book exams are not as bad as they first seem. They are an excellent method of testing your knowledge of the law, and their presence on your law course adds an incentive to study, research and revise your topic areas. After all, if you would like to pursue a career in the legal world, you need to know the law! The secret is to prepare well, revise well, and have a strategy in place to answer law exam questions. It is unlikely that you will see the questions in advance when you undertake a closed book exam, and it is this apprehension that makes students very nervous. Preparation and revision is the key to successful closed book examinations, helping you to keep calm and in control when a difficult question appears and you have no option but to attempt it.

Advice for closed book exams

- Revise the topics most likely to come up in the exam, and revise them well in advance. A slow build-up of knowledge is longer-lasting knowledge.
- Control your nerves by finding a coping technique that works especially for you.
- Become acquainted with past exam questions to take away the 'shock factor' when you sit down to your first question.
- Develop a strategy for choosing which questions to answer.
- Research new developments in your topic areas during revision time to enhance your notes and breathe new life into your old revision methods. You may remember the law better.

Exam questions

Part of the fear for law students is not knowing what they are going to be asked in their exam. In law, lecturers and exam boards have two favourite kinds of questions: case studies and essays.

(a) Case studies

Case study questions seem slightly more friendly than essays, as they consist of a case study or a story involving people, injuries, loss of earnings, psychiatric injury, criminal offences, breached contracts, etc. The student is expected to advise each party of his or her liability in law. The trick is to identify the relevant area of law, and then apply the principles within that area of law correctly to the parties involved. Slight analysis of the law is involved in these questions, to illustrate that you can grasp some wider legal issues and flaws in the law, but in general your examiner will be looking for the correct application of case law and legal principles. Criminal law, tort law, land law and employment law often use case study exam questions because these topics can be quite practical. Below is an example of a criminal law case study exam question.

Question 1

'Amelia and Ben are married. Before Amelia married Ben, she was in a relationship with Ryan. Amelia and Ryan's son, Freddie, lives with Ryan and Ryan's new partner Sienna.

Amelia and Ben are having marital difficulties. Ben strongly believes that the function of marriage is to bring up children. He would very much like to have children with Amelia, but has recently discovered that he is infertile. Their only option for a child of their own is donor insemination but Amelia is strongly opposed to this for religious reasons. Ben has become severely depressed as a result, but has refused to take any medication.

One day, Amelia receives a letter from Ryan. Amelia can tell it contains a photograph, so she puts it to one side, planning to open it later. Unfortunately, before Amelia can look at the letter, Ben opens it. It contains a photograph of Ryan, Freddie and Freddie's new baby sister, Georgia. Ben is deeply upset. He tears the photograph up and puts it in the rubbish bin.

　　When Amelia returns home, she cannot find the letter and she asks Ben where it is. He tells her he has destroyed it, because he cannot bear to have pictures of Freddie in the house. Amelia is furious and tells Ben that she is leaving him. "I cannot live like this any more. I have a son, and I love him. You make me pretend he does not exist. You're useless anyway, any real man would be able to give me another baby." Ben just explodes. He runs up to Amelia, puts his hands around her throat and strangles her.

　　Ben has been charged with murder. He does not deny that he intended to kill Amelia, but is putting forward the defences of provocation and diminished responsibility. Consider whether these defences are available to him.'

Notice how there are several topics combined into one question: murder, voluntary manslaughter, provocation and diminished responsibility. Case study questions often do this: it is your lecturer's way of testing your ability to pick out and separate different areas of law and deal with them in a logical and sequential order. Additionally, case studies may contain an intricate story and many parties – as there can be in real life – and you may need to draw diagrams on the back of your exam paper to help you understand who links to whom and who is liable for what. It is best to deal with one party at a time. The question only asks you to consider the defences of provocation and diminished responsibility in relation to Ben's behaviour, so the task is not as overwhelming as it first seems. However, because many students do not read the question properly, they do not adopt this focus in their answer, and lose marks.

Advice for case study exam questions

- Read the question twice – case studies can be complicated when there are several parties and several injuries, breaches, etc.
- Draw pictures or diagrams on the back of your exam booklet of each individual's liability and mental state. Piece the parts together like a jigsaw before you begin your formal answer.
- Be very clear what is being asked of you. You may be given a clue, such as *'Discuss Roger's liability for murder'* or *'Has Peter frustrated his contract with Sally?'* Other times, you will not be given any clue, such as *'Does Lisa incur any liability?'* or *'What offences has Mike committed?'* In these instances, you need to pinpoint any potentially wrongful behaviour and identify an offence as well as the blameworthiness of each party.
- Handle one party at a time if you feel it will be easier for you. If you can identify an individual who definitely satisfies all the legal tests, apply the law to this individual first, and simply refer back to the previously explained case law for the next individual. You do not need to repeat yourself unless you have a new point to make.
- Keep a look out for any potential defences or hidden issues woven into the facts of the case study. For example, an individual may stab someone to death whilst drunk. This opens the criminal law defence of intoxication. Or, a man may make a counter-offer before his neighbour accepts the original offer. Counter-offers usually cancel original offers.
- Do not forget to conclude, stating whether you think each individual has liability and for what. Do not forget that the main aim of case study questions is to ascertain whether the

student can apply the law to the culpable acts of individuals and discuss whether they are liable. Pass your judgement in your conclusion.

(b) Essays

Essays are often seen as great tests of a student's memory and academic strength, but they are easier than case studies in a few ways. An essay requires the student to simply discuss or analyse a small area of law, without having to consider the liability of any individuals, or having to untangle the complex structure of party incidents. The words *'discuss'*, *'critically analyse'* and *'evaluate'* will probably appear in the short essay question. See the examples below:

'Critically assess the law of murder and the current proposed reforms.'

'Analyse the law of consideration and its role in formation of a contract.'

'Discuss the ways in which the current terrorism laws protect the citizens of the United Kingdom.'

Essay questions require deeper analysis, critical thinking, research and evaluation skills than case study questions. This is the price you pay for not having to untangle a large scenario and consider the liability of four people at the same time. However, as long as you have a good understanding of the main principles that underpin a certain area of law, and as long as you have revised your case law and some additional legal theories, there is no reason why you cannot achieve very high marks in an essay question. Structure and legal reasoning is key in essay questions, and the examiner is expecting to see a fluid argument – and contrasting arguments – throughout your answer, with a sound conclusion at the end that draws together all your preceding arguments. Consider an essay question to be a mini-assignment.

Advice for essay exam questions

- Solid and well-prepared revision is required for essay questions. Case law only will not suffice for the deep analytical commentary that your examiner is expecting to see.
- Legal theories and principles need to be criticised and evaluated. These require you to project your own views about the topic. Do you have any?
- When you put your own legal reasoning forward, you need to back it up with some kind of legal authority. Reference to a judgment or an academic article will be welcomed by your examiner, as long as you use it appropriately to support or rebut your arguments.
- When you conclude, make sure your thoughts back up the questions in your introduction. Have you proved your points/answered your own questions?

(c) Confusing directions

Whether you are faced with case study questions or essay questions in your law exam, written directions relating to how many questions you are allowed to answer sometimes cause frustration and panic. Usually, students are directed to answer a selection of questions, and it is these directions that can be confusing. See the examples below:

'Answer 2 questions from a choice of 6 (50% weighting for each).'

'Answer 3 questions from a choice of 5 (equal percentage weighting to each).'

'Answer the only question in Section A (compulsory) (50% weighting) and answer 2 questions from Section B from a choice of 7 (25% each).'

'Answer the only question in Section A (compulsory) (50%) and one question only from Section B from a choice of 6 (50%).'

'Answer all parts of Section A (multi-choice) (20%), plus 2 questions from Section B from a choice of 6 (40% each).'

As you can see, students need a bit of time at the beginning of their exam simply to work out which questions to answer! It is worth taking the first five minutes to decide this, as it is vital that you answer the questions that you can handle confidently.

Advice for essay exam questions

- Reword these directions if you don't understand them.
- Put your hand up and ask the invigilator present at the exam to clarify the directions for you.
- Jot down on the back of your exam paper how many questions you are allowed to answer, how much each question will weigh, and then carefully pick your questions.

Strategies and exam technique

There is an old saying: *'fail to prepare, prepare to fail.'* This is true of exams. You need a strategy in place to ensure that when you are finally faced with your exam questions, you do not panic and jump in without thinking your answer through. Additionally, whilst you are writing your answer, you need excellent exam technique to ensure that your answer is well structured and your timing is spot-on.

Your law lecturers will have marked many exams. If you are studying A-level law, your lecturer will mark your assignments, but your exam will be written by and returned to an external exam board. If you are studying LLB-level law, your lecturer will not only write your formal exam, but will also mark your exam paper before it is sent to an external moderator for confirmation.

Lecturers at undergraduate level law are looking for certain things in your exam answer. Whilst all lecturers mark slightly differently, the skills and knowledge they are looking for remain the same. Look at the quotes below from law lecturers. Can you spot any recurring themes in what they are looking for in exam answers?

Professor Christopher Gale (sports law, human rights law):

'Answer the question asked rather than writing all you know about a subject. Structure an answer like a story – introduction (what you are going to do); middle (doing what you said you'd do); conclusion (answering the question and explaining what you've done).'

Dr William Onzivu (environmental law):

'Identify and understand the relevant law applicable to the subject, topic or question. Explore the reasons for the law and how it applies to a given situation. Practise your skills to assess, examine and analyse. Discuss the law and the issues. Be able to justify alternative viewpoints.'

Have you noticed any recurring themes? Your law lecturers want to see the following things in your exam answers:

- demonstration of understanding;
- analysis;
- evaluation;
- answer the question!;
- further understanding, ie further research;
- depth rather than a broad sweep;
- a structured answer, not scattered points.

It is easier said than done when you are faced with a complex exam question in time-restrained conditions. However, if you have a strategy prepared and excellent exam techniques (see below), you will be more likely to develop a strong and legally authoritive answer (and not panic!). Remember, in a law exam, it is depth not breadth that attracts marks: your answers should be specific and deep, not broad and shallow.

(a) Time and weighting

Have you made the following mistake?

> 'I read the questions and I knew I could answer 3 out of 5 so I started work on the first one straight away. Before I knew it, an hour had passed, and even though I had written loads for the first answer, I only had 45 minutes left for two more questions of the same weight. By the time I finished my second question, I had only 10 minutes left for the third, and I was so angry at myself because I knew I couldn't submit anything worthwhile. I could see all my marks falling away.'

Students often fail to finish their answers in exams, meaning that they lose *many* marks. It is perfectly possible to complete every question in the allocated time and achieve a high mark, so where do students go so wrong? Time management is key. When your exam starts, first work out how much time you have overall. Secondly, work out how many questions you have to answer to complete the exam. Thirdly, consider the weighting of each question. For example, if your third question only weighs 10% of the exam, you can give that question less time than your second question, which may be worth 40% of the exam. Fourthly, allocate a time slot to each question and stick to it no matter what. If you go over your time allocation whilst you are writing your answer, finish off your current sentence, leave it, and come back to it when you have finished your final question. Students too often spend over half the allocated time on their first question, leaving minimal time for the next two or three questions. If you are strict with your time allowances, you are more likely to pick up more marks because you have attempted every question. This strategy may take a few minutes, but it actually saves you a lot of time in the long run and it will pick up many marks.

> *Question 1: 50%, 1 hour, 2pm – 3pm.*
> *Question 2: 25%, 30 minutes, 3pm – 3:30pm.*

Because exams are designed to test not only your legal knowledge but your application of legal skills, it is vital that you choose the questions that you feel you can answer very well. If there are particular case study scenarios or essay topics which would reflect your range of academic talents, knowledge of the law, and research and writing skills, mark these questions as 'sure bets' and carefully analyse the remaining questions for their potential to make you look good too. Pick the questions that will do you justice.

If you find that you can perform really well at one particular question and distinctly 'average' at the rest of the questions, you must still stick to your time allocation for each question (allocated according to their weighting). If you can write reams and reams for question one, you are not allowing yourself enough time to write a solid answer for questions two and three, cheating yourself out of marks. You do not want to be caught up in a scrambled rush at the end of your exam as you try to begin your answer for question four. Additionally, if you attack the most obvious issue first, the rest of your answer risks being weak. Be very strict with your time allocation – you will be given enough time to provide a very good answer for the full number of questions.

What if you finish your exam early? This does not happen very often – particularly if you have revised thoroughly – because you will have so much material in your head that you will want to write down on paper. But many of us have seen a student leaving the exam hall way before the time was up, and wondered whether that student had simply finished early or given up completely. If you finish your whole exam with 45 minutes or more to spare, you have probably omitted a considerable amount of material from your answers. Do not leave the exam hall if this happens to you: stay and read through your answers, checking for gaps in knowledge and flaws in your application of the law. Think back to your lectures – have you missed or forgotten about any major legal principles? Have you included some legal theories? Are there one or two more cases which could still be applied? Even if you are able to increase your overall grade by three or four marks, this may take you into the next classification category.

(b) Read the question

This seems very simple – almost patronising – advice, but law lecturers continue to be baffled by how many students do not read their exam question correctly. Students often assume that the directions in their exams one year will be the same as they were the previous year. Additionally, during the panic and adrenaline of entering an exam hall and being faced with unseen questions, students tend to identify the easiest question at first glance and jump straight into their answer without checking the questions thoroughly. The costliest mistakes are usually made at this stage when it comes to case study questions, because many law students will do the following things:

- write about a topic that seems to feature in the case study but is not relevant and/or not in the actual question at the bottom of the page;
- write about the liability of the wrong individual;
- write about the wrong offence;
- write about the wrong defences;
- write about the wrong area of law.

It is conceded that not all exam questions explicitly state what the relevant area of law is, and not all exam questions state which offences and defences are relevant either. This is done to encourage the student to pick out the relevant law for him- or herself and to identify the hidden issues (there will always be some). There are usually big hints in the case study scenario to tell the student which area of law, which offences and which defences are relevant, but because students normally skim the exam question and scenario only once, *they do not pick them up*. So make sure you allocate the first five minutes of your exam to read the question – and the details of the case study – very thoroughly to find all the hidden issues.

It may also be wise to confirm which verbs ('doing' words) and key subject words appear in your question. What do you actually have to 'do' and 'to what'? It is excellent practice when you first read your questions to highlight or underline the key words in each question to identify exactly what each question requires you to do. After highlighting the task in each question, you may realise that the question is asking you to do something completely different to what you originally thought, and you may need to leave that question and pick another one. Look at the examples below from both case study and essay questions:

'Explain the ways in which Keisha may be liable for Fred's injuries.'
'Discuss the law relating to terms of a contract.'
'Critically analyse the above statement in relation to unfair contract terms.'
'Illustrate the ways in which the Hospital Trust is liable for negligence in relation to Nailah's injuries.'
'Evaluate the rules regarding statutory interpretation and state whether they are just and reasonable.'

The verbs ('doing' words) and key subject words from the questions above are as follows:

Verbs:	Key words:
'Explain ...'	'Injuries ...'
'Discuss ...'	'Terms of a contract ...'
'Critically analyse ...'	'Unfair contract terms ...'
'Illustrate ...'	'Negligence in relation to injuries ...'
'Evaluate ...', 'State ...'	'Statutory interpretation ...'

As you can see from the above table, in the first few minutes of your exam it may be worth simply jotting down what you actually have to do. For example, in the question below:

'Discuss the law relating to terms of a contract.'

you are required to *discuss* the specific area of express and implied terms in contract law. A discussion is a rounded essay, which looks at both positive and negative aspects of a topic, and brings in arguments and theories from all sides. This is quite different to the verbs 'illustrate' or 'state', which merely require some description, not the deep analytical skills that will attract the highest marks. A merely descriptive answer will not attract very high marks, no matter what the question requires.

Verb in question:	Your task:
'Explain ...'	Describe and make clear the law, giving details and explanations.
'Discuss ...'	Talk about and argue a point of law. Debate, deliberate.
'Critically analyse ...'	Examine and scrutinise the law. Question and consider the principles.
'Illustrate ...'	Demonstrate and show why something is as it is. Point out how something works.
'State ...'	Tell the examiner what the current position is. Show principle in simple terms.
'Evaluate ...'	Assess, weigh up and calculate the law and its main principles.

Do not forget! Case study questions are different to essay questions in that essays require a deep critical analysis of the law, whereas a case study requires the student to apply the law to a fictional scenario with only limited academic criticism. If your case study answer turns into an essay answer, or vice versa, you will quickly begin to lose marks. Be sure of the nature of the question from the very beginning and stick to the format required.

(c) Structure your answer

Law lecturers rarely see an excellent structure to an exam question, simply because the panic and adrenaline in the exam hall pushes a student into writing as quickly as possible without planning what he or she will write in advance. When a student does not plan his or her answer in advance, it shows on the page when he or she begins writing. New ideas emerge halfway through the answer and are 'squashed in' to the margins or between the lines. Arrows appear all over the page, instructing the examiner that the paragraphs are in the wrong order, and the argument at the beginning does not flow through the whole submission, coming to a completely different conclusion at the end. The overall impression is one of laziness, lack of care, effort, attention, research, structure and knowledge. All the correct information may be there, but the examiner will not be able to make any sense of it. Many, many students make this same mistake, and it means many unnecessary marks will be lost.

A good structure will attract marks, because your lecturer or your examiner will be able to follow your arguments clearly, they will get the impression that you have considered the presentation of your answer, and they will consider your logical sequence to be proof that your thoughts are clear and correct. Take the example below:

'Discuss the law relating to terms of a contract.'

Express and implied terms are in themselves two separate fields, so it may be a good idea at the beginning of your exam time to draw out with your pencil on the back of your exam answer booklet both areas separately and which cases you intend to use for each. This will give your answer some initial structure. Secondly, you may like to jot down some immediate ideas that come into your head about express and implied terms, such as unusual cases, main principles, most recent articles, and exceptions to the rules. This adds further depth to your answer. Finally, jot down some concluding thoughts, although these may also come to you as you are writing your answer.

Perfect essay answer structure:

1. Introduce the topic
Introduce a particular idea
Introduce a principle
Introduce a theory

2. Main section
Describe and explain main principles underpinning the field
Mention the important theorists, cases, judgments, etc
Argue the main points, discuss the main issues
Demonstrate your knowledge of any exceptions to the rules
Show a wide range of research and reading

3. Conclude
Draw together your arguments

Advice for structuring your answer

- Draw a mind map or a brainstorm of all your ideas once you have decided on a question.
- A good introduction will make the examiner cautiously optimistic about you. It is your way of reassuring the examiner that you can identify and discuss the relevant topics in an orderly and structured manner.
- A sound middle to your answer will demonstrate your knowledge of legal principles, case law, legal theories, exceptions to the main rules, and your application and analytical skills.
- In your middle, your descriptions and references need to be accurate. You must demonstrate that you know the key cases, main legal principles, and how they apply to the question. You must explain why judges or theorists came to their conclusions.
- Also in your middle, you need to present arguments for and against the main legal principles. Perhaps you know of an article that argues against the leading case judgment? This shows the examiner further reading.
- A sound conclusion will pull your key ideas together and will summarise the present law, before coming to a conclusion. Remind the examiner of the central point to your answer. Have you proved liability in the case study? Is the area of 'terms' in contract law satisfactory?

Describing *main principles* and the *exceptions to the main rules* are vital content to include in a law exam answer. Most social science subjects appreciate this type of knowledge about the field, but in law this deep level of critical thinking will attract the highest marks.

Below is an excellent example of an *essay* introduction. Would you have thought to write something like this when faced with an essay exam question?

> *'Discuss the law relating to terms of a contract'*
>
> 'Terms of a contract' refers to both express and implied terms in a contractual agreement. These can be separated into two very specific areas. 'Express terms' are terms expressed verbally or otherwise by either party, and are incorporated into the contract before signing. 'Implied terms' are implied into a contract by statute, and are also agreed upon by the parties before signing. This essay will discuss the origins of both express and implied terms in the law of contract, and the redress available when either type of term is breached by the contracted parties.

Below is an excellent example of a *case study* introduction. Would you have thought to write something like this when faced with a case study exam question?

> *'Explain the ways in which Keisha may be liable for Fred's injuries.'*
>
> It appears from the facts that Fred has sustained a broken leg as a result of Keisha's act of assaulting him with a crowbar. This is the offence of assault occasioning actual bodily harm under s 47 of the Offences Against the Person Act 1861. It also appears that Keisha was intoxicated at the time of the assault. This answer will explore the *actus reus* and *mens rea* of the said s 47 offence and will apply the legal principles to Keisha's behaviour to ascertain whether she is liable for Fred's injuries. In addition, the defence of intoxication will also be explored and it will be discussed whether Keisha can rely on this defence when charged with assault occasioning actual bodily harm.

Notice how both introductions have identified the main issue and outlined the scope of the answer. The examiner will appreciate being told from the outset what topics you are about to explore, and it shows that you can identify the correct area of law when given a complex scenario to detangle.

This strategy may take a few minutes at the beginning of your exam, but it will improve your answer so greatly that you may pick up *significant* marks. Remember – just one extra mark can cross the boundary between one classification and another.

(d) Show your research

When it comes to essay questions, good levels of legal research and evidence of further reading count for many extra marks. Students are often not clear about what exactly they need to incorporate into an exam answer compared to an assignment answer when it comes to research and references. After all, assignments require a very high level of research and references, but in an exam you usually have no access to such legal materials. How much are you supposed to remember? Perhaps this student view is familiar:

'I try hard to incorporate as many cases and articles into my law assignments as I can, as they help me with my critical analysis of the topic. But I can never remember all of the references in an exam, and I'm worried that I'll lose marks if I forget to put the page reference of the case or article.'

There is good news. Your law lecturers do not expect you to remember exact case references such as *R v Jones* [1980] 2 All ER 678. The case name and year will suffice for the same mark: *R v Jones* (1980). How many cases you would like to revise is up to you, but the more the better because case names instantly attract marks and illustrate well-researched legal principles.

Case facts are a bone of contention for students in law exams. It is often unclear how much information is required when using a legal authority such as a leading case. Are case facts relevant? Do they pick up marks or lose marks for being a waste of time? How much is too much? The answer is, keep case facts brief. They do not show the examiner that you can apply and analyse legal principles; they merely show the examiner that you can remember case facts. This is not an academic skill; it is merely evidence of a good memory. The only time when case facts will be relevant is when your case study scenario in your exam is identical to the facts of a leading case. In this instance, you can make a direct comparison to the case law and use the real case as evidence when showing the examiner what the likely outcome of the law will be.

Articles from legal journals also provide excellent evidence of further legal research, but students tend not to include them very often because they are either unsure about whether they are relevant, or simply cannot remember them during their revision. The full reference of an article is not required for an exam answer, as long as the examiner can recognise the authority that you have used. For example, in an assignment you would need to state the article reference in full: Levinson, D, 'The Shortfalls of the Sale of Goods Act 1979' (1998) 4 CLQ 452. In an exam, the examiner only needs the vital information: Levinson, 'The Shortfalls of the Sale of Goods Act 1979' (1998) CLQ.

In general, incorporating legal authorities into your exam answers makes them look professional, polished and well researched. They demonstrate your understanding of the law much better than if you were simply to state your opinion, which may be right or wrong:

Do not include any legal material in your answer which is not directly relevant to your question. You will not receive any extra marks for it, and writing it down and explaining it will waste several minutes of your valuable time in the exam hall. Each question has a clear and strict focus. The trick is to identify the focus and stick within the scope of the question. It is tempting when you have revised a particular legal theory off by heart to include it in your answer because you think there may be a *slight* chance that it is applicable to the question, but this is a risk if you are running out of time. It will interrupt the structure of your answer, making the overall submission look weak and patchy.

(e) Nerves

How do you feel about exams? Bad performance is almost always linked back to nerves in some way. Negative worries and fears can scramble your thoughts on examination day, and you will not be able to think as clearly and as logically as you would if you were confident and positive. Take the test overleaf to find out how you feel about exams.

 **Self-assessment** **How do you feel about exams? Plot your present position on the line with an X:**

A positive attitude:

I recognise that my expertise is growing. _ _ _ _ _

I can imagine hearing the news that I achieved a good pass. _ _ _ _ _

I will never have to revise this again if I pass! _ _ _ _ _

I can find a point of interest in every law topic. _ _ _ _ _

I will gain so much by passing my exams. _ _ _ _ _

I can imagine myself writing a really good answer. _ _ _ _ _

I like to remember the times I did better than expected. _ _ _ _ _

I can identify areas of my exam technique that have improved. _ _ _ _ _

I have learnt so much by revising and completing exams. _ _ _ _ _

I like the fact that I *know* my subjects. _ _ _ _ _

I like to think about what I'll do after the exam. _ _ _ _ _

I like to revise for my exams with my friends. _ _ _ _ _

I feel competent, capable and intelligent. _ _ _ _ _

I have learnt from my previous bad performances. _ _ _ _ _

I pace myself and know what I can handle. _ _ _ _ _

I can cope well with the pressure on me to perform well. _ _ _ _ _

I am confident that I can face any exam question. _ _ _ _ _

I can exercise good self-discipline during exams. _ _ _ _ _

My family and friends support me. _ _ _ _ _

I know that I can perform well when I put the work in. _ _ _ _ _

I have sorted my work into different piles and lists. _ _ _ _ _

I stay away from university until exam day to concentrate. _ _ _ _ _

A negative attitude:

I don't understand how exams help me to learn the law.

I can imagine hearing that I have failed.

I may as well leave my revision until the re-sits in the summer.

I hate all my law topics – they are so boring.

All I need to do is to pass these exams.

I can see myself staring at the clock and feeling stuck.

I've always been rubbish at exams.

I don't have an exam technique.

I don't feel I have learnt anything.

I don't really *know* my subjects.

I'll probably be re-sitting these exams.

All my friends are ahead of me when it comes to revision.

All my friends are cleverer than me.

I dwell on the times when I performed worse than expected.

I put too much pressure on myself.

I hate the spotlight being on me and my capabilities.

I feel nervous and uncertain about the exam questions.

I feel hungry and restless and get easily distracted.

I worry about letting others down.

I have no faith in myself and my own performance.

I am totally overwhelmed by how much there is to do.

I get nervous when hearing rumours about the exam.

How do you feel about your attitude towards exams after taking this test? Are you pleased with yourself, or do you feel as though you have so much work to do that you are not quite sure how to put things right?

....

....

....

....

....

....

Exams cause different levels of stress in each student. Some students take impending exams in their stride, some students are not bothered and do not take them seriously, and other students simply fall apart with the pressure. Clearly, any type of stress that causes you to panic is bad stress that will affect your ability to perform well during your intense revision period and in the exam hall on the day itself. Work out what stresses you and take control of it:

What are your stress triggers?

Tick the boxes below.

- [ ] I have many other pressures in my life and things are mounting up.
- [ ] I have a shortage of money and don't know how to handle it.
- [ ] I have had a bereavement and am not coping very well.
- [ ] My family situation has recently changed and I can't concentrate.
- [ ] I simply lie awake worrying about the exams and how I'll fail.
- [ ] I get really frustrated when the cases and statutes won't stay in my head.
- [ ] I haven't been taking care of my health and my body isn't functioning properly.
- [ ] I set myself unrealistic goals and get upset when I don't reach them.

- [ ] I have family responsibilities as well as my studies.
- [ ] I am in a difficult relationship that distracts me from my studies.
- [ ] I have lost my job and searching for a new one is taking up all my time.
- [ ] I have just had to move house and don't have time for my exams right now.
- [ ] I feel guilty when I'm not working but I can't make myself work.
- [ ] I have physical stress symptoms such as shaking, sweating and feeling sick.
- [ ] I'm irritable, moody, snappy and rude to those around me.
- [ ] I think everyone is doing better than I am and I feel like a failure.

Have you ticked many of the stress triggers above? If you have identified some instances which worry you and cause you stress, what can you now do to limit their effect on you, or to eliminate them completely from your life?

De-stress!   Done!

Try the methods below to help yourself feel better during the exam period.

Set priorities. What is most important in your life right now? Make a list, and dedicate your energy to tackling any urgent tasks so your revision and exams do not suffer.   [ ]

Sleep properly. Everyone has their own sleep cycle, but do not stay up too late during the exam period.   [ ]

Manage your time. How well have you stuck to your revision schedule? Have you done enough work?   [ ]

Be organised. Sort out your university work from all the other demands in your life and allocate your time accordingly. Remember, if you perform well in your exams, you have the whole summer free.   [ ]

Take breaks. If you over-revise, your brain will shut down and you will stop remembering facts and cases. A little bit over a long time builds a stronger foundation of knowledge than 'cramming' at the last minute.   [ ]

Look at your own attitude. Are you giving yourself an unnecessarily difficult time? Are you really doing enough to improve matters? Is your drive and enthusiasm as strong as it could be? If not, change these for the better.   [ ]

Dream about success. Remember how it feels to win that prize, to get the answer right, and to know that your hard work has paid off. Fantasise about graduation day with all your friends. ☐

Get rid of extra energy. Do something active on the weekends to take your mind off everything and release all your stress. Hanging out with your friends will help with this because they are in the same position as you. ☐

Analyse your private thoughts. Are you feeling negative about your impending exams? Why? Are you feeling self-conscious about your exam performance? Why? Are you doing anything to combat your negative thoughts and lift yourself up into a confident and hard-working firecracker? If not, why not? ☐

Take care of your body. Drink plenty of water to nourish your brain – carry a bottle everywhere if necessary. Cut out coffee, junk food, cigarettes, and any other substances which affect the chemicals in your brain. ☐

Reward yourself. If you achieve even small goals, you should plan a small reward, particularly if it took a lot of time management and effort to finish an afternoon of revision. This may be 30 minutes a day when you do something on your own just for you. ☐

Schedule

Months before

One of the positive aspects of taking examinations is that you know they are coming from the very beginning of your course. Assignments are sometimes issued unexpectedly and it is difficult to plan around them, but exams happen in a fixed exam period every term.

- Find out how many exams you have and in which subjects.
- Find out the dates of your exams.
- What type of exam are they?
- Find past exam papers and mock exam questions for practice.
- Approach your friends to form study groups and meet once a week.
- Design a revision strategy as early as possible.

It may also be worth developing a little 'exam schedule' alongside your revision schedule, to remind you of the tasks that lie ahead:

My Exam Schedule		
Subject:	Module:	Weighting:
Length:	Date:	Time:
Venue:	Materials:	
Further information provided by lecturer about exam:		
Revision strategies in place:		
Personal exam strategies to improve on:		

A week before

You will be in the middle of deep revision by this stage, and you can start testing yourself and asking your friends or your family to test you on your favourite topics. Tension, however, will be building, particularly if you need a certain mark in your exams to achieve the classification of degree that you are striving for.

- Keep with your revision schedule now more than ever.
- Remind yourself that in a week's time it will all be over for good and you will never have to revise that topic again!
- Get some daily exercise in the morning or in your break in the afternoon to detach yourself from all the case names and statute sections flying around in your head.
- Study buddies are still a good idea at this point, but avoid friends who have done no revision at all, as they will look to you for help and will slow you down
- Alter your diet slightly in the days before your exam. Sugar and sweets cause blood sugar levels to swing violently, so settle for fruit, vegetables and complex carbohydrates such as brown bread, brown rice, brown pasta and potatoes for a wide-awake feeling and excellent energy levels.
- Think positively. If you are sticking to your revision schedule as planned, you can look forward to leaving the exam hall feeling good and looking forward to the summer with your friends.
- Take care of domestic and personal arrangements – clear your diary the week before your exams of anything that can wait an extra week.
- Stay away from social events just for this week. No late-night parties, no excessive drinking. Take early nights, and don't be afraid that you are missing time with your friends – if your friends are serious about their studies too, they will join you in doing the same thing.

On the day!

Exam day is nerve-wracking for even the most serious of students. If your revision schedule has gone to plan, you should wake up feeling 'completely ready for it'. You will want to test yourself to the maximum to see whether you really are competent and up for the challenge, and you will feel so much better – and proud – once it is all over.

If your revision schedule has not gone to plan, or you have not done any revision at all, you will wake up feeling nervous.

- Set your alarm one hour early and set a second alarm as a back-up just in case your first alarm does not go off for whatever reason.
- If you think you cannot make it to your exam for health reasons, get a note from your doctor; otherwise you will be failed, and re-sits sometimes only carry a basic 'pass or fail' mark.
- Make sure that you have everything that you need for your exam: pen (and a spare), pencil with a rubber, your student card, and water if you need any.
- Make sure you enjoy a good breakfast to keep you awake all day. Many students drift off in afternoon exams because of the silence, the heat and the boredom. You need to stay awake!
- Get the earlier bus, or leave your home earlier in the car. It is unlikely that the exam invigilator will let you into the exam hall if you are over five minutes late, and this will completely mess everything up. Fancy more revision and a re-sit in the August 'heatwave'?
- Continue with your positive thoughts right up until you open your exam paper. *'I can do this. My answers will flow. I will pass. I have worked really hard. I know everything I need to know ...'*

- Stay away from nervous, edgy and stressed students. They will panic you and put you off. Stay in a quiet corner as you wait to enter the exam hall and sort your thoughts logically in your head.

In the exam!

Students make some silly mistakes when in exams. Make sure you do the following to ensure a smooth ride:

- Check that you have the correct exam paper.
- Don't forget to fill out your personal details at the beginning of the exam.
- Make your handwriting perfectly clear; otherwise the examiner will not mark it.
- Turn up to the correct exam! Check the room, date and time.
- Don't forget your student card, open book exam materials, and something to write with (and a back-up).
- Plan your answers carefully before writing them.
- Watch the clock meticulously and allocate a time slot for each question depending on its weighting.
- Write the number of your question clearly at the top of your answer, and take care of the other little details which ensure a clear structure.
- Do not include material that is not relevant to the question.
- Do not turn case study answers into essay answers, or vice versa. This will lose marks.
- Always attempt a final question. If you miss one question out of a compulsory four questions, you have already lost 25% of your whole mark.
- Check spellings when you have finished.
- Do not leave the exam hall if you finish early. If you finish 45 minutes early or more, you have probably not answered the questions properly and have omitted considerable material.

What now?

Examiners and/or your lecturers receive a large pile of exam scripts to mark, and they do not read them all meticulously because there is simply not time. Usually, there are only a few minutes available for each paper, so your marker is not as thorough as he or she would like to be.

Your marker will read your introduction and conclusion to get a feel for your argument, your line of reasoning, the topic(s) you identified, your concluding thoughts, and any other legal principles you have chosen to explain. Secondly, your marker will skim your whole answer to check for correct application, critical analysis, legal research, discussion of theories and any original ideas. An estimated grade will pop into your marker's head based on what he or she has seen on first impressions. This is why your exam answer must have a clear structure – markers only glance at exam answers briefly and form an opinion without reading your work in great detail. It must make a good first impression.

To ensure that the mark you receive is representative of the work you put in, exam scripts can also be second marked before they are sent to external moderators to confirm your grade, and there are often exam boards at law schools which confirm all the exam marks too. It takes some time to return the exam mark to the student.

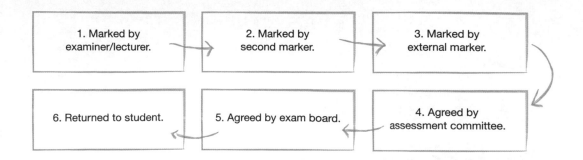

7

Professional communication

Learning outcomes

> To understand what 'professional communication' means
> To identify how and where professional communication differs from everyday communication

> To develop an ability to use formal means of professional communication
> To be able to evaluate yourself and others in the context of professional communication

If you are enrolled on a course to study law, you will be expected to communicate in a legal way. If you wish to establish a legal career after your course, your employer will expect excellent professional communication skills, both in writing and in verbal interactions.

The legal field is notoriously professional and strict – you cannot interrupt a judge! You must harness the skill of communicating professionally in a legal context before your law course comes to an end. Employers will not take you on if you cannot write a simple law letter, or interview a client in a professional manner. Additionally, your exams and assignments require a legal tone in your answers, and you must express yourself clearly. Can you do this effectively yet?

Self-assessment

How confident am I with legal communication? Tick the statement that applies to you...	This applies to me	I still need to do/ master this
I can write professional letters to external companies	☐	☐
I can talk on the phone with external companies	☐	☐
I have worked in a job where I had to wear a suit	☐	☐
My verbal skills with my peers are excellent	☐	☐
My assignments put forward a professional tone	☐	☐
In my exams I can communicate myself clearly	☐	☐
I can conduct an interview professionally	☐	☐
I am understanding of the needs of others	☐	☐
My lecturers tell me that my arguments are clear	☐	☐

My current weaknesses:

....

....

....

....

7.1   WRITING FOR LEGAL PRACTICE

You may have already had the opportunity on your course to communicate professionally in a legal context – perhaps you have secured a work placement? Or perhaps you have worked in the law before? If you have not had such opportunities then you must practice legal writing on your law course. Solicitors and other legal professionals write a lot of letters, whether on paper or via email. And don't think that just because solicitors communicate via email that it will be any less professional: it must be just as skilled and clear.

 Below are some examples of the types of legal writing that you will come across in practice. In the space below, explain and define the nature of each document, identify whether a solicitor or barrister would normally prepare the document, and identify the relevant audience. Some research may be required.

Document:	Description/ definition:	Prepared by a solicitor or barrister:	Audience:
Letter	Record of information required/received or advice given	Solicitor	Client, other professional, witness
Letter before action/ letter of claim			
File note/ attendance note			
Instructions to counsel			
Brief to counsel			
Counsel's opinion			
Pleadings/ statements of claim			

Document:	Description/ definition:	Prepared by a solicitor or barrister:	Audience:
Will			
Contract of sale			
Transfer of registered land			
Conveyance			
Lease			

We will now examine some of the key features of effective writing in legal practice in relation to some particular types of documents. This is not a detailed or comprehensive guide, as those of you who go on to the Legal Practice Course or Bar Professional Training Course (BPTC) will study this in more detail later. It is intended rather as an overview, highlighting some key similarities and differences between writing for academic and professional purposes.

As with other forms of writing, you need to consider the appropriate legal language and style for your audience. Remember: be clear, concise and correct.

In legal practice, just as in your legal studies, it is important to consider a number of key questions:

- Who is your audience? To whom are you writing and why?
- Why are you writing and what outcome do you want to achieve?
- What are you writing? Are you using the appropriate language and style, and is your writing clear, concise and correct?

In legal practice it is probably even more important to bear these factors in mind, because if you fail to write effectively, it is not only you who will suffer. In legal practice it is also your client, your firm or livelihood, and professional reputation that may suffer!

Letters

(a) Letters to clients

In legal practice you may spend a considerable amount of time writing letters to clients, advising them on particular issues and keeping them up to-date about progress. So you will need excellent letter writing skills, and remember that whilst you will need to explain things clearly, you will generally not be required to include all the legal detail and background as you would if you were writing an academic answer to an essay or problem question on the same subject.

Remember to address the client appropriately, use a short heading clearly describing the subject of your letter, avoid clumsy openings and endings with redundant words and use the active voice so that your letter does not sound too impersonal or remote.

Generally you should sign your letter to a client using 'Yours sincerely', having addressed the letter to him or her personally. However, be aware of your own firm's practices and conventions and the requirements set out by the professional body for the contents of client care letters.

Below is an example of a professional letter, but many firms and practices have their own standard layout which you should follow:

Practise writing your own in the box below:

For an example, visit our **Companion Website** at www.palgrave.com/law/legalskills.
Remember:

  'Dear Sir or Madam' = Yours faithfully
  'Dear Mr Smith' = Yours sincerely

(b) Letters of claim, and letters to other professionals

A letter of claim (formerly known as a letter before action) is a letter sent to the other side in a legal dispute before any legal proceedings have been issued, setting out details of your client's claim. It is normally sent to the other side's solicitor or the defendant direct.

The Civil Procedure Rules set out some pre-action protocols that include specimen letters which you will also need to take into account when drafting any such letter. You may also need to write to solicitors acting for the other side in connection with ongoing litigation, and during negotiations to settle a contentious matter, or agree a contract or other document in a non-contentious matter, such as the sale and purchase of a house or the granting of a lease. Many of the same principles apply, but you would normally start a letter to the other side's solicitors, 'Dear Sirs', and end, 'Yours faithfully', with the name of your firm, rather than 'Yours sincerely'.

As well as having a short heading describing the matter, in a letter during negotiations for a contract or possible settlement of a contentious matter, you will also need to be aware of when to use the words 'subject to contract' or 'without prejudice'. 'Subject to contract' generally makes it clear that negotiations are ongoing and there is no agreement until formal exchange or completion of the formal contract document. 'Without prejudice' allows parties to negotiate without the risk of damaging their case should the matter go to court, as no such correspondence can be referred to in legal proceedings should negotiations fail.

In longer letters, it may well be appropriate to use headings and numbered paragraphs as in a report.

 Some of your lecturers will have practised law before. Ask one of your lecturers to show you some examples of professional letters they used to write, to give you an idea of how they can vary and how complex they can be.

(c) Instructions to counsel/briefs to counsel

'Instructions to counsel' are documents prepared by solicitors for a barrister (counsel). They may be necessary when a solicitor seeks detailed advice or a second opinion from a barrister about an issue relating to liability, advice on quantum (the possible level of damages) and the chances of success.

A 'brief to counsel' is the document where a solicitor instructs a barrister to represent the client in a court hearing.

With both types of document, effective writing is key. You can of course assume a greater level of legal understanding when writing to a barrister, and your legal language should reflect this. However, particularly when asking for advice on issues of liability, you should explain your own opinion and clearly identify particular questions and issues upon which you are seeking advice. It is also crucial to include and list all additional documents that are relevant, such as witness statements, experts' reports and relevant documents. Use appropriate headings and numbered paragraphs.

Activity In the boxes below, write some notes to a barrister on the left side in the same way as you would talk to your friends in a social context. In the box on the right, write the same notes in a much more professional manner. Are you better at this than you thought?

(d) Counsel's opinion

This is the barrister's response to instructions where the barrister will set out in writing and give his or her advice on issues of law, liability, evidence and procedure. Again, the principles of effective writing apply, and headings and numbered paragraphs may well be appropriate.

Drafting legal documents

There are many situations where lawyers are required to prepare a legal document, such as a contract or statement of claim. A legal document may relate to a variety of matters covering different areas of law, such as the sale and purchase of land, goods or a business; the creation of a lease, a partnership or company or a will; the appointment of an employee, agent or franchisee. Whilst the general principles for effective writing also apply to this type of document, it is important to remember the aim of the document and what you want to achieve for your client.

In order for your contract, for example, to do this, it will need to be not just comprehensible but also comprehensive. That is, as well as being easily understood, it has to ensure that any possible eventualities are provided for and potential disputes avoided. For example, in a long-term sale of goods contract, you may need to include provisions to deal with the consequences of delay, unforeseen events preventing delivery and the increase in the cost of raw materials from suppliers. This can add to the length and complexity of such documents. In a document of this nature, it will often be necessary to include a 'definitions' section explaining the meaning of particular words, and the language you use will need to make reference to and be governed by any relevant legal provisions or rules.

In addition, the main audience will not necessarily be just the client but the other side, his or her solicitor and potentially the court or arbitrator in case of a dispute, so the language used may be more complex that might be expected in a communication addressed solely to the client.

The art of good drafting is all about getting the balance right between comprehensibility and comprehensiveness. Drafting is an area included on LPC and BPTC courses, and there are also many excellent books and online packages of precedents, access to which is vital to most lawyers. Indeed, many firms of solicitors have their own banks of precedents. However, any precedent has to be used with care and should be amended and tailored to the particular facts and needs of your client, taking into account any changes in the law.

In terms of structure, a clear and logical order is required, as with other forms of writing, and, again, headings and numbered paragraphs are appropriate.

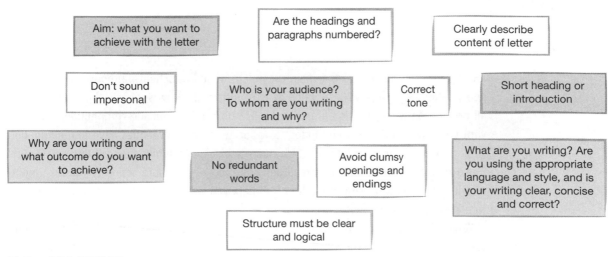

7.2 MOOTING

Mooting is a strange word; many students will not be familiar with the word 'mooting' until they begin their law course. What 'mooting' means in modern legal terms is to engage in a mock legal appeal – whether in criminal or civil law – where one or more interesting points of law are engaged. A courtroom scenario will be set up in one of your tutorial rooms, and a judge, two senior counsels, two junior counsels and a court clerk will be nominated to act out a real law appeal.

The current English phrase 'a moot point' means something which is capable of being seen and decided in more than one way. Moots are often about points of law, and many cases in real life are decided in this way. A 'point of law' can sometimes come down to the meaning of a simple word or phrase in a case or a statute, which could mean the difference between winning and losing the case for the parties, depending on how the word or phrase is interpreted. These points of law are usually the main matter of debate in a moot, derived from case law or statutes, and barristers will wrangle with each other to submit that the word or phrase in question means something different to what the other party is arguing, taking the focus of the argument back to the original, dictionary meaning of the word. Moots emphasise to students the fact that the law can sometimes balance on a simple point. Mooting is different from a mock trial, which simply focuses on giving evidence and examining witnesses.

What does 'consideration' in contract law really mean?

Has my client really 'assaulted' the appellant?

The actors amongst you will greatly enjoy mooting, as you will have the opportunity to dress as barristers, hold an audience, and present your legal argument to the judge. You may be in a law school where mooting is compulsory, for example as part of a Legal Skills module. If this is the case, you will have no choice but to take part, but it is a very positive experience. If mooting is not compulsory on your course, there will probably be the option to take part in a moot through your Student Law Society. Mooting involves lots of skills that you will find very useful elsewhere, and your confidence will grow as a result. For those of you who wish to practise law one day, mooting is where your performance skills start to develop!

Why moot?

Mooting may not be part of the main curriculum of all law schools, although most provide opportunities to engage with mooting at least informally. How seriously the moot is taken will depend on whether it is an assessed piece of work, an outside competition, or a 'fun' event with your friends in your Student Law Society. Many universities have formal mooting competitions and mooting teams, which create special opportunities to visit the Royal Courts of Justice and appear in front of a real High Court judge! The more seriously you take mooting, the more you will learn, the better the mark you will receive and, in all probability, the more likely you will enjoy it.

You will learn a lot about the particular area of law that you are researching for your counsel argument, and you will learn a lot about court procedure, court etiquette, and how to compose a thorough, concise legal argument. It will also look good on your CV if you have mooted, especially if you have been successful in regional or national competitions, when it comes to looking for jobs.

Before you begin to quake in your boots at the thought of playing a barrister in front of all of your friends and your lecturer, remember that this kind of practical experience is good for you on many different levels. Professionally, the advantages are endless. For those of you who aim to hold an audience in a court of law one day, the very serious business of presenting your argument to a magistrate or a judge requires professionalism, an element of showmanship, confidence, thorough research and a quick mind. Would you know what to do if a judge asked you a question that you could not answer? Would you know how to present yourself in a court of law? Is it appropriate to say 'Hi' to a judge or magistrate? All of these rules you will need to learn during your legal studies before you go out into the real world of legal practice. Remember, if you are a barrister or a solicitor, your clients are depending on you to help them out of their legal predicament.

Other professional advantages of mooting, apart from the practice, include the following:

- professional presentation skills;
- excellent etiquette;
- thorough research skills;
- good time-keeping;
- uplift in confidence;
- attention to detail;
- broadened legal knowledge;
- affirmation of your career goals.

These skills may not seem to important while you are trying to complete coursework, attend lectures, and sort out your exam revision, but employers who look for excellent people skills (which is in most fields of work) will require some evidence that you can present yourself professionally with courtesy and respect. Mooting requires all of these special traits and more.

To be able to stand in front of a judge, develop a sound legal argument, and listen to and respond to another senior counsel, shows hard work, dedication and integrity. As a law graduate, you are expected to learn these skills as part of your law degree. Research skills also come to the fore during mooting, and so you will notice the benefits of mooting in your legal studies right away. You will find that you will be paying intricate attention to case judgments, undertaking detailed research into additional relevant cases to collect a more 'rounded' argument and to add to your knowledge in the field, and you will be presenting all your findings – and suggesting original reforms – in a concise way that makes perfect legal sense. Your marks will probably improve as a result of your dedication to mooting because the legal skills you learn – both academic and professional – are many.

The layout of a moot

In a moot, it is important that your tutorial room is set up in a way that allows everybody to see and communicate with each other clearly. The clerk has particular importance when it comes to laying out your courtroom – he or she needs to be able to help the judge and direct all the counsels.

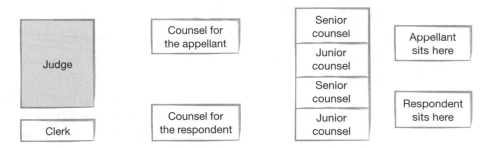

Roles!	
What does each party do in a moot?	
Judge	<ul><li>watches over proceedings and requests to hear the arguments of the counsels;</li><li>listens to the arguments in turn;</li><li>asks questions of both senior and junior counsels;</li><li>negotiates with the clerk to read evidence and check timings;</li><li>weighs up both arguments and delivers a judgment;</li><li>announces which party has won at the end.</li></ul>
Senior counsel – appellant	<ul><li>very important role – starts the moot by introducing all the parties to the judge;</li><li>presents the first point of appeal to the judge on the appellant's behalf;</li><li>may have a right to reply to the respondent's arguments.</li></ul>
Junior counsel – appellant	<ul><li>introduces the second point of appeal to the judge on the appellant's behalf;</li><li>summarises both points of appeal from the appellant team to the judge.</li></ul>
Senior counsel – respondent	<ul><li>presents the first point of appeal to the judge on the respondent's behalf;</li><li>addresses the arguments raised by the senior counsel for the appellant (who may have a right to reply).</li></ul>

Junior counsel – respondent	• introduces the second point of appeal to the judge on the respondent's behalf; • addresses the points raised by the junior counsel for the appellant. • summarises both points of appeal from the respondent team to the judge.
Court clerk	• keeps time and alerts mooters of time left; • passes evidence to the judge; • finds page references in documents for the judge to read.

What does counsel for the appellant really do?

Counsel for the appellant has a really important job. As the name suggests, the appellant is *appealing* from a previous decision, and so sets the agenda for the whole moot by giving reasons and presenting evidence (usually case law) as to why the previous decision should be overturned in favour of the appellant. Counsel for the appellant will have to construct legal arguments without knowing what the respondent is going to respond with, and this is why the appellant has a right to respond at the end of the moot.

This is difficult – the senior counsel for the appellant will have to think on his or her feet once the respondent arguments have been concluded to try to rebut what has been said. To combat this difficulty, a good mooter in the appellant senior counsel position could anticipate what the respondent is going to say and try to incorporate this into his or her legal arguments. This is a clever card to play, and makes the work of the respondent counsels much harder because the appellant will already have rebutted their arguments before they have even stood up!

What does counsel for the respondent really do?

Counsel for the respondent has a difficult job. As the name suggests, counsel is responding to the arguments put forward by the appellant as to why the previous decision should be overturned. If counsel for the respondent fails to rebut one of the submissions of the appellant, counsel is seen to be accepting that the appellant was correct on that point. Counsel for the respondent must therefore see the skeleton arguments of the appellant before the case begins, in order to craft and tailor an appropriate response. This is why the appellant has a right to reply at the very end. After responding to the appellant's main arguments, counsel for the respondent has a second job – to advance arguments as to why the previous decision should hold firm.

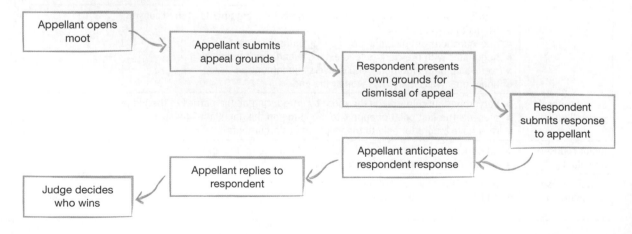

Counsel for the appellant can anticipate all of these arguments but may be wrong. A clever card to play in the respondent senior counsel position is to take a completely unexpected line of reasoning, or present a totally unique legal argument. Counsel for the appellant will be left stunned and will not know how to respond at the end!

Junior counsel for both sides have the same stresses to contend with but deal with the smaller points of law.

Example moot scenario

Below is an example of a mooting scenario. In regional and national mooting competitions, mooting cases are usually very complex with specific timings and an integration of legal topics, and the fictional incident is usually based on real case law which has to be researched in depth. A very simple scenario is provided below to get you started and to help acquaint you with the process of mooting and the work involved.

Activity:

Jack wrote a letter to Rose, asking her if she would like to buy his old Ford Fiesta. These are the terms of the offer:

> *'Dearest Rose,*
> *I offer to you my beloved Ford Fiesta for the bargain price of £300. This is an offer just for you as I know you collect old Ford Fiestas. If you do not wish to accept this offer then please tell me so I can make the offer to Fred in seven days' time. If I do not hear such things from you, then I will await your £300 within the week.*
> *from Jack.'*

Jack posted the letter to Rose but she was on holiday in Blackpool. When she returned two weeks later she received a legal letter, claiming that Jack was taking legal action for the £300. Jack argued that his genuine offer had been accepted, and he won his case, so Rose appealed to the Court of Appeal. Jack won again in the Court of Appeal, so Rose has now appealed to the Supreme Court. Rose is now the 'appellant' and Jack is now the 'respondent'.

- Jack argues that this is a proper offer under the rules of *Carlill v Carbolic Smoke Ball Co* (1893). He also argues that because the offer stated that silence was acceptance, Rose had accepted the offer with her silence. His arguments were accepted in the lower courts.
- Rose argues that silence is not acceptance under the rule of *Felthouse v Bindley* (1863). Additionally, she argues that she cannot accept an offer if she has no knowledge of it.

Task:

In your group of eight, pick a judge, an appellant and a respondent, a senior counsel for each side, and a junior counsel for each side. Don't forget the court clerk to control proceedings. For the purposes of this exercise, the senior counsel handles the bigger legal arguments/points, and the junior counsel deals with the smaller legal arguments/points. The case is called *Rose v Jack*.

Timeline:

Draw a timeline below of the sequence of events between Rose and Jack.

Getting started on a moot

Once you have received your scenario, it will be a huge help to your team if you create a timeline of events, just to make it clear in your mind what happened when. In contract law cases involving communication, timing is especially vital.

Next, it would be helpful to jot down the main facts. What do you know to be true? What is a little unclear? What are the main issues, and what are the smaller issues? What questions will be raised by the other side?

	Appellant (Rose)	Respondent (Jack)
Main known facts to be argued		
Unclear issues for each party		
Smaller issues for the junior counsel of each side		
Questions which may be highlighted by the other side		

Building your argument

If you are acting for the appellant, you need first to submit your grounds of appeal, before anticipating and disproving what the respondent might say. If you are acting for the respondent, your task is the opposite – you need to prove the appellant wrong first, before submitting your own grounds for a dismissal. The mooting scenario will provide references to relevant cases – this is the biggest hint you will get as to where to start your research. You cannot create a legal argument without your legal authorities.

	Point of law/main argument to submit to court	Main legal authorities to support argument
Appellant senior counsel		
Appellant junior counsel		
Respondent senior counsel		
Respondent junior counsel		

How important is research in a moot?

Vital! In preparing for your moot, you will need to research the appropriate law and write out an argument – or series of arguments – applying the relevant law to the facts of your scenario to illustrate why you think your client should win. In doing this, you will also become aware of the strengths in the appellant's/respondent's case which your opponent is likely to advance. You can then think of how you can undermine these arguments.

Case law is the foundation and content of your argument – the judge will be expecting you to use the law as authority to support your submission. You will need to read the relevant cases very carefully to ascertain why they helped or hindered your party in the lower courts. Were they interpreted correctly? Can a new approach be taken? You will need to present to the judge passages from the relevant cases to prove that they help your client's position.

For example, the appellant could use legal authority in the following way:

'Your Lordship, in the case of *Felthouse v* [pronounced 'and'] *Bindley*, reported in volume 142 of the 1863 England Reports at page 1037, Mr Justice Willes states at page 1040 – which is page 15 of your bundle my Lord – that "silence does not amount to acceptance".'

Notice how a new word has popped up – 'bundle'. When you are mooting, you must collect all of your legal authorities (ie case judgments) in one package, and give the judge a tightly bound copy. The full judgment of your case(s) must be provided, but the relevant quote should be highlighted. The judge can then decide for himself if the case you have chosen is indeed relevant.

Full cases I am going to need in my bundle:

....

....

....

....

....

You can see from the quote above that moots take a considerable amount of time. The judge must be directed to the relevant case, the relevant page, and the applicable quote must be read to him. This will probably happen several times during one submission, but each counsel only has approximately 10 minutes to speak. Therefore, your arguments must be concise and straight to the point. Do not waste time flitting from one case to another every other minute – pick some strong authorities and build your submission upon those.

Both sides will deal with the larger, obvious cases, but sometimes there may be other legal authorities that can help a client's position. For example, in response to the argument above about the judgment in *Felthouse v Bindley*, the respondent could pull out a new case, *Yates v Pulleyn*:

> 'Your Lordship, in the case of *Yates v Pulleyn*, reported in volume 237 of the 1975 England Reports at page 183, Lord Denning states at page 192 – which is page 27 of your bundle, my Lord – that "acceptance can be in any form".'

As you can see, moots can be complex, and they require an intricate understanding of the law. However, if you construct your argument clearly and use two main arguments for your grounds of appeal rather than several smaller ones, you are less likely to become confused, and more likely to present a strong case.

In the box below, jot down any additional cases that each side could use to present a novel and unique argument. Additionally, you may wish to make a note of any loopholes that the other side might identify in the new legal arguments. This will help both sides to build a stronger submission.

	Alternative argument to submit to court	New legal authorities to support argument
Appellant senior counsel		
Appellant junior counsel		
Respondent senior counsel		
Respondent junior counsel		
Potential loopholes in arguments:		

The formalities of mooting – speaking

Speaking in a moot is almost a special art, which takes practice to learn. It is not until you find yourself standing before the judge that you begin to realise how important the etiquette of the court is. Only one person speaks at a time, and that person must stand. Once you sit down, the judge knows that your submission is finished and he or she will then direct the next party. When you are standing, you have audience of the court, and no one else can interrupt you. It is considered rude to talk in court when another person is speaking, but sometimes it may be necessary to whisper to your senior/junior counsel if a particularly important issue arises. This is one of the really important lessons to be learnt from a law course – every person has a right to speak and be listened to, and every other person has a right to reply politely.

Counsel for the appellant speaks first, and this is what you say:

'My Lord/Lady, I am [Matthew] and I appear for the appellant, Rose, who is the appellant in this matter. My learned friend [Daisy] appears for the respondent Jack.'

- *Always* stand to speak to the judge, and *never* interrupt him!
- Be clear when addressing the judge.
- Refer to the judge as 'Your Lordship' or 'Your Ladyship'.
- Refer to cases as 'Smith and Williams' rather than 'Smith versus Williams'.
- The judge can question you at any time, so answer him or her politely.
- If you disagree with the judge, do it politely using legal authority to support yourself (ie case law).
- Thank the judge if he or she points something out to you.
- Ask the judge for permission, ie 'with Your Lordship's permission I will now move on to my second point ...'.
- Do not say what you think or feel, say what you 'submit' or 'suggest'.

Activity Write down in this space how you will open your moot (ie what you will say):

....

....

....

....

The formalities of mooting – timing

Timing is important during a moot. Turn up early and check that you have everything in place to submit a perfect argument.

The judge will decide who speaks and when. Sometimes judges prefer to hear both counsels on one side before swapping over, and sometimes judges like to alternate between sides, ie senior counsel for the appellant, then senior counsel for the respondent. The judge will usually tell you how he or she is going to proceed, but the senior counsel for the appellant always speaks first.

- Introduce yourself and all the other parties if you are the senior counsel for the appellant.
- Ask the judge if he or she wants them, then provide a brief summary of the facts of the case.
- Outline the grounds of appeal.
- Put your argument (with legal authority, ie case law) forward.

Nerves

Mooting is nerve-wracking in front of your peers, let alone in front of a real judge in a national mooting competition!

Write down in this space how you feel about mooting in front of your peers:

....

....

....

....

....

....

....

Presentation skills are vital when it comes to delivering your moot, and the formality of a moot often makes students even more nervous than they would normally be, especially if they are dressed up in gowns! Why, then, would anyone want to do this if they did not have to?

There are a number of reasons:

- It can be fun – especially if you enjoy working with your 'pair'. You develop research skills and teamworking skills which can be invaluable in life and not just as a lawyer.
- You sharpen up your advocacy and public speaking skills, which are clearly important for a solicitor or barrister but also useful for people who have to advance points of view in other types of work.
- It is good on a CV and helps give you confidence.
- It may give access to other outside competitions which, in turn, expose you to other ideas and opportunities. After all, outside competitions often involve members of the profession.
- It helps you to learn the law and think as a lawyer.

7.3   ADVOCACY

Although 'advocacy' is usually taken to mean 'speaking in court', advocacy also means representing someone or a particular point of view, and can often take place away from the legal profession – in the ordinary commercial workplace for example, or simply at a tennis club meeting where you want more money spent on marking out the courts!

It is also true to say that the skills underpinning any type of advocacy are transferrable to many other situations – planning what you are going to say, placing your arguments in a logical order, seeking a way to impress with your delivery, and being able to respond quickly to changes in circumstance (such as when it becomes obvious that the court is not following or agreeing with your carefully structured argument).

So, advocacy can be taken as a form of public speaking, although everyone will be able to think of cases where points are put forcefully in writing – a form of written advocacy.

Would you like to be a solicitor, barrister or judge? These roles require advocacy skills. In this box, describe the advocacy role that you believe each of these professional people perform, and consider whether you could do it every day as part of your permanent job:

....

....

....

....

....

A lot of people think that only those with 'the gift of the gab' can be effective advocates. In truth, while some people seem to have a winning way early in life, almost anyone can learn to be an effective public speaker if they work at it and are masters of what they have to say.

Self-assessment Honesty checklist!

Tick the skills you have and give yourself a mark out of 10 if you feel you can successfully apply the skill in practice:

Mark out of 10:

Present. I feel I can present myself professionally in a courtroom. ☐

Articulate. I know that I can present arguments clearly and logically. ☐

Observe. I have been to courts before and I could see how the manners were different than in normal social interactions. ☐

Prepare. I am good at preparing materials in advance – I don't miss a thing. ☐

Dress. I can look professional and set an excellent example when in a professional situation. ☐

Critical. I can find loopholes in arguments, and I can read a case or a decision and pick faults with it. ☐

Reflect. I learn from bad experiences to ensure that my next experience is better. ☐

Argue. I can put together solid arguments that are strong, forward-looking and logical. ☐

Act. My presentation skills are excellent, and I have no problem speaking in front of an audience, no matter how superior they are. ☐

Conclude. If I notice that an argument is not going well for me, I can find a way around it, or an alternative solution. ☐

Speak. I can always think of something to say, no matter what is thrown at me! ☐

The ancient Greeks created a vast body of literature on this, way back in the fourth century BC.

How you stand – or sit – to make your points is important. If standing, as advocates usually do, it is important to strike the right pose.

Manners!

Look at the quote below. This kind of behaviour is to be expected in a court room. Could you and your peers behave in this way in your next tutorial?

'Usually standing straight or leaning very slightly from the waist does it, the head should be held up (even if glancing down at papers), shoulders back, standing still rather than swaying from side to side. Hands should never go in pockets, nails should not be bitten, if tissues are needed, the errant nose should be blown quietly and as unobtrusively as possible. Hand should be down, unless holding notes (which should be somewhere between waist and chest) or making a particular point – fingers should not be pointed but a thrust of a pair of spectacles can be effective as can, very occasionally, theatrical gestures such as an outstretched arm.'

If you are sitting, as you may very well be in a tribunal or if you are making your point at a meeting or conference, much of what is written above holds good – sit up straight and do not slouch. Do not talk down to your shoes. Do not fiddle with your fingers. The same sort of strategy can be adopted to make people look at you, hear what you say and not be distracted.

 Make notes in this box as to how you feel about courtroom etiquette:

....

....

....

....

Delivery

Whether standing or sitting, a good-humoured demeanour will always help. A brief smile to the judge or other people you are speaking to is pleasant, open and well mannered. Making eye contact is again a plus point – although you have to keep looking around and selecting your target more when you have a body of people in front of you rather than a single judge. Not only does this portray you in a good light, it should also help you pick up signals if anyone is not understanding you and give you the opportunity to approach your argument from another standpoint that may be understood. Smiles and nods in return are polite, but do not necessarily mean you have convinced your audience! Frowns and sighs usually mean they are bored or not agreeing with you and should be your clue to moving on or trying to make your point in another way.

> Your Lordship…
>
> **YOUR LORDSHIP!**

You need to make sure you can be heard. If you follow the advice above, you will at least not be talking to your shoes, but your volume needs to be adjusted to take account of your settings – clearly you need to speak louder when in a large room than when sitting across a desk from someone. Usually, if there is difficulty in hearing you, you will be told, but it can be off-putting for you, so better to try and start with a sufficiently loud delivery.

Even if you can be heard, your argument will be difficult to follow if you rush through your points at the speed of light. Early in your career, you are probably aware of people watching you and want to get it over as soon as possible, but remember the point of you being there is so that people look at you, listen to you and, hopefully, are convinced by what you say. Repeatedly remind yourself to slow down and, for dramatic effect, a short pause can bring wandering attentions back to the point you are about to embark upon.

> Gobble…gobble… gobble……

> Your Lordship………If I may begin……

You need also to vary the tone of your delivery. A flat monotone is likely to have your audience drifting away in their minds, and a high-pitched rant is likely to have them wanting to cover their ears to protect their hearing. Loud enough is one thing; a variety in delivery is another and will help to keep the attention of your audience. If you see heads beginning to nod or windows being gazed out of, do not be rude or churlish with your audience but try to put some variety into your delivery. If you sound enthusiastic about a point you are making, rather than weary and cynical, there is every chance you will hold your audience's attention and, hopefully, get them sympathetic to your arguments.

Virtually all of the above improves with practice. 'Keep practising' is the motto here! Involve yourself in moots, become a member of committees, see how your arguments and techniques hold, impress friends when you are debating where to go out, and adjust your advocacy delivery strategy in the light of what works well. Keep honing for various situations and circumstances, and continue with this throughout your life, and you will have the makings of a decent advocate – at least as good as anyone else.

Activity In the space below, list the fears you may have about performing as an advocate, whether in a full-time job, or as part of a moot with your peers:

....

....

....

....

....

....

Preparation and research

None of the notes above makes reference to the value of preparation and research into your subject. Even though you hardly need research to suggest to your friends that you go to Place X rather than Place Y, you will have a reason for suggesting X based probably on research and preparation. You may advance its cause because it is closer, cheaper, newer, louder, quieter or for whatever reason, but you will be suggesting it because you want to go there based on something you have experienced before or based on something someone whose judgement you trust has told you – that is the research here.

Preparation is knowing when to suggest your favoured destination – before anyone else can speak or after a lot of alternatives have been suggested and not met with much enthusiasm. You get to know when to speak based on your knowledge of the group you are talking to – whether friends or a bench of magistrates or a High Court judge. Some of this preparation can come from observing others, but personal involvement at the earliest opportunity is likely to help you most – and there should not really be much to lose by speaking out in a tutorial or even in a moot at university.

In courtroom advocacy, preparation includes not only knowing your audience but being sure of your subject. You need to know the facts of a case, the participants in the events, the law relating to all of these and what decision you want the court to come to. Of course you can have props and reminders in front of you, but you should need those only for reasons of comfort, affectation or 'first night nerves' – you should know what you want to say and not be looking for the case or the paragraph of a case you want to use as you are speaking.

Activity Fill in the empty boxes:

Preparation is key!		
Know your audience		Know the relevant law
	Be sure of your subject	
Know the previous decisions		Know the facts

Timing

As in mooting, timing is also likely to be relevant – you will be given a specific number of minutes in which to speak. Work out what you want to say and practise – whether in front of the mirror or in front of friends. If you come in exactly on time, you are lucky! You may finish early, which is not a crime as long as you are sure there is nothing else you need to be saying – do check this through. Far more likely, you will overrun.

Do not be tempted to make time up by speaking more quickly, but instead make sure that unnecessary repetition is removed, that unnecessary explanations of basic concepts are cut out and that your arguments follow logically from one to the next. In doing this, it is very likely that your time target will come into sight, and a little more adjustment using the same process should make it achievable.

Activity Prepare an oral presentation on an area of the law with which you are comfortable and familiar, using the tips above. Practise in front of a mirror – and evaluate your performance honestly.

Next ... team up with a group of three or four friends or colleagues and find somewhere you can sit around comfortably without being overheard or seen. Each of you make a presentation on the area of law of your choice for five minutes, and then receive feedback from the others about how you looked and sounded and the impression the points you were making made on them.

Next ... taking on board the points made by colleagues, try the whole thing again ... a number of times!

7.4 CLINICAL LEGAL EDUCATION

The acquisition of legal knowledge is one of the main intended outcomes of an LLB programme, or indeed any law course. However, knowing the law is not the same as practising the law. About half of the students enrolled on the LLB pursue a professional legal career, but the acquisition of legal knowledge is only one of the steps these students have to take in order to enter the legal profession and succeed. There are many more things to learn and skills to develop in order for a law graduate to become a successful lawyer.

Law students will acquire most of the required practical skills in their Legal Practice Course (LPC) or Bar Professional Training Course (BPTC) during their period of vocational training, which are the usual career steps for prospective lawyers following university graduation.

The university degree is usually a first step, which offers some fundamental knowledge on specific legal subjects (contract, tort, criminal, land, equity and trusts, etc) and an introduction to essential legal skills (research, writing, problem solving etc), which can be used to support the later career steps. At university level, the intended outcomes are achieved through a combination of teaching and assessment methods and student activities, such as writing essays, being involved in group work and oral presentations, and participating in moots and mock trials. Most universities also run specific legal skills modules aimed at introducing students to essential legal skills, research projects focusing on research skills, and career development modules helping with career planning and management.

Activity **In the space below, list your feelings about undertaking work experience during your law course. How important is it to your future career?**

....

....

....

....

....

A large part of an LLB programme is based on theory, offering little practical knowledge and experience. Students seeking to become professional lawyers leave university having little knowledge of what they will meet when they become solicitors or barristers. This vacuum existing between theory and practice creates problems in the process of gradual transformation from inexperienced young individuals to well qualified and skilled lawyers.

This is a problem identified long ago in the United States. Universities sought to address it through the introduction in undergraduate law programmes of law clinics which seek to combine theoretical legal knowledge with some practical work experience. In this way it is hoped that the gap that traditionally exists between the theoretical knowledge provided in the undergraduate law programmes and the practical knowledge and experience required by the legal profession can be filled.

UK universities adopted clinical legal education (CLE) more recently, and its use is expanding throughout the country. Some universities have included CLE in the curriculum, while others run clinics outside of it.

What is clinical legal education?

Clinical legal education is a concept which, due to the various forms and aims it can have, is hard to define accurately. According to the UK Centre for Legal Education, CLE has been used to encourage learning which is experiential in design and focused on enabling students to understand how the law works in action (see www.ukcle.ac.uk/resources/trns/clinic/one.html). The desired learning outcomes are achieved through the use of either real (ie 'live client') or simulated cases. The student performance in the clinic may also be assessed.

(a) Live client clinics

'Live client' clinics seek to involve students in real legal cases by allowing them to provide legal advice and other assistance to clients, subject to appropriate supervision by academics or lawyers.

The clients could be members of the local community or the general public, and the students' involvement could take various forms, ranging from mere provision of information on legal rights and obligations to partial or full client representation, depending on the programme's educational objectives. The clinic may be designed to handle cases in any area of law or only those in specific areas. The cases may be as simple as filling out forms and drafting documents (council tax, social security benefits, etc) or more complex, involving legal advice and/or representation (criminal offences, immigration, employment disputes, etc).

Other student activities taking place in the context of law clinics could involve campaigning in the community to raise awareness of legal rights and responsibilities on issues that may interest the community, or delivering courses and seminars to educate people on legal matters.

The law clinic may be located within the university or hosted by an external institution or organisation. It may be funded by the university or an external body.

Other 'live client' programmes involve work placements where students are placed to work for a defined period in an external organisation under the control and supervision of that organisation.

Self-assessment Would you like to work in a law clinic? Would it further your future career? Note your thoughts below (further information is provided in Chapter 9):

....

....

....

....

....

(b) Simulation clinics

These clinics do not involve 'live' cases but seek instead to enhance student learning by simulating real cases. Simulated cases include, among other things, problem solving, the handling of legal documents, and preparing cases for court. They are designed in terms of structure and complexity to be as realistic as possible. However, it is obvious that students involved in simulated cases do not experience the same level of exposure to legal practice and strong feelings as students involved in live cases do. On the other hand, the scenarios considered in simulation clinics are realistic and complex enough to provide valuable experience of the application of practical legal strategies.

Simulation may be particularly useful to students who for various reasons do not feel confident enough to expose themselves to a real-life version of their university-acquired legal knowledge and skills in live clinics. These students, though, will still benefit from their involvement in the realistically simulated legal scenarios in the clinics. Also, simulations could be designed to test specific legal skills or achieve specific learning outcomes, which may not always be achievable in live clinics where the content of the cases and the associated learning experience of the students are not fully controllable and predictable.

The objectives of CLE – 'why do I need it?'

The educational objectives of a law clinic vary and depend on the model of law clinic used, in association with the specific objectives set by the university.

General objectives of CLE programmes include:

- improved knowledge of:
  - o the English justice and court system,
  - o professional practice and ethics,
  - o substantive law and practical application of law;
- support to students in their career decisions;
- social objectives:
  - o inform members of the community on significant legal issues;
  - o popularise law;
  - o improve people's access to the English legal system;
  - o provide basic legal support and related assistance to members of the community who are unable to gain direct access to legal services.

Overall, law clinics could be used to achieve a wide range of aims in different areas. However, in order to maximise student benefits as well as running the clinic more efficiently and achieving consistent results, it is prudent for the designers of the clinic to set out specific and clearly identifiable objectives for the operation of the clinic, as well as to design appropriate tasks to achieve these objectives. The objectives should be clearer in those clinics where the performance of participating students is assessed.

It should be stressed, though, that since many of the law clinics handle real cases of varying legal significance and complexity, it may be hard to fully predict the whole range of learning outcomes resulting from participation in the clinic.

Skills acquired

Employability

Hard work

Professionalism

Motivation

Dedication

The participation in a law clinic could lead to the acquisition of new skills or improvement of existing essential legal skills. The list below contains some of the areas where students are expected to acquire or improve their skills as a result of their involvement in clinical activity.

(a) Research

Students joining CLE have already developed some research skills from their participation in academic modules where legal research is required to successfully meet the learning outcomes of the module and pass the assessment. Adequate research skills are essential to any lawyer, and CLE offers students the opportunity to improve these skills by researching new areas of law beyond those taught in academic modules or by digging deeper into existing areas. Research taking place in CLE covers substantive law and legal processes, professional practice and the operation of courts, tribunals and essential public services.

Also, research experience in clinics helps students to improve their ability to draw up comprehensive research plans, to evaluate sources and evidence, and to link their research activity to the adoption of logical, practical steps to resolve disputes.

Lastly, due to the increased complexity and realistic nature of the cases, research in clinics is often multi-dimensional and multi-disciplinary. Students dealing with real (or simulated) cases must research all issues that will allow them to successfully handle the client's claim, including evidence, legislation, documents, the operation of the court or tribunal that will decide the case, legal representation of the client, and available remedies. Depending on the nature of the dispute, research on areas beyond law, such as science and technology, may be required too.

 An example of a landlord–tenant dispute is set out below. This kind of case may come your way in a law clinic. Make a note of the tasks you may have to complete:

'This case involves a landlord–tenant dispute about a residential property where the clinic undertakes to provide legal support to the tenant. The students involved in the case must be able to complete research in a number of areas: on the evidence to support their client's claim (eg the tenancy agreement, information about the current state of the property and the nature of the dispute etc); on applicable statutory and common law principles which determine the rights and responsibilities of the landlords and tenants in residential property disputes; on links between the facts, legal principles and rules on which the legal argument will be built and developed (eg if legislation protects the tenant from the landlord's claim for a big rise in the rent for the property); on remedies available to the tenant against the landlord; on the court or tribunal that will hear the case and on the relevant processes; on the documents that will be needed to be filed with the court or tribunal; on the way that the case will be defended in court; on the code of practice that will have to be followed regarding the preparation of the case and its presentation in the court.'

(b) Critical thinking and evaluation

Participation in CLE helps to improve critical thinking and evaluation skills. Students participating in CLE will learn to distinguish between relevant and irrelevant facts, legislation, case law and legal theories. During all stages of their involvement (from the collection of evidence to the development of the legal arguments and presentation in court), students must be able to critically assess the gathered information and use only what is necessary to secure the desired outcome for the case. All law modules provide opportunities to acquire and develop critical thinking and evaluation skills, but CLE experience, which involves real-life scenarios, offers the opportunity to test and further develop existing critical thinking and evaluation skills.

(c) Problem solving

Real cases in live clinics often involve complex issues, unpredictable developments and uncertain outcomes. The ability to solve problems is essential in the legal profession, and CLE offers students the opportunity to rigorously test their problem-solving skills. Problems that need to be solved may include the selection of legal arguments that will support the client's case, the selection of evidence, and the handling of impatient and uncooperative clients.

Self-assessment I would handle an uncooperative client by ...

(d) Drafting

The drafting of documents is an essential part of working on real legal cases. Drafted documents could include simple letters or statements, or formal court documents such as a claim form. Students participating in CLE will acquire skills and experience in the drafting of a wide variety of important documents.

(e) Interviews

Interviewing the clients of the clinic is an exciting student experience. The interviews will help students to collect information about the facts of the case and establish a plan to work with the client. Codes of professional conduct are followed during interviews, and students may also receive training from lawyers or other experts. Students usually participate in interviews in groups, which helps them to cope with the task and improve their interview skills more effectively.

Self-assessment When faced with an emotional client during interview, I would ...

....

....

....

....

(f) Negotiation

Negotiation is an essential skill that will be acquired or improved through participation in CLE. Negotiation can take place at various levels and in various formats. Students may have to negotiate with their clients about the legal strategy to be adopted in order to achieve a specific outcome in the case. They may have to negotiate with the other side for an amicable settlement of the dispute, or negotiate with public bodies and authorities (eg police, local authorities) on behalf of their clients. Effective negotiation skills are essential for successful lawyers, and negotiation in various forms is required in almost all types of legal case. CLE helps to test and improve these skills in realistic work conditions.

(g) Advocacy

Advocacy incorporates a number of skills that are essential in day-to-day legal practice. Formal presentations (written and oral), clear communication, witness examination and persuasion are vital elements of successful advocacy, and many students will have the opportunity to improve these skills in the context of law clinics where they will be called upon to handle their clients' cases. After hearing the facts of the case, students will have to design and implement a plan for the defence of the client.

- They will have to identify the main directions of legal support and representation available to the client and convince him or her that the proposed directions are the most appropriate for his or her case.
- Then, they will have to advance and defend the client's case in the appropriate court or tribunal.
- They will have to ensure that the whole case is handled in a professional manner.

Students undertaking live client representation receive training and support from lawyers or legal experts, and their work is usually subject to supervision. Also, students can work on the cases in groups, which helps to enhance students' learning and increase their confidence. Advocacy, by involving formal acts of presentation, is perceived by most students as a very difficult and at times very scary activity. Participation in law clinics helps to ease these fears and offers students a valuable opportunity to test their skills and abilities and receive feedback on them. However, not all clinical programmes provide full client representation.

Self-assessment If faced with the prospect of playing a role in real-life advocacy, I would feel ...

....

....

....

....

In many clinics, the handling of cases is limited to identifying the legal issues and providing the client with advice on the steps he or she will have to take to resolve the dispute, such as identifying the legal nature of the dispute, indicating the court, tribunal or other authority appropriate to hear the case, and guiding the client regarding the selection of an appropriate lawyer. In clinics where simulated cases are used, student exposure to 'real' advocacy is even more limited, but nevertheless some aspects of advocacy (eg preparing persuasive legal arguments to resolve the artificial dispute, written presentation etc) are present.

(h) Group work

In clinics, students usually handle cases in groups, which gives them the opportunity to develop group working and interpersonal skills. In a professional environment, lawyers often have to work in groups to handle important or complex cases. Group work includes a number of skills such as participating, sharing, persuading, respecting and helping. The interaction with other group members in the clinical context helps students improve these skills and at the same time enhances their learning of law. Students already carry out group work in the context of the LLB programme and other undergraduate law programmes, but the clinical experience, in dealing with real legal scenarios, offers a more advanced experience.

Self-assessment Group work in a law clinic

| 'I could do this' | 'I would feel out of my depth' |
Why?	Why?
....	....
....	....
....	....
....	....
....	....
....	....

(i) Practical knowledge

One of the main advantages of law clinics is that they offer practical knowledge, which students are greatly lacking in their academic modules. The theoretical knowledge offered on law courses is essential to introduce students to the law and its operation, but practical knowledge is equally important, not only for further enhancing the learning experience for the students, but also for demonstrating the practical utility of the theories. In simple terms, a good lawyer is not one who possesses adequate knowledge of law but one who can use this knowledge to provide solutions to disputes.

(j) Professional conduct

Law clinics follow codes of conduct which introduce students to the world of legal ethics and codes of practice. The relevant rules will regulate a number of professional exchanges, including client relations, confidentiality and disclosure, litigation and advocacy and other essential areas of lawyer activity. Students will learn from this that in clinics they must not only resolve legal disputes as lawyers do, but they must also behave as lawyers do.

Self-assessment Areas where participation in CLE could help to develop and improve skills are set out below. Tick those which you already feel confident about:

- ☐ research
- ☐ critical thinking and evaluation
- ☐ problem solving
- ☐ drafting

- ☐ interviews
- ☐ negotiations
- ☐ advocacy
- ☐ group work

- ☐ practical knowledge
- ☐ professional conduct

Benefits

The benefits from the use of clinical legal education are multifaceted and concern the students, the university and the surrounding community.

Student benefits

Students have the greatest benefit. It is not only the acquisition and improvement of legal skills or the opportunity to be involved in the practical application of law in the clinics that offer growth and confidence. Participation in clinical work by handling cases of individuals, many of whom are disadvantaged and marginal members of society and deprived of access to professional legal advice, raises the social awareness and social responsibility of students. This in turn lifts the levels of self-confidence and satisfaction of students, which adds positively to their overall university experience and increases overall student performance in the curriculum.

Additionally, participation in clinics strengthens interaction between students and their clients, fostering strong interpersonal relationships. Further, clinics usually involve real lawyers working in their professional capacity, which offers students the opportunity to establish links with law firms and gather experience of working in the legal profession, which is the desired career destination for most law students. Even for those who do not intend to qualify and practise, the transferable skills acquired will be useful to them, whatever career destination they decide to take.

Institutional benefits

For the institution which sets up and runs the clinic (usually the law school of the university), the benefits can also be significant. Law clinics can attract external funding for their original set-up and subsequent operation, and add a new stream of income for the institution. The existence of a successful law clinic, in offering the opportunity for practical experience and links to law firms, may attract more students to the law programmes of the university and additional income. The clinic can also help to develop and maintain ties with the local community and strengthen the social role of the university in the area. All these benefits may be reflected in the league tables, thus raising the status and prestige of the university at a national level.

Benefits to the community

The local community benefits from the operation of a law clinic in its area because the clinic can be used to offer legal advice and support to its most disadvantaged members. It can also be a source of useful information about law, which affects the lives of individuals in the community.

The extent of the benefits of a fully-operational law clinic depends on a variety of factors, most importantly the availability of sufficient funding to support its operations, staffing, supervision, training and the existence of clear and, as much as possible, specific aims. In a live clinic situation, cover has to be built in for lawyers to carry on cases which have started when students are away from, or have left, the university.

 My Law Clinic Diary
Record the benefits of your participation in a law clinic below:

Skills expected	Level of achievement (1–5)	My notes
Research		
Critical thinking and evaluation		
Problem solving		
Drafting		
Interviewing		
Negotiating		
Advocacy		
Group work		
Professional conduct		

Case studies

The following case studies show how law clinics work in practice.

Example 1: *University of Bristol* (www.bristollawclinic.co.uk)

The University of Bristol Law Clinic was established in 1995 as a non-profit organisation, having as a main aim the provision of free legal advice and assistance. The recipients of the clinic's services are those unable to obtain legal advice and support from other sources. The clinic is staffed by students of the University, who are sponsored and trained by a law firm. The clinic is run by an executive committee of students of the Law School, subject to control and supervision of academic staff of the law school and a qualified lawyer. The clinic provides a broad range of services in a number of law areas including contract, employment, consumer protection, tax and property, but it does not handle criminal, personal injury or family disputes. The services offered extend to full representation.

The clinic operates a 24–hours answer-phone service to receive public requests and it can be reached by email as well. The case will be assigned to two or more members of the clinic, who will then arrange a meeting with the individual requesting the clinic's assistance to collect information about the facts. The clinic members will research the legal issues and, after consulting an appropriate lawyer, will send a letter to the client containing the clinic's legal assessment and advice. If the clinic is unable to handle the case, it will help the client to find a suitable lawyer.

All members of the law clinic are required to observe a strict confidentiality policy and follow a code of professional conduct and ethics.

Example 2: *Northumbria University* (www.studentlawoffice.co.uk)

The Student Law Office (SLO) has been operational since 1991, in its present form since 1996 and in its current location since 2003. The SLO offers a wide-ranging legal service from initial advice through to full representation. It is for both professional and practical purposes a solicitors' practice. Cases that come to the SLO (by direct client contact or referral) are handled by the SLO administrator, who records case details. These details are then passed to the supervisors (qualified members of law school staff who teach in the SLO) who will decide if the case is potentially of interest for their firm and if their firm has the capacity to take the case on. If so, an appointment is offered and the case is allocated to a student firm. If not, the administrator informs the client and offers alternative sources of help where appropriate.

Where an initial interview does take place, this will be conducted by the students who then report back to the supervisor (a qualified solicitor or barrister). The supervisor will, in consultation with the relevant student firm, decide whether the case can be taken further and if so what needs to be done. The client is advised by the students accordingly. Where a case cannot be taken on, the students must advise the client of the fact and the reason. The students are

supervised in every aspect of their work, and nothing can leave the SLO for a client or third party without the approval of a supervisor.

The SLO holds the Legal Services Commission's (LSC) Quality Mark in Employment, Housing and Social Security at the Specialist level and the LSC Quality Mark at the General Help level.

The caseload of the SLO falls into three broad areas:

- housing;
- employment;
- general civil (with emphasis on welfare benefits, family, consumer and criminal injuries compensation).

The SLO also takes on a sizeable number of miscarriage of justice cases, as well as general human rights work and some commercial litigation.

The SLO is funded from internally generated money (from university and school budgets). Some cases attract public funding and/or costs generated in litigation, and any such funds received are used as a contribution towards the general cost of the operation.

Example 3: *University of Bradford*

Like a number of other universities, this simple model is a third-year option undertaken by approximately 15 students each week. Students are matched by staff with external legal providers – firms of solicitors, Citizens Advice Bureaux, specialist immigration advisers, etc – and work with them for approximately 48 hours in one semester. They are assessed by a work of reflection on what they have gained.

This model is cheap for the University to resource, it gets students into the local legal community, but has no implications for ongoing cases, which continue to be run by solicitors. In reality, the student has provided 'free labour' for the firm's cases for a period of time, but hopefully has gained valuable experience from the time spent there.

Other law clinic models

Gaining the sort of experience set out above is very valuable. There are, however, other ways by which a similar end can be achieved – this time usually as an extracurricular activity rather than an assessed one.

Two well-known initiatives that universities can align themselves to are the 'Innocence Network UK (INUK)' and 'Streetlaw'.

(a) INUK

The Innocence Network UK (INUK) is the coordinating organisation for member Innocence Projects based in UK universities.

The network has three core aims:

- *Educate.* To encourage and support the creation and subsequent running of member Innocence Projects in UK universities.
- *Research.* To conduct and facilitate research into, among other related things:
  - o the causes of the wrongful conviction of the innocent;
  - o the barriers to attempts to overturn these convictions in the Court of Appeal or by application to the Criminal Cases Review Commission;
  - o the associated harmful consequences of wrongful conviction on victims, their families, friends and society as a whole.
- *Communication.* To inform public debates about the wrongful conviction and imprisonment of innocent people. INUK will communicate findings from the activities of member Innocence Projects and research, with the objective of improving the criminal justice system and preventing future wrongful convictions.

(b) Streetlaw

Its name may conjure up images of a gripping, prime-time, vigilante-based soap opera, but Streetlaw is in fact an increasingly popular form of pro bono work, most often undertaken by law students.

The concept came from the USA where it is run by Street Law Inc (www.streetlaw.org), and it dates back to 1972. It is an interactive presentation to educate an identified group about their legal rights and responsibilities in relation to a particular issue or area of law.

Lawyers and law students can use their time and legal expertise to benefit the community without needing to give specific legal advice. The target audience gains a better understanding of their rights and responsibilities in relation to the identified issue and are less likely to develop legal problems and more likely to seek help where required.

A Streetlaw session also provides an opportunity for those delivering it, as well as those receiving it, to understand more about a particular area of law (this is why it is particularly popular with law schools as part of clinical legal education). Streetlaw sessions can be easier to organise than clinics as there is no individual legal advice given so no indemnity insurance issues.

Law students usually deliver Streetlaw sessions with the support of academic tutors and/or qualified lawyers. However, Streetlaw sessions can also be delivered or supported by qualified lawyers. It is crucial that appropriate supervision is provided to students and trainees by tutors and/or qualified lawyers. The audience for Streetlaw sessions can vary immensely: from primary and secondary schoolchildren to senior citizens to residents' associations.

Is this experience for me?

Will it benefit my studies and my career?

The Streetlaw model has been used to look at many different issues, including sessions for teenagers regarding the law on 'stop and search' and in relation to DJing, or working with resident associations on housing issues.

Involvement in some practical legal work, whether in a formal law clinic, by means of some other academic module or just as a voluntary activity, clearly has benefits for students and the community alike. The university may also forge contacts and take its own mission forward.

The end position is not always positive – some students who have undertaken practical legal work suddenly realise that it is not the sort of thing they want to do for the rest of their working lives. This can result in a change of career planning before study on the LPC or BPTC, and so the saving of money does make this a worthwhile and positive, if unexpected, filter.

Activity Investigate your institution's involvement with law clinics and select the model of clinical legal education that is preferable for you. Research this model in terms of its contribution to student knowledge and experience of practical aspects of law. Also seek to identify practical issues around the operation of the model. Who is managing it? Does it allow students to represent clients before public authorities or the courts? Does it use real or simulated cases? Present your findings to one of the lecturers involved, or to the head of the School if your institution is not currently as engaged in this matter as you would like.

8

People skills

Learning outcomes

> To understand and appreciate the role of networking in strengthening professional skills in the study and practice of law

> To understand and appreciate the importance of teamworking and leadership skills in law and other careers

> To explore and understand the principles and practices of negotiation in enhancing professional skills

> To explore and understand the importance of interviewing and advising skills in law and other careers

When you enrol on any law course, you are also signing up to be part of a great network of peers and professionals. It is vital that you communicate with your peers in teamwork. It is excellent for your career prospects if you can network with legal professionals when you come into contact with them, and it is essential that you can harness the two other fundamental skills in this field of law: negotiation and interviewing.

On your law course, you will mostly interact with peers and lecturers (who may be legal professionals themselves, ie lay magistrates, solicitors, etc). Engaging with these individuals during your law course or degree will equip you with the tools that you need to communicate effectively with other legal professionals throughout your entire legal career.

 People skills

Tick the statement that applies to you...	This is me	I could do this more
I can network with others more senior than me	☐	☐
I can make strong connections to help my studies/my job/my career	☐	☐
I seek out those who can help me, and I follow their advice	☐	☐
I can work in a team effectively	☐	☐
My leadership skills are excellent	☐	☐

Tick the statement that applies to you...   This is me   I could do this more

I can negotiate with my peers when we are working together   ☐   ☐

I feel I can/could negotiate with upset or angry clients   ☐   ☐

I can interview people effectively   ☐   ☐

I can get the best out of a person during an interview   ☐   ☐

My action plan:

....

....

....

....

....

8.1 NETWORKING

Networking is not just a personal activity. Good networks operate as systems within network communities. Network communities refer to groups of people who regularly gather together online or offline to talk, build, play, read, write, work, have fun, browse ... Networking communities are not just fixed or uniform; they are always evolving and exhibit diverse interests. They may also be virtual.

Successful networkers know how to connect to other people and groups effectively.

Use the boxes below to think about your own networks. You may be a member of informal networks, such as friendship groups, or more formal ones, such as clubs or societies.

My informal networks   **My formal networks**

1 ....   1 ....

2 ....   2 ....

3 ....   3 ....

4 ....   4 ....

Why network?

'It's not WHAT you know, it's WHO you know that counts.'

The quote above may sound unfair or calculating, but think of it in another way: if no one knows about your skills, talents and projects, who's going to help you make the best of them? Networking is essential for making the most of what you have to offer throughout your studies and for finding and maintaining careers and strengthening professional links.

Networking can help you find hidden opportunities and can set you apart from the competition. Networking often introduces you to people you would not otherwise meet and can help you to overcome shyness and minimise the fear of rejection.

People with strong networks get more things done more effectively; they learn from others with different knowledge or experience, and they are able to use their network as they seek to move through their studies and in their careers, whether in a planned way or if a crisis looms.

Most people actively develop and maintain their network of friends and family. The same principles apply to university and the workplace. Law students are often reluctant to network beyond their circle of friends and fellow students. Perhaps we fear we would be 'using' other people, or we are daunted by the prospect of having to 'work' in a room of strangers at a conference or event. However, in today's world, the ability to develop and maintain a broad network of 'professional friendships' is a critical skill for law students when seeking any kind of professional career following their degree.

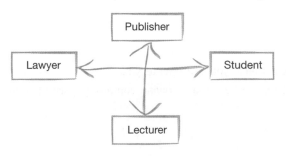

The good news is that networking doesn't need to be difficult or a chore. It can be an enjoyable and rewarding part of your professional development. You're probably already part of more networks than you realise. Now that you know a little bit more about networking, go back to the list of networks you made above and see if you can add any more.

You might want to expand your networks for the following reasons:

- Networking enables you to meet new people such as customers, partners, investors, mentors and friends.
- Networking provides information to help you make informed decisions.
- Networking can enhance access to expertise and resources that you may be lacking.
- Networking can lead to getting the job of your dreams, being promoted within your firm or making a career move.
- Networking helps solve legal challenges and problems by acting with others.
- Networking enables the exchange of ideas and experience.

Not only do businesses have brands but people do too. Your personal brand is the full and complete message you give to others about yourself.

Networking for law students

A good place to start is to map out your current networks. You have already listed your networks earlier in this section. To see how well networked you are, try making a list of all the people you know and then categorise them according to the relationship you have with them. The beginning of your list could look something like this:

Name	Category
Joe Bloggs	School friend
William Onzivu	Work colleague
Ania Sample	Swimming club, school friend

Add your list of close friends here who you feel could support your studies and career in the future:

Name	Category
....	....
....	....
....	....
....	....
....	....
....	....
....	....

Studies show that, in their daily lives, individuals have about 250 people in their circle of acquaintances. As you establish new contacts you can update your list, and if you do this electronically you will be able to sort the list by category giving you a handy list of connections for whatever purpose you require.

Building networks

A really easy way to build your networks is to join an organisation or society. You might want to think about joining your student law society, which should give you access to more experienced students, other universities and legal professionals as well as organised events which in turn might lead to more networking. It is important to choose the right networking group, and a number of considerations can help in making the appropriate choice. Questions to ask include:

- Is the group relevant to your goal for networking?
- Are the group organisers able to fully share information about participants, roles and other internal operations of the group?
- Are attendance and meetings and events compulsory, and is membership good value for money? Will it be costly?
- How much time is needed to commit to membership of the group?

Before deciding which organisation to join, think about why you want to build your networks and what sort of things you might like your networks to help you with. You can use the table below to get you started.

Reason for building network	What help might this network offer?	Possible organisation/society/club to join
Get to know fellow law students	*Advice on university work, finding summer placements, what courses to choose, attending careers events*	*Student Law Society*

Reason for building network	What help might this network offer?	Possible organisation/society/club to join

Strong ties, weak ties, connectors

In networking, strong ties are those you have direct connections to. Weak ties are those you relate to indirectly, ie you are connected to them through others. Psychologists believe that weak ties are more beneficial and networking extensively with weak ties gives you better access to information or other resources that you were not already aware of. It is therefore worth putting the effort into networking with those contacts you do not yet know very much about.

Weak ties could be potentially more beneficial than strong ties.

Virtual community networks

Online exchanges and access to virtual communities present important networking opportunities for law students. The following are some of the virtual forums for networking that may be of interest to you.

Blogs

There are millions of blogs in the virtual world, and you can carefully choose legal blogs that increase your access to other students, lawyers or resources that can improve your studies and career prospects, and share knowledge and experience for mutual benefit. Caution must be exercised because most blogs are openly accessible; other interested parties such as prospective employers may use it to find information about you as a potential candidate. You may also wish to set up your own blog, but you must be prepared to devote skills and other resources to set it up.

Beware that many employers now check blogs.

Forums

Like chat rooms, forums help to share knowledge and exchange ideas. There are many forums out there for law students and professional lawyers. Try searching the Internet for some and list them in the space below. By regularly commenting on forums and leaving your link, you can be regularly picked by search engines that help to improve your professional rankings. Your attributes, skills, competencies and achievements can be recognised by prospective employers and others.

Interesting and useful forums to keep up to date with:

....

....

....

....

....

....

....

....

Wikis

Wikis allow a group of people access to your site to review, change and add information. They are an excellent form of networking because members from the legal profession, or group or country, or even from the whole world, can have access to them, creating networking activities that lead to potential jobs, promotion or other positive career changes.

Social and business networking sites

Social networking sites such as MySpace are, of course, very popular and can be useful for building useful contacts. LinkedIn provides an important network tool for career and business development. It provides a forum to stay in touch with professional partners, colleagues, find a job, hire people or ask for or demonstrate expertise.

Electronic mailing lists

Electronic mailing lists enable discussion between its members without joining a discussion forum. Members simply reply by email to the group and the conversations provide excellent networking opportunities.

> *Sign up to professional newsletters, blogs and other sites for networking by opening an email address devoted entirely for this purpose.*

Networking in action

Three are plenty of opportunities to network as a student. All clubs and societies you join are likely to have social events as well as other activities, and your university is quite likely to hold careers fairs, talks and other events. Some law firms hold corporate events for potential training contract applicants, and you may be able to take part in other events or training days through your part-time work. All situations where you are with a group of people provide opportunities for networking. In such situations, there are a number of pointers which can help make you a successful networker:

- You get out what you put in. Take the initiative: introduce yourself to some new people.
- Be frank: have a keen desire to contribute what you have and show an interest.

- Listen and understand the other person and his or her story. Only then can you know what to give and expect to be given.
- Share knowledge, expertise and contacts. Share your experiences and provide your business cards if you have some. The more you give, the more you will receive.
- Have clear goals to achieve during the events. Think about what information you might want to get or how many new people you would like to meet.

Creating a good first impression

Making a judgement in advance or adhering to stereotypes can often be unconscious but can obscure our attempts to network. The world of work is becoming more diverse and multicultural, and it is important that you are able to connect with people from diverse backgrounds. Smartness and compliance with the requirements of the event, such as the dress code for an evening dinner, are very important. It is important to speak clearly and intelligibly.

Overcome your often powerful and unconscious stereotypes.

Good communication

In any good networking conversation, introduce yourself but give the other person an opportunity to respond. Share your goals and your commonalities, asking for what you want and sell yourself early in the process of conversation. If you meet a group, integrate into the group and join the conversation. Listen carefully and ask thoughtful questions but do not interrogate. Maintain interest and, if you do not get a positive response, give a fair reason to leave and move on.

Make the other person feel comfortable and avoid discussing irrelevant subjects. Ensure that you ask what you want.

Dealing with potential rejection

Fear of being rejected or shunned may prevent us from networking. When someone says no, there may be underlining reasons for this when attempting to network. The best option is to maintain confidence, and attempt to reconnect later or with others. A change of strategy or potential targets will yield positive results.

If you do not get a positive response, depart politely.

Following up and managing your network

It is important to follow up after a networking event. An easy way to keep track of people you meet is to note down where you met them, and a little something about them, to help you remember them, on the back of the business card or in a note. It is also important to have a system to record all business cards as soon as you receive them. You could file them like index cards, or you could transfer the information to an electronic address book. To maintain active presence with online networks, as well as face-to-face networking, use email or phone to maintain contact. You are more likely to gain from the network if you are also putting something in, so get involved. If you receive information that might be useful to the network, pass it on.

When you have accomplished the following, tick the box:	Done!
I have drawn up a map of my current connections	☐
I have written up plans to build my network	☐
I have identified my strong ties, my weak ties, and my connectors	☐
I have found, logged on to, and become established in virtual community networks	☐
I have joined relevant electronic mailing lists so I am kept up to date	☐
I can now create an excellent first impression	☐
I have excellent communication skills	☐
I can deal well with potential rejection	☐
I can follow up and manage my network effectively	☐

Towards successful networking

Set specific networking goals

Identify the people you want to meet, plan on how you will meet them and set a timetable by which you will achieve these networking goals. For example, before attending a professional association meeting, review the list of attendees and identify the specific contacts you would like to make before the meeting is over. If you set your goals before you attend the event, you are much more likely to achieve them. For example, you will often find that one of the people you earmarked to meet is standing in line in front of you at the registration table.

Focus completely on others' needs when trying to establish professional relationships

Ask open-ended questions and really listen to what is important to them. As you listen you will find ways to help by offering information, resources and other people that can address your contact's needs. For example, you may find that what the person you are speaking to needs most at this moment is a new apartment, a good book to read or a business referral. The more you find ways to help others, the more your network will thrive. Do you remember the last time somebody helped you with something that was important to you? As human beings we have a healthy need to reciprocate any time someone has done something of value for us. This is the real key to effective networking – helping others to get what is most important to them. In addition, by focusing completely on others when networking, you will take the pressure off yourself and be more comfortable initiating your new professional relationships.

 Ask your friends how they feel about their own networking skills, particularly in relation to the headings above. Take note of their concerns, and then advise them on how to improve. What did you tell them? Write your guidance in the space below. What has this helped you to learn about your own networking style?

Practise small talk

Before you attend a networking event, have at least three conversation starters. These 'ice-breakers' can include comments on current laws and business events. Be creative and guard against discussing trivial matters such as the weather – it is hard to develop a meaningful dialogue when substance is lacking and you have no sincere interest in the topic. Try to keep up with the media by reading a quality newspaper. This information will provide you with good leads for initiating networking conversations. But remember to focus on understanding the contact's needs as soon as the initial conversation has begun.

Follow up within 48 hours with all new contacts

New contacts will form their opinion of you based upon your initial follow-through, or lack of it. It is best to take the initiative in developing the professional relationship. Specifically, it is best to take the contact's card (rather than giving them yours) and say, 'I'll call you later this week'. By taking responsibility for follow-through, the 'ball is in your court' and you take the pressure off the contact. Try to get into the habit of calling or writing to new contacts within 48 hours of meeting them. You will give them the impression that you are an organised professional and that they can count on you. In addition, the longer you postpone your follow-up, the harder it is to do it.

Maintain your professional relationships

It is critical to keep in touch with your contacts on a regular basis. Reconnect with them at least once every six months. If you constantly think about how you can help others, you will come up with information, resources and other people that can be valuable to your contacts. A great way to maintain connections is to leave voice mail messages or send emails just to 'touch base'. End each message or conversation asking how you can help your contact. You will be surprised how often you can do something to help them achieve their goals! Nurture these relationships when you do not need them, so they are there for you when you do need them.

'Hi! We met at the conference three months ago; I was wondering if you would be interested in ...'

Take one action a day to initiate and maintain networking relationships

Get in the habit of calling, meeting or writing to one contact a day. This will enable you to proactively manage your career. By constantly establishing new *professional* relationships and nurturing existing ones, you will be in the stream of information, opportunities, resources and information.

Don't overlook your networking pearls

You may assume that only *professionals* at a certain level can help you with your career – this is not true. One example that stands out in my mind is of a barrister we will refer to as Rianna. When she was seeking a new job opportunity, one of the first people she called was a High Court judge for whom she did part of her pupillage. He had been on the bench for over 25 years and knew hundreds of lawyers. Unfortunately, as much as he wanted to help, the judge had no useful suggestions or contacts to recommend to Rianna. The person who turned out to be the most helpful was the judge's secretary. She had worked with him for many years and kept in touch with all his former pupils. The secretary gave Rianna the names and numbers of former pupils who had successfully pursued various legal careers and others who were looking to hire for their law firms. This secretary is a perfect example of a networking pearl! A networking pearl is always willing to connect people to resources that can help them achieve their goals.

Respect your contact's name and time

Always ask for permission before using or referring to someone's name. Courtesy will show that you are respectful and will encourage that person to help you more. Be considerate and always ask, 'is this a good time for you to talk?' before launching into a conversation. If someone helps you towards one of your own goals, remember to thank them with a quick call or email.

Self-assessment Honesty checklist!

Tick the skills you can perform and give yourself a mark out of 10 if you feel you can successfully use the networking skill. The higher your score, the better networker you are (maximum score 140).	Mark out of 10:
☐ Am I confident in approaching strangers and people I do not know?	
☐ Do I find it easy to keep a conversation going?	
☐ Am I assertive and confident in asking for what I want from others?	
☐ Do I possess an efficient means/mechanism/system that enables me to search and reach all contacts with speed and ease?	
☐ Do I have a wider circle of friends with diverse backgrounds and interests?	
☐ Do I always ensure that I speak to as many people as possible during an event and not just the same person I came with or someone I'm more familiar with?	
☐ Do I enjoy having diverse experiences such as travelling, other professional activities, etc?	
☐ Do I often connect and interact deeply and persuasively with others and share with others key information about myself?	
☐ Do I remember the particulars of people I have met, such as names, places, events and other details, to reconnect to people I have previously interacted with?	
☐ Do I find it easy to ask for help when I need assistance?	
☐ Do I share my contacts freely with others and do my best to assist others when I can?	
☐ Am I an active member of organisations, societies, professional clubs, citizen groups and other networks that encourage common purpose, share my interests, and whose membership involves likeminded people?	
☐ Do I actively connect regularly with others within my networks even when I do not need them, and do I assist them when necessary?	
☐ Do I possess relevant technology to facilitate my network?	

8.2 LEADERSHIP SKILLS

Leadership is undoubtedly a major factor in the success or failure of teams. It does not matter whether the team is 'run' by one leader throughout or whether the leadership role is shared and passed around. The issues discussed here apply equally in both cases.

What is leadership?

Leadership is the influencing of the behaviour of a person or a group in a way that is focused on objectives and results in order to bring about the completion of a common task. There are a number of different leadership styles, and they can be broadly categorised as follows:

- *Authoritative leadership style.* The 'I am the boss' approach, which usually has a strict regime of orders. Team members are there to implement orders given by the leader and do not normally work independently. This approach to teamworking is not likely to impress the other team members!
- *Patriarchal leadership style.* The 'I will take care of everything' approach, adopted by leaders who want team members to empathise with decisions made but can leave leaders vulnerable to doing all the work themselves
- *Cooperative/participatory leadership style.* The 'What does my team think?' approach. Team members are involved in the decision-making process, decisions are not directed from the top but are made taking the suggestions and concerns of members into account. This requires a greater degree of independence and responsibility on the part of the team members and better social skills from the leader. This sort of leadership is what you should aim for when working in groups throughout your studies. It also allows for a relatively easy handing over of leadership responsibilities to another member of the team.
- *Permissive leadership style.* The 'It will all work out' approach. There is no leadership in the strict sense; the leader presents possible solutions and coordinates the team but does not expressly direct. This approach can also work well in study group situations but becomes problematic when the team cannot agree or has other problems.

In order to be an effective leader, you need a number of skills. First, it is important that you have a good grasp of your subject area or discipline. This will give you credibility within the team. You also need good social skills to allow you to communicate well and manage any conflict that might arise in the team.

How to manage conflict and keep the peace in teamwork situations

Praise

Team members are likely to work much more effectively if they feel like their contribution to the team is valued. As a team leader, you should praise members for their work and effort but make sure this does not end up being patronising. If you are praising team members in front of others, make sure that by praising them you are not putting down others or belittling their efforts.

Sketch a picture in the box of what you consider to be an excellent leader. Give the person special traits that make him or her an efficient leader, such as 'empathy' and 'enthusiasm'.

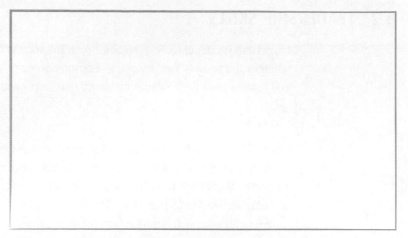

Criticism

Constructive criticism can be a very powerful tool in managing group dynamics and avoiding serious conflict. It does, however, require careful thought and good social skills. You should make sure that any criticism is timely and not delayed. It means very little if you criticise something that happened ages ago. You should also make sure that you criticise the action rather than the person responsible for the action. Remember this is about getting a job done, not about assessing one person. Thinking carefully about what you want to say and how you will say it will help you stay calm when delivering your criticism. It can also be really useful to have some suggestions for how to resolve the issue and/or improve next time up your sleeve. This will reinforce the fact that the team is committed to the same objectives and helping each other.

Clarifying expectations can avoid the need for criticism or can simply clear up misunderstandings that resulted in criticism becoming necessary in the first place.

Conflict is normal

It is really important to remember that conflict in teams is normal and can be a positive driver for development and creativity. If you all agree with each other, you are not challenging each other or developing your ideas. Conflict can bring problems to light and allow teams to search for new solutions, new ideas and new ways of dealing with situations. This can be a very rewarding process and can lead to some exciting academic work.

Conflict does need to be managed though, and conflict management often results in power struggles within the team. If you can, do not get drawn into power games but instead seek open and honest dialogue with the team to resolve any issues. In order to manage conflict successfully, it is useful to deal with conflict in three stages:

- *Step 1*: diagnosis and analysis of the conflict – what are the issues?
- *Step 2*: planning and preparation – how can this conflict be dealt with; what are possible solutions; how can they be raised in a constructive way?
- *Step 3*: carrying out – meet the team specifically to resolve the conflict and try to encourage an open and honest discussion.

The following activity will help you think about effective leadership and whether you have the skills to be a good leader.

Activity Use the boxes below to list situations in which you are either being led, or assume a leadership role yourself and evaluate those situations:

Situations in which I am being led	What could be improved?

Situations in which I lead	What could be improved?

Note your leadership skills below and explain how you can evidence these skills:

Leadership skills	How can I evidence them?

Once you have completed these tasks, you can discuss within a group which skills you are missing and how you might be able to develop them.

8.3 NEGOTIATION

Negotiation is an art, and a very useful personal and professional skill to have. Remember when you negotiated with your friend about a night out when he or she had other plans? Remember when you negotiated with your lecturer about an appropriate time to visit him or her about assignment feedback? Negotiation skills are with us from a very early age, when we learn that we can get around out parents by telling them things that they want to hear, ie 'I promise I'll take our new dog for a walk every single day!' or 'If I clean the windows, can I have extra ice cream?'.

The law requires negotiation skills on a whole different level. Big businesses fall out, couples get divorced, and the solicitor is the one who has to talk to both sides to reach an agreement. Do you think you could do it? It is a difficult skill to master, but it will make you an excellent 'people person' once you harness it.

We all negotiate. Negotiation basically refers to the way in which two or more people apply their efforts to reach an agreement. You are therefore quite likely to negotiate with your friends, family and peers all the time. The reason for negotiation may range from a trivial matter such as a family discussion, to a breached multi-billion pound contract, and it involves two persons or more representing a variety of interests. In negotiations, the parties recognise that they do not have any control over the other party, and so the best way to reach an agreement is through negotiating.

Negotiation is not an easy term to define but can be described as 'getting what you want from others through persuasion'.

Activity When was the last time you negotiated? This can be professional or personal. Write details in the space below.

....

....

....

....

Types of negotiations

Negotiations can be classified into two categories: adversarial and problem solving.

(a) Adversarial negotiations

In adversarial negotiations, the parties are attempting to resolve questions which have arisen between them. There may already be a real or potential dispute between the parties who have opposing positions on the issue. The aim is to find a compromise with which both parties are happy. You will often find this sort of negotiation in legal practice. Because litigation is usually expensive and protracted, negotiation is encouraged as a strong alternative and helps to resolve a dispute before it gets to full trial or before the commencement of the litigation process. Many civil cases are resolved this way.

(b) Problem solving

In problem-solving negotiations, parties are seeking to establish the ways by which their future relationship will be defined and exercised. For example, when two people wish to contract to sell specified goods between them, they will wish to agree on clear terms to ensure that the required activities are undertaken smoothly and to avoid any future disputes between them. When dividing up a group work task, teams will negotiate who does what and by when. Problem-solving negotiations are often referred to as planning negotiations.

Seven features of negotiation in law:

- *Common purpose*: negotiation involves two or more parties who need each other to achieve a desired outcome.

- *Differences in opinion*: parties commence negotiations with different opinions or objectives.
- *Shared convergence on negotiations*: parties consider negotiation as an effective means to resolve their differences;
- *Flexibility*: each party believes they can persuade the other to change their positions.
- *Potentially acceptable outcome*: even if parties do not get their ideal outcome, both retain the hope of an acceptable outcome.
- *Existence of real or potential influence over the other party*: each of the parties have some real or imaginary influence over the other's actions.
- *Interaction*: the negotiation process involves interaction between people as well as interests.

(Boyle, F, Capps, D, Plowden, P and Sandford, C (2005) *A Practical Guide to Lawyering Skills*, Cavendish, p 258)

Basic factors affecting negotiations

(a) Human behaviour

Serious negotiations require social interaction, and therefore an appreciation of human behaviour including sociological and psychological factors. These factors affect human behaviour, and a basic knowledge of these factors is essential for effective negotiations.

(b) Methods of communication

An understanding of verbal exchanges and their underlying meanings is also essential. In negotiations, statements may be made which at first seem clear. However, they may refer to something deeper than that, or have a hidden meaning. Besides verbal exchanges, non-verbal exchanges such as disbelief, anger, expression of pleasure or loss of temper and exaggerated body movements, etc, all affect the success of negotiations and let one side know how the other is really feeling.

Activity Think about the last time you negotiated, or an instance on your course where you may need to negotiate, and explain it in the space below. How well did you do/do you think you will do?

....

....

....

....

(c) Consideration of personal needs

As much as a negotiator represents his or her client's needs, he or she also needs to consider and be understanding of the opposition's direct and indirect needs. These include a client's underlying interests and how they may be satisfied, and the opposing party's underlying interests and how they may be satisfied. Understanding the needs of the opposite side helps to influence your interaction.

(d) The type of negotiation

Different kinds of negotiations involve many different participants and/or unique considerations which may influence the negotiations process. They must be taken into account when a negotiating strategy is being developed.

Preparation for negotiations

Knowing your own situation and as much as possible about your opponent's circumstances is very important. You need to be fully prepared with regard to knowing all the relevant facts and applicable law, and identifying potential arguments and counter-arguments. It is also important to clarify your assumptions and those of the opponent.

Furthermore, when negotiating with peers on your course or professionals at work, it is important to establish your tactics and strategy. Carefully plan your methodology, and adopt a versatile plan that can be changed when required (for example when unexpected concessions are made by the opponent). Imagine a road map with various routes from opening position to the ultimate objective and be prepared to change routes in response to opponent tactics.

Establish an aspiration level – where do you want to end up after negotiations? This is a crucial factor, because negotiators who start with high aspirations usually do better than those who do not. Increase your aspiration levels.

 Look at the map. You can see that there are alternative ways to reach an agreement in this situation. Fill in the blanks at the end of the arrows coming off the road. How many alternative solutions can you think of?

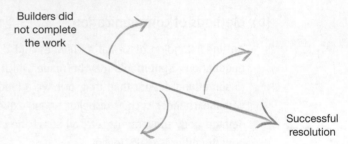

Builders did not complete the work

Successful resolution

Negotiators will initially seek a high but reasonable starting position, that will not cause the opponent to lose all interest. This bolsters their confidence when they begin the negotiation process and causes an uncertain opponent to reconsider his or her evaluation of the dispute in favour of the confident party. Negotiators draft a logical rationale to explain each part of their argument.

You must develop a bargaining strategy which will ultimately culminate in a 'final offer' that is sufficiently tempting to your opponent.

Activity **Think back to the last time you negotiated with a person to derive a benefit from them (eg washing your dad's car for money). How did you negotiate with that person? Did you use any special tricks, or take advantage of a particular emotion? What stages did you go through as the negotiator?**

....

....

....

Know your negotiation – styles, strategies, ethics and skills

Negotiation is not just about persuading people, or 'twisting their arm' into something that they do not want to do. There are different ways to negotiate, particularly in a professional and legal context. Styles can vary from friendly to confrontational, and strategies can range from open and honest, to aggressive and demanding.

(a) Negotiation styles

A negotiation style is the overall approach to negotiation (see Charles B Craver (1993) *Effective Legal Negotiation and Settlement*, 2nd edn, Michie). Negotiators usually develop their own styles of negotiation. However, while more experienced lawyers will employ a style that adapts to the question at hand, negotiations are often categorised into whether they are cooperative or competitive. Most negotiators often use both styles. An experienced negotiator will vary his or her style in accordance with the subject matter of the negotiation and the style of the other negotiator. In a more social context, if you knew that your friend had particularly strong beliefs, how would you change your negotiation style when you wanted to reach a controversial agreement with him or her?

Competitive (aggressive) style

A competitive negotiator typically takes extreme positions, focuses attention on to his or her demands, is reluctant to explain the basis for positions taken or to share information, and is likely to use arguments and threats as negotiation tools.

Cooperative (friendly) style

In contrast to a competitive negotiator, a cooperative negotiator is likely to take a less extreme approach and is likely to explain his or her position in light of the needs or expectations of his or her client. He or she tends to share information freely with the other side, providing justifications for the demands made, and seeking such justifications from the other negotiator by using reason and logic as negotiation tools.

Both approaches have been considered as effective in obtaining the appropriate results for negotiating parties. Which type of negotiator would you be?

Activity Get in a group with your friends and split into two sides. One side wants to seek the death penalty for a convicted murderer, and the other side wishes to rehabilitate the murderer. Each side must use both of the above negotiation styles, and switch styles after 15 minutes. Which style was the most effective, and why?

(b) Negotiation strategies

Your lecturer may one day give you a contract law or a tort law scenario to figure out in small groups. If you have to present a mock trial and play the lawyer, or even voice your opinions to your class about how you will solve the scenario, you will need a strategy when talking to both parties. Effective negotiation requires detailed strategic planning by the negotiator and his or her client. A negotiator and his client need to talk about a wide range of issues before a strategy is adopted, including: issues which may help or hinder the negotiation, the initial positions to be adopted and how these can be developed, alternative avenues to investigate that would be reasonable for the client, and final positions that would make everybody happy. In addition, the planning process should establish, where possible, various compromise positions between the initial and final positions which are acceptable alternative ways of dealing with the matter. It should be clear that the final position on any given issue may be subject to change in light of any decisions made on other issues. Can you see how flexibility is key to negotiating?

There are five commonly used negotiating strategies outlined below: competitive, cooperative, integrative (or problem-solving), avoiding, and accommodating. Negotiation strategies must be distinguished from negotiating styles. A negotiation strategy is a separate and distinct concept from the negotiator's personal characteristics: a strategy is the negotiator's planned and systematic attempt to move the negotiation process forward towards a resolution which is favourable to his or her client's interests. Strategy and personal style can of course be frequently intertwined. A negotiator who has an aggressive personal style will succeed in causing his or her opponent to lose confidence in him- or herself, or his or her case, and as a result the negotiator will be able to win substantial concessions (some leeway) from the other party, a goal of the competitive strategy. Usually, a negotiator's personal characteristics positively correlate with his or her preferred negotiating strategy.

The competitive strategy

The competitive negotiator tries to maximise the benefits for his or her client by convincing the opponent to settle for less than he or she otherwise would have at the start of the negotiation process. In a competitive strategy, all the gains for your own client are obtained at the expense of the opposing party. This strategy aims to convince the opposing party that his or her 'alternative' suggestions are not as advantageous as he or she had previously thought. Competitive tactics are designed to break the opponent's confidence in his or her case, thereby inducing him or her to settle for less than originally asked. The competitive negotiator moves psychologically against the other person, with behaviour designed to unnerve the opponent. Competitive negotiators expect similar behaviour from their opponents and therefore can sometimes mistrust them.

The cooperative strategy

The cooperative negotiator will grant concessions in order to create both a moral obligation on the opposing side to reciprocate and a relationship built on trust that is helpful to achieving a fair agreement.

The cooperative negotiator views concessions as a positive negotiating technique, which is designed to match the opponent's aim of reaching a fair and just agreement. This also maintains an accommodative working relationship. Users of the cooperative strategy believe that cooperative negotiators are motivated by collective desires to reach a fair solution. Cooperative negotiators assert that the other, more competitive strategy often leads to resentment between the parties and a breakdown of negotiations. Cooperative strategies therefore include any strategies that aim to develop trust between the parties and that focus on the expectation that both opponents will match concessions ungrudgingly. Central to all cooperative strategies is the question of how the negotiator should respond if the opponent does not match his or her concessions and does not reciprocate his or her goodwill. The major weakness of the cooperative approach is its vulnerability to exploitation by the competitive negotiator. The cooperative negotiator is severely disadvantaged if his or her opponent fails to reciprocate his or her concessions.

The integrative strategy

This is sometimes referred to as a problem-solving strategy. Both the competitive and cooperative strategies focus upon achieving as many concessions from the other party as possible. These concessions may move the negotiations closer to a favourable outcome for the negotiator, but each concession diminishes somebody's satisfaction with the potential outcome. Integrative bargaining, on the other hand, attempts to reconcile the parties' interests and thus provides benefits to both. Integrative bargaining usually happens where the parties' interests are not directly opposed, and the benefit in one area for one party does not necessarily result in the loss in another area for the opponent. Instead, the parties use a problem-solving approach to invent a solution which satisfies the interests of both parties.

- *People*: separate the people from the problem.
- *Interests*: focus on interests, not positions.
- *Options*: generate a variety of possibilities before deciding what to do.
- *Criteria*: insist that the result be based on some objective standard.

Avoiding and accommodating

Besides the three main strategies, avoiding is a strategy which seeks to avoid real progress. Those using this strategy do not often wish to engage in negotiation at all. It may also involve continued cancellation and postponement of negotiations.

Accommodation is a strategy that involves agreement to the other side's proposals and is at a practical level useless as a strategy for negotiation:

 Think back to your last successful negotiation, whether social or academic. Fill in the boxes with your different negotiation experiences.

Negotiation style and strategy	My experiences and examples
Competitive (aggressive) style	

Negotiation style and strategy	My experiences and examples
Cooperative (friendly) style	
The integrative strategy	
The avoiding strategy	
The accommodating strategy	

Which strategy can be used?

There is no one strategy that is better than the rest, and a negotiator cannot plan, and use, one strategy for a whole negotiation. The strategy selected depends on the issue being dealt with at the time, the personality of the negotiator and the client, and the way the negotiator reacts to the demands of the opposite party. The following factors illustrate how different strategies are applicable to different scenarios:

- What is the approach used by the other side? An integrative approach can only work if both sides are willing to use it.
- Do both parties wish to continue a relationship? A party will be less disposed to adopt a competitive approach and opt for a cooperative or integrative approach if he or she wishes to maintain a connection. A competitive approach will be less favourable in these circumstances.
- What are the goals of each party? If a case is tried in court, the range of outcomes is more certain and restricted (such as an injunction). Adopting a cooperative or an integrative approach may expand the range of options.
- What is the importance of reaching an agreement and avoiding trial? If a client's case is strong, it is easy to opt for a competitive strategy and, if not, a cooperative/integrative approach will be the option.
- Instructions from clients. A client could set a starting point for negotiations beyond which he or she cannot go, and this could be used to adopt an appropriate strategy. For example, a client may demand £50,000, and any less would see his business go under.
- The stage of negotiations. Negotiations often flow from competitive to cooperative, and on to an integrative or problem-solving approach.
- What is the main issue? Simple issues such as the price to pay for goods are appropriate for a competitive strategy, whereas a multilateral negotiation between countries will require a more cooperative and problem-solving approach.

- The negotiator's preference. A negotiator may have a preferred approach in relation to style in order to reflect his or her personality. If a lawyer considers the other side competitive, there is no point in maintaining a cooperative approach.

Activity 'The Negotiator'

In the box below, make a note of the advantages and disadvantages of the two negotiation styles and five negotiation strategies:

	Advantages	Disadvantages
Competitive (aggressive) style		
Cooperative (friendly) style		
The competitive strategy		
The cooperative strategy		
The integrative strategy		
Avoiding		
Accommodating		

(c) Ethical issues in negotiations

Telling the truth   Lying, deliberate misleading, and concealing something that should have been disclosed is unacceptable in your studies and in practice, as it breaches professional codes of conduct for both solicitors and barristers. Exaggeration of a party's case can undermine negotiations, and it will poison the atmosphere which should be conducive to fair exchanges. However, a negotiator is under no duty to disclose facts that are adverse to his or her case.

Honesty to the party you represent   Honesty is required in dealings with the client and other lawyers. All the parties involved must be aware of the strengths and weaknesses of the case as well as the realistic chance of success.

Use of threats   Threats such as *'If you cannot deliver what I want, I will end the negotiations'* are unacceptable. Any situation where one party says that he or she will act in a way that is damaging to the other is a threat. In fact, professional conduct requires that lawyers do not make such threats.

The client is in charge A lawyer acts on behalf of his or her client and cannot negotiate without that client's authority. If a lawyer makes a negotiating decision without the client's authority, the decision must be ratified by the client.

Confidence Inexperience can be a problem where confidence is a concern, but this problem can be put to rest by preparing well.

A competitive negotiator The best option with which to confront an aggressive negotiator is to adopt the same tactics, before then shifting to a more cooperative approach.

Last-minute changes Sometimes, new facts become evident at the last minute. A turn of events should not lead to a panic. The best course of action is to ask for a break, to reassess the situation, and to proceed accordingly or even request for postponement of negotiations. Negotiators often use surprises in an attempt to disorient or disorganise the opposing party. They may introduce previously unanticipated matter. Again the best option is to request time to respond to new material by taking a break or adjourning.

Stalemate Some negotiations often end up in a complete stalemate. Both parties are simply not ready to give way on certain issues, and it becomes a waste of time and resources to attempt to pursue further negotiation.

In such situations, negotiators can take a break, adjourn, or postpone the sessions. In many large, multilateral negotiations, the best option is to break up into smaller groups to search for creative solutions to the stalemate, and to emphasise the shared purpose and achievement so far. During this stage, adopting a cooperative style and strategy as well as an integrative option may be best.

Lack of clarity Some negotiators often retreat behind subtle words and actions to disguise and hide information. The key is to listen carefully and seize the opportunity to question information which is unclear.

Activity In the space below, list five positive and five negative acts or characteristics that your negotiator – that you employed – could do to support your case, and could do to damage your case:

Positive practice

....

....

....

....

....

....

....

....

Negative practice

....

....

....

....

....

....

....

....

(d) Negotiation skills

How good are your negotiation skills? Could you listen calmly to somebody when he or she was being aggressive towards you?

Get your party or your client the results they deserve   Getting results and acting for your client should inform all of your negotiation strategies and aims. The negotiator must always act in the best interests of his or her client.

Maintain focus and objectivity   It is important to remain objectively focused and not become personally and emotionally involved. In this way, you provide an atmosphere of calmness in order to deal with emerging problems, and it enables a negotiator to focus on the interests of the client.

Active listening   To respond effectively in negotiations, listening skills are important. Negotiation requires concentration and the ability to sum up, with accuracy, your opponent's views before responding to them. This enables parties to be creative, and to appreciate each other's positions. If you talk over the opposing negotiator, you appear impatient and unprofessional.

Body language   Changes in someone's facial expression, demeanour or posture may demonstrate his or her thoughts. However, not all eye signals mean deception, and not all hand movements illustrate the rejection of an argument. Caution must be exercised, and not too much should be read into every body signal. This is because cultural and other differences may have an influence on the underlying meaning behind a person's body language.

Questioning   Appropriate questioning enables the best information to be obtained from the other party. Interviewing skills are useful for better questioning in negotiations.

Persuasion   If you express yourself with clarity and you appreciate the views of the other party, you will be more likely to be able to persuade the opposite party to see your point of view.

Honesty and politeness   Honesty in negotiations is an ethical and professional requirement and must be adhered to at all times. Moreover, it is important to maintain politeness and to avoid stalemates that often occur when parties become rude in their actions. This is difficult, of course, when tempers fray. A negotiator must be able to handle highly emotional issues.

Effective preparation   A negotiator must know his or her case very well and be able to respond to questions from the opposing party on the spot. Adopting a negotiating plan that takes account of the key demands of both clients is important. Effective preparation means that the negotiator must be ready to prepare, access, obtain, receive and analyse the information given to him or her in order to shape his or her negotiation strategy.

Self-awareness and prudence It is important to detach yourself and assess your actions to avoid getting emotionally involved in the case. It is also important to examine the strengths and weaknesses of your client's case and be realistic about what is achievable and what is not achievable. Exaggeration of your client's case could lead to a loss of credibility with your opponent, and lead to a stalemate.

Self-assessment

Skills for negotiation	How I would apply these skills and how I could improve them
Getting myself, my party or client the results	
Maintaining focus and objectivity	
Active listening	
Body language	
Questioning	
Persuasion	
Honesty and politeness	
Effective preparation	
Self-awareness and prudence	

Negotiations in practice: step-by-step

Step 1: Exchange personal and professional information Include name of law firm or agency of negotiating team, education and professional backgrounds, legal or negotiating experience relevant to the subject matter.
Step 2: Establish tone of negotiations: competitive, cooperative, etc Explore the tone of negotiations based on initial information, venue and first exchanges. A quick grasp of subtle presentations by the opposing party can help you to assess how to proceed.
Step 3: Seek as much information from opponent as possible But be careful not to disclose confidential or prejudicial information to protect your own bargaining power.
Step 4: Decide what information you need to disclose to the opponent to facilitate the negotiation Keep answers to your opponent's questions short, to avoid unintended verbal and non-verbal gestures. Information you provide in response to your opponent's questions will usually be perceived as being more credible than information you voluntarily disclose in an unsolicited manner.
Step 5: Carefully ask information-seeking questions Broad, less direct, and open-ended questions tend to elicit the most information. Only begin to narrow your questions during the final stages of the information retrieval process. 　　Try to maintain good eye contact during this phase and restate answers to your question to verify them.
Step 6: During negotiations, plan and employ 'blocking techniques' to avoid answering opponent questions about highly sensitive areas Simply ignore probing questions and move on to other areas you would prefer to discuss. Answer only the beneficial part of a complex question, ignoring threatening portions of it. 　　Furthermore, you can answer your opponent's question with a question of your own. For example, in response to, 'Are you authorised to pay £10,000?', you could simply ask your opponent, 'Are you willing to accept £10,000?' If the question is inappropriate, rule the question out of bounds as an improper inquiry.
Step 7: Observe carefully and probe the opponent to ascertain his or her perception of the situation, because it may be more favourable to your own side than you had anticipated Watch carefully how the opposing negotiator handles and talks about certain documents, evidence, views and aims. Is he or she giving anything away?
Step 8: Look out for non-verbal communication Non-verbal communication is an important source of information during a negotiation. Observe your opponent carefully while you are speaking and when he or she is speaking, and watch your and his or her non-verbal actions. For example, facial expressions of pleasure, anxiety, relief, twisting of hands as an indication of frustration, sitting on the edge of a chair, indicating interest, prolonged hand shakes, open or uplifted hands, and crossed arms all give away either a genuine wish to negotiate, or a strong desire to win. 　　Furthermore, clenched teeth often indicate anxiety, anger or frustration, whereas warm eye contact can establish rapport, and intense staring can be aggressive and intimidating.
Step 9: Negotiating games and techniques We've all used them! Negotiating games are used as psychological ploys to make our opponent respond in a beneficial way that is not necessarily based on wholly rational considerations. These include false flattery to induce a concession, faked weakness to evoke sympathy, and faked anger to produce guilt. Other tactics include statements such as, 'If it weren't for you'; 'I've got you'; 'So what', and 'Yes but'. Making false demands and concessions, faked boredom, passive and aggressive responses and reaction of uproar to statements all try to influence an opponent's position to achieve a settlement.
Step 10: Psychological entrapment Do not become so caught up in the negotiation 'game' that you find yourself compelled to achieve a final agreement no matter what the cost. Recognise when you are engaged in a losing battle and attempt to minimise your losses using any information you have obtained from the negotiation process. There is usually an alternative to 'no settlement'. Never continue a negotiation merely because you have expended a substantial amount of time and/or resources, particularly if you are doing so in an effort to 'punish' your opponent.

Specific negotiation issues

There is the question of whether a client must be present during negotiations. It is generally preferable not to have your client attending negotiating sessions, but your client must be kept informed during negotiations.

Achieving breakthrough in negotiations

Professor Michael Watkins of Harvard University advanced seven principles of successful international negotiations (Watkins, M and Rosegrant, S, 'The Seven Principles of Breakthrough Negotiation', Alternatives to High Cost Litigation, vol 20, March 2002). These principles can also be applied to domestic negotiations:

Self-assessment Tick these seven steps to 'successful negotiations' when you feel you have harnessed these skills effectively:

Skill:	Done!
1 Successful negotiators shape the structure of their negotiations	☐
2 Negotiators must organise efficiently and adapt quickly in order to learn	☐
3 Good negotiators are masters of process design	☐
4 Good negotiators must foster an agreement when possible but adopt forceful tactics when necessary. 'We make you an offer you cannot refuse.'	☐
5 Effective negotiators anticipate and manage conflict	☐
6 Effective negotiators build momentum towards agreement	☐
7 Effective negotiators lead from the middle	☐

Essential negotiation checklists

When you find yourself engaging in a negotiation on your course, use these checklists to help you. Evaluating yourself will significantly improve your performance for next time.

Checklist A   *Pre-negotiation: Negotiation Preparation Form*

1 Your minimum settlement point (lowest result you would accept).
2 Your target point (best result you might achieve). Is your target high enough? Never commence a negotiation until you have mentally solidified your ultimate goal.
3 Your estimate of your opponent's minimum settlement point.
4 Your estimate of your opponent's target point.
5 Your factual and legal leverage with respect to each issue (strengths and weaknesses of case). Prepare logical explanations supporting each strength and anticipate ways in which you might minimise your weaknesses.
6 Your opponent's factual and legal leverage regarding each issue.
7 Your negotiation strategy (agenda and tactics). Plan your anticipated concession pattern carefully to disclose only the information you intend to divulge and prepare principled explanations for each planned concession.

8 Your prediction of the opponent's negotiation strategy and your planned counter-measures. You may be able to neutralise your opponent's strengths and emphasise his or her weaknesses.

9 Information you hope to learn during the negotiation.

10 Information you are willing to reveal during the negotiation.

Checklist B   *Post-negotiation: Evaluation Checklist*

1 Was your pre-negotiation preparation sufficiently thorough?

2 Was your initial aspiration level high enough?

3 Did your pre-bargaining prognostications prove to be accurate?

4 Which party dictated the contextual factors such as time and location? Did these factors influence the negotiations?

5 Did the information phase develop sufficiently to provide the participants with the knowledge they needed to consummate an optimal agreement?

6 Were any unintended verbal or non-verbal disclosures made?

7 Who made the first offer? The first 'real' offer?

8 Was a 'principled' initial offer articulated by you? By your opponent?

9 How did the opponent react to your initial proposal?

10 Were consecutive opening offers made by one party before the other side disclosed his or her initial position?

11 What specific bargaining techniques were utilised by your opponent and how were these tactics countered by you?

12 What particular negotiation devices were employed by you to advance your position?

13 Did the opponent appear to recognise the various negotiating techniques you utilised, and, if so, how did he or she endeavour to minimise their impact?

14 What other tactics might have been used by you to advance your position more forcefully?

15 Which party made the first concession and how was it precipitated?

16 Were subsequent concessions made on an alternating basis?

17 Were 'principled' concessions articulated by you? By your opponent?

18 Did successive position changes involve decreasing increments and were those increments relatively reciprocal to the other side's concomitant movement?

19 How close to the mid-point between the initial real offers was the final settlement?

20 How did time pressures influence the parties and their respective concession patterns?

21 Did either party resort to deceitful tactics or deliberate misrepresentations to enhance its situation?

22 What finally induced you to accept the terms agreed upon or to reject the final offer made by the other party?

23 Did either party appear to obtain more favourable terms than the other side, and, if so, how was this result accomplished?

24 What could the less successful participant have done differently?

25 Did the parties resort to cooperative bargaining to maximise their aggregate return?

26 If no settlement was achieved, what might have been done differently with respect to client preparation and/or bargaining developments to produce a different result?

8.4 INTERVIEWING AND ADVISING

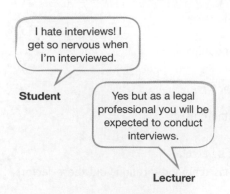

Student

I hate interviews! I get so nervous when I'm interviewed.

Lecturer

Yes but as a legal professional you will be expected to conduct interviews.

In this section we will look at what these skills are and why they are important, when you are likely to use these skills and, briefly, how to exercise these skills effectively. They are both skills that are very important in legal practice and are studied in detail on the Legal Practice Course and Bar Professional Training Course. However, they are used in many other situations outside legal practice and are useful to consider as a law student. Indeed, interviewing may form part of a legal skills course at undergraduate level, and there are interviewing competitions open to law students at undergraduate level as well as those at postgraduate level.

Interviewing

An interview is a form of oral communication, like a conversation or a presentation, but it is not exactly the same. An interview is a way of attaining information from a person for a particular purpose.

Self-assessment How many interviews have you had? Jot down your memories here, and why you think you were successful/unsuccessful:

....

....

....

....

....

....

....

....

....

....

....

....

....

Lawyers must have excellent interviewing skills because they talk to clients every day as part of their job. Many clients who need to see a solicitor have a difficult issue that will not go away without legal intervention, and so some clients may be emotional or angry. A lawyer must get the best information out of his or her clients without upsetting them, and, most importantly, the lawyer must be kind, understanding and approachable at all times.

Complete the table below to identify some of the key differences between an interview and a conversation:

	Conversation	Interview
What is the nature of the subject matter?	Selected by both parties and can cover many issues	More focused and specific with a limited number of issues
Is there a dominant party?		
Who directs/leads it?		
What is the nature of the relationship between the parties?		

Having completed the above table, it should be apparent that an interview is different from a conversation. It is a conversation with a purpose in a non-social setting where one party has a leading role.

 Interview another student on your course about why they are studying law and what aspects of the course they find most challenging and why. Then both complete the following questionnaire:

Interviewing Exercise Questionnaire

Names   Interviewer: ....

Interviewee: ....

How well do you know the other person? ....

....

What information was given/obtained? ....

Was the information obtained with ease/difficulty? Why? ....

How much talking did the interviewer do? ....

How much talking did the interviewee do? ....

What sort of questions were used? ....

Was any non-verbal communication used? ....

What do you think are the main interviewing skills required and how would you assess the interviewer's skills?

....

Key skills

To be a good interviewer there are three main skills required: listening, understanding non-verbal communication, and questioning.

(a) Listening

You must be a good listener. You need to concentrate and be seen to be concentrating. This requires the interviewer to make eye contact and can include both *passive* and *active* listening techniques.

Passive listening:	**Active listening:**
Silence	Key word repetition
Non-committal responses, eg 'I see', 'Ah!'	Paraphrasing
Nodding	Summarising what has been said
Smiling	

(b) Understanding non-verbal communication and body language

Experts say that only a small percentage of meaning is derived from the words used. The rest is derived from how words are spoken, including non-verbal communication. It is important as an interviewer to be aware of your own and others' body language in order to understand the words being used and to help you establish a rapport with the interviewee. Body language includes facial expressions, hand and leg movements and positions, posture, distance, pace and tone of the voice.

Activity Allocate the non-verbal gestures into the empty boxes below which contain possible meanings. As you are doing this exercise, imagine what impression you would get if your interviewer used any of these positive and negative gestures:

Gestures		
Crossed arms	'Steepling' (finger tips together)	Smiling
Scowling	Pointing upwards	Avoiding eye contact
Head tilted	Staring	Clenched hands/fists
Nodding gently	Lots of eye blinking	Chin stroking
Leaning away	Table thumping	Leaning slightly forward
Hand over mouth	Pointing/jabbing finger	Hands visible and turned up
Fidgeting	Leaning over other person	Wandering gaze

Possible meanings	
Receptiveness	Confidence
Defensiveness	Thoughtfulness
Aggression	Anxiety
Boredom	

(c) Questioning

There are many different situations where you may be involved in an interview. You may be an interviewer or an interviewee. The interview may be in legal practice or in some other situation. How many interview-type situations can you think of?

Job interview	Dissertation meeting	Witness interview
Police interview	Employment appraisal interview	
Doctor–patient consultation	Solicitor–client interview	Others

We have already identified that an interview is a conversation with a purpose. Consider what is the main purpose of all of the above interview-type situations. For example, in a job interview the interviewer is seeking to check information supplied on the CV and to find out if the candidate is suitable for the job. In a solicitor and client interview, the solicitor is finding out what legal problem needs solving or what legal issue needs addressing. In most of these situations, the main purpose of the interview is to find out information. In order to do this, the interviewer has to ask questions. Good questioning technique helps the interviewee explain and explore an issue. Poor questions can confuse an interviewee and mean that full information is not obtained and the purpose of the interview not achieved.

There are several different types of question that can be used including:

OPEN QUESTIONS
These invite the interviewee to tell his or her story, eg 'Tell me about your accident'; 'What exactly does your current job involve?'

PROBING QUESTIONS
These encourage development and further explanation of an issue, eg 'How?' 'When?' 'Why?'

MULTIPLE QUESTIONS
These are questions of more than one type or more than one of the same type. These should be avoided as they tend to confuse the interviewee.

LEADING QUESTIONS
These questions suggest the answer and should be used sparingly in an interview but can be useful to show active listening and to seek confirmation of understanding.

CLOSED QUESTIONS
These are narrow questions asking for specific information, eg 'Were you wearing a seatbelt?' 'How long have you worked for your present employer?'

In an interview, it is usually best to start with open questions and move to probing and closed questions and then end with more open questions to check you have obtained all the information. However, you may have to alter this approach to adapt to a particular situation. For example, if the interviewee is nervous or reluctant, closed questions may be more appropriate. As with other forms of communication, good questions should be clear and concise in order to be effective.

In addition, as the main purpose of the interview is to obtain information, as an interviewer you may well need to make some notes during the interview and after the interview to help record the facts, aid recall and plan further action. Any notes made during an interview should be brief, well spaced in order to allow for additional material to be added, and should not detract from the information gathering, so ensure you maintain eye contact as far as possible during the interview.

Interview planning and structure

As with other forms of communication, preparation and planning are important to help you achieve the aim of the interview. When preparing, you need to consider your surroundings to ensure that the environment is suitable, your desk is clear and you will be uninterrupted. You should also think about the purpose of the interview and what information you are seeking. It is often a good idea to have a list of questions you need to ask, even if it is just a list in your head. Indeed, in legal practice there are checklists available tailored to different types of legal matters that you can use as prompts.

You should also have a clear structure to your interview. Rather like an answer to an assessment, your interview should have a beginning, middle and an end.

Beginning
Introductions
Icebreaking – ask about journey, weather etc. Some small talk to help relax the interviewee
Explain the interview structure/purpose

Middle
Appropriate questions to discover information and make notes
Supply information and advice as appropriate

End
Summarise information obtained and advice given
Check no further queries from the interviewee
Check interviewee's understanding
Explain next steps

Activity Now repeat the interview exercise at the beginning of this section with a different student, but this time ensure that you plan and structure your interview properly. Make a checklist of questions, and also give your fellow student advice on how to deal with the challenging aspects of the course. How did it go? Did you see an improvement in your skills?

....
....
....
....
....
....
....
....

Advising

It is important to remember that an interview does resemble a conversation and that it is a two-way process. Whilst the main aim of an interview is for the interviewer to obtain information, another aim of the interview is for the interviewee to be given information and advice. For example, in a job interview, the interviewee may want more information about the job or the employer and is usually given the opportunity and indeed expected to ask questions. In a solicitor–client interview, the client will be seeking advice about a particular legal problem or procedure. This is where in legal practice you will need to use your skills of analysis and problem solving to enable you to explain any legal issues and options available to your client.

At the very least, the interviewee will need to be given a summary of the information obtained as the interviewer understands it and information about the next steps. Just as in the case of written communication, you will need to make sure any explanation is as clear as possible and appropriate language is used. You may also need to follow up the interview by conducting further research, considering any further information you receive following the interview and then putting your advice in writing. For further information, see the earlier sections **5.1** 'Legal language', **5.4** 'Writing effectively' and **7.1** 'Writing for legal practice'.

9

Career planning and development

Learning outcomes

This chapter provides the tools to help you plan and develop your career from start to finish. Law graduates can go into a wide range of careers, so all career options are considered. By the end of this chapter you will be able to:

> identify a wide range of law and non-law related career options
> reflect upon your career-related skills, interests and motivations
> choose a potentially fulfilling career

> plan a strategy for entering your career
> develop your skills through work experience and volunteering
> promote yourself effectively in applications

The career planning process

Help – where do I start?

Career planning can be daunting, especially at a time when there are so few jobs and so many graduates. The good news is that the modern recruitment market is very flexible and law graduates can go into almost every career there is, so you have a world of opportunity.

However, with so much choice, finding a fulfilling role can be very challenging. This chapter divides the career planning process into six discrete manageable steps, and helps you systematically tackle them one at a time. These steps are shown alongside.

Six steps to success

The first step to finding a fulfilling career involves identifying the wide range of careers that law graduates can go into. As you embark on your legal studies you should realise that your degree can be a passport into a diverse range of exciting law and non-law related occupations.

Once you have identified a wide range of interesting careers, you can then find a role that matches your skills, interests and motivations and plan how to get your foot in the door. The next stage is to develop your skills through work experience, volunteering and extracurricular activities, and to undertake any further study that may be required. Finally, you need to promote yourself in a CV, an application form and an interview.

Take your time to research each element of the process before moving on, and soon you will be in control of your own career.

9.1 RESEARCHING YOUR OPTIONS

The world is your oyster

The majority of graduates end up in careers not directly related to their degree subjects; this is because employers often rate skills ahead of subject knowledge. Therefore, law graduates can enter a wide range of law and non-law related occupations. You could become a solicitor or a barrister, but you could also train to be a legal executive or a teacher, a politician, a journalist, an accountant or any of thousands of other occupations. Therefore, before choosing a particular career, you owe it to yourself to research as wide a range of options as possible.

See what's out there

Try to research as wide a range of careers as possible and expand your horizons in terms of the type of career you are prepared to consider. Allow yourself to dream. If a role exists then someone has to do it, so why shouldn't it be you? Various ways of researching careers are listed below.

Use your university's careers service

Most universities and training providers have careers services that can help you in a range of ways. They are staffed by professionals who can give you information and advice on any careers-related matter. You should also be able to see a careers adviser. Don't be worried if you have no idea what you want to do in your career, or you feel lost and worried, just arrange an appointment and ask for help.

Research your options
Look into a wide range of law and non-law related careers

Choose a role
Take stock of your skills, interests and motivations and identify a fulfilling career

Plan your strategy
Research what you need to do to turn your dream into reality

Work experience
Identify a wide range of work experience opportunities

Further study
Research the various postgraduate study options

Applications and interviews
CVs, application forms and interviews

Six steps to planning your career

Research your options

Choose a role

Plan your strategy

Work experience

Further study

Applications and interviews

The career planning process

Careers services also usually run fairs and events where you can talk to people from a wide range of organisations. Sign up for these in order to find interesting career options. Don't be afraid to walk up to employers at careers fairs and ask what sort of jobs they recruit for (and what they involve). From October onwards every year, your university careers service will also have free graduate job directories outlining the vacancies on offer from most of the major employers. Some directories list vacancies across the board; others focus on graduate opportunities in a specific sector.

Look up career planning websites

There are numerous career planning websites. Some good places to start are listed below:

- Graduate Prospects – www.prospects.ac.uk: A general student and graduate career planning resource with detail on every aspect of career planning
- Jobs4u Careers Database – www.connexions-direct.com/jobs4u: This website includes an excellent database of occupations, including less glamorous roles such as legal secretaries which you may consider both as a career pathway and work experience
- Inside Careers – www.insidecareers.co.uk: A very well written resource summarising the jobs in different sectors
- University of Sussex careers website – www.sussex.ac.uk/cdec: a good HE resource linking career planning to the university experience

Use a search engine

Spend an evening or two seeing what ideas spring to mind when you Google different searches, such as 'interesting jobs' or 'exciting careers'.

Talk to people

Simply talk to people you know and ask for help, for example:

- Ask your friends what they want to do after university.
- Ask your family what they think you'd be good at.
- Chat to people you know about their jobs.
- Talk to lecturers and tutors about what they suggest.
- Find out what previous graduates from your course have done.

Look at job websites/newspapers

See what professional jobs are on offer in a wide range of sectors and identify the ones that excite you. Some useful websites and newspapers are listed below:

- Get – www.get.hobsons.co.uk
- Target jobs – www.targetjobs.co.uk
- The Guardian newspaper – http://jobs.guardian.co.uk
- The Times – http://jobs.timesonline.co.uk
- The Telegraph – http://jobs.telegraph.co.uk
- Milkround – www.milkround.com

Follow your skills and interests

Think about what you are good at and look up relevant jobs. For example, if you are good at organising things, look up administrative jobs; if you are good at helping people in trouble, look up counselling jobs or community work. Also, think about things you enjoy doing, and look for relevant roles. For example, if you like rugby, you could find out about becoming a rugby development officer or, if you like the theatre, how about becoming a stage director?

For more about the skills linked to a law degree and corresponding careers, see our Companion Website.

Look at postgraduate opportunities

Research masters courses and the careers they lead to, and see if any of them interest you. However, before commencing a course, make sure that the qualification will actually help you find a way into your chosen career.

Use your social networks

Social networking offers a whole new perspective to researching careers. For example:

- See what your old friends are doing.
- Find out what people from your school have done.
- Join common interest/career-related groups.
- Just get in touch with people who look interesting and ask them for help.

LinkedIn at www.linkedin.com is a very useful professional networking site. For more details on some interesting social networks, see our Companion Website.

Widen your horizons

Try to get involved in a range of new activities so you can get more ideas. For example, you could join a student society, volunteer with a charity or travel overseas.

Self-assessment Which interesting career ideas have you identified?

....
....
....
....
....
....

Becoming a solicitor (in England and Wales)

What's involved?

Solicitors work directly with individuals or organisations, providing legal advice in an attempt to find solutions to their problems. Their work can be broadly classified as being either 'contentious' or 'non-contentious', ie as featuring disputes and court cases or advising clients. They usually specialise in specific practice areas and work in a wide range of firms and organisations. Solicitors also have increasing opportunities to represent their clients in the High Court as Higher Court Advocates (a role which used to be the sole domain of barristers).

What's the attraction?

This is probably the most popular career aspiration amongst law students, largely because there are a wide range of roles to suit most people, there are opportunities in every part of the country and abroad, and there is a large number of training contracts for newly qualified graduates. Many solicitors are also well paid. In 2010 the minimum yearly salary for trainee solicitors was £18,950 for those based in London and £16,500 for those outside the capital, but many trainees earn much more. Newly qualified solicitors earn about £32,500 on average, and partners in commercial firms tend to earn in excess of £100,000 per annum.

The skills required

To enter this profession you will need a wide range of legal and transferable skills, such as good teamwork and communication skills, because of the close working relationship with colleagues, clients and other legal professionals. Many of the key skills required to be a solicitor are outlined below – take some time to reflect on when you have recently demonstrated them at work, at university, or in your spare time:

- relationship building
- organisation
- teamwork
- commercial awareness
- verbal communication
- intellectual ability
- stamina
- research
- written communication
- attention to detail

Solicitors' practice areas

Solicitors tend to specialise in specific practice areas, and some of the more popular of these are outlined below. You can research the full range of specialisms on the Chambers and Partners website: www.chambersstudent.co.uk and read personal trainee accounts on www. lawcareers.net. Try to identify the areas of law that you would most like to practise.

Banking and finance

Lawyers in this sector help corporations and individuals with financial transactions, contracts and regulatory issues. They will meet their clients to discuss their financing requirements, then assist with structuring the deal. They are expected to come up with creative ideas to maximise the benefit to their clients and to ensure that everything is conducted within the law. Trainee banking solicitors tend to perform a wide range of tasks for a specific partner; these may include liaising with clients and other lawyers, drafting documents and performing due diligence. If you want to enter this sector you will need the capacity to understand complicated financial agreements, have sound commercial awareness and be able to demonstrate high-level negotiation skills.

Capital markets

This role involves support for all parties involved in the trading of securities such as shares and bonds. Solicitors in this sector usually advise banks, companies and/or governments on how to raise funds on the markets. Trainees support other lawyers by researching the intricacies of company law, drafting documents and arranging meetings. Good trainees who are prepared to put in the hours can progress quickly and gain a great deal of responsibility. New entrants should have the intellect to quickly understand complicated financial instruments and be enterprising, well organised and driven.

Commercial

Commercial solicitors negotiate and draft contracts for a wide range of clients including High Street businesses, local authorities and large corporations. Their work involves overseeing standard form contracts, conducting due diligence and drawing up intricate agreements. Commercial solicitors often liaise with other specialist lawyers. As with other legal specialisms, trainees do their fair share of research and drafting work, and may work on specific contracts from start to finish. Technical legal skills, commercial awareness and communication skills are key in this sector.

Commercial property

Property lawyers deal with the legal issues surrounding the transaction of real estate, and with all types of buildings and land from housing estates to shopping centres. Lawyers often focus on one specialism within property, such as residential property, retail or social housing. The work involves drawing up contracts, negotiating sales and leases, managing property transfers, helping developers get their projects off the ground, and undertaking due diligence on a building's investment potential. To enter this sector you should be able to multi-task, and have good attention to detail, and be able to liaise with a wide range of partners and clients on the phone and face to face. Trainees are often given their own files and a great deal of responsibility.

Construction

Construction lawyers advise the parties involved in building works, such as landowners, developers, engineers and contractors. The role involves both contentious and non-contentious elements as solicitors in this field negotiate contracts, liaise with other legal professionals and resolve disputes primarily through arbitration. Trainees perform a wide range of duties including attending meetings, carrying out research, managing their own projects and attending court/taking witness statements. New entrants to this profession need a genuine interest in construction, a positive and pragmatic approach, people skills and drafting skills.

Corporate

Corporate lawyers are employed by companies, financial institutions and wealthy individuals. They advise on every aspect of company law including forming new companies and the role of directors, and manage complex corporate transactions such as mergers and acquisitions, corporate restructuring, and rights issues. New trainees support their colleagues in a number of ways, for example by conducting research and due diligence, forming new companies and drafting documents. You will have the capacity to work in teams under great pressure and should have a strong intellect with good analytical skills. You should also be flexible and have a real understanding of the technical and commercial issues faced by your client. Twenty-hour days are not uncommon.

Criminal

Solicitors in this sector either defend or prosecute clients in the UK's criminal courts. Solicitors work primarily in the magistrates' court, but can also represent their clients in the Crown Court alongside barristers. They also attend police stations and prisons, prepare their cases by liaising with all other interested parties, such as witnesses and other solicitors, and attend conferences with clients' barristers. The work is often fast and frantic, and criminal solicitors deal with a huge number of cases related to theft, assault, drugs and driving offences. This area of law may suit you if you have excellent advocacy skills, an ability to form relationships with a wide range of people, a flexible attitude and a thick skin. New trainees carry out each element of the job under supervision. Quick learners are given early responsibility.

Dispute resolution/litigation

This role involves helping clients resolve differences with other parties, either in a trial or before it gets that far. Commercial disputes cut across all legal areas and are increasingly resolved out of court through arbitration or mediation. Lawyers in this sector advise their clients on the strength of their claims and liaise with prospective defendants to try to find a resolution. If this fails, they prepare the client's case for trial and instruct barristers if they are required. At this stage, the job is usually more about preparing a case for court than appearing in front of a judge. You will need good organisation skills, a calm nerve and sound commercial awareness. Trainees will spend much of their time sifting through paperwork, drafting correspondence and conducting legal research.

Employment

Employment solicitors advise employers and employees on all legal issues related to the workplace. They advise organisations about their general employment practices, such as contracts and pay scales, and help clients on either side in a dispute through mediation, in employment tribunals or at the High Court. Thus, a key characteristic of this role is that the work is both non-contentious and contentious. Employment legislation is regularly updated so there is always work in this sector for solicitors who are willing to keep up with the changes. You will need excellent communication skills, the ability to think on your feet and a sensitive manner. Good trainees are often given a great deal of early responsibility, including the preparation of employment tribunal cases, researching legal developments and drafting letters.

Environment

Lawyers in this sector advise clients on UK and European environmental law. They work at a range of organisations and regulatory authorities such as local authorities, charities, non-government organisations, the Department for Environment, Food and Rural Affairs and the Environment Agency. Environmental specialists often work closely with other professionals such as construction lawyers to conduct due diligence on the environmental implications of new initiatives. New recruits tend to conduct research and communicate findings to colleagues and clients, so analytical skills are at a premium along with the ability to explain technical issues and commercial awareness.

Family

Family lawyers deal with legal issues related to personal relationships, children and inheritance. Many tend to either specialise in matrimonial law or child law. Private work often boils down to representing clients as they seek a fair distribution of finances after a divorce and/or custody of their children. Clients may fund their own cases or they may be legally aided. Public work revolves around representing local authorities, guardians, parents and children themselves in cases related to children who are cared for by the state, or who may be taken into care. Trainees usually conduct research, draft documents such as divorce petitions, and attend court and client meetings. Family solicitors require good negotiation and advocacy skills, patience and sensitivity.

Human rights

Solicitors in this sector moderate the powers of the state against the rights of the individual. This balance has become ever more contentious in England and Wales since 2000 when the European Convention on Human Rights became enforceable in UK courts. Throughout the last decade an increasing number of private firms have started to deal with human rights issues. One role in this sector is to help clients appeal decisions made by public bodies. This involves gathering evidence, conducting legal research and representing clients in tribunals and courts/instructing counsel. Other duties may include conducting judicial review proceedings against the government, and representing overseas clients. Many clients are legally aided so this is not a particularly lucrative field; therefore solicitors tend to enter this sector because they have a burning passion to ensure that people's human rights are upheld. This is a very competitive area to enter, so graduates should gain relevant postgraduate qualifications and/or relevant experience and will need to demonstrate advocacy skills, an ability to balance idealism with commitment, persistence, analytical skills and sensitivity with clients.

Intellectual property (IP)

IP lawyers help clients develop and protect their patents, trade marks, design rights, brands, copyright and confidential information/data. Non-contentious work includes searching for existing UK, European and international patents or trademarks and establishing ownership, developing new IP rights and drafting commercial contracts to allow the use of a client's IP right. Contentious work involves drafting letters to prevent others from using a client's IP right and taking them to court. Solicitors often focus on either the non-contentious or the contentious elements of the role. New trainees often review legislation, draft letters, liaise with clients and research IP rights. Patent research often requires relevant technical knowledge so scientific/engineering graduates are often in high demand. Other requisite skills include excellent drafting skills, attention to detail and an enquiring mind.

Personal injury (PI)/clinical negligence

Solicitors in this expanding sector deal with compensation for injury and ill health arising from accidents, negligence and disease. Solicitors tend to specialise in particular areas, such as negligent hospital treatment or car accidents. Firms usually advise either claimants or defendants. Claimants are individuals or groups of people conducting a class action; defendants include insurance companies, local authorities and the NHS. Solicitors establish who they think is responsible for an injury and calculate a fair financial penalty for the loss of income and expenses. If a level of compensation cannot be agreed, claimants will institute a court hearing, and solicitors on both sides will handle the case and instruct counsel (barristers). Trainees attend meetings and court proceedings, take statements, conduct research, support fee earners and often conduct simple cases under supervision. Skills required include negotiation skills, the facility to understand technical detail and good people-skills.

Private client/charities

Private client solicitors support individuals rather than businesses. The work involves financial planning (including wills and probate) and the management of trusts and taxes. Many private client firms also advise charities; this involves advising on charity law and a range of commercial and property issues. Trainees often liaise closely with clients and are often given early responsibility to run their own small caseloads. You should have good knowledge of tax, be able to empathise with clients and have superior interpersonal skills.

Residential property/conveyancing

Arranging residential sales and leases, managing property and conveyancing provide the bread and butter income for many solicitors in High Street firms. The work involves liaising with clients and other professionals, conducting 'searches' to find out if there are any major hidden factors which may affect the sale of a property and coordinating the exchange of contracts.

Sports

Sports lawyers advise individuals and organisations on laws related to their endeavours and help them make the most of their commercial rights. Advice could cover a wide range of matters including contractual negotiations regarding employment, promotion and sponsorship, intellectual property questions regarding merchandise, and issues such as libel and reputation management. Applicants should demonstrate sound commercial awareness and attention to detail, as well as a passion for sport. This sector may be the one for you if you also have good interpersonal, negotiation and analytical skills.

My story: Richard Jobes (trainee solicitor at a regional firm in Yorkshire)

My firm, like many mid-sized commercial law firms, covers the expected areas: corporate, commercial, competition, dispute resolution, property, employment, insolvency and private client. Trainees at the firm are expected to complete three six-month seats in the 'core' areas: corporate, property and litigation, along with a fourth one of your choice (I opted for competition law).

I can honestly say I've enjoyed my training contract a great deal. I feel I've been given a good level of responsibility – either preparing long documents or dealing directly with clients – but always aware that my work or advice was being well supervised. It's been a little like learning with a safety net, which I think is a good way to build confidence and raise

your game. The thing I've come to enjoy most is that traditional duty of many a trainee solicitor: research. It feels like an area in which I can make a genuine contribution. As subjects can often be very technical it can be challenging, so determination is required to do a thorough job. Yet, those demands are what make it rewarding.

Ultimately I hope to specialise in litigation (with an emphasis on property litigation) at this firm.

To view other trainees' experiences search www. youtube.com using terms such as 'trainee solicitor' or look at the websites of law firms/organisations in the sector you want to enter (see www.solicitors-online. com).

Where solicitors work

Solicitors work in a wide range of settings, often dictated by the type of law they want to practise. As a general guide, the larger the firm, the more they focus on commercial and corporate areas of the law.

High Street firms

These small firms usually have less than a handful of partners and can be found in every corner of England and Wales. They tend to help business and private clients in areas such as employment law, landlord and tenant issues, property, crime, family law, wills and probate and immigration. Many of their clients are legally aided, which means that publicly funded agencies foot the bill for the service provided, not the client, so they are relatively low paid. However, they do get a very varied role with a great deal of early responsibility and an opportunity to directly help people in need. You may want to target this sector if you are driven by a strong desire to help people, if you are flexible and a good communicator with a wide range of people.

Regional hubs

These firms range in size but are primarily based in one region; for example a regional firm may have only about 15 partners and two offices in one city, or more than 70 partners, four offices in and around a particular region, and one in London. Regional firms engage with a broad range of commercial and private client work, and many provide corporate advice to high profile clients and other large organisations. Consider this sector if you are committed to living and working in a specific area, if you want high quality, challenging work and you want to work closely with clients at an early stage in your career.

National firms

National firms have offices across the country and usually offer the broad range of legal specialisms. Local offices tend to offer an expertise in local issues and often have a particular national and international expertise (many also have a substantial presence outside the UK). Therefore, their clients can rely on local solicitors and national experts to look after their manifold interests. This sector attracts trainees who enjoy challenging work and want to be leaders in their field, but also want to have a great deal of contact with local clients.

City circles

Large city firms are often labelled as 'silver circle' firms or 'magic circle' firms according to their size and international outlook. These firms also specialise in corporate and commercial work with a financial focus. The larger firms have upwards of 200 partners and trainees in London, and a substantial international remit with offices all over the world. Choose this career path if you have excellent legal and transferable skills, you enjoy working hard for a good salary, want opportunities to travel and work overseas and want to train in a firm with a wide range of internal career opportunities.

The American invasion

The Americans are not coming over to the UK – they have arrived! Scores of US firms have set up shop in London, focusing on financial and corporate work within an international context. You should approach these firms if you are academically outstanding, possess high-level legal and transferable skills, want the highest salaries in the sector, expect to work hard for your money, and want to work in a more intimate atmosphere than many City firms.

Niche practices

Some firms specialise in one specific area of law, such as aviation, media or intellectual property. They often start life as offshoots of larger, general practice firms. You should consider specialist firms if you have excellent academic grades, excellent legal and transferable skills, a genuine interest in the specialism and relevant qualifications/experience (eg a science degree if you want to join an IP law firm).

In-house

In-house lawyers work directly for large companies and organisations such as banks, utility/ entertainment companies, special interest groups and public sector organisations such as universities. Solicitors in this sector cater to the diverse needs of their organisations and therefore tend to work in a much wider range of specialist areas than most of their colleagues in private practice. Focus on this area if you have experience/interests in the work of the organisation, want a diverse workload and challenging work with a good work–life balance.

Public law/government

Solicitors work in a range of regional, national and European governments and various intra-government organisations such as NATO and the United Nations. UK local authorities usually have their own legal departments with up to a dozen solicitors who advise on local issues and policy developments. The central Government Legal Service (GLS) employs about 2,000 lawyers to staff the various UK government departments and usually recruits about 25 trainees each year. The work involves advising Ministers, interpreting existing laws, drafting new legislation and litigation; and advising on the issues faced by all large organisations, eg employment problems and contract negotiation. Join this sector if you enjoy politics and public law, if you do not enjoy the commercial trappings of working for a private law firm and want a varied role with a good work–life balance. You should have excellent organisational skills and good attention to detail.

The Crown Prosecution Service (CPS)

The CPS employs solicitors as Crown Prosecutors to prosecute people in England and Wales who have been charged with a criminal offence. Crown Prosecutors advise the police on whether a case is viable, prepare the case for court and often deliver advocacy during the trial. They can be very busy, often working on scores of magistrates' court cases in any one day. You should look here for a training contract if you do not like the commercial aspects of practising law, have strong communication skills, have commitment to the public nature of the role and want a family-friendly working environment.

Other sectors

Solicitors also work in a range of other sectors including Her Majesty's Court Service (as legal advisers), Law Centres, The Law Commission and the Legal Services Commission.

Qualifying as a solicitor

The traditional route

Most students become solicitors through the following three-stage process:

1 *The academic stage.* To pass this stage you need a qualifying law degree gained within the last seven years (including a 'senior status' law degree) or another UK (or Irish) degree followed by a law conversion qualification called a Graduate Diploma in Law (GDL) or Common Professional Exam (CPE). The full list of qualifying law degrees and conversion courses can be found on the Solicitors Regulation Authority website (www.sra.org.uk/students). Graduates who are studying law or who have studied law on a non-qualifying degree programme may also be able to get partial or total exemption from the GDL/CPE. Details on how and when to apply for law conversion courses are provided in the further study section of this chapter.

2 *The vocational stage – the Legal Practice Course (LPC).* This is a postgraduate law course designed to prepare you for practice, which has recently been divided into two stages that can be studied full time or part time at more than one training provider. There is a wide range of LPC courses offered across England and Wales. More details on the LPC and information on how and when to apply can be found in the Further Study section of this chapter.

3 *The professional stage – a training contract.* Training contracts are best described as the 'on the job training' or 'legal apprenticeships' required to become a fully qualified solicitor. The vast majority of traineeships are provided by private law firms. A handful of training contracts are also offered by the Crown Prosecution Service (CPS), the Government Legal Service (GLS), local authorities and in house at a range of private and public institutions such as the Financial Services Authority.

The traditional route to becoming a solicitor

> **1. The academic stage**
> A law degree, or another degree followed by a law conversion qualification
>
> ↓
>
> **2. The vocational stage**
> The Legal Practice Course (LPC)
>
> ↓
>
> **3. The professional stage**
> (a) A training contract
> (b) The Professional Skills Course (PSC)

Most full-time training contracts last for two years, during which time you will get experience of at least three different practice areas. Students with 'time to count' (relevant work experience) can qualify in 18 months. Firms traditionally offer four six-month placements in different departments called 'seats', but contemporary firms are increasingly designing their own unique study patterns. Roughly 6,000 training contracts are provided each year. Some small firms have only one or two openings, whereas larger firms may have over 100 vacancies.

Other training opportunities include:

- modular training contracts whereby you can work towards your training contract at more than one firm (very rare);
- part-time training contracts whereby you work part time (very rare);
- part-time study training contracts (PTSTCs) that allow people, who are already working in a legal environment, to undertake their training contracts without leaving their jobs (or their

salaries!). Half of the time spent working in this scheme counts towards a training contract, so PTSTCs tend to take three to four years to complete. Many employers are unaware
of this training option, so PTSTCs are often arranged by students already in legal roles, such
as paralegals and legal clerks. This training route has become increasingly popular over
the last few years.

Find out more about getting a training contract at **9.4**, 'Planning your strategy'.

During your training contract you are also expected to pass the Professional Skills Course
(PSC), covering three core modules in client care and professional standards, financial and
business skills and advocacy and communication skills, and a range of other electives.

The legal executive route

A long-standing alternative to the traditional route to becoming a solicitor is to first become
a legal executive. This route was initially designed for non-graduates, but it is increasingly
becoming more popular with law graduates because training contracts are becoming harder
to find and legal executives' roles are quickly being assimilated with the duties undertaken
by solicitors.

The legal executive career is outlined later in this chapter. Once you have joined the
profession, you just need to top up your ILEX (Institute of Legal Executives) Professional
Qualification in Law and complete the LPC. You don't usually have to complete a training
contract. Find out more about the legal executive route to becoming a solicitor either on the
ILEX website (www.ilex.org.uk) or the website of the SRA.

New developments

The training required to become a solicitor is currently under development. Those students
who prepare for these changes are bound to have more success in finding a fulfilling career.
Keep up to date with developments by regularly looking on the Solicitors Regulation Authority
website (www.sra.org.uk/students) or by talking to a careers adviser at your university or
legal training provider. The SRA is currently considering an exciting new form of training,
called work-based learning, which it recently piloted. The scheme involves more objective
and rigorous assessments and more flexibility in terms of the contract provided to trainees. If
adopted, it is hoped that this scheme will open up the profession to a more diverse group of
trainees who currently cannot gain a training contract.

My story: Nicola Speight (LPC student with a part-time study training contract)

The partners at my firm recently agreed to give me a training contract and I began the part-time study training contract (PTSTC). One thing I must say is that I have found that the PTSTC is not widely heard of. I had accidentally found it whilst researching the routes to qualification on the Law Society's website. My firm did not have any knowledge of the existence of the PTSTC and I had to provide them with all the information. I understand there are very few people actually signed up to a PTSTC. My main advice to anyone who is in a similar position to me would be to see if your employer will take you on under a PTSTC as soon as possible as you can count the final two years of a law degree with two years part-time LPC.

Becoming a trainee has really challenged me at my place of work. Having spent 10 solid years commercially focused I was initially moved to my first seat in Private Client which involved drafting wills and setting up trusts. After a year there I was moved to Clinical Negligence dealing with claimant-based medical negligence claims.

Further information about becoming a solicitor

You can find out more about every aspect of training to be a solicitor on the following websites:

- General guide to legal careers produced by Chambers and Partners – www.chambersstudent.co.uk
- Popular guide to every aspect of legal training published by LawCareers.Net – www.lawcareers.net
- The website of the Solicitors Regulation Authority – www.sra.org.uk/students
- The Junior Lawyers Division of the Law Society – www.juniorlawyers.lawsociety.org.uk
- Quick reference for students thinking of becoming solicitors published by Target Jobs – www.targetjobs.co.uk/law-solicitors/faqs.aspx

Becoming a barrister (in England and Wales)

What's involved?

Qualified practising barristers provide advocacy or specialist opinions under instruction from other legal professionals. They have the right to appear in all English and Welsh courts.

What's the attraction?

Students who are attracted to this role are usually excited about the idea of representing clients in court. Many practising barristers relish the prospect of using their intellect to debate important issues in high-pressure situations. Many barristers are also attracted by the prospect of becoming a well-known expert in one specific area of the law. As most barristers are self-employed, this is also a career for those who enjoy working on their own as well as in a team.

This is an extremely competitive career. The majority of students who start the training to become practising barristers do not succeed in this aim. Therefore, before choosing this path you should take some time to assess your motivations and chances of success. You should also be aware that solicitors currently have increasing opportunities to represent their clients in the High Court as Higher Court Advocates, so the differences between the roles of solicitors and barristers are becoming increasingly blurred. The earnings for self-employed barristers in chambers range between £10,000 for newly qualified criminal barristers to £120,000 and more for civil barristers with five years' experience.

The skills required

The following skills are especially important:

- confidence
- eloquence
- the ability to improvise and 'think on your feet'
- the ability to work independently
- the ability to persuade
- the ability to construct an argument
- the ability to run a business
- the capacity to work long hours when required

If you are considering this career, think of times when you have recently demonstrated each of these skills.

Barristers' practice areas

Like solicitors, barristers tend to specialise in specific practice areas, and some of the more popular of these are briefly outlined below. Other specialist areas of law which barristers can enter are admiralty and shipping, civil, construction, environment/planning, European Union and international, landlord and tenant, human rights, intellectual property and media. You can research the full range of specialisms on the Chambers and Partners website: www.chambersstudent.co.uk, and read personal case studies on www.lawcareers.net. Try to identify the areas of law that you would most like to practise.

Chancery

Chancery revolves around legal reasoning. Traditional chancery involves cases related to land law, trusts, probate, tax and charities. Commercial chancery covers financial and business disputes in areas such as intellectual property (IP), tax, professional negligence and company law. This is a highly complex area in which barristers must unravel complicated technical legal issues and explain them clearly to lay clients and solicitors. Barristers in this field spend less time than many of their peers in court and more time researching, drafting and negotiating. New entrants to the career are often given junior roles on large cases or are allowed to cut their teeth on low value cases such as insolvency applications. To succeed in this area of the bar, you will need excellent verbal and written communication skills, analytical skills, and an exceptional intellectual ability.

Commercial

The commercial bar primarily covers issues of contract or tort within commercial disputes. Clients range in size from small regional firms to giant multinationals. As with other areas of the law, mediation and arbitration are quickly becoming as important as litigation. Commercial barristers take the leading role in advising solicitors and lay clients on strategy throughout a case, and work closely with solicitors to sift through mountains of paperwork to find crucial pieces of evidence. Pupils tend to conduct research, write opinions and attend solicitor/client conferences and gradually get the chance to take on small cases. Barristers also usually develop an expertise in a particular industry. To become a commercial barrister you will need high-level advocacy skills, a strong work ethic and an ability to build rapport with people.

Common law

Barristers in this sector deal with cases linked to law that is developed through decisions of courts (precedent) rather than legislation. Like commercial law, most cases revolve around tort and contract. Chambers which focus on common law are often subdivided into practice groups, each focusing on specific specialisations such as employment, personal injury, discrimination, family law and crime. Chambers in this sector also take on a number of commercial cases. Advocacy is at the heart of this branch of the profession, as is variety, and you will work in a wide range of courts and tribunals. Juniors gradually get more responsibility in lower value cases if they are up to it. To enter this sector, you will need excellent all-round advocacy skills, you will have to be good at multi-tasking, have sound interpersonal skills and the ability to work quickly and effectively.

Criminal

Criminal barristers are instructed by solicitors to advise and provide advocacy for clients prosecuted for criminal offences, and can work either for the defence or the prosecution. However, the Crown Prosecution (CPS) increasingly prosecutes its own cases. Barristers work mainly in the Crown Court on serious cases such as supplying drugs, assault and murder. The work can be extremely varied, hectic and demanding. Pupils and juniors start by helping their supervisor in court and conducting research/drafting case summaries and quickly move onto handling their own cases in the magistrates' court and sometimes even in the Crown Court. The relationship between master and pupil is central to a new barrister's success. The key skills required in this sector are confidence, the ability to reassure clients, an ability to get on with difficult people (not just the judges but also the clients!), the capacity to 'think on your feet', good advocacy skills and the ability to assimilate facts quickly.

Employment

Barristers in this sector deal with all cases relating to breakdowns in the employer/employee relationship. These include cases related to breach of contract (such as when an employer is accused of not giving enough notice when dismissing an employee), statutory employment rights (such as race, age and sex equality) and disputes between employers and trade unions. Barristers mostly work alongside solicitor advocates in employment tribunals and the Employment Appeals Tribunal. Applicants can only generally afford junior barristers, whereas respondents often employ more experienced counsel. Pupils tend to perform a great deal of administrative tasks and conduct research for their pupil masters. Junior barristers also work on other civil and commercial cases. To succeed in this sector you will need an ability to get on with a wide cross-section of society, from senior executives to shop stewards.

Family

Family barristers work on all cases related to children (including local authority intervention) and family members in dispute. Cases are heard in the county courts and the Family Division of the High Court, but mediation is usually tried first. New pupils tend to start by learning how to complete the relevant paperwork and go on to handling their own cases. Junior barristers often act on cases involving private law children work and injunctions. If you want to enter this sector you will need the capacity to keep up with the relevant legislation/case law and have a good understanding of financial instruments, pensions, trusts and mortgages. You should also be able handle a wide range of cases under pressure, to communicate tactfully with people who are often very stressed, and have good teamwork skills, as you will usually be working in close partnership with judges, solicitors, social workers and clients. Entry to this sector is intensely competitive.

Personal injury/clinical negligence

Barristers in this blossoming sector act on civil cases involving accidental injury, illness, incapacity, disease and death. Most cases involve road traffic accidents, accidents in the workplace and medical malpractice. Junior lawyers spend a great deal of time in court dealing with small claims; their more senior colleagues spend less time in court and more time preparing more serious cases and planning the strategy for how cases will be presented. To succeed in this sector you need to be able to reassure clients, be a creative thinker and have the capacity to understand complex technical issues.

Public

This sector revolves around all issues related to the legality of the powers, practices and decisions made by public bodies. Junior barristers often spend a great deal of time in tribunals; experienced barristers spend more time preparing for complex cases in the higher courts. To get into this sector you will need a good understanding of current affairs and knowledge of how the UK is governed, good problem-solving skills, the flexibility to quickly turn your hand to a range of cases and a high intellect (as indicated through good academic grades). Entry to this sector is also extremely competitive. Opportunities at the Government Legal Service (GLS) are outlined below.

Tax

Tax law barristers advise clients on how to efficiently plan their taxes and help draft specific tax schemes. They also represent clients in disputes related to all forms of taxation including income tax, capital gains tax, inheritance tax and value added tax (VAT). Most barristers represent taxpayers, but you may also get the opportunity to represent Her Majesty's Revenue and Customs (HMRC). There is less court work in this sector than others as much of the work involves advice and drafting specific tax schemes. The laws related to taxation are continually updated so professionals in this sphere need to be able to keep up with the changes. Tax law barristers also need good communication skills in order to work efficiently with solicitors, accountants and clients. You should also enjoy research.

Where barristers work

Students can call themselves barristers as soon as they pass their postgraduate training qualification. Therefore, barristers work in a wide range of organisations from supermarkets and chip shops to chambers and government departments. The more professional workplaces are outlined below:

Chambers

The Holy Grail for most prospective barristers is to work with a group of other barristers in independent practice at premises called 'chambers'. The vast majority of practising barristers work in this sector. The barristers in each 'set' of chambers are self-employed but, by working together, they are able to share the costs of practising, for example by hiring a barristers' clerk. Chambers are located across England and Wales. They range in size and tend to focus on specific legal areas. You can identify chambers that specialise in certain types of law in your area at www.legalhub.co.uk. Many sets of chambers are also described at www.chambersstudent.couk and www.lawcareers.net.

The Crown Prosecution Service (CPS)

The CPS recruits barristers as Crown Advocates. Criminal barristers find the workload to be very similar to their role at the Bar. In other words, they have a similar level of independence, work long hours, and are very busy. Find out more at www.cps.gov.uk.

The Government Legal Service (GLS)

Lawyers at the GLS advise ministers, interpret existing laws, draft new legislation, litigate and provide advice related to the issues faced by all large organisations, eg employment problems and contract negotiation. There is limited scope for advocacy. Find out more at www.gls.gov.uk.

Other sectors

Barristers work in a range of other organisations, including large public and private organisations (as in-house lawyers), large firms of solicitors (in their in-house litigation departments), magistrates' courts (as legal advisers) and the Law Commission (as research assistants and lawyers).

Qualifying as a barrister

(1) The academic stage

Prospective barristers need a 2:2 (the minimum requirement may soon be changed to a 2:1) in a qualifying law degree or a degree in any other subject from a UK or Irish university and a law conversion qualification (a Graduate Diploma in Law or a Common Professional Exam) that must have been completed in the last seven years. As with trainee solicitors, graduates who are studying law or who have studied law as part of a non-qualifying degree may also be able to get partial exemption from the GDL/CPE. Find out more about the academic stage of training on the Bar Standards Board website (www.barstandardsboard.org.uk).

More details about law conversion courses are provided in the Further Study section of this chapter.

(2) The vocational stage

(a) The Bar Professional Training Course (BPTC): In 2010, the new Bar Professional Training Course (BPTC) replaced the existing Bar Vocational Course (BVC). This course prepares students for practice and is offered full time or part time at a range of institutions across England and Wales. The Bar Standards Board is currently planning to introduce an aptitude test as part of

Becoming a barrister

1. The academic stage
A law degree, or another degree followed by a conversion course often called a Graduate Diploma in Law (GDL)

↓

2. The vocational stage
The Bar Professional Training Course (BPTC) and 12 'qualifying sessions' at your Inn of Court

↓

3. The professional stage – pupillage
A year's work experience under the tutelage of an experienced barrister

the application process for this course in order to reduce the numbers of students who enrol. More details on the BPTC, and information on how and when to apply, can be found in the Further Study section of this chapter.

(b) Qualifying sessions at an Inn of Court: In order to be called to the Bar (to become a qualified barrister) you need to complete 12 'qualifying sessions' at an Inn of Court, involving lectures, advocacy courses and moots.

(3) The professional stage – pupillage

Although you are allowed to call yourself a barrister after the vocational stage of qualification, you are not allowed to set up in chambers as an independent practising barrister; to do this you need to complete a one-year apprenticeship called a 'pupillage'. Pupillages are mostly provided by barristers' chambers and involve practical training under the supervision of an experienced barrister. During the first six months (the 'first six') pupils shadow their 'pupil master'; during the second period (the 'second six') they are usually given their own cases. Pupillages are extremely difficult to obtain. Find out more about getting a pupilage at **9.4**, 'Planning your strategy'.

What are the Inns of Court?

The Inns of Court are ancient societies that provide education, mentoring opportunities and support for their members along with bursaries and scholarships (for GDL students, BPTC students and pupils). You have to join an Inn of Court by the end of May in the year you start your BPTC. Your four choices are Inner Temple (www.innertemple.org.uk), Middle Temple (www.middletemple.org.uk), Gray's Inn (www.graysinn.org.uk) and Lincoln's Inn (www.lincolnsinn.org.uk). Prospective barristers often join the Inn that offers them the largest sponsorship deal for their GDL or BPTC.

Further information about becoming a barrister

- General student guide to legal careers produced by Chambers and Partners – www.chambersstudent.co.uk
- Popular guide to every aspect of legal training published by LawCareers.Net – www.law-careers.net
- The Bar Standards Board website – www.barstandardsboard.org.uk
- Simple step-by-step guide on The All About Law website – www.allaboutlaw.co.uk

Other legal roles

Law graduates go into a number of other law-related roles, and many of these are outlined below. Find out more about some of these career options on the Skills for Justice Website at www.skillsforjustice.com.

Legal executives

Legal executives are not subordinate legal assistants, but are lawyers in their own right. They are entitled to directly charge clients for the work they have done. Legal executives work in a range of sectors, from solicitors' firms to the Crown Prosecution Service and local authorities. They tend to specialise in one area of law and perform much the same tasks as solicitors in the same sector. The main specialisms are civil and criminal litigation, family law, conveyancing, public law, private client work, and corporate and commercial law. Salaries start at about £14,000 for new entrants to the profession, whilst qualified, experienced practitioners can expect to earn over £35,000, and City salaries can get much higher than that.

This is quickly becoming an increasingly attractive alternative to becoming a solicitor, for the following reasons:

- Legal executives have recently gained greater status. They are allowed to represent clients in court, to become partners of law firms and to become judges.
- The costs of qualifying to be a legal executive are a tiny fraction of those to become a solicitor.
- You can earn while you learn. Most trainees study part time whilst they are working because you just need to find a legally-related job in order to train.
- Most qualified and experienced legal executives can become solicitors without having to find a training contract.

To become a fully qualified legal executive (called a 'fellow' of The Institute of Legal Executives) you need to pass the Institute of Legal Executives (ILEX) membership exams, be a member of ILEX and work for five years in qualifying legal employment (two of which have to be undertaken after you qualify). Law graduates can claim exemptions from some of the ILEX examinations. You can study full time and part time for the ILEX exams at a range of colleges, and there is an ILEX Graduate 'Fast-Track' Diploma for graduates with a qualifying law degree.

The skills required for this profession are similar to those needed as a solicitor; however, candidates must have a strong ability to manage their own careers as soon as they leave university. Find out more about being a legal executive, and where you can study, at the website of the Institute of Legal Executives: www.ilex.org.uk.

Licensed conveyancers

Licensed conveyancers are specialists who deal with all legal matters related to buying and selling property. The role includes drafting contracts, liaising with all interested parties, and conducting searches. Licensed conveyancers usually work in private practice or at a firm of licensed conveyancers. Salaries for trainees start at about £15,000 whilst qualified and experienced professionals earn around £25,000 upwards. To qualify as a licensed conveyancer, you first need to gain a Council for Licensed Conveyancers (CLC) 'Employed Licence'. To get this you have to pass the CLC Professional Qualification and gain a minimum of two years' supervised on-the-job training. To gain a full licence, you then need to remain in a relevant job for another three years. At this point you will be allowed to set up in business for yourself.

Most students study for their exams whilst in relevant employment, but you can undertake your CLC Professional Qualification before looking for work in the sector. Law graduates can gain exemptions from some of the examinations and practical training; all applications for exemptions are dealt with by the CLC. Most new entrants to this profession start in some sort of an assistant conveyancing role, but these positions are currently hard to find due to the severe recession in the property sector. Find out more at the website of the Council for Licensed Conveyancers: www.conveyancer.org.uk.

Patent attorneys

Patent attorneys help people secure patents and enforce the intellectual property rights they provide. They usually work in specialist private firms or large manufacturing organisations. Typical duties include studying new inventions and processes alongside existing patents to see if a new patent could be granted, writing patent drafts in precise legal terms to be submitted to patent offices, applying for patents and defending and enforcing intellectual property rights resulting from a patent. British patent attorneys generally deal with the UK Patent Office and the European Patent Office, so travel is often necessary.

New trainees earn about £20,000 a year, and experienced practitioners can name their salary. To qualify as a Patent Attorney, you need to pass the exams set by the Chartered Institute of Patent Attorneys (CIPA) and undertake two years' experience. However, the exams are very difficult to pass, and trainees usually take four to six years to qualify. To enter this career you will usually need a scientific and/or technical degree and language skills (especially French and German). Patent law firms recruit graduates as trainee patent attorneys, and the application process is very competitive. Find out more at the website of the Chartered Institute of Patent Attorneys: www.cipa.org.uk.

Trade mark attorneys

Legal professionals in this role help clients protect and enforce their trade mark rights and support them with intellectual property issues such as copyright and licensing. Their role involves researching new trade marks and making sure that proposed trade marks are not already in use. They also manage, protect and enforce intellectual property rights, negotiate in disputes regarding trade marks, and take action on trade mark infringement.

Trade mark attorneys work in private practice (often alongside patent attorneys), in large companies and in firms of solicitors in specialist trade mark departments. The qualification route to become a trade mark attorney is currently under review; find out more at the website of the Institute of Trade Mark Attorneys: www.itma.org.uk.

Paralegals

Paralegals are professional legal practitioners who are not fully qualified solicitors. Some perform repetitive, straightforward tasks such as managing documents, arranging meetings and preparing letters, whilst others have more challenging roles, for example liaising with clients, conducting legal research, preparing court papers, assisting in court and taking witness statements. The role is gradually becoming more professional so being a paralegal can be a career in its own right with its own set of qualifications, but, for an increasing number of LPC diplomates, it has become the first step on the career ladder to gaining a training contract. Although, if you choose this route to becoming a solicitor, try not to give potential employers the impression that you only want paralegal work until you can get a training contract somewhere else!

You can find paralegal work at employment agencies and by contacting firms directly with speculative applications. However, be warned, this is a competitive market, and you will probably need some experience to get your foot in the door. You will probably have to undertake a couple of short-term, casual appointments before securing a challenging long-term role. Salaries start at about £14,000 and experienced staff earn between £25,000 and £40,000. Find out more about opportunities as a paralegal on the website of the National Association of Licensed Paralegals: www.nationalparalegals.com.

Legal publishing (editorial, sales/marketing)

You may find work for one of the specialist legal publishers, or for a publishing house with a specialist legal arm. Many firms in this growing sector produce hard law and directory publications and news and features magazines with online content. Others focus on academic textbooks and monographs. Find out more about publishing at the Graduate Prospects website: www.prospects.ac.uk.

Crown Prosecution Service (CPS) caseworker/associate prosecutor

Caseworkers are employed by the CPS to assist lawyers. Lower level caseworkers perform administrative tasks; more senior colleagues liaise with the police and summarise evidence, prepare cases, maintain case notes and attend court. Salaries start at around £16,000 per year and rise to about £26,000. After six months in the job caseworkers are allowed to apply for training contracts and then become Crown Prosecutors, so this could be one way to become a solicitor if other methods have failed. Find out more about this role on the CPS website: www.cps.gov.uk and on the Connexions job database: www.connexions-direct.com/jobs4u.

Barristers' clerks

Barristers' clerks are professionals who manage the business activities and day-to-day running of barristers' chambers. Some of their key roles are allocating cases to the appropriate barrister and balancing the workload for all barristers in the set, agreeing fees, finding work for the barristers, keeping accounts, and planning a case/liaising with other barristers, solicitors and clients. Junior clerks earn about £13,000 per annum and experienced senior clerks generally earn between £25,000 and £55,000 a year. Junior clerks are trained by their more senior colleagues. Junior positions are recruited through specialist agencies and roles are advertised on the Institute of Barristers' Clerks' website (www.ibc.org.uk). Find out more about this occupation on the Connexions job database: www.connexions-direct.com/jobs4u.

Legal secretaries

Legal secretaries provide skilled administrative services to legal professionals and therefore tend to work in the offices of solicitors, barristers, large organisations and courts. As well as an interest in law, you will need good typing skills, organisational skills and good attention to detail. Salaries start from around £13,000 and can reach £30,000 a year. For many, the role of legal secretary can represent a satisfying career in its own right, but it can also be the route into a number of more challenging roles such as becoming a paralegal, a legal executive or even a solicitor. Find jobs in local and national newspapers, through recruitment agencies and on the website of the Institute of Legal Secretaries and Personal Assistants: www.institutelegalsecretaries.com.

Court administrative officers

In this role you will help with the day-to-day business of a court. Typical duties involve dealing with the public, booking court hearings, making sure that judges, magistrates and lawyers have the right paperwork and following up the court's judgments. Salaries range from roughly £15,000 to £22,000. New recruits are trained on the job and some court administrative officers become legal executives. You can find vacancies by contacting your local courts (contact details for all courts in England and Wales are available on the website of Her Majesty's Court Service: www.hmcourts-service.gov.uk), looking in local newspapers and on the websites of Jobcentre Plus (www.direct.gov.uk) and the Ministry of Justice (www.justice.gov.uk). Find out more about this role at the Connexions job database: www.connexions-direct.com/jobs4u.

Court reporters

Court reporters take down word-for-word accounts of court hearings for official court transcripts (usually using stenograph machines). Legal knowledge is not necessary but may be an advantage. Find out more about this role on the Connexions job database: www.connexions-direct.com/jobs4u and on the website of the British Institute of Verbatim Reporters: www.bivr.org.uk.

Company secretaries

Company secretaries ensure that organisations comply with all financial and legal regulations. Find out more on the Graduate Prospects website: www.prospects.ac.uk, and on the website of the Institute of Chartered Secretaries: www.icsa.org.uk.

Outdoor clerks

Outdoor clerks perform a range of ancillary tasks for legal firms, such as taking witness statements, conducting legal research and transcribing witness statements. This is a great way to network with legal professionals and develop your career. Find a position by networking with legal employers, sending speculative applications and through legal recruitment agencies. Find out more at www.lawcareers.net.

Other popular careers

When planning your career it is important to appreciate that many law graduates also go into a wide range of fulfilling careers not directly linked to the legal process. A small selection of the more popular choices is listed below. You can find out more about your options at www.prospects.ac.uk, www.connexions-direct.com/jobs4u, www.milkround.com, www.targetjobs.co.uk, www.monster.co.uk and www.get.hobsons.co.uk.

Careers in advertising, marketing and public relations (PR)

Many law graduates are attracted to this competitive sector because it is perceived to be glamorous and exciting. Some large firms offer graduate training programmes, but most new entrants to this profession have to compete for junior roles by gradually building up their CVs and developing essential skills and contacts.

Careers in advertising include advertising account executives/account handlers, account planners, copyrighters, media buyers and media planners. Find out more about careers in this sector on the website of the Institute of Practitioners in Advertising at www.ipa.co.uk and the Creative and Cultural Skills website: www.creative-choices.co.uk.

Careers in marketing include marketing officers, marketing executives, market research interviewers, market researchers and brand managers. The digital marketing sector is currently expanding so graduates with good IT skills are especially welcome. Find out more about careers in marketing on the website of the Chartered Institute of Marketing at www.cim.co.uk and the website of the Institute of Direct Marketing: www.theidm.com.

PR careers include communications officers, press officers and PR officers. Find out more about careers in PR at www.connexions-direct.com/jobs4u.

Two other useful resources for researching this sector are the Guardian's media portal at www.guardian.co.uk/media and www.skillset.org/careers. Your careers service may also carry useful magazines such as 'Campaign', 'PR Week' and 'Marketing' and books such as the Hollis UK *Public Relations Annual* and *The Creative Handbook* published by Centaur Media plc.

Careers in the armed forces, security and emergency services

Law degrees clearly prepare graduates for security-related roles. Many organisations such as Her Majesty's Revenue and Customs have management fast-track roles open to graduates, whilst others, such as the police, have development schemes that are open to graduates once they have been hired. Careers in this sector include the following roles:

- Police officers (see the police recruitment website at www.policecouldyou.co.uk)
- Immigration officers (see the UK Border Agency's website at www.ukba.homeoffice.gov.uk)
- Customs officers, excise officers and tax inspectors (see the website of Her Majesty's Revenue and Customs (HMRC) at www.hmrc.gov.uk)
- Officers in the armed services – graduates are recruited through a series of interviews and practical and written tests (find out more on the careers websites of each of the arms of the armed services – www.armyjobs.mod.uk, www.raf.mod.uk/careers/jobs and www.royalnavy.mod.uk/careers)

- Intelligence analysts with the Government Communications Headquarters (GCHQ) – gathering electronic and digital data and protecting the government's communication and information systems (see www.gchq-careers.co.uk)
- Intelligence officers – MI5 (see www.mi5careers.co.uk)
- Operational officers – MI6, the Secret Intelligence Service (see www.sis.gov.uk)
- Prison officers (see www.skillsforjustice.com and www.hmprisonservice.gov.uk/careers andjobs)

Other roles in this sector include scene of crime officers, forensic computer analysts, trading standards officers, environmental health officers and health and safety inspectors. Find out more about these roles on www.prospects.ac.uk.

My story: Lisa Cherkassky (HE lecturer)

I always wanted to be a teacher. I took the Post Graduate Certificate in Education (the Post Compulsory Education version) after my law degree, which is a nine-month training course in a further education college to become an A-Level lecturer.

When I graduated from my PGCE(PCE) I went back to university to complete an LLM in Criminal Law so I could teach in higher education instead. One of my professors during my LLM helped me to publish a case note and, combined with my experience of

teaching A-level Law, I got an interview to be a lecturer in law at Bradford University.

I have become aware since starting my job that most academics these days have PhDs, which I would like to achieve through publication in the next 10 years. I have to publish a few articles every year, which takes up a lot of time and adds pressure. I prefer the teaching part, and I greatly enjoy interacting with the LLB students. I consider them as friends.

Careers in education and training

The academic rigour of law degrees prepares graduates for a career in the classroom. It is worth noting, however, that to teach law in a secondary school (children aged from 11 to 19) you generally need to train in another subject on the curriculum (usually a humanities subject). Careers in this sector include the following roles:

- Primary and secondary school teachers (find out more on the website of the Training and Development Agency for Schools at www.tda.gov.uk, the website of the Times Education Supplement at www.tes.co.uk, and the Teach First website at www.teachfirst.org.uk, which has information about combining a short teaching assignment with a long-term corporate career)
- Further/higher education lecturers (see www.prospects.ac.uk and the university jobs website, www.jobs.ac.uk)
- Teachers of English as a foreign language (see Cactus TEFL at www.cactustefl.com)
- HE advice workers/careers advisers/education administrators (see www.prospects.ac.uk)

Careers in financial services, insurance and pensions

Many of the modules involved in a law degree, such as taxation, prepare graduates for a life in the City. The larger recruiters in this sector usually recruit new graduates through two-year training programmes. Some of the careers you could go into are listed below. For more information on these occupations, and many others in the sector, look for the job profiles outlined on the website of the Financial Services Skills Council at www.fssc.org.uk.

- Chartered accountants (see the website of the Institute of Chartered Accountants in England and Wales at www.icaew.com)
- Chartered certified accountants (see the website of the Association of Certified Chartered Accountants at www.uk.accaglobal.com/uk/students)
- Chartered management accountants (see the website of the Institute of Chartered Institute of Management Accountants at www.cimaglobal.com/Our-locations/UK)
- Chartered public finance accountants (see the website of the Chartered Institute of Public Finance and Accountancy at www.cipfa.org.uk)
- Actuaries (see the Actuarial Profession website at www.actuaries.org.uk)
- Corporate careers in banking and finance such as retail bankers, investment bankers, financial traders, stockbrokers, commodity brokers, financial advisers and financial risk analysts (see the Inside Careers website at www.insidecareers.co.uk and www.discoverrisk.co.uk)
- Insurance brokers, account managers, claims inspectors, risk surveyors and underwriters (see the Inside Careers website at www.insidecareers.co.uk and www.discoverrisk.co.uk)
- Chartered tax advisers (see www.prospects.ac.uk)

Careers in public administration and politics

Many law graduates end up in this sector, especially those interested in public law. Some roles, such as through the Civil Service Fast Stream and those in public health management, have structured graduate trainee schemes, but to get into political roles you will need extensive work experience.

- Civil Service administrators/executive officers (www.civilservice.gov.uk/jobs)
- Civil Service fast streamers (www.civilservice.gov.uk/jobs/faststream)
- Local government administrators: see your local council's jobs listings, the JobsGoPublic website at www.lgjobs.com and the website of the National Graduate Development Programme (NGDP): www.ngdp.co.uk
- Health Service managers (see opportunities with the NHS at www.nhscareers.nhs.uk)
- European Union (EU) administrators (see www.europa.eu/epso)
- Political researchers/constituency organisers – many people enter this sector after a period of voluntary work experience. Find useful resources on the University of Kent's Careers Advisory Service website at www.kent.ac.uk/careers

Other career options

Other popular roles for law graduates include the following:

- Management consultants (see www.insidecareers.co.uk)
- HR managers (see www.personneltoday.com)
- Events organisers (see www.prospects.ac.uk)
- Environmental consultants (see www.environmentalcareers.org.uk, published by the Chartered Institution of Water and Environmental Management)
- Librarians (see the website of the Chartered Institute of Library and Information Professionals at www.cilip.org.uk)
- Museum curators (see the website of the Museums Association at www.museumsassociation.org and the Creative and Cultural Skills website: www.creative-choices.co.uk)

- Health and safety inspectors (find out about trainee roles on the website of the Health and Safety Executive at www.hse.gov.uk/careers and at www.civilservice.gov.uk/jobs)
- Newspaper/broadcast journalists (see the websites of the National Council for the Training of Journalists at www.nctj.com and the Broadcast Journalism Training Council at www.bjtc.org.uk)
- Radio producers (see the websites of the National Council for the Training of Journalists at www.nctj.com and the Sector Skills Council for Creative Media at www.skillset.org)
- Probation officers (see www.skillsforjustice.com)

Self-assessment Pick an interesting industry sector outside of law and identify the skills you have gained on your law degree that could help you to be a success:

....

....

....

....

....

....

....

What to do next

Now you have researched a range of occupations, you can make an informed choice as to which career to pursue. The next section shows you how to do this.

9.2 CHOOSING A ROLE

It's your life

With such a wide range of possible careers to enter, it can be daunting to find a role that will be both suitable and satisfying. A good way to find a truly fulfilling career is to create a snapshot of what you are good at, what you enjoy, and what you want from life. An understanding of these elements will help you assess the various careers you may want to enter and to find a career path which will be successful, enjoyable and fulfilling.

Research your options

↓

Choose a role

↓

Plan your strategy

↓

Work experience

↓

Further study

↓

Applications and interviews

The career planning process

What are your strengths? (your skills)

In order to find a job you will be good at, you first need to identify the skills you have to offer. There is no point in planning to be a ballerina if you have one bad knee and two left feet!

Many skills, such as teamwork and research, can be used in a wide range of contexts – these are called transferable skills. The easiest way to assess your transferable skills is to reflect upon your recent achievements at university, at work or during your interests/extra-curricular activities. For example, good grades at university may indicate that you are good at researching information, or a promotion at work could show that you have good interpersonal skills. Most law graduates will have developed skills related to research, critical analysis, presenting an argument, expressing themselves orally and in writing, paying close attention to detail and solving problems.

Your skills audit

Try to identify your key skills in the space provided. Think deeply about what you can personally offer an employer but, if you're struggling, use the prompts provided for inspiration and ask your friends and family what they think you're good at. The longer you take on this activity, the more you'll get out of it.

- Are you good at retaining a great deal of information?
- Are you a quick learner?
- Can you multi-task?
- Are you good in a high-pressure situation?
- Are you good at serving/helping people?
- Are you good at communicating with people in person?
- Are you good at communicating with people in writing?
- Are you good at making presentations?
- Can you work independently?
- Can you work well in a team?
- Are you good at sharing ideas/feelings?

- Are you good at organising things?
- Are you good at organising people?
- Are you good at organising events?
- Can you easily build rapport with new people?
- Are you good at motivating people?
- Are you good at persuading people/leading people?
- Are you good at advising people?
- Are you good at teaching/training others?
- Do you have good listening skills?
- Are you good at solving problems?
- Are you good with numbers?
- Are you good at analysing information/research?
- Are you good with IT?
- Can you easily adapt to new situations?

Self-assessment **Identify your skills:**

....

....

....

....

....

....

....

To assess your skills, see the quiz on our Companion Website.

My story: Susan Davies (law graduate and primary school teacher)

I studied law at university because I was expected to choose a highly academic degree and career. I chose a good university and really enjoyed the subject, got a good 2:1 and secured a training contract with a big City law firm because they agreed to pay for my Legal Practice Course (LPC). I never once sat down and assessed whether I had the skills to succeed in such an environment and, more importantly, whether I'd enjoy it.

Unfortunately, I never enjoyed my time as a trainee. I liked law as an academic exercise, but the job was just too sales-based and cut-throat. I was not cut out for the commercial environment. Consequently, even though I finished my training contract and became a solicitor, I never practised. I randomly applied for a range of alternative roles without much success and eventually worked at a music store in London for 10 years which I loved.

As I got older I started to understand myself better and to appreciate what I was good at and what I enjoyed. I carefully researched a wider range of careers and thought that I would like to be a teacher. I volunteered in a classroom for a year and really enjoyed it, so I signed up for a Post Graduate Certificate of Education. I finally became a teacher when I was 34 and I have never looked back. It's hard work, but I enjoy every moment. My advice would be that you only live once, don't be too much in a rush and take some time to find a career that you would enjoy. Good luck.

What do you enjoy? (your interests)

Of course, being good at something doesn't necessarily mean you want to do it for the rest of your life. For example, you may be good at working with children, but do you want to do it every day? The more time you take to assess the things you enjoy, the more chance you have of finding a career that corresponds.

Your interests audit

This time, list the things you would enjoy doing in your career. Try to come up with your own unique list of interests but, if you get stuck, use the prompts provided.

- Do you want to work in an area related to your hobbies?
- Do you enjoy working in an office?
- Would you prefer to work outdoors?
- Are you happy to follow directions?
- Are you only really happy when you're in control?
- Do you like helping people?
- Do you like teaching/training people?
- Do you like working with colleagues?
- Do you like working on your own?
- Do you enjoy meeting new people?
- Do you enjoy motivating people?
- Do you enjoy organising people?
- Do you like leading people?
- Do you enjoy building relationships with people?
- Do you enjoy persuading people?
- Do you like IT?
- Do you like making presentations?
- Do you enjoy organising things?
- Do you enjoy organising events?
- Do you like analysing data?
- Do you like working with numbers?
- Do you like things to stay the same?
- Do you prefer change or consistency?
- Do you enjoy solving problems?

....

....

....

....

....

....

To assess your key interests, complete the quiz on our Companion Website.

What do you want from life? (your motivations)

The final way to assess yourself in relation to career planning, and perhaps the most important, is to identify what is important to you in life, ie your motivations or values. For example, is it more important for you to have a good work–life balance or to make as much money as possible?

Once you have weighed up your motivations, you can look for corresponding careers. For example, if money is more important to you than anything else then you need to look for a well-paid career such as investment banking, whereas if helping the community is more important to you then you may want to be a social worker.

Your motivations audit

Try to identify your top 10 personal career motivations in the space provided.

- Do you value the freedom to make your own decisions?
- Do you value contact with others?
- Do you want to define your own workload?
- Is a structured career path important to you?
- Is job security important?
- Do you want to create new ways of doing things?
- Do you want to build your own business?
- Is it important for you to provide a service that people need?
- Do you want to make a positive difference to the community?
- Do you want to make loads of money?
- Do you want a high standard of living?
- Is it important for you to have a good work–life balance?
- Do you value flexible working practices, eg the opportunity to work outside normal hours/work at home?
- Do you want a job that does not get in the way of your family life?
- Do you want to travel or stay in your local area?
- Do you want to be an expert/specialist?
- Are you excited about learning and developing?
- Do you have specific talents you want to use?
- Is it important for you to be creative?
- Do you want respect/status?
- Do you value responsibility?
- Do you want to work in a fast-paced environment or a slow, peaceful one with few pressures?
- Do you want an exciting role or would you prefer routine?
- Do you value variety?
- Do you want to be the boss or would you prefer not to have the responsibility?
- Do you value personal development/promotion?

Identify what you want from life:

....

....

....

....

....

....

To assess your personal motivations, complete the quiz on our Companion Website.

Matching yourself to possible careers

One way to take the pressure off yourself is to identify a range of attractive careers rather than just one specific role. This approach can be very positive because it allows you to identify a number of possible occupations and to keep your options open.

Start by linking your skills, interests and motivations to the list of interesting careers you identified at the beginning of this chapter. Career profiles for most careers can be found at www.prospects.ac.uk or www.connexions-direct.com/jobs4u. In this way, create a shortlist of interesting occupations that stand out from the crowd.

Once you have identified some interesting careers that match your skills, interests and motivations, get out there and talk to people who do those jobs and find some relevant voluntary roles/work experience. You will only get a true picture of an occupation by putting yourself in that position. For example, if you're considering teaching as a career, you really need to spend some time in a classroom. Your university careers service should be able to help you get some useful contacts/work experience.

Take your time to assess a wide range of possible career options. Students often rush this process because they are understandably worried about what they are going to do after leaving university. Law students sometimes quickly decide to be commercial solicitors just because it's an obvious choice, without ever considering if there are other careers that would be more fulfilling.

Making a decision

We all make decisions in our own unique ways. In order to find a fulfilling career you need to recognise your own decision-making style and to plan accordingly. Some of the more common decision-making strategies are outlined below; try to identify your own personal style and consider how you can maximise your chances of finding a fulfilling career using this approach.

Intuitive

Intuitive decision makers choose options which 'feel right' at a particular moment in time. People with this decision-making style often have a good emotional attachment to the career they go for but may choose an occupation without looking at all their options or making sure that the role they have chosen fits their unique skills, interests and motivations. If this is you, make sure you do your research and get some work experience before following your gut instincts.

Systematic

People with this decision-making style carefully weigh up all their options and make well-thought out decisions but can often take no account of how they actually feel about the jobs they are considering. If this is you, continue carefully researching your options but get away from the websites for a while and talk to people who work in the roles you are considering, get some relevant work experience and carefully assess whether you actually enjoy doing the job.

Hesitant/paralytic

Career planning can be too scary for many students, so they often bury their heads in the sand and hope that the whole thing goes away. If this sounds like you, it may help to carefully plan each step you're going to take to choose a career and give yourself strict deadlines. It may also help to ask a friend or a careers adviser to help keep you motivated. Once you start taking positive steps you may well feel much more energised and in control of the situation, and soon you may actually be excited about finding a fulfilling future.

Impulsive/spontaneous

People with this decision-making style often leap before they look. They find out about an interesting career one day and apply for a job the next. If this is you, congratulate yourself for being so proactive but try to find some time to assess what you actually want to do in the long term. You could mentally picture yourself where you want to be in 20 or 30 years and carefully research your next move by talking to people in your chosen role or seeing a careers adviser.

Fatalistic

The motto for fatalistic people is 'what will be, will be'. Graduates with this decision-making style often just fall into a career (or don't!) without doing any research at all. They may just get a job after university and stick with it, or go for a role just because it is linked to the degree they are studying (such as becoming a solicitor). These people often get itchy feet a few years after they leave university because they are not being fulfilled, and face what is called a 'quarter century crisis'. This is a modern term describing the frustration of twenty-five/twenty-six year olds who are doing menial tasks or boring professional roles and now want to move on and find something more interesting and well paid. If this sounds like you, one way to inspire yourself is to get any job so there's money coming in, get some help from a careers adviser, and allow yourself to dream about what you actually want from life. In this way, you can then carefully plan your next moves and make it happen.

Compliant/dependent

Some people avoid decisions like the plague and let other people rule their lives. People in this category may choose a certain role just to please their parents or their friends, but will probably not succeed in the job they go into or enjoy it very much. Therefore, if you focus on a particular career just because someone else wants you to follow that path, try to make sure that the role really suits you before you start applying. No one wants you to be miserable (hopefully!).

Deviant

People in this category are usually happy to ask for advice on careers only so they can do exactly the opposite. This implies a healthy desire to take personal control of the career planning process, but it is ignorant of the insight that research into websites and the advice of others can provide. Your mum does not always know best but you should at least consider what she (and everyone else) suggests!

Self-assessment

(a) What type of decision maker do you think you are?

....

....

....

....

....

....

....

....

(b) How can you maximise your chances of finding a fulfilling career using this approach?

....

....

....

....

....

....

To determine your own decision-making style, complete the fun quiz on our **Companion Website**.

A step-by-step approach

One way of making career planning less daunting is to break the process up into a sequence of discrete manageable tasks and to set yourself mini-goals along the way. A sample action plan using this approach has been shown below; try to draw up your own personal plan alongside. Set yourself specific targets relevant to your personal circumstances and your unique decision-making style, and set a realistic timescale. For example, instead of planning to research 'a range into of career options', try to research a specific number of occupations over a fixed time period.

Activity Draw up a personal action plan for finding and choosing a fulfilling career:

A sample career choice action plan

Step one: Assess yourself
Take a week or two to list your top 10 skills, interests and motivations

↓

Step two: Research your options
Take a month to list about 30 interesting career choices from a wide range of sectors

↓

Step three: Make a shortlist
Take a few weeks to match your skills, interests and motivations against your range of interesting career options to come up with about six outstanding career choices. Make sure you find roles that match all three elements. For example, some jobs on your list may suit your interests and motivations, but not your skills, and others may be enjoyable but they may not deliver the lifestyle you want.

↓

Step four: Narrow down your search
Find a way to talk to people in the jobs on your shortlist and see if you can shadow them at work for a day or two to see which of the roles you are considering is the most attractive. This step could take a few months to complete

↓

Step five: Confirm your decision
Get some work experience/a voluntary role in your chosen field to make sure you've made a good choice. This step could take a few months to complete, so the sooner you start planning your career the better.

Your personal career choice action plan

Step one: ....
....
....

Date to be completed: ....

Step two: ....
....
....

Date to be completed: ....

Step three: ....
....
....

Date to be completed: ....

Step four: ....
....
....

Date to be completed: ....

Step five: ....
....
....

Date to be completed: ....

Online tools to match yourself to a career

- Assess yourself using the skills and interests assessment tools on the DirectGov website – www.careersadvice.direct.gov.uk
- Link your specific skills, interests and motivations to career options on Prospects Planner at www.prospects.ac.uk
- View the excellent career skills section on the MindTools website – www.mindtools.com
- Try the free personality tests on the Hire Success website – www.personality.net
- Access the wide range of self-assessment and profiling tools for HE students on the careers website of the University of Sussex – www.sussex.ac.uk/cdec

What to do next

Once you have decided to focus on a specific role, the next step is to plan a strategy to get your foot in the door; this is covered in the next section of this chapter.

9.3 PLANNING YOUR STRATEGY

The need to plan

Once you have chosen to pursue a particular career, you need to carefully plan your next steps so you can stand out from the crowd and succeed in your aim. The process is like finding a destination on a map and planning your best route to get there. The challenge is that most graduate careers are very competitive to enter, especially in a global economic downturn. The good news is that a bit of planning and preparation will very quickly give you an advantage over many of your peers.

Typical graduate paths

Graduates are recruited in different ways depending on a range of factors such as the traditional graduate path in the industry, the size of organisations and the state of the economy.

The career planning process

Most graduates start their careers by working in voluntary, junior, temporary or casual roles and work their way into more senior roles. For example, if you want to work in the film industry, you may get your foot in the door as a 'runner', or if you want to be a licensed conveyancer, you may start your career with an estate agent or by getting an administrative job in a conveyancing firm.

In some sectors, many of the larger graduate recruiters employ graduates directly onto training schemes. These are structured programmes in which new employees are trained for a year or two in a range of roles. The key recruitment period for these schemes is usually some time between October and February for contracts starting in the following autumn, but every firm has its own timetable (which may fall outside this window), and organisations are increasingly recruiting all year round.

Organisations often recruit students and graduates into a range of specialist positions that are not necessarily linked to their core business because they need professionals in a range of sectors, for example, energy firms may need legal trainees. Furthermore, many graduate employers recruit students and graduates from a wide range of degree programmes because they value general employability skills over subject specific knowledge, for example an accountancy firm may be attracted to a law graduate because of the communication skills he or she has developed.

Graduate training programmes are very competitive, so anyone interested in following this route should build up their work experience in their first two years at university. Many employers who run graduate training schemes expect graduates to have at least 280 or 300 UCAS points and a 2:1.

Students should start looking for relevant programmes at the start of their final year of study. Graduates are usually welcomed within two or three years of leaving university. You can find graduate training schemes by looking at the general career planning websites such as www.prospects.ac.uk, www.milkround.com, www.targetjobs.co.uk, www.monster.co.uk and www.get.hobsons.co.uk, or by picking up general and sector-specific graduate jobs directories from your university careers service (usually available from October onwards).

Five keys to success

Develop your skills

Skills are central to the recruitment process. Some of the skills required by graduate employers will be closely related to a specific role, such as an ability to conduct an audit, or to type quickly, but many of them will be common to all careers, such as teamwork and organisation. These are called transferable skills.

By the time you graduate, you should strive to gain all the sector-specific and transferable skills required in the specific career you want to enter. You can develop these skills through a successful academic career, through your willingness to take on extracurricular activities and, most importantly, through your work experience. You should have general work experience and more focused experience related to the career you want to enter. For example, if you want to find work as a corporate solicitor, some experience at a corporate legal firm and/or financial institution would be very beneficial.

During the three (or four) years of your degree, you have time to start building up your experience from scratch. You could start by looking for part-time casual opportunities, joining a few clubs or societies on campus and keeping your eyes open for any interesting volunteering opportunities. During your second year, you could then identify the career you want to enter and look for relevant opportunities and a position of responsibility in a club or society on campus. Finally, you should aim to undertake some form of placement or sustained work period at the end of your penultimate year of study. Once you finish university, you may also need to volunteer or work in lowly paid jobs before you can get into a more substantial role.

Some of the more common transferable skills required by graduate employers, and what they involve, are shown below. Try to identify how you can develop these skills whilst you are at university.

Get some help with understanding and developing your skills on the University of Bradford's Career Development Services website at www.careers.brad.ac.uk/student/skills, on the MindTools website at www.mindtools.com, and ask for help from a careers adviser at your university or postgraduate training provider. View the personal experiences of other students and graduates on www.youtube.com using a search term such as 'transferable skills' or 'employability skills'.

Build your networks

Who you know is as important as what you know. Your contacts can make the difference between finding a fulfilling career and being frustrated at every turn. You can ask for help from your contacts in a number of ways, for example to research careers in general, to find out more about a specific role, to plan the best way to start your career, to get work experience or even to get a job.

The key to networking is to realise that we all know people who know other people. For example, your mum may have a friend who is a solicitor, or your friend's brother may be a teacher, or your employer may know an accountant. Get in touch with as many contacts as you can, and ask for a five-minute chat and some help. At first it can be scary approaching people, but professionals are usually happy to help, and if you don't ask, you don't get!

For more suggestions on how to network, see our **Companion Website**.

Consider more study

Some careers require you to have other qualifications as well as your bachelor's degree, such as specific technical certificates (for example in touch typing or Photoshop), postgraduate degrees (such as a Master's in shipping law) or vocational qualifications linked to specific occupations (such as the Legal Practice Course to be a solicitor or a teacher training certificate). Find out more about further study options later in this chapter, but be aware that further study will not necessarily improve your chances of getting into most careers.

Boost your grades

Good A-level and degree grades are usually required to get into a graduate training programme. If you are having trouble with your studies, don't just let things slide, speak to someone. You could start with your personal tutor or your lecturer. However, if you graduate without the requisite grades to join a profession through the normal graduate path, all is not lost. In this case, you could see if organisations will accept mitigating circumstances (unlikely), or do your research to see if work experience will improve your chances through some other route into the profession. For example, to get into a graduate training programme to become a chartered accountant at one of the larger accountancy firms, you often need about 300 UCAS points and a 2:1 in your degree. If your grades are not up to this standard, maybe you could plan to work in a relevant role for a year or two and then enter the profession through a smaller accountancy firm (which may have more flexible recruitment procedures).

Set some goals

Research your chosen career and find out:

- how people are generally recruited into the career you want to enter;
- the grades, experience and any further qualifications that may be required;
- how people specialise in your chosen sector;
- whether you need any postgraduate qualifications and, if so, what, when, and where you can study;
- how you can gradually build up your skills and experience whilst you're at university.

In this way you can draw up a strategy to succeed in your career aims, setting yourself mini-goals along the way and plan when and how you are going to apply for your first role.

Activity Identify where and how you can develop some of the key transferable skills required by employers:

Transferable skills required by employers	What these skills involve	Where and how can you develop these skills (eg at work, in a student society or in a voluntary role)?
Commercial awareness	Commercial awareness is an appreciation of the business and financial elements that affect a particular organisation and how you can influence them. Some things to consider are the economy, the sector in which the organisation operates, competitors and marketing priorities.	
Teamwork	Teamwork is all about effective collaboration that enables a group of individuals to perform at a high level. It revolves around a balance of contributions based on people's abilities, hard work, coordination, communication, support and respect.	
Communication	Good communication is a two-way process involving unambiguous transmission of messages and clear reception. Therefore, it revolves around: • effective presentation including an ability to tailor information to the needs of the audience; • good active listening skills, such as checking that you understand someone correctly.	
Initiative/ problem solving	Welcoming personal responsibility for taking actions, solving problems and meeting targets, and logically finding solutions.	
Planning and organisation	Planning and organisation involves focusing on everything that's required to achieve a goal and ensuring that you deliver on time and on budget. Planning skills embrace a clear vision, an ability to create a realistic action plan and self-management. Organisation skills include a capacity to research, prioritise, keep records and manage time.	
Computer literacy	• The ability to use common word processing programmes, spreadsheets and databases, to surf the web and use common email packages. • The confidence to adopt new hardware and software.	

Getting into law

Legal careers are like all other graduate roles in that they are competitive to enter, and employers expect you to have total focus and all the necessary skills. The routes to qualification for a number of legal roles are currently under review, so it incumbent on you to keep up with the changes and plan the route into your chosen career that best suits your personal circumstances. This section focuses on the professional stages to becoming a solicitor and a barrister, ie training contracts and pupillages. Details on work experience and the postgraduate qualifications you need to become a lawyer (ie the GDL, LPC and BPTC) are outlined later in this chapter.

Getting a training contract

What are your chances?

Securing a training contract to be a solicitor is a very competitive process and is currently the most challenging stage to becoming a solicitor. A traditional rule of thumb is that about 30% of people get their training contracts sorted out before they start their Legal Practice Course (LPC), roughly 30% get them when they are on their LPC, and around 10% arrange them in the year after they finish. At the time of writing, we are in a global economic slowdown, so many firms are cutting back on recruitment whilst other firms are offering paralegal roles to LPC diplomates instead of training contracts, with a view to offering training contracts in the future to those who do well.

What do they look for?

Legal employers look for confidence and the following attributes:

- high-level skills such as communication, client interaction and commercial awareness, as proven through work experience, academic achievement and extracurricular activities;
- a real and demonstrable commitment to the firm/organisation and its legal specialisms.

When to apply

Most larger firms tend to recruit trainees in July or August a full two years in advance. This means that law students can make their first applications during their second year at university, and non-law students in their final year. Some smaller regional or national firms offer training contracts one year in advance. Many local firms advertise for trainees as and when they are needed, and these are often given to people who have already gained their LPCs. Even though many firms tend to recruit at specific times, training contracts in all sorts of firms and organisations are still advertised all year round, so you should always keep your eyes open for vacancies.

Where are they advertised?

Most large firms advertise their vacancies in a range of publications that are easily accessible to students and graduates, such as the Chambers and Partners website: www.chambersstudent.co.uk and www.lawcareers.net. Smaller firms may choose to advertise their vacancies more locally, for example they may recruit candidates directly through careers services at universities and postgraduate training providers, and at careers fairs and other careers events. They may also choose to recruit internally or wait for speculative applications. Most employers look favorably on candidates who have completed some work experience at their firm, especially those involved in formal placement programmes (generally open to law students at the end of their penultimate year of university study, and non-law students at the end of their degrees).

Planning your strategy

Training contracts are difficult to secure. They are usually offered to students with excellent academic grades and relevant skills and experience. Therefore, the first step to achieving your aim is to ensure that you get the best possible grades during your degree and postgraduate study. Don't underestimate the benefits of a First or a 2:1. Many students use the scattergun approach to apply for training contracts. In other words, they apply for as many of them as possible and hope that they get lucky. This method usually fails because applications are bound to be vague and unconvincing. A better way to find a training contract is to use the following strategy:

(a) Develop your skills and experience

Employers expect you to prove yourself through your work experience and your extracurricular activities. You need to gradually build up your experience and contacts so you can stand out from the crowd by the time you put together your applications. You could start by just chatting to solicitors, getting involved with your university's student law society and taking up some relevant voluntary work. Work experience of any sort will also make you eminently more employable but, as you progress through your degree, you should look for more relevant and formal work experience opportunities. Most universities and postgraduate training providers have careers services that run events to introduce students to legal professionals and help you find work experience. In the autumn term you can also chat to solicitors at law fairs across the country; these are advertised on the Chambers and Partners website: www.chambersstudent.co.uk.

(b) Focus your career search

Take some time to identify where you want to work, how you want to specialise and for whom you want to work (the type of firm or organisation). These decisions will clearly be influenced by personal factors, such as where your family and friends are based or where you're going to university, but you should also be realistic – there are not many magic circle firms in Great Yarmouth! If you make an early decision as to where you want to live and work, this will allow you to choose a postgraduate training provider in the same region, and this, in turn, will give you the chance to build up local contacts and work experience.

In order to get a good idea of the type of law that suits you best, read about the different firms and specialisms, have a chat with some real-life solicitors and look for some relevant work experience. Some students target certain firms simply because they offer funding towards the GDL or LPC. This is understandable because these courses are very expensive, but you should only apply to firms if you are really interested in the types of law they practise, or you might end up in a very unfulfilling role.

(c) Enhance your work experience

Look for work that is relevant to the legal sector you want to enter. For example, you may want to look for a summer placement in your chosen type of firm, or look for work in a relevant industry (such as an investment bank if you want to get into corporate law, or a refugee advice centre if you want to practise immigration law).

(d) Target specific firms

Once you have relevant experience, you are ready to apply for a training contract. Start by looking for training contracts with firms or organisations in your region that specialise in your favourite areas of law (see the solicitors online website: www.solicitorsonline.org.uk) and try to meet recruiters at law fairs and other careers-related events, then send off well-focused applications.

If all else fails

If you have been trying to get a training contract for some time and have not succeeded, you should re-evaluate your strategy and make sure your applications are up to scratch. Try to avoid just sending out hundreds of applications and hoping for the best; this strategy rarely works because the majority of untargeted applications are poor. Why not give your career's service a call and ask for help. If you still cannot secure a training contract, even after you have improved your applications, you may want to look for paralegal work and build up your skills and experience until firms find you irresistible.

What if I get a 2:2?

Intellectual ability is central to success as a lawyer, but so too is general aptitude and, in many

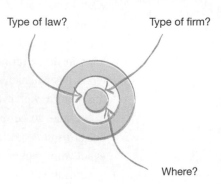

To get a training contract it helps to target where you want to work, and what you want to do

cases, commercial acumen. Larger firms may not consider applicants with a 2:2 degree, but medium-sized and smaller firms may do so, especially if you have a great deal of relevant work experience.

After your training contract

Most trainees are kept on at the end of their contracts, but not all. On the other hand, you may decide to seek pastures new for your own reasons. Either way, the end of your training contract is a watershed moment, when you should consider whether a position at other firms or organisations would better deliver your career motivations, such as a good work–life balance, a higher salary or a more obvious route to partnership.

My story: Clementine Foster

I originally studied Classics at Newcastle University but I always had an interest in entering the legal profession. In 6th form I arranged vacation placements with two law firms and I was lucky enough to work in several different departments which meant that I was exposed to a variety of different practices.

In my final year on the Classics course I arranged a further work experience placement with a local firm of solicitors and I quickly realised that a career in law was for me.

What initially attracted me to becoming a solicitor as opposed to a barrister was the opportunity to work closely with my clients and I always knew that there would always be the opportunity to do some advocacy work as well.

Armed with a 2:1 in Classics I headed across the road to the University of Northumbria to do the CPE (Common Professional Exam) and the LPC (Legal Practice Course). During my time on the LPC I applied for a number of training contracts, but whilst I obtained good grades I found it very difficult to get past the interview stage due to the stiff competition. Nevertheless, I didn't let this to deter me.

I joined a local firm in 2006 as a paralegal in the Technical Team. At that time the firm didn't operate a training contract programme but I knew that the experience I gained working at such a firm would be invaluable. I started off assisting a senior fee earner, carrying out basic tasks such as preparing disclosure statements and court bundles. After six months or so I was running my own caseload that consisted of mainly defended matters. My responsibilities included negotiating settlements, drafting witness statements and applications, preparing cases for trial. I also undertook some advocacy work as well.

In 2009 I was promoted to a more senior role as Legal Officer and then in July 2009 I was offered a training contract with the firm. I started my training contract in October last year and due to my previous experience I will qualify in just 18 months (as opposed to the usual 24 months).

This is an incredibly exciting time for me partly because I am so close to achieving my goal of qualifying as a solicitor, but also because I know how difficult it is to secure a training contract these days. From my own personal experience, if you want it enough and you put the hard work in there is no reason why you cannot fulfil your ambition (and I am proof of this!).

Getting a pupillage

What are your chances?

If you think that getting a training contract is competitive, you haven't seen anything yet! Over recent years only about 25% of students who started their Bar Vocational Course (BVC) got a pupillage to become a practising barrister, and, even then, many of them could not find a seat in chambers (often called a tenancy) when they finished. Your chances may grow over the coming years if the Bar Council succeeds in its aim of significantly reducing the number of applicants who are accepted onto the new Bar Professional Training Course (BPTC), which recently replaced the BVC. However, entrance to the profession is always bound to be very competitive because it is very popular.

What do they look for?

Pupillage providers (mostly chambers) look for people who stand out from the crowd and have exceptional skills that are relevant to the areas of law that they practise. Successful candidates typically have a great intellect, exceptional communication skills and an ability to persuade people and carry an argument. Applications are also welcomed from people who have excelled in some area of their lives outside of their academic study, such as mooting champions or mature candidates who have had successful careers away from the Bar.

Where are they advertised?

The General Council of the Bar's Pupillage Portal advertises all vacancies on its website: www. pupillages.com. Chambers stipulate on this website whether they want you to apply direct or through the portal's central online application system. You can apply to as many chambers as you like if they do not use the centralised application system, whereas, each year, you can only apply to 12 sets of chambers that use the portal, and one more through clearing. Most chambers offer pupillages which last for the full year but some only offer vacancies for six months, which puts the added burden on you to find a second six-month pupillage so you can qualify.

When to apply

Chambers that take applications outside the Pupillage Portal will have their own recruitment timetables. The Pupillage Portal usually accepts applications in March every year, and clearing usually runs from the middle of August to the middle of September. Most pupillages are advertised in the calendar year before they start; some of the top commercial sets have a two-year lag. Find out the key dates for the current recruitment round at www.pupillages. com.

Planning your strategy

Before you choose to be a barrister, ask yourself if you can afford it, if you can develop the necessary skills and if you have the commitment to succeed. Read about the profession in detail, talk to barristers at careers-related events and keep in mind that solicitor advocates nowadays have many of the same opportunities to represent clients in court as barristers. If you are still convinced that this is the career for you then you need to do everything in your power to make it happen. There are a number of things you can do to stand out from the crowd; many of these are outlined below:

Choose your specialism

Research the different legal specialisms practised by barristers and try to identify the ones that are most linked to your skills, interests and motivations.

Get plenty of work experience

Look for general legal work experience such as mooting, marshalling and mini-pupillages and then get some experience related to the type of law you want to practise (see the 'Develop your skills' section above). Try to find things that make you stand out from the crowd, such as a Stage at the European Union or an internship at the United Nations.

Find something in which to excel

Get involved in activities at which you can excel, either at university or in the wider world, and seek achievements which will shine out on your CV.

Network

Build relationships with barristers through your personal relationships, by taking part in activities at your Inn of Court, by going to careers events and pupillage fairs and by asking for help from your careers service. This will help you target chambers appropriately and may open doors into valuable work experience.

Know the law

Keep up to date with legal, commercial and current affairs, particularly those related to the Bar.

Put together targeted applications focusing on skills

Make sure your applications are targeted at the nature and ethos of the chambers (or other organisations) you are applying to and clearly demonstrate your skills, commitment and experience.

My story: Tahir Khan (barrister responsible for recruitment at a large set of Chambers)

There is a wide variety of work in the legal sector and many different skills are demanded by recruiters in the individuals they select. The Bar as a profession has always tended to specialise in advocacy and so when recruiting, the emphasis is on skills that can be employed in contested court work whether it be jury advocacy or litigation in the civil or family courts.

The popularity of courtroom dramas and the public's appetite for them reinforces the perception that those embarking upon a vocation at the Bar must possess a flair for the theatrical. Being able to speak confidently in public is therefore an essential pre-requisite for those wishing to practise in the adversarial system that has made British Justice the envy of the world.

Trainee barristers are required to undertake an apprenticeship known as pupillage. But the demand for pupillages far outstrips their availability. Chambers recruitment is intended to ensure that only those with real ability and potential are offered pupillage. The future of a set of Chambers depends on the calibre of those recruited into Chambers.

A prospective pupil's academic achievement is the foundation on which Chambers will entertain an application. What really matters is a strong showing at degree level and on the Bar Vocational Training Course. Some Chambers insist on a minimum 2:1 degree but many others take a more flexible view and will not dismiss a candidate with a lower class of degree.

It is important for candidates for pupillage to demonstrate a real desire to practise at the Bar, and having a track record

of legal-based work experience (mini-pupillages) will fulfil this criterion. Most universities now partake in 'mooting' competitions and have debating societies. Those with an aptitude and natural ability for thinking on their feet and public speaking can shine in this environment and in the process demonstrate that they have what it takes to be an advocate.

When taking on someone as a pupil, Chambers are making a huge commitment, both in financial terms (pupillages are funded) and because a recently graduated entrant into Chambers can expect to spend typically 20 years with the set of Chambers that they join. Those responsible for recruitment when assessing an interviewee for pupillage often ask themselves, 'How will this person fit into these Chambers?' Prospective pupils must have a life beyond their love of the law. Foreign travel, extracurricular activities, social conscience and other outside interests all combine to make a rounded and personable individual who will be regarded as a positive asset to Chambers.

In the challenging legal profession of today, the fierce competition for pupillage allows Chambers to be much more demanding of applicants than hitherto was the case. For the successful few, the future often holds out a vocation that is both financially rewarding and personally fulfilling.

To view trainees' experiences look at the websites of chambers in the sector you want to enter (see www.legalhub. co.uk for a full list of chambers).

If all else fails

If you cannot get a pupillage, you have a range of options including the following:

- Keep on building up your work experience and improving your applications/interview technique and re-apply.
- Look for a role as an in-house lawyer or seek opportunities at large corporate firms of solicitors.
- Work for two years as a paralegal and cross-qualify as a solicitor by taking the qualified lawyers' transfer test (see the Solicitors Regulation Authority website: www.sra.org.uk/students).
- Look for other quasi-legal roles or non-law careers.

After your pupillage

Once you have finished your pupillage, you need to find a chambers to accept you as a 'tenant'. You may be offered a tenancy where you have been a pupil, but this is certainly not guaranteed. If you cannot find a tenancy, you may be able to work at a set of chambers on a more casual basis on a 'third six' or as a 'squatter'.

Activity

1 What career are you interested in pursuing?

....
....
....
....

2 What steps could you take while you are at university to boost your chances of success? (Consider work experience, volunteering, networking, improving your grades, signing up for additional qualifications, going to careers events ...)

....
....
....
....
....
....
....
....
....
....
....
....
....

9.4 WORK EXPERIENCE

What is it?

Work experience is any activity that can develop your skills. It comprises anything from a day's voluntary work to a structured summer-long placement.

Why you need it

You may believe that you have all the necessary skills and commitment to be a success in a particular field, but employers need proof. Any skills gained during work experience are especially transferable to the workplace and are therefore highly prized.

The career planning process

What you can do

Anything and everything

All work experience, however unskilled or casual, is valuable because you can use it to prove to employers that you have the skills they require. For example, a blue chip company recently recruited an applicant who was able to demonstrate his communication skills by outlining how he calmly and efficiently pacified angry drunk customers in his role in a fast food restaurant.

Voluntary/pro bono work

All sorts of organisations, from schools to the London Organising Committee of the Olympic and Paralympic Games, require volunteers. Getting involved with the community in this way is a great way to develop your skills, meet new people and make good contacts. Your university or postgraduate training provider may have an office that could help you find suitable opportunities. Three national volunteering organisations that can help you find opportunities in your area are Student Volunteering UK at www.volunteering.org.uk, YouthNet at www.do-it.org.uk, and Community Service Volunteers at www.csv.org.uk.

There are numerous legally-related roles in which you can assist and advise people for free. You could look for your own role by approaching charities or support groups, or try some of the following organisations:

- The Citizens Advice Bureau (www.citizensadvice.org.uk) – CAB advisers help people with a wide range of problems including legal issues. You can also sign up for their Adviser Training Programme
- The Refugee Council (www.refugeecouncil.org.uk) – get involved with activities to support refugees, from teaching football to teaching English
- Law Centres (www.lawcentres.org.uk) – provide administrative support for legal advisers who give free advice to people who live or work in their area

- Victim Support (www.victimsupport.co.uk) – help support witnesses and victims of crime
- The Free Representation Unit (www.fru.org.uk) – help clients in tribunals

Find out about a wide range of additional voluntary opportunities on the Chambers and Partners website (www.chambersstudent.co.uk) and www.probonouk.net.

Many law schools and most postgraduate training providers also have pro bono offices that organise relevant voluntary opportunities for students. For example, you may get an opportunity to raise legal awareness in local communities, respond to legal enquiries from the general public, or represent clients in selected tribunals. Before you sign up for a particular postgraduate training provider, see what pro bono opportunities they can offer.

Temporary/part-time work

Most universities have some sort of 'job shop' that offers part-time job vacancies both on and off campus and an office that can point you towards local voluntary opportunities. A walk around town with a simple CV may also unearth interesting options in places like shops, restaurants, cinemas and theatres.

Employment agencies offer general vacancies or jobs in a specific sector, and may be able to find you work, especially in the summer holidays. Agencies in your area may be listed in your local paper, at your careers service or online at the Recruitment and Employment Confederation's website: www.rec.uk.com. You could also try the JobCentre Plus website at www.direct.gov.uk, or your local paper.

Another approach would be to ask your friends, family and colleagues if they know anyone who will give you a job or a chance to volunteer, or you could send speculative applications to organisations where you would like to work. Some organisations recruit students at certain times of the year, such as shops and the Royal Mail at Christmas and children's holiday camps over summer.

Many students also look for overseas work during their holidays or at the end of their course, such as volunteering in an East African village or teaching English in South Korea. Find out more on the 'Explore working and studying abroad' and 'Gap Year' sections of Prospect's website (www.prospects.ac.uk). Your university careers centre will also probably have useful books such as Lonely Planet's *Gap Year Book*.

Other useful resources include the Employment4Students website (www.e4s.co.uk), the National Council for Work Experience website (www.workexperience.org) and www.summer-jobs.co.uk.

Legal employers often employ administrators, call-centre operatives, receptionists and other support staff; this may be a great way to get your foot in the door. Vacancies are often advertised in regional newspapers or through local agencies, but they may also be passed directly on to your university's careers service and your law school. You can also send speculative applications to firms in your region that specialise in your favourite area of law (find relevant firms on the solicitors online website: www.solicitors-online.com). Small and medium-sized firms are usually more open to this approach than large corporate entities. Alternatively, you could ask your contacts if they will let you shadow them for a day or two and then see if you can talk your way into a real job.

Going about getting a work experience placement isn't as daunting as it seems. Sometimes it's simply about being in the right place at the right time! For those of us who aren't that fortunate there's a few rules of thumb.

Research – where is it that you want to work, or more precisely who would want you to work for? There are tons of firms out there that are willing to take on students, after all you are going to be working for them for free!

Arrange to speak to someone at the firm, be it through a letter, an email or a phone call, or you could even drop in if you're feeling confident. In my experience the last approach has worked best. It shows you're dedicated and it's harder for firms to say no when you turn up at their door.

CV – take one with you – it is likely you will be asked for it.

Impression Dress smartly and be polite to everyone you meet, from the receptionist onwards. You never know who might put in a good word.

Finally, Good luck!

Extracurricular activities

Nothing shows your commitment more than getting involved in extracurricular activities. For example, you could join a Student Union Society and get a role on the committee, such as treasurer or events organiser. You could also help out at events organised by your department or show prospective university students around on open days. There are numerous opportunities you could get involved with both on and off campus, so be proactive and find something that you would enjoy doing, then ask if you can get involved.

Most universities have a student law society, but if yours doesn't, why not start one? Student law societies offer a range of training and networking events that will help you build up your legal knowledge and skills. If you can get into a role on the management committee then this will also look good on your CV.

Some of the activities you could get involved with, which may be organised by your student law society or by your law school, include:

- mooting/debating competitions, which involve working with a partner to present an argument;
- client interview competitions, in which students interview and counsel actors who pretend to be clients.

You could also contact your local court to ask if you can visit them and/or get some work experience, or you could ask them about opportunities to shadow a judge (called marshalling).

Mentoring

Some organisations and universities offer mentoring opportunities that put their students in touch with supportive professionals in the field they want to enter, especially people who are under-represented in the workforce, such as ethnic minorities or the disabled. This is a great way to develop confidence, to find out more about an industry, to make useful contacts and perhaps even to get your foot in the door. See what your university has to offer, and contact professional bodies in the sector you want to enter (such as your local Law Society) to find other opportunities. A number of other legal groups also offer support to students, such as the Black Lawyers Directory, which supports ethnic minority students in their first two years at university (www.onlinebld.com). You can create your own opportunities by contacting legal associations directly and asking for help; these can be found at www.infolaw.co.uk or www.venables.co.uk. The Law Society also lists special interest groups and regional law societies at www.lawsociety.org.uk.

Employer events

Many of the larger graduate recruiters offer 'taster days', training events and competitions to students who are interested in careers in that sector. For example, the Civil Service has a role-play policy game called 'Dunchester millions', and many of the larger law firms offer open days. Many firms and organisations also visit university campuses in the autumn and spring terms. Look out for employer events on your careers service website, on the Graduate Prospects website: www.prospects.ac.uk, or by looking directly on specific organisation websites.

Summer placements and other structured work experience

Any sort of structured work experience on your CV will impress employers. Many larger organisations offer summer placements, primarily for students at the end of their penultimate year at university. These placements are usually advertised seven to nine months in advance, and are very competitive to secure. Other organisations rely on speculative applications and their own networks to find recruits.

Your route will depend on the sector you want to enter. For example, if you want to get into publishing, you may have to use your contacts and send out speculative applications or get any work in a role that is relevant (such as proof-reading or working in a bookshop), whereas if you want to work in accountancy, you may focus on organised placement opportunities.

Here are a few ways of finding interesting placement options:

- Look directly on organisation websites.
- Visit the vacancies page on your careers service website.
- Look up work-experience jobs directories available at your careers service.
- Identify interesting firms which offer graduate training programmes and look at their websites to see what placement opportunities they provide (you can find graduate training programmes on www.prospects.ac.uk and in graduate jobs directories available from your university's careers service).
- Apply speculatively to organisations you want to work for and ask your contacts for help.
- Look up industry-specific websites that may have opportunities, such as Skillset at www.skillset.org (the industry body that supports skills and training for creative media industries in the UK). You can find useful links for each sector on the Graduate Prospects website at www.prospects.ac.uk.

Your university may also offer structured projects for students over the summer months; ask about this at your careers service. One national organisation that offers organised summer projects is Shell STEP (www.shellstep.org.uk). Other interesting options are the business internship programme in New York organised by the Mountbatten Institute (find out more on www.mountbatten.org), and the SEO Internship Programmes in investment banking, technology and corporate law (see www.seo-london.org).

Formal legal vacation schemes

Work placements at law firms are an invaluable opportunity to get first-hand experience of being a lawyer and to confirm your career decision. They are also a great way to build a relationship with an employer and maybe even get a training contract.

Most medium and large commercial/corporate firms run paid summer placements for students. Law students are traditionally welcomed in the summer recess at the end of their penultimate year at university, whilst non-law students are usually accepted in the summer months at the end of their degrees, ie before they start their GDL. However, every firm will have its own recruitment procedures, and candidates may well be considered at other times; for example, law graduates may be taken on at the end of their degrees. During these placements, students get a chance to do some real legal work, meet trainees, associates and partners and join in on a range of social events.

Many firms also run short placements over the Christmas or Easter period that may be open to a wide range of university students or even students on their GDL or LPC.

Students could also look for placements in organisations relevant to the type of law they want to practise; for example, students who want to work in the corporate sector may want to get some work experience in a financial institution, whilst future public lawyers or barristers may want to undergo a traineeship with the European Union. If you want to further your career in a smaller public legal services firm, where structured placements are few and far between, you may have to look for placements in larger firms which most closely match your plans, or send speculative applications and get help from your contacts to secure some sort of unstructured work experience at a local firm. Local Crown Prosecution Service offices also offer work experience opportunities to suitable candidates who send in their CVs.

Employers often use summer placements to identify excellent training contract candidates, so the application process is very competitive. Placements are usually advertised from around November in the year before they take place, and the early bird often catches the worm. Placements at the larger law firms are listed on the Law Careers.Net website at www. lawcareers.net and the Chambers and Partners website at www.chambersstudent.co.uk. They are also listed in hard copy in the 'Training contract and pupillage handbook' and the 'Student's guide to careers in the law' which you can pick up from your careers service during the autumn term.

You should carefully identify the opportunities that most closely match your career aspirations and produce high quality applications that clearly demonstrate your commitment, skills and experience.

Mini-pupilages at barristers' chambers

Mini-pupillages are short-term work experience opportunities at barristers' chambers which usually last for a week or two and are sometimes formally assessed. They are a valuable opportunity to shadow barristers in their day-to-day activities and build a relationship with individual barristers and sets of chambers. You can apply for as many mini-pupillages as you like. Find advertised vacancies on the Law Careers.Net and Chambers and Partners websites listed above or apply speculatively to local sets of chambers. Find local chambers at www. legalhub.co.uk.

Activity Identify some specific work experience opportunities you can get involved in during your studies:

Voluntary work

....

....

Temporary/part-time work

....

....

Extracurricular activities

....

....

Employer events

....

....

Formal placements/mini-pupillages

....

....

9.5 FURTHER STUDY

Is it right for me?

Further study may develop your skills, enhance your employability, and be very fulfilling, but it can also be a boring, expensive, and a waste of time!

The best reasons to take up further study are:

- You enjoy the subject.
- It is a necessary step to get into the career of your choice.
- You have researched your career fully and have found a course that will definitely enhance your opportunities.
- You want to develop a specific skill (such as learning a certain type of software) that you enjoy or will help you get into your chosen career.

Other motivations that may not be so good are:

- You have no idea what you want to do after university so you want to delay the inevitable (the year or so will probably pass by very quickly and you will still be undecided, but even deeper in debt!).

The career planning process

- You have a vague idea that any further study will improve your career chances (this is often not true).
- You just want an excuse not to leave the place where you have studied or are too afraid to go out into the big bad world (further study will probably be a very expensive way of delaying the inevitable).
- Your tutor wants you to do a PhD in his or her department (he or she may get an excellent researcher, but is it right for you?).

If you are considering taking up further study, carefully assess your motivations, research the courses on offer and the opportunities that will be presented before you make your decision, and try to get some objective, impartial advice (for example, speak to a careers adviser).

What are your options?

- **Taught masters (Master of Arts/Science)**
These are generally one year (or two year part-time) taught courses. Students tend to either focus on an area of their bachelor degree that they enjoyed, or a new subject where they can use the skills they have gained to prepare for a particular career, for example in journalism or IT.

- **Masters in business administration (MBA)**
Executive education primarily tailored for graduates who already have some experience in the workforce and want to develop their careers in management.

- **Masters by research (MRes)**
These courses combine a taught course with intensive training in research methodology, and are often a precursor to a career in research.

- **Doctor of Philosophy (PhD)**
PhDs take three years or more to complete and are usually the first step to a career in research. They involve new research in a specific field resulting in a thesis and an oral exam (viva). New route PhDs combine research with discipline-specific and generic training in a wide range of subjects including law.

- **Vocational courses**
Many careers, such as teaching, social work and becoming a solicitor, barrister or legal executive, require you to undertake specific diplomas, certificates, masters or PhDs. These courses may be subsidised, or you may receive a grant (but not always) and usually have some sort of central application procedure.

- **Short courses**
Learn specific skills linked to the sector you want to enter such as web authoring software or bookkeeping.

Finding and choosing a course

You can find thousands of courses listed at Graduate Prospects' dedicated further education website: www.prospects.ac.uk/links/postgrad or at www.findamasters.com/www.findaPhD.com. Vocational courses tend to have their own central application procedures, such as initial teacher training courses that are coordinated by the Graduate Teacher Training Agency at www.gttr.ac.uk.

The factors to consider when choosing a course are:

- Does the course cover what you want to study?
- Is the course any good?
- Is the course well regarded?
- Will you get help with your career?
- Does the teaching style (and/or research support) suit you?
- Does the course attract funding?
- Do you want to live in that area?

Costs and funding

Courses typically cost between £3,000 and £10,000 a year upfront (for UK and European Union students). Living expenses cost upwards of £13,000 a year in London and about £10,000 everywhere else in the country. Therefore, further study can be a very expensive option and should be researched thoroughly. You should carefully consider whether the monetary outlay matches the benefits gained from the course.

Most people pay for their own postgraduate study, but some financial support may be available from a range of sources as follows:

- *The Research Councils* – the government-funded agencies responsible for supporting research in the UK (contact the course provider to see if the course you are interested in attracts Research Council funding)
- *Institutional funding and employment* (contact the course provider)
- *Bursaries and grants* – these are usually offered for vocational courses such as teaching or social work (contact the course provider or research the course on www.prospects.ac.uk/links/postgrad)
- *Charities, foundations and trusts* (look up the Association of Charitable Foundations' website at www.acf.org.uk or 'Funderfinder' at www.funderfinder.org.uk)
- *Loans* (find out about Career Development Loans on the Government's website: www.direct.gov.uk)

When to apply

Courses have different deadlines, but you should be prepared to apply well in advance. Applications for many postgraduate courses open in the autumn in the year before the course starts, and places can fill up pretty quickly.

The Graduate Diploma in Law (GDL)

The GDL, often called a Common Professional Exam (CPE) or Postgraduate Diploma in Law (PgDL), is a postgraduate diploma that is equivalent to a law degree. It is the course you need to take if you want to become a solicitor or barrister but have a non-law qualifying degree (or qualifications/experience deemed to be equivalent to a non-law qualifying degree by the SRA). It is offered by a large number of training providers across the UK (a full list can be accessed at www.lawcabs.ac.uk). The course is aimed primarily at non-law graduates from UK and Irish universities; however, students who have studied law as part of a non-qualifying law degree may be able to get exemptions from parts of the GDL by applying to the Solicitors Regulation Authority or the Bar Council before they start their course. The course comprises study into the so-called seven foundations of legal knowledge, which are land law, the European Union, equity and trusts, tort, contract, crime and public law. You can study for the GDL full time for a year, part time for two years (during the day/evening or weekends), or even from home. Find out which modes of study are offered and where on www.lawcareers.net.

Most people pay their own way, but many of the larger graduate recruiters will pay for your course fees and even provide your living expenses if they have already given you a training contract. If you plan on being a barrister, you may also be able to secure funding from an Inn of Court (see the funding section for the BPTC). Applications for part-time and distance education courses study should be made directly to the institution. Applications for full-time courses need to be made through the Central Applications Board (CAB) at www.

lawcabs.ac.uk. Applications received by the beginning of February in the year the course starts are usually considered immediately, and offers are sent out at the beginning of March. Applications received after this date will be considered in early April, and all subsequent applications are considered by institutions immediately after they are received. Refer to www.lawcabs.ac.uk to check the exact timetable for applications in the year you want to study. All applications are considered by the individual institutions, not the CAB. In your applications, course providers expect you to demonstrate why you have chosen law as a career and your commitment to the course.

A 2.2 will probably not hold you back from getting onto a GDL course, but it will make it difficult (though certainly not impossible) to secure a training contract.

The Legal Practice Course (LPC)

The LPC is the vocational stage of training to be a solicitor that is designed to enhance students' practical knowledge and skills. A full list of providers can be found at www.lawcabs. ac.uk. Most students undertake an LPC after they have gained a qualifying law degree (within the last seven years) or a GDL, and complete this stage of training before they embark on a training contract.

The LPC incorporates the following elements:

- *The foundations of legal practice* comprising ethics, skills, taxation, trusts and tax planning, principles of EU law and probate and administration of estates
- *Compulsory subjects* comprising conveyancing, business law and practice, litigation and accounts
- *Optional subjects* as provided by your course provider
- *Skills* – legal research, drafting, interviewing, negotiating and advocacy

The compulsory and basic elements of practice on the LPC have recently been disengaged from the optional elements so that LPCs can now be undertaken in two freestanding stages, which can be taken at more than one provider. The SRA hopes this development will allow students to start their training contracts after simply completing the compulsory elements of the LPC, but most firms are currently hesitant to adapt to these changes.

Like the GDL, you can study for the LPC full time for a year, part time for two years (during the day/evening or weekends), or even from home. Find out which modes of study are offered and where on www.lawcareers.net. Before choosing a course, look at the profiles of LPC courses compiled by the SRA (www.sra.org.uk), and visit the college. LPC providers charge fees from about £6,000 to over £11,000. If cost is a major consideration, you can find out the exact fees for each institution on the Law CareersNet website at www.lawcareers.net.

As with the GDL, some LPC students secure sponsorships from future employers if they start their course having already arranged a training contract, but most students have to foot the bill themselves, or draw funds from the bank of mum and dad. A comprehensive list of specific legal funding options is published on the Chambers and Partners Website – www. chambersstudent.co.uk.

Applications for part-time and distance education courses study should be made directly to the institution. Applications for full-time courses need to be made through the Central

Applications Board (CAB) at www.lawcabs.ac.uk. Applications received by the beginning of December (along with references) in the year before the course starts are usually considered immediately, applications received from December to March are considered at the end of March, and all subsequent applications are considered by institutions as and when they are received. Check on www.lawcabs.ac.uk for the exact timetable for applications in the year you want to study. All applications are considered by the institutions, not the CAB.

As with the GDL, a 2.2 will probably not hold you back from getting onto an LPC course, but it will make it difficult (though not impossible) to secure a training contract.

The Bar Professional Training Course (BPTC)

The BPTC has recently replaced the Bar Vocational Course as the second stage of training to be a barrister. The course builds on the legal knowledge and skills developed during a qualifying law degree or GDL and prepares students for a career at the Bar. Like the LPC, the course takes one year to undertake (two years part time). Fewer than 10 course providers are dotted around the UK (find them on the Bar Standard Board's website at www.barstandards-board.org.uk).

The skills you learn include casework skills, legal research and advocacy; the knowledge elements of the course include civil litigation and remedies, criminal litigation and sentencing and evidence.

The BPTC is currently in a state of flux. The new elements which are due to be incorporated are an aptitude test on entry (probably only to be included on a voluntary basis), a new syllabus and a restriction on entry to graduates with a minimum 2:1 grade. Up-to-date details of the new course can be found at www.lawcareers.net.

BPTC providers charge fees up to about £14,000. You can find out the exact fees for each institution on the Bar Standards Board's website. Chambers and Partners provide useful reports on each of the BPTC training providers on www.chambersstudent.co.uk.

Substantial scholarships for students on the GDL and BPTC are provided by four historical organisations known as the Inns of Court. These are Inner Temple (www.innertemple.org.uk), Middle Temple (www.middletemple.org.uk), Grays Inn (www.graysinn.org.uk) and Lincoln's Inn (www.lincolnsinn.org.uk). You must join one of these Inns by the end of May to be entitled to start a BPTC in September.

BPTC applications are made through the Bar Council's central applications system at www.barprofessionaltraining.org.uk. The first round of applications usually opens in October and closes in January. Once applications have been considered, offers are usually made in early March. Unsuccessful applications and late applications are then put in a clearing pool in early April and considered by the course providers.

Activity Use the links from this section to identify some specific postgraduate courses related to the careers you are considering, and complete the following table:

Possible career options	Relevant postgraduate courses	Where you would like to study	When you need to apply	What the application entails

9.6 APPLICATIONS AND INTERVIEWS

What employers look for

Success in any field is down to three things – your skills, commitment and knowledge. Whether you want to be a football player, a politician or a lawyer, you will only succeed if you have the ability to do the job, you want to do it and you know what you're doing. Therefore, employers look for candidates who excel in each of these three areas, as shown below.

As the diagram shows, graduate employers often rate skills and commitment above knowledge because they think that if you have the right potential and attitude then you will soon learn what's required.

The career planning process

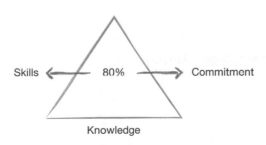

What employers look for

Proving your skills

Employers expect you to prove you have the skills they require; these will be explicit skills linked to the specific role (such as an ability to write websites if you want to go into digital marketing) and transferable skills which are used in a number of roles (such as commercial awareness and teamwork).

Many students and graduates find it very difficult to demonstrate that they have the skills required in a position, even though they clearly have them. To prove you have a skill you need to demonstrate two things:

- A specific (not a general) example of *when* you have performed the skill to a high level. For example, you may have demonstrated teamwork skills supporting a particular customer in your part-time job, organising a specific event for your student society or by motivating a particular colleague in a sporting activity. Try to identify experiences from every walk of your life, but focus on examples from your work experience.
- *How* you demonstrate the skill well. For example, you may have demonstrated your teamwork skills by listening to colleagues, supporting them and taking personal responsibility, or you may have demonstrated organisation skills by planning carefully, setting yourself strict targets and regularly assessing your progress.

It can be very difficult to reflect on your skills in this way, especially if you have never tried it before, but persevere because this is the easiest way to add value to your applications and stand out from the crowd. Employers who see where, when and how you have demonstrated the skills they require are very quickly going to invite you in for an interview. In the table below, revisit the skills exercise shown earlier in this chapter, and try to identify specific examples of when and how you have demonstrated some of the key transferable skills required by employers.

Proving your commitment

Many applicants think that they can pretend that they've always wanted a particular role, even if they've never even given it thought, but their applications are usually shallow and unconvincing. In order to succeed in your applications, you need to demonstrate that you have:

- done your research about the career, the industry, the role and the organisation;
- carefully assessed that the position suits your skills, interests and motivations;
- gone out of your way to get some experience to confirm your career decisions.

Proving your knowledge

Make sure you understand any technical aspects of the job you're applying for, such as the National Curriculum if you want to be a teacher, or an understanding of relevant recent legislation if you want to be an employment lawyer.

Transferable skills required by employers	What these skills involve	Specific examples of *when* and *how* you have demonstrated each of these skills
Commercial awareness	Commercial awareness is an appreciation of the business and financial elements that affect a particular organisation and how you can influence them. Some things to consider are the economy, the sector in which the organisation operates, competitors and marketing priorities.	*For example, by boosting sales in your part-time job.*
Teamwork	Teamwork is all about effective collaboration that enables a group of individuals to perform at a high level. It revolves around a balance of contributions based on people's abilities, hard work, coordination, communication, support and respect.	*For example, by supporting a struggling colleague in a university project.*
Communication	Good communication is a two-way process involving unambiguous transmission of messages and clear reception. Therefore, it revolves around: ● effective presentation including an ability to tailor information to the needs of the audience; ● good active listening skills, such as checking that you understand someone correctly.	*For example, by listening to clients in a professional role and addressing their needs.*
Initiative	Welcoming personal responsibility for taking actions, solving problems and meeting targets, and logically finding solutions.	*For example, by proactively developing more efficient procedures at work.*
Planning and organisation	Planning and organisation involves focusing on everything that's required to achieve a goal and ensuring that you deliver on time and on budget. Planning skills embrace a clear vision, an ability to create a realistic action plan and self-management. Organisation skills include a capacity to research, prioritise, keep records and manage time.	*For example, by successfully completing a complicated project on time in your part-time job.*
Computer literacy	● The ability to use common word processing programmes, spreadsheets and databases, to surf the web and use common email packages. ● The confidence to adopt new hardware and software.	*For example, by quickly learning new technology during a hobby.*

What makes a good CV?

Good CVs are marketing tools which briefly demonstrate that you have the specific skills required by an employer. They are your shop window advertising designed to catch the attention of recruiters and persuade them to give you an interview.

No two jobs or organisations require exactly the same skills, so you should change your CV each time you send it. For example, a bar job may require an ability to change a barrel of beer and good communication skills, whereas a vacancy as a legal executive may demand attention to detail and good legal skills in a specific field. It's hard to imagine a single CV that could simultaneously prove that a person has the attributes required in both of these roles! Even similar firms offering comparable roles will require slightly different attributes. If you take time to spot exactly the requirements for each post, and amend your CV appropriately, you will soon stand out from the crowd.

When to use a CV

Use a CV as part of your application when asked to do so by an employer. It is also useful to have it ready at careers fairs and events and at networking opportunities. If the CV is not targeted at a specific organisation, try to focus it on the industry you are interested in pursuing.

What to include

Your personal details

Include your email address, home address and phone numbers, but not your age, date of birth or national insurance number (unless they have been specifically requested). If you go home in the holidays, provide both your home and term-time addresses and the dates when you will be at each. Non-EU nationals allowed to work in the region should include their nationality and state that they have permission to work in the UK.

Personal profile/career objective (optional)

Personal profiles are short summaries of a candidate's relevant experience and therefore promote key skills and experience. Career objectives are brief statements that link a candidate's ambition to a specific role. They are usually unnecessary if you have written a convincing cover letter, but if you want to re-emphasise some element of your experience or career plans, make sure what you write is specifically related to the organisation and the role you are going for, and is written in the third person (eg describe yourself as a 'law graduate' rather than 'I'). For example, you could write:

> 'Recent law graduate with excellent grades and experience at two leading corporate firms seeking a training contract in a well respected local Birmingham firm that specialises in general commercial and corporate work.'

A summary of your education

Include the following:

- Details of where and when you went to school, college and university and what you studied, but you may want to summarise all your GCSEs (see example CVs).
- Your expected grades/actual grades (if they are very poor you may decide not to include them).
- An outline of what you studied (if relevant to the job you're going for).

A summary of your work experience

Include all your work history including paid work, voluntary experience and even any opportunities you have had to shadow someone at work. Outline the duties you performed in each of your roles that are relevant to the post you are targeting. If you have a lot of work experience, you may want to break this section up into two smaller sub-categories such as 'Relevant work experience' and 'Additional work experience'. If you are going for a legal job, you could have a section entitled 'Legal work experience'.

Positions of responsibility/achievements (include at your discretion)

Employers are impressed by candidates who have the commitment to succeed in a specific field outside their degree studies. If you have things to shout about, for example if you are the Secretary of the Student Law Society or you have gained an award for volunteering in your community, list them in this section, and outline your relevant achievements.

Additional skills

Outline any extra relevant skills that you have not covered elsewhere in your CV, such as IT skills, foreign language ability or a driving licence.

Your interests

List your interests that show you in the best possible light, such as those in which you have to socialise with others, for example in a rugby club, or where you have been ambitious and outgoing, such as during your overseas travel.

Details of your referees

Provide details of your referees or a statement indicating that you will provide the details on request. Include the address, email address and phone numbers for one academic referee and one professional referee (such as your supervisor at work).

Other possible sections

Your CV is your own personal marketing tool so you can include any sections you want; you don't have to copy everyone else! For example, you could have a section on 'Pro bono work', 'Legal interests' or 'Additional legal qualifications'.

Some general rules

The wonderful advantage of a CV is that you can tailor it to emphasise your best qualities and lessen the impact of your weaknesses, but there are some general rules, and these are outlined below:

- Your CV should be no more than two pages in length, even if you have years of experience, and it should be typed, well-formatted and the dates should be easy to see.

- All entries should be in reverse chronological order, ie the most recent experiences should be placed first as they are more relevant.
- You should promote yourself in the best possible light, but you should not be dishonest.
- Use a readable font size.
- Use short paragraphs (3/4 lines max) and break up long paragraphs using bullet points.
- Allocate space according to the importance of the information (eg your GCSEs should take up a lot less space than your degree).
- Leave plenty of white space, ie do not try to squeeze in as many words as possible.

Use positive words

Make sure you make the most of your achievements by describing them using positive, active words such as those listed below:

ability	calculate	dedicated	efficient	friendly	judgement
accomplished	can-do	demonstrate	empathy	fresh	keen
achieving	capacity	dependable	encourage	generate	knowledgeable
accountable	careful	design	energetic	goals	launched
accurate	caring	determined	enthusiastic	guide	leadership
acknowledged	clearly	develop	enquiring	happily	lively
actively	collegiate	devise	ensure	hardworking	logical
adaptable	committed	devoted	enterprising	help	maintain
advanced	composed	diligent	establish	highly	manage
ambitious	comprehensive	diplomatic	excel	honest	mature
amenable	concise	determined	experienced	implemented	motivated
analysed	conduct	diligent	expertise	improve	negotiate
analytical	coordinate	discerning	evaluate	independently	nurture
approachable	considerate	discipline	explain	influence	objective
appreciative	confident	discover	faculty	initiative	observe
aptitude	cooperative	dynamic	flexible	innovative	open
articulate	create	eager	fluent	inspire	opportunity
assemble	creative	edit	focused	interested	
assist	decisive	effectively	form	intuitive	

You should also identify key words in the personal specification for the role and use them in your CV. For example, if the job description uses the word 'innovative' three times, you should also use it three times!

Use short sentences

In order to promote yourself in the best possible light, you need to outline your experience and sell your skills using short punchy statements as demonstrated below:

'Liaised closely with colleagues to restructure the manufacturing process, resulting in a record increase in productivity.'

'Demonstrated a strong ability to lead a team through good organisation, encouragement and hard work.'

CV styles

Although you can use any style you want in a CV, there are two types that most students and graduates use – the traditional/chronological CV and the skills-based CV. Both types of CV should be designed to prove that you have the appropriate skills for the role you are targeting. The traditional CV directly links each of your experiences to the skills you want to promote, whilst the skills-based CV briefly lists all your experiences and then has a separate skills profile that demonstrates your skills from all walks of your life. An example of each type of CV is shown below.

Four steps to constructing your CV

Step 1: Identify the skills required

Start out by identifying exactly what skills are required in the job you're going for:

- Carefully read the job advert, the job description and the selection criteria (if they are provided).
- Look on the organisation's website.
- Talk to employers at careers fairs and events, and ask them what skills they look for.
- Research the employer profiles at your careers service and www.prospects.ac.uk.
- Use your contacts to get in touch with someone at the organisation (or a similar organisation).
- Look up application-related blogs (such as www.thestudentroom.co.uk/www.wikijob.co.uk) and see what help you can get. You could also Google phrases like 'KPMG application' or 'army interview', and see what comes up.

Activity Find a graduate-level vacancy in the sector you want to enter, and use the sources of information above to identify the specific skills that are required:

Vacancy details   The skills required

....

....

....

....

....

....

....

....

....

....

....

....

Step 2: Identify when and how you have demonstrated the relevant skills

Remember to identify specific examples and outline how you have personally demonstrated each skill to a high level.

Step 3: Choose a CV style

Choose a style (traditional or skills-based) that best relates your skills and experience for the specific role. Students with extensive experience tend to prefer the chronological CV.

Step 4: Put pen to paper and create a masterpiece

Put together an effective marketing document that clearly outlines where, when and how you have demonstrated the skills required in the job you're going for.

Checking your work

Once you have finished your CV, use the following checklist to check your work:

- Have you outlined specific examples of *where and when* you have demonstrated the skills required in the specific role?
- Have you outlined *how* you have demonstrated each of the required skills to a high level?
- Have you used positive action words and key words from the personal specification?
- Have you clearly highlighted the main points?
- Have you checked the spelling and grammar?
- Are the dates easy to see?
- Is your CV short (2 pages), attractive and easy to read?
- Have you whetted the reader's appetite?

The one-minute test

One way to make sure that you have targeted your CV appropriately is to ask a friend to look at it for one minute and tell you what skills you are trying to prove. If he or she identifies the correct skills then you know that you are on the right track.

Example CVs

Two example CVs are shown on the following pages.

Traditional CV

A traditional CV for a law undergraduate aimed at a non-law job requiring the following skills: analysis, research, organisation, flexibility, customer service, teamwork, working under pressure and working with a wide range of people.

Clear, attractive font

John Stonchouse

07367 215578

j.stonehouse555@hotmail.com

Home Address:	18 Nunsome Road London NW9 8EP	**Term address**: (From October 10)	23 Tin Crescent Derby DE24 4YH
Tel:	020 8353 6832	**Tel:**	01332 642 347

Address with dates if you go home in the holidays

EDUCATION

Highlight the key points

2009–present University of North Derby, LLB (2:1 expected)

Relevant modules

Identify elements of your degree that are relevant to the job you're going for

- Legal skills (including teamwork, organisation and drafting correspondence)
- Legal research (including library and online research and statistical analysis)

Skills gained

Outline how, when and where you have demonstrated the skills required

Research: Demonstrated the capacity to use a wide range of resources including web-based resources, library books/periodicals and obscure texts, and the ability to check findings thoroughly using more than one source of information.

Teamwork: Successfully completed first-year group project by working closely with team colleagues, demonstrating an ability to listen, sharing ideas positively and providing encouragement, resulting in the highest grade achieved for that module (82%).

Allocate space according to the importance of your qualifications (more for your degree than your A-levels)

2003–2009 Camden School for Boys, Kentish Town, London
A levels: History (A), Geography (B), Maths (B)
GCSEs: 8 subjects at grade B or above, including English Language and Maths

WORK EXPERIENCE

Summer 2008 Management Assistant: Nosco Superstores Head Office, London

Try to get your key work experience on the first page

Job description: Coordinated a small research project team looking at branding for local stores. Researched the local market trends for teenagers and young students to see how Nosco could target its promotions more effectively.

Briefly and positively relate your work experience to the skills required

Skills gained

Organisation: Demonstrated an ability to plan carefully, organise resources efficiently and meet deadlines, resulting in a well-received report that has become a national blueprint for student research projects.

Analysis: Conducted and collated research from a range of sources to develop an integrated new marketing strategy resulting in a project that has markedly improved Nosco's promotions in the area.

Try to get the key skills on the first page

Customer service: The foundations of success in this project were the ability to listen to customers, to respect their choices, and to address their needs.

Oct 2007–June 2008 Volunteer with Care Volunteers, North London

Job description: Supported a wide range of community projects including shopping for the elderly and cleaning up a local council estate.

Skills gained

Flexibility: This was an extremely challenging, yet fulfilling role in which every activity required a new set of skills. Successfully completed each task by working hard, being open to ideas and listening to advice.

Working under pressure: Demonstrated an ability to work with a wide range of people and a thick skin when the going got tough.

Oct 2007–Sep 2009 Sales Assistant: Nosco Superstores, Camden, London

• Assisted customers in a fast-paced, pressured environment
• Dealt calmly and sympathetically with customer complaints
• Promoted to supervisor in charge of customer relations

Summer 2007 Usher: ACD Cinemas, Camden, London

• Managed the flow of customers
• Ensured the safety of patrons, including the elderly and the disabled

POSITIONS OF RESPONSIBILITY

Vice President, University Arts Society: Maintaining membership and organising new events and activities.

Captain, University Rugby Club: Rejuvenated the university's rugby club by increasing the membership and organising a tour of Ireland where we even managed to win a match.

INTERESTS AND ACTIVITIES

Travel: Backpacked across India during the summer holidays before university, developing an understanding of different cultures.

Sport: Play rugby and football and have learned how to get the best out of a team.

ADDITIONAL SKILLS

Good knowledge of Word, Excel, spreadsheets and databases
Clean driving licence
Basic German

REFEREES

Academic
Dr B. E. Learned
Personal Tutor
School of Law
The University of North Derby
Stamford Street
Derby DE1 2SF
01332 642 432
learned@nderby.ac.uk

Professional
Mr M. Manager
Director
Brand Research
Nosco Superstores
Head Office
London W1 7PT
0208 654 3456
manager@noscos.co.uk

Make sure dates are easy to see

No need to go into detail for older/less relevant jobs

Use short punchy statements and positive action words

Optional section

Relate your positions of responsibility and interests to the skills required

Outline any other relevant skills you may have which are not addressed in the personal specification

Include all contact details and make sure you've asked your referees for permission before submitting their details

Skills-based CV

A speculative, skills-based CV for an undergraduate targeting work experience at a regional commercial firm of solicitors requiring the following skills: written communication, verbal communication, interpersonal skills, organisation, legal research skills, flexibility and commercial awareness.

Xang Yu
Personal details

Make sure your headings are clear and easy to see

Address: 23 Feast Road
Plymouth PL4 3DF

Nationality: British / Singapore
Permitted to work in the UK

If you were born overseas make it clear that you have permission to work in the UK (if you have)

Tel: 01752 675 398

Mobile: 07968 574 647

Email Yu@devon.ac.uk

Education & Qualifications

2008 – Present: University of Devon, predicted grade 1st / 2:1

Completed second year modules

Career Development: 72%   EU Law: 69%
Criminal Law: 62%   Legal Research: 68%

Legal employers usually expect you to include your grades if you are still studying for your degree

First year modules

Contract Law: 66%   Legal History: 65%
English Legal System: 62%   Legal Skills: 62%
Public Law: 71%   Practical Legal Skills: 59%

Good grades at university demonstrate intellectual ability, commitment and a good understanding of black letter law.

2006 – 2008: Truro College of Further Education, Devon
A-levels: Politics (B), History (A), Mathematics (B)

2002 – 2006: St. Barnabus High School, Singapore
7 GCSE O-levels (including Maths and English)

The top page should briefly and positively outline your key experiences and achievements

Legal Work Experience

If you have legal work experience why not include a 'Legal work experience' section?

Summer 2008: General assistant, Edgar, Allen and Poe Solicitors, Truro, Devon
Duties included: Drafting letters, communicating with clients, legal research, conducting environmental searches and general administrative duties such as filing, printing, and IT support.

Summer 2007: Work experience, Edgar, Allen and Poe Solicitors, Truro, Devon
Duties included: Shadowing partners and fee earners and providing administrative support on a number of high profile cases.

Avoid outlining your key skills here as you have a skills profile overleaf

Additional Work Experience

9/2007-present: Waitress, Singha Restaurant, Truro, Devon
Duties include: General waiting duties and recently promoted into a management position in charge of part-time staff and customer care.

Extracurricular activities
I currently represent the University of Devon at a range of local and national mooting events and am the Vice President of the Student Law Society.

Skills profile

Use positive words and short, punchy sentences

Provide examples from your work experience, your education and your interests/ extracurricular activities

Outline **how** you have demonstrated the relevant skills to a high level

Written communication

Good academic grades demonstrate my capacity to effectively describe complicated legal principles and precedent. At Edgar, Allen and Poe Solicitors I was praised for my ability to quickly and accurately draft letters for clients.

Verbal communication

Always demonstrate an ability to listen empathically, share ideas positively and take instructions. For example, at Edgar Allen and Poe Solicitors I was regularly asked to telephone clients to elicit information. On these occasions I carefully listened to instructions from my manager and spoke in a friendly and reassuring tone to clients to find exactly what I needed to know. I can also speak two foreign languages: Chinese and Malay.

Interpersonal skills

I am positive, outgoing and friendly and enjoy working with a wide range of people. Since I arrived at university I have gone out of my way to make friends and build networks with legal employers. For example, I currently work closely with a mooting partner from a very different cultural background with whom I have carefully built rapport and confidence, resulting in a very positive relationship and a good record in competitions.

Organisation

I currently use excellent organisation skills to juggle a part-time job with my degree studies and extracurricular activities. My degree is currently my most important commitment so, every month, I plan the time I need to devote to my studies, assess my progress and consistently gain good grades.

Legal research

Each skill should be outlined in no more than six lines

Throughout my degree I have demonstrated a strong ability to research primary and secondary sources of law, such as Acts of Parliament, statutory instruments and Halsbury's Statutes. Furthermore, I am able to find authoritative legal commentaries and EU cases and legislation, and can use the major online legal databases including Lawtel, Westlaw and LexisLibrary.

Flexibility

I enjoy learning new skills. For example, as Vice President of the University of Devon Student Law Society, I have organised a range of events that have required close liaison with employers and professional bodies. At first this was daunting, but I soon learnt to ask for help, work hard and reflect upon my performance in order to improve, and this year I am organising the biggest law fair the university has ever seen.

Commercial awareness

Having worked at a commercial firm in a competitive market I appreciate the need to constantly build business and promote new services to existing clients. At Edgar, Allen and Poe Solicitors I enjoyed finding ways to network with local businesses and regularly attended the local Chamber of Commerce.

Additional skills

Driving licence
Confidence with Word, Excel, Access and various legal databases

Make sure you address every skill required in the specific job you're going for

References

Available upon request

Supply contact details for your referees unless you have a good reason for withholding them

Application forms

Employers use application forms so they can easily and fairly assess the skills, knowledge and commitment of a large number of applicants. The questions are designed in such a way as to encourage applicants to focus on the attributes required in the role, so they are usually more revealing than CVs.

Before putting pen to paper, confirm with yourself why you want the job, in other words research the role and assess how it suits your specific skills, interests and motivations. The more confident you are about why you want that specific job and why you are suited to it, the more chance you have of proving this in your application.

Recruiters tend to ask questions about your contact details, qualifications, experience, skills, knowledge, interests and motivations, and usually give you just a few hundred words to provide your answers. You should use short, punchy sentences, positive words and key words from the personal specification and avoid too much scene setting. Most applications fail because of poor spelling and grammar and because the questions are poorly answered – don't fall into this trap.

Questions about your qualifications and experience

These questions focus on your studies and your duties throughout your work experience. You should complete these sections with reference to the job you are going for. For example, if you are going for a job as a teaching assistant, you should relate your education and work experience to the skills you would need as a teacher.

Questions about your commitment

Employers often test your commitment through direct questions about why you have chosen the career/role. Some common questions are as follows:

- Why have you chosen xxx as a career?
- Why have you applied for this role?
- What attracts you to our firm?

Your answers to these questions should demonstrate that you have done your research, you have carefully assessed that the specific role suits you, and your experience has confirmed your decision. You should always keep to the word limit. Two examples are shown below:

Clarify exactly what they are asking (in this case – why do you want to work at Hambles and what attracts you to its training programme?)

Demonstrate that you have done your research

Question: Why do you want to train at Hambles? (200 words)

Answer: I want to train at Hambles because my skills are eminently related to your firm, and I am attracted by the exciting range of opportunities available within your progressive training programme. This interest was fired when I spoke to your partner Stephen Hughes when he recently visited Sussex University.

My relevant skills include a strong intellect, good communication skills and strong commercial awareness, which I demonstrated at a city firm last summer, thus confirming that I had chosen the right career path.

The opportunities that attract me about Hambles are:

- Your 'balanced growth potential' mission statement that directly links domestic growth to international strategy

- Your dynamic structure that efficiently focuses resources on areas of growth
- Your commitment to the individual, as shown by gaining Lawyer2C's 'employer of the year' award

Your training programme catches my attention because it offers a flexible attitude on seats according to the personal interests and needs of trainees and because it will develop my skills to pursue a corporate career at a leading international firm. As recently noted by Law magazine: 'Hambles puts the needs of its trainees first and prepares them for the rigours of a corporate legal career.'

Question: Why do you want to train to be a chartered accountant and what attracts you about the area of accounting you have chosen? (150 words)

Answer: I want to be a chartered accountant because I hope to use my analysis, communication and project management skills in a client-focused business setting, and want a career that is constantly challenging. At Rafik and Company last year I enjoyed working closely with a local firm and enjoyed developing some significant strategies to minimise its tax burden.

I want to train in your tax service line because I would greatly enjoy keeping up to date with tax policies and procedures and using my creative problem-solving skills to ensure that the organisations I represent stay one step ahead. I am also impressed by the range of opportunities offered within this service line at your firm, in particular the chance to support not-for-profit companies, charities and overseas organisations. Furthermore, I am excited about the prospect of working within your renowned 'green tax' consultancy arm.

Questions about your skills

Questions about your skills are central to the recruitment process. These questions are often long and complicated, for example, a typical question might be: 'Tell us about a time you had trouble communicating an idea to someone else. What were you trying to explain and how did you eventually get your point across?' Your answers to these questions are key to your chances of success, but they are often answered very poorly.

How to answer these questions

In order to prove a specific skill on your application form, you should focus on *how* you have demonstrated the skill well, not just on what you have done. For example, if you are asked to give an example of working in a team, outline how you have personally worked well with the other members in a team (for example, you may have listened empathically, encouraged colleagues and taken individual responsibility). You should use recent and relevant examples from every area of your life, ie your work experience, your education and your extracurricular activities/interests, and you should stress your personal contribution. One way of answering these questions is to use the CAR method outlined below.

The Context, Action, Result (CAR) method for answering skills-based questions

Context (10% of your answer) – Briefly outline the situation and your task

Action (80% of your answer) – Outline in detail how you personally demonstrated the required skill

Result (10% of your answer) – Show how your input led to a successful outcome

Some good answers to skills-based questions using the CAR method are set out below.

Question: Tell us about a time when you have worked as a member of a team. Describe your personal contribution and how you faced any problems that arose (150 words).

Answer: I worked as part of a close-knit team responsible for designing a new sales strategy during my work experience at Meters Insurance last summer.

At the beginning of the project I brought people together to ensure that everyone's views were taken into account. As the work progressed I also encouraged colleagues and demonstrated my commitment by completing my assigned tasks ahead of schedule.

One problem that arose was that some team members were not completing their tasks on time. I knew our manager was getting upset so I approached my struggling colleagues in a quiet corner and offered my help and support. It became clear that some of them were unclear of their duties and were too scared to come forward. I pointed them in the right direction, reassured them and boosted their confidence and, in this way, developed an excellent new strategy that is still being used today.

Question: At Alsburst we need trainees who are good communicators. Tell us about a time when you have persuaded someone to accept your point of view (200 words).

Answer: I recently used my communication skills in my role as the President of the Norfolk University Law Society to persuade Tinstey and Co to sponsor our annual mooting competition.

At first the corporate sponsorship partner declined our invitation to support our inaugural event citing the recession as the limiting factor. I contacted her to say thank you for considering our request and took time to listen to her concerns. It turned out that her budget had been slashed and she could not even afford her firm's annual litigation conference. I empathised with her and asked her to give me a week or two to find a creative solution that could solve both our problems.

In the following days I persuaded the Law Faculty that it would be a good idea to let Tinstey have their conference at a reduced rate on our main campus and, in doing so, increase our links with employers. I rang the corporate sponsorship partner and suggested this idea. She accepted this solution and was then able to sponsor our event, which was a great success, to the extent that Tinstey have agreed to sponsor the event over the next five years.

Personal statements

Some application forms request a general statement outlining your suitability for the role and/or what attracts you to the position. Here are some tips:

- Research the occupation and the firm, and make sure you make a reasoned argument as to how you would fit in.
- Take your time to identify the skills required.
- Prove that you have the skills required by providing a specific example of when and how you have demonstrated them to a high level.
- If you are provided with a person specification, systematically link your personal statement to the attributes required. In other words, if a person specification states that the firm needs someone with 'energy and enthusiasm', write a paragraph outlining how you have demonstrated exactly these attributes. You may even consider using the criteria listed in the person specification as headings in your personal statement.

- Provide the information required – each application form requires slightly different information, so don't just cut and paste a previous statement you have written without making amendments.
- Use short sentences and paragraphs with positive words.

Online applications

Many graduate employers now expect you to apply online. Unfortunately, online applications are often filled in carelessly; here are some guidelines for ensuring your applications are up to scratch:

- Familiarise yourself with the organisation's system.
- Don't rush the answers.
- Save the answers regularly.
- Copy answers into Word (or any other format) to save them in case the system crashes.
- Print your answers out to check them.
- Save your work and return to it later so you can reflect on what you've written.
- Don't leave the form to the last minute as computers and networks regularly crash.

Directly contact the employer if you have any questions, for example, if you don't have the grades required but you have mitigating circumstances, or if you have a disability which means you need an alternative format.

Further study applications

Postgraduate course providers expect you to prove that you will succeed in the course and that you have a genuine interest. You should research the curriculum and teaching methods provided and prove your suitability through your previous study, employment and personal experience. In all law-related postgraduate course applications, you should show an understanding of the career you want to follow, why you have made your particular career choice and why you will succeed on the course and in your career.

Covering letters

When to use one

You should always send (or email) a covering letter with your CV or application form unless you have expressly been told not to, or there is no facility to do so with an online application.

What to include

Your covering letter should include your name and address, the name and address of the person to whom you are sending your CV (always send it to a named person) and a brief and positive outline of what attracts you about the post and your key attributes (which you have outlined on your CV or application form). Just like your CV, your covering letter should be targeted at the specific role for which you are applying. If you are sending your CV as an attachment to an email, send the covering letter as another attachment.

Points to bear in mind

- If you are emailing your cover letter as an attachment along with your CV or application form, list your attachments in the body of the message so they don't go unnoticed.

- Good grammar and spelling are absolutely essential, so get your letter spell-checked and checked by a friend or a careers adviser.
- Always use a professional tone and be careful not to be overly familiar.
- Try to use a writing style that is suited to the career you want to enter, eg covering letters for advertising roles may be more expressive than those for roles at a traditional law firm.
- Make sure you address the letter to the correct person and that you spell his or her name, and the name of the organisation, correctly.

Suggested structure

Use one side of A4 and highlight relevant skills and experiences using the following structure:

Your Full Name and Address

Name of person to be contacted
Person's title
Address of organisation
Date

Dear (Mr. / Mrs. / Ms.) Xxxx,

APPLICATION FOR THE POSITION OF... (Ref. no.)

Paragraph 1: Introduce yourself positively and explain how you heard about the opportunity (avoid informal statements such as 'Hello, my name is Joe Smith and I am writing this letter ...').

Paragraph 2: Explain why you are interested in the opportunity and the organisation. Demonstrate that you have researched the role and have assessed why you are keen.

Paragraphs 3/4: Outline why you are suitable. Draw the reader's attention to your key skills and experiences that are outlined in full on your CV.

Paragraph 5: Include a polite and positive ending.

Yours sincerely

(If you have addressed the letter to 'Dear Sir/Madam',
close your letter with the statement 'Yours faithfully'.)

Your signature
Joe Smith

Interviews

Why employers use them

Employers interview candidates whose applications stand out from the crowd. The purpose of the interview is to make sure that potential employees have the requisite skills, commitment and knowledge to succeed and they fit in with the culture of the organisation.

Types of interview

The two most common types of graduate interview are telephone interviews and panel interviews. Employers increasingly use telephone interviews as the first stage in the recruitment process. They are usually conducted by relatively junior members of staff or human resources personnel and last for about half an hour. Questions are not usually too searching at this stage as organisations just want to see if you are a serious candidate. They evaluate this by assessing how much you know about the organisation and the industry, how much you have reflected on what attracts you to the role and whether you are fully aware of what you have to offer. Successful candidates are then usually given a panel interview soon afterwards.

Panel interviews are usually held at one of the organisation's offices and involve two or more interviewers who usually take turns to ask searching questions. Panel members may include senior managers and recruitment professionals. These interviews usually last for 45 minutes or a full hour, during which time you will have the opportunity to comprehensively prove that you are the right person for the job.

Skills-based questions (why they should choose you)

Recruiters usually test your skills by asking for an example of when you have demonstrated a certain skill to a high level, or they may ask you what you would do in a particular situation/scenario. For example, they could ask you to 'tell us about a time you have worked in a team and achieved a good result', or they may ask 'Imagine you are in one of our teams and one of your colleagues is not pulling their weight, what would you do?' Other examples of skills-based questions include:

- 'Tell us about a time you solved a difficult problem for a customer or client.'
- 'Tell us about a difficult project you have successfully managed.'
- 'What do you think is the key to good communication?'
- 'Tell us about a time you have demonstrated good commercial awareness.'

To prepare your answers for these questions, research the skills required in the occupation and the specific post you have applied for using the resources listed in the CV section of this chapter. Think of times when you have demonstrated the skills in different aspects of your life, ie at work, at university or during your extracurricular activities/interests, and assess how you performed them to a high level. For example, if you are asked about your organisational skills, you could give an example of compiling a sales report during your work experience at a call centre, where you planned carefully, set specific goals and reviewed your progress throughout the project to make sure you completed the report effectively and on time.

Commitment-based questions (why you want to work for them)

Skills alone are not all you need to succeed in a job. Candidates also need the passion and drive to succeed. Therefore, interviewers usually also ask a range of questions to test your knowledge of the vacancy, the organisation and/or the industry, because people who are serious about the particular career should know the answers to these questions. Example commitment-based questions are shown below:

- 'What do you know about our organisation and our competitors?'
- 'How has this industry been affected by the recession?'
- 'Why have you applied for this job?'

- 'Why do you want to be a ...?' (whatever the job is)
- 'How does your degree relate to this position?'

Prepare for these questions by researching the organisation, the role and the industry, and reflect upon how they suit your specific skills, interests and motivations. For example, if you are asked why you are applying for a particular post at a firm specialising in employment law, you could say that you really enjoyed studying the subject at university and working on employment law cases during your work experience last summer. Furthermore, you could stress that you especially like the challenging nature of the work, the need to keep up to date with continuous legal developments and the interaction with a wide range of other legal professionals.

Knowledge-based questions

Questions in this category test technical capabilities and knowledge related to the industry you want to enter. For example:

- 'What is the national literacy strategy?' (for prospective teachers)
- 'Do you think the banks are responsible for the recent recession?' (testing your commercial awareness)
- 'Tell us your opinion about an event related to our industry that's recently been reported in the media.'

To prepare for these questions, make sure you keep up with current affairs in your chosen sector.

Law interviews

Interviews for training contracts, pupillages and placements focus on skills, commitment and knowledge, just like all other graduate interviews. Scenario questions are usually linked to current legal or ethical dilemmas. For example, you may be asked searching questions on how a recent law change may affect local businesses or what you would do if you noticed that the other side in a contract negotiation had inadvertently added a zero to a contract worth £50,000 to make it worth £500,000. Law interviewers ask you these challenging questions not just to test your legal knowledge, but also to see if you can back up your opinion calmly and logically under pressure (a key legal skill).

For some more common interview questions, see our **Companion Website**.

Your weaknesses

If recruiters ask you about your weaknesses, tell them what you have struggled to do in the past, but outline how you have improved and what you have learned. For example, you could say that, when you started university, you sometimes focused too much on one commitment to the detriment of others, but that you quickly learned how to carefully plan your schedule, so that now you are able to focus on key priorities and also get all your other work done on time.

Questions for them

At the end of the interview, you are usually given some time to ask the panel some questions of your own. This is an excellent opportunity to demonstrate your research and your interest in the firm. Try to ask genuine questions which have come to mind during your research that will have a direct impact on your role should you be employed. Avoid questions about pay and holidays and vague questions about the organisation's plans and aspirations. For example, if you are going for a training contract interview, you may ask if you will have a mentor or how the firm organises the professional skills course.

Preparing for the day

Even if you have researched the role and the organisation thoroughly and are fully aware of you skills, you should also:

- Practise, practise, practise – think of different questions and answer them in your head, practise with your family, your friends, careers advisers, the cat, anyone.
- Read through your CV/application form so you are ready to comment on the things you wrote.
- Contact the organisation if you have any questions about who you are going to be interviewed by and what the interview will involve.
- Research your interviewers on the web to get an idea of their professional interests so you can refer to them in your answers and questions.
- Double-check the location of the interview (and when you are supposed to arrive) and plan your route to the interview so you arrive in plenty of time.
- Try on your old suit to make sure it fits, or buy some new clothes, and make sure your shoes are shiny, get a haircut and eat well (your brain is the first thing to suffer from a poor diet!).

Performing on the day

Get a good night's sleep and, when you wake up, go through the following routine:

- Have a good breakfast/lunch.
- Dress smartly.
- Get to the location a good hour in advance but don't go in.
- Use your spare hour to go over your research and your answers to the questions you are expecting.
- Attend the interview 10 minutes early.
- Be nice to everyone, including the receptionist – you never know who might be watching!

Body language
- Shake hands firmly
- Smile
- Walk upright and confidently
- Sit up straight
- Look into the interviewers' eyes while they are asking their questions and scan the faces of the panel while you are providing your answers
- Address the interviewers using their names

After the interview

However well you performed at the interview, make sure you immediately contact the organisation (usually by email) to thank them for such an interesting and enjoyable experience. If you do get the job, make sure the pay and conditions are acceptable (you may need to negotiate). If you are not successful, ask for feedback from the interviewers on your performance so you can improve in the future. You could also ask if you could pop in to ask for advice on how you could develop your career, or even ask if you could shadow someone in the organisation for a day or two. Who knows, they may give you a job after all!

Find out more about succeeding at interviews on the websites listed at the end of this chapter.

Assessment centre exercises

Larger employers (including many in the legal sector) now use a vast array of additional techniques to find the best graduates. The most common assessment tools are briefly outlined below; find out more on the websites listed at the end of the chapter.

Psychometric tests

Psychometric tests are multiple-choice questionnaires usually designed to test your verbal and numerical reasoning skills, ie your ability to draw conclusions from information and data. Candidates are given a tight timeframe, so you will probably not have the luxury to check your work thoroughly. Therefore, you need to strike a balance whereby you can work as quickly and accurately as possible. Your careers service will probably be able to give you some sample questionnaires and may even run practice psychometric tests under exam conditions.

Presentations

Employers often ask candidates to make a short presentation to a panel. You will either be given a topic in advance or on the day. Either way, you should use visual aids appropriately and focus on the needs of the specific audience. For example you should:

- use a large font on any visual aids which everyone can see;
- look at the audience, not the flipchart or PowerPoint presentation;
- use as few slides as possible (if you are using PowerPoint) and don't read from the slides (your audience can read for themselves!);
- avoid jargon;
- speak clearly and stick to the deadline.

A good general rule is to break the presentation up into three parts as follows:

1 A short introduction (tell them what you are going to tell them)
2 The key issues (tell them what you want them to know)
3 A summary (tell them what you've just told them)

Some people get very nervous about presentations, and this often holds them back on the day. If this is you, practise as much as possible at university and prepare for the presentation at the assessment centre comprehensively, ie go over and over what you are going to say, and how you're going to say it, so you can almost do it in your sleep!

Group exercises

These are activities in which you will be put into a group of five or six people to solve a practical problem or discuss a current issue and present your findings. The issues involved are not usually too taxing as employers are really looking for your ability to work under pressure, to work collaboratively and to be creative and well organised. Prepare for these activities by identifying how you work well in a team and by carefully planning how you will demonstrate your key attributes to the assessors. For example, if you are good at encouraging people, you could focus on praising colleagues and introducing shy people into the discussion.

In-tray exercises

In these exercises you are given a pile of papers (either real or virtual) such as emails, faxes, letters, phone messages and reports, and asked to respond based upon their relative importance. You may also have to cope with more paperwork being delivered whilst you're working.

Case studies

Some employers ask you to work individually or in a team to analyse a real-life business situation and come up with an effective strategy. You are usually given time to assess a great deal of information from a range of sources, such as official reports, tables and newspaper cuttings, and then asked to make a presentation and answer some searching questions. Employers are not really looking for a specific 'correct' strategy in these situations because they are really assessing your ability to analyse problems, prioritise tasks and put forward effective arguments with clarity and tact. You can prepare for these activities by keeping up to date with current affairs and reflecting upon the implications of key business events. You can also find practice resources at your careers service on the websites listed below.

Further information about applications, interviews and assessment centres

- Sussex University's career development website – www.sussex.ac.uk/cdec
- The University of Kent's Careers Service website – www.kent.ac.uk/careers
- Manchester University's student website – www.studentnet.manchester.ac.uk
- The University of Bradford's Career Development Services website – www.careers.brad.ac.uk
- The University of Edinburgh's website – www.ed.ac.uk/schools-departments/careers
- The Open University Careers website (find advice on law interviews) – www.open.ac.uk/careers
- The Target Jobs law website – www.targetjobs.co.uk/law-solicitors

Summary

As a law student you can choose from a wide range of careers but, to achieve success, you need to take steps to target a specific role and develop a strategy to make sure you stand out from the crowd.

There are a number of things you can do to plan for a successful and fulfilling career; these are outlined below.

1 **See what's out there:** Law graduates go into numerous law and non-law related careers, but many students and graduates limit themselves to the obvious choices. Make sure you are aware of all your career options before making a decision.

2 **Assess yourself:** Take some time to identify your skills, interests and motivations. After all, if you don't know the answers to these questions, you may struggle to find a role in life that is truly fulfilling.

3 **Choose a role:** Once you have researched all your career options and have assessed what you want from a career, you can identify a shortlist of possible occupations that you'll be good at, you'll enjoy and which will give you what you want from life, be it a family, a flat in Knightsbridge or a Ferrari (few of us can have all three!).

4 **Plan your strategy:** Figure out what you need to do to succeed in your aim. You will need to target a specific career path, build up your work experience and extracurricular activities and develop a network of professional contacts who can help. You may also need to sign up for some postgraduate study.

Work experience is absolutely crucial in today's recruitment market, so you should endeavour to build up your CV during your time at university. You can volunteer, take part in extracurricular activities, such as mooting competitions, and get some part-time/vacation work. You should also aim to get some sort of formal placement at the end of your second year.

Finally, to kick-start your career, you need to put together applications that are positive, well written, and targeted at the post you're chasing. This means clearly conveying your relevant skills, commitment and knowledge.

Bibliography and further reading

Chapter 1

Harris, DJ (1998) *Cases and Materials on International Law*, London: Sweet & Maxwell

Aust, A (2005) *Handbook of International Law*, Cambridge University Press

Chapter 2

Clinch, P (2001) *Using a Law Library: a Students' Guide to Legal Research Skills*, 2nd edn, Oxford: Oxford University Press

Elkington, A et al (2007) *Skills for Lawyers*, Guildford: College of Law Publishing

Foster, N (ed) (2009) *Blackstone's EU Treaties and Legislation 2010–11*, 21st edn, Oxford: Oxford University Press

Magrath, P (2007) 'Introduction: the Incorporated Council's 135 years of law reporting for England and Wales' in *The Law Reports and the Weekly Law Reports: Special Issue,* 4th reprint, London: Incorporated Council of Law Reporting for England & Wales, pp ix–x

Ministry of Justice (2008) *Judicial and Court Statistics, 2007, Cm 7467* available at http://www.justice.gov.uk/publications/docs/judicial-court-stats-2007-full.pdf

Simmonds, A (2007) 'Researching Case Law' in Elkington, A et al (2007) *Skills for Lawyers*, Guildford: College of Law Publishing, pp 42ff

Slapper, G (2007) *How the Law Works: a friendly guide to the legal system*, London: Collins

Wilson, S and Kenny, P (2007) *The Law Student's Handbook*, Oxford: Oxford University Press

Woodley, M (ed) (2005) *Osborn's Concise Law Dictionary*, 10th edn, London: Sweet & Maxwell

Further reading

Clinch, P (2001) *Using a Law Library: a Students' Guide to Legal Research Skills*, 2nd edn, Oxford: Oxford University Press

Elkington, A, et al (2007) *Skills for Lawyers*, Guildford: College of Law Publishing

Wilson, S and Kenny, P (2007) *The Law Student's Handbook*, Oxford: Oxford University Press

Chapter 3

Chaterjee, C (2000) *Methods of Research in Law*, 2nd edn, London: Old Bailey Press

Elkington, A et al (2007) *Skills for Lawyers*, Guildford: College of Law Publishing

Holborn, G (2001) *Butterworths Legal Research Guide*, 2nd edn, London: Butterworths

Blaxter, L, Hughes, C and Tight, M (1998) *How to Research*, Buckingham: Open University Press

Collis, J and Hussey, R (2003) *Business Research: a practical guide for undergraduate and postgraduate students*, 2nd edn, Basingstoke: Palgrave Macmillan

Denscombe, M (2002) *Ground Rules for Good Research*, Maidenhead: Open University Press

Saunders, M, Lewis, P and Thornhill, A (2007) *Research Methods for Business Students*, 4th edn, Harlow: Prentice Hall

Silverman, D (1993) *Interpreting Qualitative Data: Methods for Analysing Talk, Text and Interaction*, London: Sage

SLSA (2009) 'SLSA Statement on Ethical Research Practice' available at http://www.kent.ac.uk/nslsa/images/slsadownloads/ethicalstatement/slsa%20ethics%20statement%20_final_%5B1%5D.pdf

Williams, K (1989) *Study Skills*, Basingstoke: Palgrave Macmillan

Further reading

Chaterjee, C (2000) *Methods of Research in Law*, 2nd edn, London: Old Bailey Press

Elkington, A et al (2007) *Skills for Lawyers*, Guildford: College of Law Publishing

Holborn, G (2001) *Butterworths Legal Research Guide*, 2nd edn, London: Butterworths

Blaxter, L, Hughes, C and Tight, M (1998) *How to Research*, Buckingham: Open University Press

Collis, J and Hussey, R (2003) *Business Research: a practical guide for undergraduate and postgraduate students*, 2nd edn, Basingstoke: Palgrave Macmillan

Denscombe, M (2002) *Ground Rules for Good Research*, Maidenhead: Open University Press

Saunders, M, Lewis, P and Thornhill, A (2007) *Research Methods for Business Students*, 4th edn, Harlow: Prentice Hall

Silverman, D (1993) *Interpreting Qualitative Data: Methods for Analysing Talk, Text and Interaction*, London: Sage

Chapter 4

Cottrell, S (2003) *The Study Skills Handbook*, London: Palgrave Macmillan

Cottrell, S (2005) *Critical Thinking Skills*, London: Palgrave Macmillan

Chapter 5

Bowden, J (2004) *Writing a Report: how to prepare, write and present effective reports*, 7th edn, Oxford: HowToBooks

Cottrell, S (2003) *The Study Skills Handbook*, London: Palgrave Macmillan

Truss L (2003) *Eats Shoots & Leaves: the zero tolerance approach to punctuation*, London: Profile Books

O'Connor, M (1991) *Writing Successfully in Science*, Taylor & Francis

Chapter 8

Networking

Hart, R (1996) *Effective Networking for Professional Success: Making the Most Your Personal Contacts* (Better Management Skills Series), Stirling Books

Håkansson, H and Snehota, I, 'No business is an island: The network concept of business strategy', *Scandinavian Journal of Management*, vol 22, Issue 3, September 2006, pp 256–70

Neal, DC, 'To market, to market: Your goal is visibility', *Business Law Today*, July/August 1996, American Bar Association

Department Legal Research Corner, Madeline Kriescher, 'Professional Benefits of Online Social Networking', *Colorado Lawyer*, February 2009

Ambrogi, RJ, 'The Future of Online Networking', *Boston Bar Journal*, January/February 2009

D'Souza, S, *Brilliant Networking, What the best networkers know, do and say*, London: Pearson Prentice Hall

Negotiation

Craver, B, 'Effective Legal Negotiation and Settlement', American Law Institute – American Bar Association Continuing Legal Education, ALI–ABA Professional Skills Course, October 27, 1989

Watkins, M and Rosegrant, S, 'The Seven Principles of Breakthrough Negotiation', *20 Alternatives to High Cost Litigation*, March 2002

Judge Eleanor Holmes Norton, 'Bargaining and the Ethic of Process' (1989) 64 NYUL Rev 993

Pendergast, WR, 'Managing the Negotiation Agenda', 6 Negotiation J 15 (1990)

Freshman C, Adele Hayes, A and Feldman, G, 'The lawyer-negotiator as Mood Scientist: what we know and don't know about how mood relates to successful negotiation' (2002) *Journal of Dispute Resolution* 1

Fisher, R & Ury, W (1983, 1991) *Getting to Yes: Negotiating Agreements without Giving In*, Penguin Books

Boyle, F, Capps, D, Plowden, P and Sandford, C, *A Practical Guide to Lawyering Skills*, Cavendish, p 258

Menkel-Meadow, C, 'Toward another view of legal negotiation: the structure of problem solving' (1984) 31 UCLA L Rev 754, pp 754–842

Interviewing and advising

Webb, J et al (2000) *Lawyers' Skills*, Oxford: Oxford University Press

Maughan, C and Webb, J (2005) *Lawyering Skills and the Legal Process*, 2nd edn, Cambridge: Cambridge University Press

Index